Influencing Social Policy

Influencing Social Policy

Applied Psychology Serving the Public Interest

KENNETH I. MATON

OXFORD
UNIVERSITY PRESS

OXFORD
UNIVERSITY PRESS

Oxford University Press is a department of the University of Oxford. It furthers the University's objective of excellence in research, scholarship, and education by publishing worldwide. Oxford is a registered trade mark of Oxford University Press in the UK and certain other countries.

Published in the United States of America by Oxford University Press
198 Madison Avenue, New York, NY 10016, United States of America.

Library of Congress Cataloging-in-Publication Data
Names: Maton, Kenneth I., author.
Title: Influencing social policy : applied psychology serving the public interest / Kenneth I. Maton.
Description: Oxford ; New York : Oxford University Press, [2017] |
Series: Advances in community psychology | Includes bibliographical references and index.
Identifiers: LCCN 2016018944 (print) | LCCN 2016026292 (ebook) | ISBN 9780199989973 |
ISBN 9780199989980 (ebook)
Subjects: LCSH: Social policy—Psychological aspects. | Psychology, Applied—Social aspects.
Classification: LCC HN28 .M374 2017 (print) | LCC HN28 (ebook) | DDC 306.01/9—dc23
LC record available at https://lccn.loc.gov/2016018944

1 3 5 7 9 8 6 4 2

Printed by Webcom, Inc., Canada

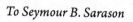

To Seymour B. Sarason

CONTENTS

SERIES FOREWORD

The **Society for Community Research and Action** (SCRA), Division 27 of the American Psychological Association, is an international and interdisciplinary organization that supports the development of theory, research, and social action. Members share a common interest in promoting empowerment, health, and well-being, with special attention to multiple levels of analysis—individual, group, organizational, community, cultural, and societal. Division members focus on an array of pressing social issues within national and global contexts (such as violence, mental health, HIV/AIDS, poverty, racism) and have developed effective social interventions to address seemingly intractable problems using a continuum of approaches from prevention to intervention to social transformation. These approaches involve diverse strategies including advocacy, citizen participation, collaboration, community organizing, economic development, prevention, education, self-help/mutual-help, sociopolitical development, social movements, and policy change. These change strategies typically share the goal of challenging and altering underlying power structures in the pursuit of social justice and community and individual well-being.

This book series, Advances in Community Psychology, is sponsored by SCRA to more broadly disseminate theory, research, and social action of community psychologists and those in allied disciplines. The overarching mission of the series is to create a publication venue that highlights the contributions of the field of community psychology and, more generally, community action, research, and practice; integrates current knowledge on pressing topics in the field; and offers the foundations for future directions.

Psychologists have long possessed the ability to use their scientific and practical knowledge to influence individuals' lives and increase their well-being. In a less well-known but equally consequential way, psychologists influence the lives of many by using scientific and practical knowledge to shape public policy.

Dr. Ken Maton's new addition to this series captures the diverse ways in which psychologists have overcome challenges and achieved policy change success. In the past, psychologists engaged in policy work have forged ahead with little train-ing, feeling their way through the dark. There has been some guidance, mostly from those outside of psychology but with some from within the field in the form of workshops, rare courses at universities, and a relatively small literature. Ken Maton's book fills a gap, giving psychologists a vast set of model narratives to guide policy endeavors, thus ensuring that psychologists who enter the policy arena will be more thoroughly prepared.

Ken Maton uses his vast expertise in psychology throughout the book. He brings a professor's and practitioner's perspective, including the refined knowl-edge he developed from teaching a course on public policy for three decades and his insider knowledge derived from the multiple policy initiatives he has worked on in the Baltimore-Washington, DC area.

Most unique is that this book represents an original product of research by a fine qualitative psychologist. Specifically for this book, Ken Maton has collected the stories of documented policy successes from applied psychologists in the United States and those whose basic research has strong translational potential. We strongly encourage the reader to look closely at the research methodology appendix; this is the single best place to appreciate the magnitude of the data col-lected, the rigorous methodology, and, more generally, the rare and arduous pro-cess by which this book came into being.

The book may be best described as a set of narrative maps to guide students, early career members, and other psychologists through the difficult but infinitely rewarding path of policy influence and change. If psychology is to have an ex-panded and enduring ethical approach to policy change, this book should be the centerpiece for the field for a very long time. Importantly, Ken Maton identified psychologists within multiple subfields including community, developmental and social psychology, thus maximizing the relevance of this book to scholars across the field.

Although this book is relevant for all psychologists who aim to influence policy, it is a most fitting contribution to SCRA Book Series. The subfield of community psychology has had an enduring interest in answering the question "How can we make a difference in the world?" To this question, Ken's book provides us with a set of tangible answers. Although some policy influence has clearly been the result of being "in the right place at the right time," Ken carefully analyzes narratives in which skills and strategies have contributed to successful outcomes, helping us think about strategies to help our research and practice become as instrumental as possible within the policy arena.

We are additionally very proud to have Ken, a premier community psycholo-gist, as an author within this book series. The book's intellectual origins fit pre-cisely with the community psychology structure of the book series. Seymour Sarason, to whom the book is dedicated, is one of the most prestigious and original community psychologists. Seymour was a professor when Ken was an undergraduate at Yale, and Seymour has since had a lifelong influence on Ken's work. The representation of theory throughout this book in the form of history, settings, the culture of the field, education, and policy itself reflects its many roots in Seymour's work, as well as Ken's own contributions to community psychology.

We thoroughly enjoyed this book and continually found ourselves learning a great deal, chapter after chapter. We hope and expect your experience will be the same.

Nicole E. Allen and Bradley Olson

FOREWORD

In 1963, I joined Seymour Sarason, to whom this book is dedicated, in the Psychoeducational Clinic housed in the Yale Psychology Department. Sarason— as a person, as a teacher, as a writer and conceptualizer—directly and indirectly influenced subsequent generations of psychologists to take on the various policy roles reflected in this book. Psychologists now function as more than research- ers: they are leaders, advisors, advocates, and serve in varied governmental roles.

The Psychoeducational Clinic was a departure for Yale, which had a first-rate department and a fairly traditional clinical program. That the Clinic was orga- nized *at all* was a mark of the respect Sarason's colleagues had for him. He had long been critical of clinical psychology's ties to psychiatry, its lack of interest in prevention, and its lack of ties to education. He took advantage of the opportunity provided by the federal government's community mental health thrust to pro- pose a new type of clinical facility. It would be tied to the schools and follow the consultation model, more or less. It would not take on an in-clinic case load, but would be directed toward helping teachers with here-and-now problems in their classrooms. That meant those of us who worked with Sarason were assigned to inner-city schools with the open-ended mission of "making ourselves helpful." We also worked in similar roles with the anti-poverty agency in New Haven. We had no training for these tasks, but we learned quickly.

One couldn't be in those settings very long before encountering the welfare system, the juvenile court, the child protection system (such as it was in those days), the child guidance clinics, the police, housing issues, urban redevelopment impacts on neighborhoods, and issues in employment. In other words, our work in these settings was inextricably linked with public policy.

The Psychoeducational Clinic had an incredible, not-to-be-missed, weekly seminar led by Sarason. We discussed and analyzed the problems we encountered on an everyday basis, and we also had many visitors from a variety of fields. They introduced us to other ways of thinking and researching. There were important spin-off projects from the Clinic, with their own policy implications; yet it was *this seminar* that legitimated engaging in the broad and interdisciplinary thinking so essential to work in the policy arena. It also validated our interests as psychologists in fields far from those studied in the psychology laboratory. In a sense, those experiences said, "Yes, those far-flung issues are psychology's business."

In the 50 years since, as this timely volume illustrates so well, many in psychology have adopted a broad perspective—in the problems under study, the research methods employed, and the theoretical concepts used to guide and interpret research. The roles they take on and the skills they use in the policy process are extensive. My colleagues are using their professional and analytical skills to build relationships with policymakers, to communicate, to conceptualize, and to actively participate in the policy process.

Today, many psychologists understand policy issues as worthy of study and action. The variety and richness of the subject matter that psychologists study, as amply illustrated in this book, show that many have overcome narrow strictures of content, methods, and roles. As a result, our field and society at large have benefitted from psychologists caring about and considering the policy implications of their research across numerous social issues and levels of analysis. I look forward to further developments as we learn more and more about the world and about ourselves, as both research workers and policy practitioners.

Murray Levine
Department of Psychology
SUNY at Buffalo

PREFACE

In my senior year of college, in the mid-1970s, I was granted permission to enroll in a graduate course on social policy taught by Seymour Sarason. Seymour invited many guest speakers from the policy world to the class; each told the story of his or her policy journey, including victories, defeats, and lessons learned. I was greatly influenced by that course, and, 10 years later, as an assistant professor, I initiated a similar psychology graduate course in policy at University of Maryland, Baltimore County (UMBC). I have been teaching this course every other year since, always inviting multiple guest speakers engaged in policy work—often psychologists. The students are always inspired by the speakers, as am I, and a number of the students over the years have been motivated to pursue policy work as an integral part of their careers, whether in academic or applied settings.

I decided to write *Influencing Social Policy: Applied Psychology Serving the Public Interest* to share with a larger audience the lived experiences of psychologists working in the policy arena, with the hope that the policy narratives will inspire the reader—as they have the graduate students—to become engaged in the policy arena. The critical challenges facing our country require innovations in social policy, and we, as psychologists, have much to contribute. Indeed we have already contributed a tremendous amount—as revealed in these pages through the policy narratives of the 79 psychologists interviewed. And, as was the case in the mid-1970s, much work remains to be done.

My father passed away while I was in college, and Seymour took me into his family, serving as a father figure. Seymour had a profound personal and intellectual influence on me and on so many others. As his colleague Murray Levine recounts in the foreword, Seymour exerted a formative influence on many areas of applied psychology and helped lay the foundation for our involvement in the policy arena. Seymour authored many books during his long career; one of the intellectual highlights of my undergraduate years was holing up in my room for an entire weekend and reading three of his seminal works in succession. The current book is a tribute to Seymour and is dedicated to him. The seeds for this book began in his graduate policy course in the chilly winter of 1975; fittingly, Seymour provides the closing quote in the final chapter.

Writing a book is a journey, and I have received help every step of the way. I am indebted first and foremost to the 79 psychologists who took time out of their busy lives to share with me their experiences working in the policy arena. I was inspired by each and every interview—indeed, conducting the interviews was one of the distinct joys of my professional life. I am thankful to Vivian Tseng from the W. T. Grant Foundation for providing a discretionary grant to fund the research. Many graduate and undergraduate students contributed to various aspects of the research endeavor; particular thanks go to the students in my graduate policy course and members of my research team who carefully reviewed chapters of the book. I want to single out for their dedicated help in this regard Tiffany Beason, Samantha Bento, Sara Buckingham, Julia Dancis, Patricia Esparza, Surbhi Godsay, Jennifer Hosler, Tahira Mahdi, and Anna Westin. I also want to thank SCRA Book Series co-editors, Nicole Allen and Bradley Olson, for their insightful feedback on each chapter; Beth Shinn for her thoughtful feedback on the book prospectus; and development editor Kate Scheinman who provided invaluable technical and substantive feedback. Finally, this journey would not have been possible without the ongoing support, love, and encouragement received from my wife, Mary Kay.

Influencing Social Policy

Psychologists in the Social Policy Arena

*The ability to work in the policy environment and bring good science to influ-
ence it, shape it, and understand how to do that is just wonderful work.*
—J. Meyers, April 15, 2013

Goals of this Volume

This volume fills a void in the literature by examining the social policy contributions of a wide range of psychologists. These psychologists work from various
vantage points (i.e., have different roles in different settings) and employ a variety of policy influence strategies and skills. Semi-structured interviews were
conducted with 79 psychologists who were asked to describe their policy influence efforts, experiences, and perspectives. Scholarship documenting policy
outcomes related to their policy work is cited whenever available. However,
little such confirmatory material is available concerning the specific policy-influence activities reported by interviewees. The purpose of this book is to provide insight into the nature of the policy process and how it can be influenced
and to portray the unique lived experiences of psychologists working in the
policy arena.

Influencing Social Policy: Applied Psychology Serving the Public Interest aims to
encourage psychologists who are interested in making a difference to become
more fully engaged in the policy world. Our presence in the policy arena is
sorely needed if we are to apply psychological principles to benefit the **public
interest**. Psychologists are in a unique position not only to conduct policy-relevant research, but also to improve the quality of life for large numbers of citizens via active policy influence efforts. Psychologists can contribute to **social
policy** change from a number of roles and settings, including as researchers in
academia, as administrators and staff in a variety of **intermediary organizations**, and as **policy insiders** working in the legislative and executive branches
of government.

Psychologists in the Policy Arena

"Exciting." "Challenging." "Unpredictable." "Essential." "Frustrating." Psychologists use these words to describe the policy arena and their work within it. Laws, regulations, and government-funded programs affect every aspect of individual, community, and national life. Many, if not all, policy changes in the public interest require new or revised social policies. Psychology can make an enduring impact, and the policy arena is an essential domain of activity. Achieving influence in this domain can be very rewarding; it is also, however, extremely challenging.

Indeed, the challenges facing psychologists as they strive to influence social policy are legion. Vested interests, partisan politics, and tight budgets are some of the external barriers to transforming innovative ideas into tangible forms of policy change. Lack of policy knowledge, limited immersion in policy networks, and the absence of professional incentives for this work are some of the internal challenges to psychology as a field. Other fields, such as economics, nursing, public health, and social work, have made greater inroads into the social policy arena than has psychology. Nonetheless, many psychologists have succeeded in contributing in important ways to policy change in the public interest. A number of their stories are told in the current volume.

The brief portraits that constitute the heart of this volume focus primarily on policy change in the United States, which is where the author of this book is based. Although the policy skills described may have relevance in other countries, the structure of government and civil society, and political and cultural contexts may differ in important ways in other parts of the world (Alfaro, Sánchez, & Zambrano, 2012; Rodríguez, 2009; Saïas & Delawarde, 2013; Serrano-García, 2005). Thus, the roles, activities, and contributions of psychologists, and the challenges faced, will likely differ.

This introductory chapter continues with five additional sections. The first of these defines key terms and provides a brief overview of psychology's historical relationship to policy work, with particular focus on contributions in the public interest. The next three sections provide an overview of the policy involvements of three subfields that constitute the primary focus of the volume: **developmental psychology**, **social psychology**, and **community psychology**. Within each subfield, pioneering policy figures, areas of policy influence, prior policy scholarship, and contributions of professional organizations are highlighted. The final section of this chapter details the research methodology used to generate the case material for the current volume and concludes with an overview of the chapters that follow.

Key Terms in the Field

The policy arena is complex and multifaceted, and there are multiple meanings to the terms that are used to depict it. A number of key terms are central to the focus of this volume. These terms are defined here, in part by contrasting them with other, related concepts, ones outside the primary focus of this volume. To become engaged in policy, one must understand the key terms used in the policy arena.

Governmental Policy Versus Organizational Policy and Practice

Government refers to the group of people who make laws and regulations and who fund services for citizens and organizations in a political jurisdiction. A **jurisdiction** can encompass towns, cities, states, and nations. **Governmental policy** refers to what government officials expect citizens or organizations within a given jurisdiction to do. As will be detailed in Chapter 2, phases of the governmental policy process include agenda setting, policy formulation and adoption, implementation, and evaluation and revision. Governmental policies relevant to psychology include those that provide funding, guidelines, and regulations affecting numerous aspects of the well-being and quality of life of citizens (e.g., child care, community development, education, health and mental health, homelessness, incarceration, and poverty).

Organizations are bounded groups composed of leaders and workers. **Organizational policy (also known as institutional policy)** refers to what organizational leaders expect members of the organization to do. **Organizational practice** refers to what organizations and their members actually do. In the case of professional staff within organizations, *practice* refers to the behaviors that help or educate clients, customers, or service recipients. Thus, organizational policies are formalized rules and guidelines, whereas practices are the application of knowledge and skills in everyday work life. An example of organizational policy and practice includes the procedures for how sexual assault is dealt with by a university or college. Governmental policies direct how all universities and colleges must address issues of sexual assault on campus and provide possible consequences if governmental standards are not followed. In some cases, these consequences may include ineligibility for federal funding. The practices and procedures developed by individual colleges and universities to comply with the policies, however, may vary widely across campuses.

Influencing Social Policy focuses on psychologists' efforts to change governmental policy—that is, to influence the decisions of governmental policymakers. Such changes will, in turn, affect the policies and practices of many organizations in a given governmental jurisdiction. Although psychologists do important work to change the policies and practices of individual organizations (e.g., a given community agency or school), this book targets change at the macro level—federal, state, and local governmental policy.

Public Policy Versus Social Policy

Public policy encompasses the entire spectrum of laws, regulatory measures, courses of action, and funding priorities enacted by government. The term **social**

policy overlaps substantially with and is subsumed by the more general term "public policy." Social policy excludes several policy areas included in public policy, particularly economic policy, foreign policy, and national defense policy. Specifically, the term **social policy** refers to governmental laws, regulations, and services that enhance the well-being of citizens. These policies cover the entire spectrum of domains affecting quality of life, including community development, crime, education, health, mental health, housing, and welfare.

Public Interest Versus Guild Interests

Within psychology, activities in the public interest aim to "address the fundamental problems of human welfare and the promotion of equitable and just treatment of all segments of society" (American Psychological Association [APA], 2015*a*). Social policies in the public interest, then, refer to governmental laws, regulations, and services that are primarily focused on enhancing the well-being of citizens who lack power and resources in various life contexts (e.g., work, family, community). Within psychology, activities guided by **guild interests** refer to efforts that influence governmental policy to advance or protect the status, power, and resources of psychologists. This volume focuses on psychologists' efforts to influence social policies where the primary intended goal is to serve the public interest, rather than guild interests.

Policy initiatives by membership organizations that enhance guild interests are often presented as efforts to enhance the public interest (e.g., reimbursement for services provided by psychologists, funding for psychology research and graduate education). In some cases, the two may indeed converge, but in others, they may diverge. A stark example of the latter, one that reveals a dark side of the pursuit of guild interests, involved behind-the-scenes efforts by officials in the **American Psychological Association** (APA) to curry favor with the Department of Defense (DOD) by facilitating the involvement of psychologists in DOD coercive interrogations (Hoffman et al., 2015). Although this secretive policy work may have served guild interests by securing the continued support of the DOD in funding for employment and research by psychologists, it ran directly counter to the public-interest priority of protecting human rights.

Active Policy Influence Versus Academic Field Influence

Psychologists who engage in **active policy influence** make concerted efforts to influence the decisions of policymakers. For academic researchers, such work may involve strategic efforts to communicate the results of their research to policymakers. This may involve a direct pathway of influence through direct communication to policymakers or an indirect pathway of influence through communication with organizations, groups, or individuals who seek to persuade or inform policymakers, including advocacy organizations and the media. Academic researchers who only seek to influence fellow academics limit communication of their findings to standard venues such as academic journals and professional conferences. Such researchers are engaged in **academic field influence** rather than active policy influence—even though in some cases their theoretical work and empirical findings may ultimately influence policymakers. For example, their results may be communicated to policymakers by others, including fellow researchers.

Policymaker Education Versus Policy Advocacy

Psychologists may seek to influence policymakers through many methods, including the provision of information such as research findings. When information is provided to inform policymakers about a particular social problem (e.g., the mental health needs of children) or to present both the benefits and limitations of a set of policy options (e.g., different approaches to school reform), such methods are educational in nature and are referred to as **policymaker education**. That is, the primary goal here is to inform and educate, not to persuade or pressure. In contrast, **policy advocacy** refers to efforts to persuade or pressure a policymaker to take a specific policy action (e.g., vote a certain way on a piece of legislation). Education may be part of successful advocacy in that enhanced understanding may be a necessary aspect of an effort to persuade or pressure someone to perform a given policy action. Advocacy, on the other hand, is not part of successful education because the goal of educational efforts is primarily to inform, not to guide a particular policy outcome (Bogenschneider, 2014). Educational and advocacy methods of policy influence are both central topics of focus in this volume.

With these guiding definitions and distinctions in mind, we now turn to a brief historical overview of the primary focus of this book, which is psychologists' active involvement in the policy arena to serve the public interest.

Historical Context: Psychology, Policy, and the Public Interest

Psychology was established as a "new domain of science" in 1879 (Super, 2005, p. 11). Thirteen years later, in 1892, the American Psychology Association (APA) was founded, with 31 members (APA, 2015b). Psychology grew over the ensuing years, both in numbers and in subfields of interest. Although some emerging subfields retained a primary focus on science, others embraced a combined mission of research and application—helping individuals and, on occasion, groups, and bringing about reforms in the larger society.

In certain historical periods, the applied and social reform focus of psychology was especially prominent; at other times, less so (Featherman & Vinovskis, 2001; Levine & Levine, 1992). During the politically progressive economic depression years of the 1930s, several new professional societies developed with an explicit focus on application. For example, the **Society for Research in Child Development** (SRCD), formed in 1933, included a joint focus on understanding child development and bettering the lives of children (Phillips & Styfco, 2007). The **Society for the Psychological Study of Social Issues** (SPSSI) was developed in 1937 by social psychologists dissatisfied with mainstream psychology's lack of relevance to contemporary social problems. SPSSI adopted an interest in testing "hypotheses regarding desirable social change" (cited in Nicholson, 1997, p. 41).

The application focus of SRCD and the activism focus of SPSSI decreased in the 1940s and 1950s as the positivist, quantitative focus of psychology increased. Reward structures and norms in many areas of psychology became increasingly focused on the generation of empirical science (e.g., publication of methodologically rigorous research in academic journals). This trend included few incentives and also featured potential disapproval for investing time and effort in application of findings in general and for forays into the "unseemly arena" of government policymaking in particular (Nicholson, 1997; Phillips & Styfco, 2007).

During the tumultuous and socially progressive 1960s, however, psychology became more visibly engaged with social policy initiatives. Policymakers called on social scientists, including psychologists, for help designing War on Poverty programs. For example, prominent developmental psychologists were asked to help design Head Start, the Elementary School and Secondary Education Act, and the Neighborhood Youth Core. Furthermore, a number of academics, including psychologists, were active supporters of the civil rights, women's rights, and anti-Vietnam War movements. Policy-relevant articles were published in the field's flagship journal, the *American Psychologist*, during the latter part of the 1960s. These articles included Seymour Sarason's (1967) call for a psychology actively engaged in social innovation and social change, Donald Campbell's (1969) call for an "experimenting society" in which social reforms would be rigorously evaluated, and George Miller's (1969) presidential address encouraging psychologists to "give psychology away" (i.e., share psychological knowledge and expertise with citizens and communities without charge). These and other exhortations on the part of psychologists reflected the zeitgeist for enhanced academic relevance to pressing social problems. Furthermore, during the 1960s, a number of new public interest–oriented APA divisions emerged, including the Division of Community Psychology (1966), later renamed the Society for Community Research and Action (SCRA), which explicitly focused on collaborative research and action to enhance the quality of life for community residents, including the use of methods such as social action, political activism, and policy engagement (Dalton, Elias, & Wandersman, 2001).

However, the liberal political landscape of the 1960s yielded, once again, to more conservative approaches to social policy in the ensuing decades, thus limiting many progressive social policies favored by social reform–oriented psychologists. Relatedly, the ample governmental funding for social programs of the 1960s gave way to more restricted funding from the 1970s onward, further dampening some of the potential for positive social policy influence. Moreover, the view that the War on Poverty programs had been oversold by social science proponents and had resulted in very limited, if any, impact reduced the enthusiasm policymakers had for the contributions of social science, including psychology (Featherman & Vinovskis, 2001).

These challenges notwithstanding, the increased focus on social policy influence that erupted in the 1960s has continued, incrementally, in the decades that followed. One reason for this continued interest in policy was the growing awareness that the fate of psychology as a field was increasingly tied up with the decisions of policymakers. In particular, drastic cuts had been proposed for governmental funding of social science research. Furthermore, the "healthcare revolution" was emerging simultaneously, and this movement to contain treatment costs and increase third-party payment for services had major implications for the future of clinical psychology and related psychology practice disciplines. Active policy influence appeared increasingly important. Thus, in 1974, the Congressional Fellowship Program was initiated by APA, providing a year-long experience working in the federal policy arena for psychologists, a number of whom then carried a policy focus on to their ensuing careers (Fowler, 1996). Additionally, new public interest-oriented APA divisions continued to emerge in the 1970s, including Division 37, Society for Child and Family Policy and Practice[2], explicitly focused on policy influence as a primary means to enhance the well-being of children and families (Achilles, Barrueco, & Bottoms, 2013).

Throughout the 1980s and early 1990s, leading psychologists continued the call for an increased, active involvement of organized psychology in the policy arena (e.g., DeLeon, 1988; Kiesler & Morton, 1988; Leshner, 1991; Maccoby, Kahn, & Everett, 1983), although challenges were also clearly noted (Bevan, 1980; Brewster-Smith, 1990; Shadish, 1984). Others strongly cautioned against such involvement, viewing the compromises and costs as substantial, with policy involvement viewed as having the potential to damage both the reputation of the discipline as a science and the integrity of individual researchers (Fischoff,

---

[2] This is the current name, not the name when founded, as is the case for a number of the other organizations listed in the succeeding paragraphs.

1990; Woodhead, 1988). Nonetheless, new APA divisions with a public interest and policy focus continued to develop during this period, including the American Psychology-Law Society (1981), the **Society for the Psychological Study of Lesbian and Gay Issues** (1985), the **Society for the Psychological Study of Ethnic Minority Issues** (1986), and the **Society for the Study of Peace, Conflict, and Violence** (1990). Also, an independent organization, **Psychologists for Social Responsibility** (PsySR), was created during this period (1982), with the initial aim of using psychological knowledge to reduce the threat of nuclear war.

In 1996, APA published the edited volume, *Psychology and Public Policy: Balancing Public Service and Professional Need* (Lorion, Iscoe, DeLeon, & VandenBos, 1996). The editors selected a number of previously published articles (1967–93) from leading psychologists—most from the *American Psychologist*—that reflected the emerging awareness of the importance and nature of policy as a focus. In addition, the first psychologist elected to the US Congress, Ted Strickland—who later became the governor of Ohio—and a number of commentators with experience in the policy arena provided their perspectives. They emphasized the need for increased involvement by psychology, the unique assets psychologists can bring to the policy arena, the challenges involved, and the need to enhance the capacity of psychologists to engage effectively in policy work (Flattau & Howell, 1996; Frank & Callan, 1996; Lorion & Iscoe, 1996; Newman & Vincent, 1996; Strickland, 1996; Tomes & Rickel, 1996). Oft-noted recommendations for psychologists included the need for an enhanced understanding of the policy process and increased cultivation of relationships with relevant policymakers. In addition, psychologists were asked to be aware of policymakers' needs and use of research; to develop appropriate communication and science translation skills; and to engage in sustained, rather than occasional, policy activity in order to achieve policy impact.

More recently, various areas of psychology have increased their efforts and continue to develop their capacity for work in the policy arena, including those with a primary focus on the public interest. *Influencing Social Policy* focuses most centrally on psychologists from the areas of *developmental, social,* and **community psychology**. These three areas were selected for primary emphasis given their extended histories of a joint focus on research and application in the public interest in multiple social policy areas. The next three sections of this chapter provide an overview of each subfield's social policy contributions to help set the stage for the case study policy influence narratives that follow.

Developmental Psychology and Social Policy

Developmental psychologists, including those trained in schools of human development and ecology, have been at the forefront of work contributing to social policies that affect children and families (Aber, Bishop-Josef, Jones, McLearn, &

Phillips, 2007; Bogenschneider, 2014; Culp, 2013; Pillemer & White, 2005; Zigler & Hall, 2000). Phillips and Styfco (2007) presented a historical overview of the maturing of the field of child development and social policy with particular focus on the contributions of SRCD (APA Division 7). Selected aspects of the contributions of developmental psychologists to social policy are highlighted here.

Social Policy Pioneers: Urie Bronfenbrenner and Edward Zigler

Developmental psychologist Urie Bronfenbrenner is well known for his **ecological systems theory of child development**, based on the premise that environmental factors are critical to child development—a direct response to the biological determinism viewpoint held by many in the mid-20th century (Bronfenbrenner, 1979). Bronfenbrenner was invited in 1964 to testify before a congressional hearing about an antipoverty bill, and then met with Lady Bird Johnson, the wife of the president, who had an interest in the development of child care programs. Bronfenbrenner was next asked to serve on the federal planning committee tasked with developing a means to address child poverty through a preschool program. Bronfenbrenner is reported to have played an influential role in persuading the group to include the child's family and community in the resulting Head Start program (Zigler & Styfco, 2010). Over the years, Bronfenbrenner contributed in many additional ways to developmental psychology's social policy efforts, both through his widely influential scholarship and through the policy-related education and training of graduate students at the Human Ecology program at Cornell University. A number of program alumni proceeded to distinguished policy-focused careers, including five who were interviewed for the current volume (Jay Belsky, Martha Moorehouse, David Olds, Laurence Steinberg, and Abraham Wandersman).

Developmental psychologist Edward Zigler conducted research on the social and emotional aspects of intellectual disability (then labeled "mental retardation") in the 1950s and 1960s. In this work, Zigler argued against the prevailing deficits perspective on non-organic intellectual disability, asserting that social deprivation and related factors, such as fear of failure and low self-esteem, played a critical role. One of his presentations was attended by Robert Cooke, an influential pediatrician and friend of Sargent Shriver, who was responsible for overseeing development of President Johnson's War on Poverty. When Cooke was charged with chairing a planning committee to develop what was to become Project Head Start, he asked Zigler (along with fellow developmental psychologists Bronfenbrenner and Mamie Clarke) to serve on the committee. Zigler was a strong advocate for including a rigorous evaluation component and later took leave from Yale University to become the first director of the Office of Child Development (now the Administration for Children and Families) and Chief of the U.S. Children's Bureau. Returning to Yale, Zigler continued to make land-mark contributions to child development social policy over the ensuing decades. He influenced policy through his scholarship, policy ideas, advisory and consul-tation roles to policymakers, development of the Bush Training Centers, and his mentoring of numerous graduate students and others who went on to devote their careers to child development and social policy work. Several of his former gradu-ate students were interviewed for the current volume: Lawrence Aber, Deborah Phillips, and Deborah Stipek.

Major Area of Social Policy Influence: Early Childhood Programs

Building on Bronfenbrenner's and Zigler's pioneering work, developmental psy-chologists have made notable contributions to child and family policy in the en-suing decades. Policy-relevant research has increased notably over the years (e.g., Phillips & Styfco, 2007), as has the number of developmental psychologists ac-tively involved in the policy arena. Developmental psychologists bring many dis-tinctive assets to policy work, including an ecological perspective, sophisticated field research methods, and a well-developed knowledge base about a population that policymakers are generally concerned with yet know relatively little about (i.e., children and youth). Developmental psychologists outside government also have the opportunity to develop relationships with supportive colleagues working as policy insiders within child-focused administrative agencies (e.g., the **Administration on Children, Youth, and Families**).

The primary area of policy influence has perhaps been government-funded programs to support development in early childhood (from birth to age 5 years), including maternal support during the first several years of a child's life and early childhood education through pre-kindergarten (pre-k). Local, state, and federal investment in early childhood has dramatically increased in recent decades, in-cluding funding for home visiting programs for pregnant and new mothers in need; early intervention programs for infants, toddlers, and young children with dis-abilities; universal preschool; Early Head Start; and Head Start (Aber et al., 2007; Raikes, St. Clair, & Plata-Potter, 2013). Home visiting programs typically provide child development and family support to at-risk mothers (e.g., low-income single parents) in their homes, prenatally through ages 2 or 3. Federal support to states for development of such programs was approved in 2010 as part of the Affordable Care Act (see pp. 64–67). Funding for early childhood has increased at the fed-eral level in recent years through doubling of funding for Early Head Start (center-based Head Start for pregnant mothers and children birth through 3 years) and for early childhood education (pre-k) through the Department of Education's Race to the Top program. Equally important, many states have increased commitment of state funds in the early childhood arena, including a focus on universal pre-k programming. Generally speaking, enhanced early childhood funding has been used to increase access to programs by low-income residents, to enhance quality of services, and to increase the continuity of services provided (Raikes et al., 2013).

The developments in recent decades appear due to a multitude of factors and forces (Phillips & Styfco, 2007; Raikes et al., 2013; Zigler & Hall, 2000). Emerging research on brain development, beginning in the late 1990s, has played an important role, capturing the attention of policymakers and citizens alike (e.g., Garner et al., 2012; Shonkoff & Phillips, 2000). Research by developmental psychologists about environmental influences on child development, along with the development and well-designed evaluations of programs, including cost–benefit analyses indicating both positive short- and longer-term benefits, have also been critical to the process. Strategic communication of research findings by researchers and intermediary organizations, the work of developmental psychologists as policy insiders, and effective advocacy by organizations at local, state, and federal levels have also played consequential roles. A number of individuals interviewed for this volume contributed to these efforts (e.g., Aletha Huston, Lindsay Chase Lansdale, Deborah Phillips, and Deborah Stipek).

Other Areas of Policy Influence, Policy Scholarship, and Challenges

Developmental psychologists have contributed to social policy changes across a wide range of policy areas in addition to early childhood education. These include enhanced access to child care (e.g., Haskins, 2005; Phillips & McCartney, 2005), child eyewitness testimony (e.g., Goodman, 1984), child-serving systems reform (e.g., Cocozza, DePrato, Phillippi, & Keator, 2013), two-generation approaches (e.g., Chase-Lansdale & Brooks-Gunn, 2014), legal status of adolescents in the criminal justice system (e.g., Steinberg & Scott, 2003), media and children (e.g., Huston, Watkins, & Kunkel, 1989; Murray, 2013), prevention of bullying (e.g., Limber, 2011), and welfare reform (e.g., Haskins, 2006).

As is the case with early childhood policy developments, the nature of the contributions has varied, including the generation of policy-relevant research and new policy ideas, hands-on advocacy, and work as policy insiders. This volume includes representative examples of developmental psychologists whose contributions have spanned a number of content areas and types of policy influence roles.

More generally, there is a growing policy-relevant literature in the area of child and family policy (Phillips & Styfco, 2007). This literature includes edited volumes that examine a wide range of child and family policy issues (e.g., Aber, Bishop-Josef, Jones, McLearn, & Phillips, 2007; Culp, 2013; Pillemer & White, 2005) and a number of policy-focused journals, including the *Future of Children* and *Social Policy Reports*. The overarching theme of scholarship is that developmental psychologists are generating high-quality research with direct relevance to child and family policy in multiple areas. In some cases, the use of such research by policymakers is documented in the literature (e.g., David Olds' research; see Haskins & Margolis, 2014). A second theme is the critical role played by child and family advocacy organizations (e.g., Children's Defense Fund, Home Visiting Coalition) in helping to bring about policy change (Culp, 2013; Haskins & Margolis, 2014; Zigler & Hall, 2000). On occasion, the role played by psychologists directly working with or for such organizations is highlighted in the literature (e.g., Knitzer, 2005). A third theme is the potential for direct policy influence exerted by developmental psychologists in expert consultant and policy insider roles (Haskins, 2006; Zigler & Styfco, 2010).

The challenges of work in the policy arena are clearly revealed in the child and family policy literature to date, including the limitations of such research and the powerful influence of interest groups and opposing forces (Phillips & McCartney, 2005). Another major challenge relates to the role of personal values and the competing roles of policy educator and policy advocate (e.g., Bogenschneider, 2014; Phillips & Styfco, 2007). The developmental psychologist often privileges the educator role, although the primary role may depend on the particular work setting (e.g., research setting vs. advocacy organization) in which the psychologist is located (Bogenscheider, 2006). Knitzer (2005), for example, recounts her explicit advocacy efforts when working for the Children's Defense Fund, a well-known and influential advocacy organization. More details about the challenges of policy work are included in Chapter 8 of this volume.

SRCD and Other Professional and Intermediary Organizations

The increased contribution of developmental psychologists to social policy over the decades can be attributed in part to the enhanced championing of such work by professional organizations, including SRCD (Phillips & Styfco, 2007). Historically, there was resistance among leading psychologists in SRCD to support policy-focused research, viewing it as inferior to or as a distraction from the mission to contribute to theory-based understanding and to the training of psychologists first and foremost as academic researchers. Over time, however, SRCD increasingly embraced the importance of applied research and active contributions to policy. Key developments include an active social policy committee, moving SRCD central office to Washington, DC, to increase policy presence, and the development of SRCD congressional fellows program, which provides a year of policy experience in the national policy arena. In addition to SRCD, developmental psychologists have contributed to social policy through involvement in many other professional organizations, including APA's Public Interest Directorate, the **Society for Research on Adolescence**, and the Society for Child and Family Policy and Practice. Furthermore, developmental psychologists influence policy through a wide range of intermediary and advocacy organizations that conduct policy work in their specific areas of expertise.

The Emerging Discipline of Child Development and Social Policy

A number of programs and training centers have formed a consortium to further the child development and social policy mission of the field (http://www.childpolicyuniversityconsortium.com). More generally, the training of developmental psychologists has reflected an increased focus on social policy. Courses and texts exist on development and social policy (e.g., Culp, 2013; Pillemer & White, 2005; Zigler & Hall, 2000). Many developmental and human development faculty members conduct policy-relevant research in multidisciplinary centers. A recent indication of the field's interest in social policy was the 2014 conference sponsored by SRCD, titled "Strengthening Connections Among Child and Family Research, Policy, and Practice" and attended by hundreds of graduate students, faculty members, and policymakers (Society for Research in Child Development [SRCD], 2014).

The evolving history of social policy involvement by developmental psychologists has some parallels in the field of social psychology.

Social Psychology, Social Issues, and Social Policy

SPSSI has a long history of involvement in social policy. The majority of members are social psychologists with an interest in pressing social issues. A special issue of the *Journal of Social Issues*, SPSSI's flagship journal, highlights a number of areas of members' contributions on the 75th anniversary of its founding (Rutherford, Cherry, & Unger, 2011). These contributions include policy-relevant work in the areas of race, sexual orientation, poverty, human rights, and peace-building. SPSSI's website, in particular its interactive timeline (http://www.spssitimeline.org/), highlights these and other aspects of the field's development, many with implications for social policy. It also includes a list of related publications (Rutherford & Livert, n.d.). Social psychologists with an interest in social issues bring many distinctive assets to the policy arena, including a distinguished history of research on policy-relevant issues, a command of theory, and the use of rigorous experimental and related research methods.

Social Action Pioneer: Kurt Lewin

Kurt Lewin was an early, influential social psychologist and one of the founders of SPSSI. His policy-relevant contributions to the discipline include a focus on the joint influence of person and environment in influencing behavior and the importance of action-research—practical, problem-focused research conducted in real-world settings so as to simultaneously enhance social betterment and social theory (Dovidio & Estes, 2007; Pettigrew, 1988). One of SPSSI's primary honors is receipt of the Kurt Lewin Award for an individual whose work represents "outstanding contributions to the development and integration of psychological research and social action." Numerous distinguished social psychologists whose work has influenced social policy have received the award over the past 65 years, including Gordon Allport (1950), Otto Klineberg (1956), Kenneth Clark (1965), Isidor Chein (1975), Claude Steele (2002), Faye Crosby (2005), Gregory Herek (2006), and Michelle Fine (2011). A number of notable developmental psychologists have also received the award, including policy pioneers Urie Bronfenbrenner (1977) and Edward Zigler (1995).

Major Area of Social Policy Influence: Court Decisions Addressing Discrimination and Prejudice

Over the decades, perhaps the most consistent contributions of social psychologists to social policy have been in the area of discrimination and prejudice. Three key examples are social policies related to school desegregation, gender equality in the workplace, and gay rights. The social science briefs cited by the Supreme Court in the landmark 1954 *Brown v. Topeka Board of Education* decision striking down school desegregation were prepared by social psychologists Isidor Chein, Kenneth Clark, and Stuart Cook (Martin, 1998). Social psychology research, cited in the brief and in the expert witness testimony provided by Kenneth and Mamie Clark, helped to make the case that there were serious, negative psychological consequences for children of color as a result of governmental policies that mandated segregated schools for black and white students. Many other social psychologists contributed to the larger anti-segregation effort, both preceding the Supreme Court decision and as expert witnesses in cases addressing challenges to the implementation of the decision (Pettigrew, 1998).

Another seminal contribution to an important US Supreme Court case involved gender discrimination (Fiske, Bersoff, Borgida, Deaux, & Heilman, 1991). *Price Waterhouse v. Hopkins* addressed the denial of promotion to partner of a female employee based on her "non-feminine" behaviors and personality characteristics. Social psychologist Susan Fiske provided expert testimony in the case and, along with several other social and industrial/organizational psychologists, prepared a court brief summarizing findings from decades of research on gender stereotyping. The Supreme Court, citing social psychological research findings, decided in favor of plaintiff Hopkins and against Price Waterhouse. It was a precedent-setting case, and social psychologists have continued to contribute to court cases involving gender discrimination in the workplace (e.g., Borgida, Hunt, & Kim, 2005; Rudman, Glick, & Phelan, 2008).

State and Federal Supreme Court decisions related to gay rights and same-sex marriage represent yet another area in which social psychologists have contributed importantly to landmark court decisions. Over the past several decades, APA has submitted multiple **amicus briefs** to these cases, building on social psychological research supporting gay rights. In most of these cases, social psychology researcher Gregory Herek has played an important role helping to prepare the social science evidence for the briefs. Furthermore, the expert testimony of Herek and fellow social psychologists Ilan Meyer and Leticia Anne Peplau was cited by California Supreme Court Judge Walker in the landmark same sex-marriage decision in *Perry v. Schwarzenegger* (Hammack & Windell, 2011). Most recently, Herek's scholarship was well represented in the amicus brief submitted by APA to the Supreme Court in the *Obergefell v. Hodges* (2015) same-sex marriage case. The Supreme Court later ruled in favor of marriage equality, a historic decision.

Other Areas of Social Policy Influence, Policy Scholarship, and Challenges

Social psychologists have contributed to many social policy areas in addition to those just cited. These contributions include affirmative action (Gurin et al., 2004), child obesity prevention (Harris, Brownell, & Bargh, 2009), community development (Cantor, 2012), cooperative learning (Johnson, Johnson, & Stevahn, 2011), eyewitness testimony (Wells et al., 2000), reducing health disparities (Smedley & Hectors, 2014), preventing homelessness (Montgomery, Metraux, & Culhane, 2013), international human rights (Cherry, Ellingwood, & Castillo, 2011), peace-building (Kimmel, 2011), preventing use of torture (Costanzo & Gerrity, 2009), prison reform (Haney & Zimbardo, 1998; Toch, 2014), and women's rights and poverty (Bullock, 2013). The nature of the contributions has varied, ranging from policy-relevant research generation, new program and policy idea development, expert consultation, advocacy, and policy insider work. This volume includes representative examples of social psychologists whose contributions have spanned a number of content areas and policy influence roles.

More generally, there is vibrant policy-relevant scholarship within social psychology, including authored books, edited volumes, and journal articles that examine a wide range of social issues (e.g., Borgida & Fiske, 2008; Bullock, 2013; Costanzo & Krauss, 2012; Haney, 2006; Lanning, 2012; Massey & Barreras, 2013; Nosek & Riskind, 2012; Toch, 2014). The content of these books and special issues of prominent journals focus primarily on reviews of policy-relevant research generating policy implications from extant theory and research and describing or critiquing current social policies. Articles in the *Journal of Social Issues,* along with those in SPSSI's two policy specialty journals, *Social Issues and*

Policy Review and *Analyses of Social Issues and Public Policy*, routinely focus on current policy concerns, providing relevant empirical evidence, policy analysis, and social psychological perspectives.

A number of social psychologists have specialized in the law and psychology area, examining the implications of social psychology theory and research for legal issues and procedures. Borgida and Fiske (2008), for example, invited authors to generate potential implications of social psychological research in multiple legal areas. Chapter authors were asked to indicate how research could serve as a guide for policy, what issues limit policy relevance, and how research can be better designed to answer policy questions. More generally, many empirical studies of human behavior in legal contexts have been published in specialty journals such as *Law and Social Behavior*.

Other types of policy-relevant research conducted by social psychologists include collaborative, evaluation, and participatory action research. Phillip Goff and his colleagues at UCLA's Center for Policing Equity conduct collaborative research studying racial profiling with police departments around the country (e.g., Goff & Kahn, 2012). Collaborations are guided in part by meetings with researchers, practitioners, and government officials to generate a research agenda to advance future research and research-based consultation on racial profiling and related topics. David Johnson, Roger Johnson, and Laurie Stevahn (2011) discuss the potential of theory-based evaluation research to influence policymakers in the area of cooperative education. Michele Fine and colleagues conducted participatory action research with prison inmates to address the need for college education programs in prisons (Fine et al., 2001).

Other chapters, articles, or books describe or analyze the active involvement of social psychologists in the policy arena and discuss any subsequent impact on policy and practice. This is particularly the case in terms of expert witness and amicus briefs for important court cases (Fiske et al., 1991; Gurin et al., 2004; Herek, 2006; Hammack & Windell, 2011) and extends to work with criminal justice administrators (e.g., Toch, 2014). Although many social psychologists work in intermediary organizations and as policy insiders, their experiences are more likely to emerge as presentations at SPSSI-sponsored policy workshops (e.g., Society for the Psychological Study of Social Issues [SPSSI], 2013) than in the published literature. Accounts of personal experience and "lessons learned" are generally not considered scientific contributions by journal editors.

SPSSI and Other Professional and Intermediary Organizations

As noted earlier, the contributions of social psychologists concerned with social issues and social policy influence have been facilitated by the mission and resources of SPSSI. SPSSI maintains an office in Washington, DC, has an active social policy committee and employs a full-time staff person whose sole function is to advance SPSSI's social policy work. Such work includes facilitating congressional briefings (in which social psychologists present findings on policy areas on Capitol Hill), preparing policy position statements, and leading workshops in social policy for members. In 1983, SPSSI established a congressional fellowship program, the James Marshall Public Policy Fellowship, to allow psychologists to gain hands-on policy experience serving as a congressional staffer for a member of Congress.

In addition to SPSSI, social psychologists have contributed to social policy through involvement in many other professional organizations, including the Public Interest Directorate of APA, American Psychological Society, **American Psychology-Law Society**, and Psychologists for Social Responsibility. Furthermore, social psychologists work to influence policy through a wide variety of intermediary and advocacy organizations that pursue policy change in their specific areas of expertise.

Both developmental and social psychology efforts have made significant contributions to public interest psychology. Their efforts have been met by a third field, community psychology, that also jointly emphasizes research and application.

Community Psychology and Social Policy

Community psychology emerged as a discipline in the mid-1960s, in response to the perceived lack of psychology's relevance to the pressing social issues facing the nation during that tumultuous decade. As such, from the start, community psychology focused on social change through community research and action, including systems change and social policy. There was also special emphasis placed on substantially broadening the applications of clinical psychology and community mental health, respectively, given the perceived incapacity of an individually focused clinical psychology to fully address the mental health needs of citizens. The field's focus on prevention and social issues has led to linkages with both developmental and social psychology. Community psychologists, including clinical-community, developmental-community, and social-community psychologists, have made substantial contributions to social policy through both applied research and hands-on policy activities.

Community psychologists bring a number of assets to policy work, including a multilevel analytical framework, social justice values, and a joint focus on research and social action (Maton, Jason, Humphreys, & Shinn, in press). This multilevel framework provides a distinct lens through which to view the complex social problems that social policies address, encompassing interrelated individual, group, family, organizational, community, and cultural influences (Dymnicki, Wandersman, Osher, & Pakstis, in press; Foster-Fishman & Behrens, 2007). This framework similarly contributes to an appreciation of the complexities of the social policymaking process. Also, the field's explicit values of empowerment, citizen participation, social justice, and social change can serve as valuable assets in the social policy arena. Community psychologists are likely to espouse strengths-based policy approaches that build on the existing strengths of populations and communities and foster the development of new ones (Maton, Schellenbach, Leadbeater, & Solarz, 2004). Relatedly, the field's focus on social change highlights the need for policies that change higher order social structures rather than simply exhorting individuals to cope with them (Rappaport, 1981).

Pioneer in Social Innovation: Seymour Sarason

Seymour Sarason, to whom this book is dedicated, was a pioneering figure in community psychology, helping to move psychology from its entrenched focus on the individual level of analysis to one also focused on organizations, social systems, and social policy (Sarason, 1971, 1972, 1974, 1986, 1990, 2006). Sarason's scholarship and consultation activities contributed to a greater focus on teachers and the school context in educational policy as well as a community-based (rather than an institution-based) approach to serving citizens with intellectual disabilities. Sarason also played a part in the shift toward greater emphasis on organizational change, coalition building, prevention, and advocacy—rather than sole reliance on individual services—as a focus for human service intervention and policy (Reppucci, 2011). Key concepts such as the culture of the school, psychological sense of community, and professional preciousness continue to guide community psychologists in their work in the public interest. Sarason mentored numerous community psychologists who, through their own policy-focused work and that of their students, maintained a policy focus as an integral aspect of the field. A number of these individuals were interviewed for this volume (Preston Britner, Heather Kelly, Edward Mulvey, N. Dickon Reppucci, Rhona Weinstein, and Jennifer Woolard).

Primary Area of Policy Influence: Prevention

Community psychologists' most enduring influence on social policy to date is their contribution to the establishment of prevention as an important area of focus. Broadly defined, this focus encompasses prevention of both psychological (e.g., depression) and social (e.g., violence) problems, as well as the promotion of well-being. Prevention was an emerging concept in the mental health field when community psychology was established in the 1960s. In the 1970s, 1980s, and 1990s, a number of community psychologists contributed to the movement to legitimize prevention as a critical area of activity within mental health and related fields. This was achieved through development and evaluation of prevention programs, generation of prevention-focused journals, completion of meta-analyses and literature reviews on prevention programs, and serving as participants and/or chairs in national task forces and commissions that produced prevention-focused books and reports (e.g., Cowen, 1983; Durlak & Wells, 1997; Mrarek & Haggerty, 1994; Price, Cowen, Lorion, & Ramos-McKay, 1988; Reiss & Price, 1996; Reppucci, Woolard, & Fried, 1999). Community psychologists have contributed to strengths-based prevention and promotion of social policies at local, state, and federal levels in a range of content areas. These include diversion from the juvenile justice system, HIV/AIDS prevention, social and emotional learning in schools, school dropout prevention, and substance abuse prevention (Association for the Study and Development of Community [ASDC], 2003; Britner & Stone, 2010; Gordon, Ji, Mulhall, Shaw, & Weissberg, 2011; Miller, 2013).

Other Areas of Policy Influence, Policy Scholarship, and Challenges

Community psychologists in recent decades have contributed to many other areas of social policy in addition to prevention at varied levels of government. These contributions include child abuse and neglect prevention (Melton, Thompson, & Small, 2001), child mental health systems reform (Huang et al., 2005), domestic violence prevention and intervention (Cook, Woolard, & McCollum, 2004), education reform (Johnson, 2011), gay rights advocacy (Pope, 2012), substance abuse and healthcare reform (Humphreys, 2012), homelessness prevention (Shinn, 2007), juvenile justice systems reform (Britner & Stone, 2010), teenage pregnancy prevention (e.g., Wilcox & Deutsch, 2013), and violence against women systemic response (Campbell et al., 2015).

The methods of policy influence include the generation of policy-relevant research and new policy ideas, evaluation research (Miller, in press), expert consultation, advocacy, and work as policy insiders (McMahon & Wolfe, in press). Child-clinical-community psychologist Gary Melton, for example, served as vice chair of the US Advisory Board on Child Abuse and Neglect in the early 1990s, contributing to new neighborhood-based strategies for child protection and the reorganization of extant federal efforts (Melton et al., 2001). This volume includes community psychologists whose contributions have spanned a number of content areas and types of policy influence roles.

More generally, there is a growing policy-relevant literature in the area of community psychology, including a number of edited and authored books as well as special issues that focus, at least in part, on the policy involvements of community psychologists. These books, edited volumes, chapters, and journal articles examine a wide range of social policy topics (e.g., Bond & Haynes, 2014; Cohen &

Ventura, in preparation; Maton et al., 2004; Miller, in press; Olson & Soldz, 2007; Sarason, 1990; Wandersman, Chien, & Katz, 2012; Weinstein, 2002). This scholarship includes several personal accounts of contributions to specific policies (Gordon et al., 2011; Jason, 2013; Meyers, 2011; Shinn, 2007; Speer et al., 2003; Starnes, 2004; Vincent, 1990; Wilcox & Deutsch, 2013; Wolff, 2013).

Examples of effective community psychologists include Rebecca Campbell, Leonard Jason, Marybeth Shinn, and Thomas Wolff. Rebecca Campbell's action research studies and policy influence efforts in the area of sexual assault contributed to important changes. These include passage of statewide legislation and procurement of federal funding directed at mandated testing of rape kits, an overhaul of Michigan's Sexual Assault Kit, a new statewide protocol for post-assault medical care and advocacy services, the SANE Practitioner Evaluation Toolkit disseminated nationally and used in multiple cities throughout the country, and trainings of government officials nationwide to change the culture of rape-victim blaming (Campbell et al., 2015).

Leonard Jason's book, *Principles of Social Change* (2013), details his career-long contributions to local, state, and national policy in three primary areas: smoking prevention among teenagers; strengths-based definition and enhanced funding for chronic disease; and community-based, peer-run residences for individuals recovering from addiction. In his policy-influence work, Jason brings to bear community-based research, collaboration with advocates, and expert consultation with policymakers. He proposes five key steps as integral to social action influence: determine the nature of the change desired, identify who holds the power, create coalitions, be patient but persistent, and measure success.

Marybeth Shinn's work (2007) highlights six key lessons related to policy influence based on her decades of work with policy administrators in executive agencies with jurisdiction over homelessness programs. The lessons are individual leaders matter, timing matters, ideas matter, costs and who bears the costs matter, government is not monolithic, and one cannot control the uses to which data are put.

Thomas Wolff (2013) provides the perspective of a locality-based community psychology practitioner. He emphasizes that opportunities to influence policy naturally arise as one works with citizens and community groups to address pressing social issues that affect them. Specifically, his work facilitating community-based coalitions in multiple regions of Massachusetts involved periodic policy influence efforts at local and state levels in the areas of health equity, housing, homelessness, sex education in schools, and welfare legislation.

The overarching theme of community psychology scholarship and policy work to date is the importance of a multilevel ecological framework and social justice values. A second theme is the use of a wide variety of research approaches, including epidemiology, qualitative and mixed methods, controlled trials, and participatory action research. In many cases, collaboration with advocacy organizations is integral. A third theme is the potential for direct policy influence exerted by community psychologists in expert consultant, coalition building, and policy insider roles.

The challenges of work in the policy arena are clearly revealed in the community psychology literature, including the tensions between social justice values and science (e.g., Price, 1989). Confronting powerful interest groups and the necessity of addressing power differentials more generally is another challenge raised (Culley & Angelique, 2011; Jason, 2013; Speer et al., 2003). The difficulties facing policy and program implementation represents a third, enduring theme, beginning with Seymour Sarason's groundbreaking work in this area (e.g., Sarason, 1971).

Role of SCRA and Other Professional Associations and Intermediary Organizations

The contributions of community psychologists to social policy have been encouraged over the years by the leadership of SCRA and in recent years by its Social Policy Committee. The Policy Committee involves members in creation of policy position statements and conducts workshops in social policy for both students and members. In addition to SCRA, community psychologists have contributed to social policy through their involvement in many other professional organizations, including APA Public Interest Directorate, APA Legal Affairs Committee, **Society for Child and Family Policy and Practice**, American Psychology-Law Society, Society for Prevention Science, and Psychologists for Social Responsibility. Furthermore, community psychologists work through various intermediary and advocacy organizations, conducting policy work in their specific areas of expertise.

The scholarly and action-focused contributions of community psychologists represent a third public interest arena of psychology's policy influence work, one complementary to yet distinct from the work of developmental and social psychologists. Taken together, developmental psychologists, social psychologists, and community psychologists whose careers have explicitly focused on influencing social policy provide a considerable breadth of policy influence coverage, both in terms of policy content areas and policy roles. At the same time, limiting the primary focus of this volume to these three subgroups allows a depth of understanding about three important policy-relevant subfields.

Research Methodology

Interview Sample

The author interviewed 79 psychologists between June 2012 and January 2015. As part of the interview, participants were asked to describe their greatest success in influencing a social policy. Forty-seven of those interviewed were working full-time in academic settings at the time of their greatest success, 18 in policy-focused intermediary organizations (American Psychological Association; National Academies; evaluation, research, and consulting firms; foundations), and 14 were working full-time as policy insiders within government. Thirty-six of those interviewed reported that their greatest policy success was at the federal level, 21 at the state level, 10 at the local level, and the remaining 12 at multiple levels, in another country, or difficult to classify.

Thirty-nine percent of the interviewees identify with community psychology (and closely related fields), 23% with developmental psychology (and closely related fields), and 17% with social psychology (and closely related fields). Another 9% jointly identify with developmental and community psychology, or social and community psychology. The remaining 13% of interviewees primarily identify with other areas of the discipline, including clinical, counseling, evaluation, measurement/quantitative, and psychology and law, but pursued careers firmly centered in public interest psychology (see Appendix A for a detailed breakdown). Although the vast majority of psychologists interviewed received degrees from programs within psychology departments, several received degrees from psychology-focused programs housed elsewhere, including child and family studies, education, and human development. The average year of PhD receipt was 1981, with a range from 1964 to 2008. Somewhat more men (57%) than women (43%) were interviewed. An alphabetical list of those interviewed, along with subfield identification(s) and year of PhD receipt is included in Appendix B.

Sampling Procedure

To identify potential interviewees, an initial pool of interviewees—developmental, social, and community psychologists actively involved in policy influence work—was generated from multiple sources. These sources included nominations from leaders within SRCD, SPSSI, and SCRA who were knowledgeable about policy work; listings of SRCD, SPSSI, SCRA, and APA policy award winners; a review of policy-related scholarship in developmental, social, and community psychology; and the William T. Grant Foundation (which provided funding for this book project). This process resulted in a list of 30 individuals. Thereafter, a snowballing sampling method was used in which interviewees were asked to nominate other psychologists actively involved in policy work. Given that the proposed volume was to be published as part of the Society for Community Research and Action Book Series, the decision was made to interview a somewhat larger sample of community psychologists than developmental and social psychologists. Furthermore, the larger number of academic, rather than nonacademic, psychologists interviewed reflects the relatively smaller pool of nonacademic than academic developmental, social, and community psychologists identified.

Potential interviewees were contacted by email. The interview was described as part of a book project to document the involvement of psychologists in the policy arena, involving a 90-minute, digitally recorded audio interview covering multiple aspects of past and present policy involvements and perspectives. Interviewees were informed that they would be given the opportunity to review and edit any quoted material to be published. A consent form was sent to those individuals who agreed to take part and a date set for the interview. The vast majority of interviews were recorded over the phone; three local interviews were conducted in person. The average interview lasted 95 minutes, with a range from 70 to 120 minutes.

Overall, 113 individuals were contacted. Twenty individuals (18%) did not respond to the invitation emails, and another thirteen (12%) declined the opportunity to take part. Of those who declined to take part, some cited extremely busy schedules that precluded a 90-minute interview, several indicated their active involvement in the policy arena was minor, and several policy insiders indicated that they did not want to be interviewed "on the record."

Interview Protocol

A semi-structured interview protocol was generated from available literature and from the author's personal experience teaching a graduate course in social policy and psychology over the course of three decades. The protocol was divided into eight sections (see Appendix C for the full protocol):

1. Personal and professional pathways to becoming involved in policy-related work
2. Policy involvement to date, including greatest success and a policy failure or mistake
3. Disciplinary background and training; benefits and limitations of policy-related work
4. Characteristics of effective and useful policy-relevant research from personal experience
5. Useful skills and policy influence tools
6. Nature of career policy influence (e.g., incremental, transformative); types of research and policy-influence efforts needed for transformative, systemic social change
7. Ideas for enhancing the policy influence effectiveness of psychology
8. Final message or theme about psychologists' involvement in policy

Interview Coding and Analysis

The interviews were transcribed and generated slightly more than 4,000 double-spaced pages. The author and graduate students content-coded the interview transcripts using qualitative research analysis software, with codes based on the various interview questions.

The brief case examples, which constitute the core of Chapters 3–7, were primarily generated by the question, *"What has been your greatest success in influencing a social policy?"* The probes that followed were:

- Please provide a detailed account of the factors and processes that led to change in this policy area.
- What role did policy-relevant research findings play?
- What types of advocacy approaches led to your success?
- What were the barriers and challenges you faced?
- What strategies did you use to address these challenges?

Many of those interviewed commented that the request to identify their "greatest success in influencing a social policy" presented difficulties. For many, this was a difficult question because multiple individuals and groups contributed to the policy outcomes they worked to achieve, so their own personal influence on the outcome was not possible to distinguish. In several cases, individuals indicated that they did not feel they had a true policy impact. Others felt that there were a number of different policy influence efforts they could characterize as their greatest success. Still others felt the term "policy success" was problematic because contributions to the passage of policy did not ensure that the implementation of the policy occurred as planned or that it led to desired outcomes, or did not take into account the reality that positive policy outcomes at the time were later reversed. In all cases, interviewees were provided the freedom to select the area of policy influence work they were most interested in discussing. In some cases, this did not involve, from their perspective, a singular, distinctive, or unequivocal policy success, as we will see in Chapters 3–7.

Overview of the Remaining Chapters

Chapter 2 provides a brief overview of the social policy process and players and the different vantage points, methods, and skills that psychologists use to influence the policy process. It sets the stage for Chapters 3–7, each of which presents multiple case examples of psychologists describing their greatest success in influencing a social policy. Chapter 3 highlights the methods and skills used by psychologists whose greatest policy success occurred while working in a university setting. Legislative, executive, and judicial branch policy successes and related policy influence methods and skills are each examined. Chapter 4 describes the policy successes of psychologists working in an intermediary policy organization setting. The policy influence successes are depicted for psychologists working for APA; the National Academies; research, consulting, and evaluation firms; and foundations. Chapter 5 presents policy successes for psychologists working within government as policy insiders. Specifically, the policy influence work of psychologists working within the legislative and executive branches is depicted.

The different types of research generated to influence policymakers constitute the central focus of Chapter 6. Four broad classes of scholarship are depicted: program evaluation, understanding phenomena of interest, research on system policies and practices, and research-based practical aids (for implementing agencies). In Chapter 7, the focus switches to career patterns of policy influence. Four career themes are illustrated: multiple involvements over time, **interdisciplinary collaboration**, leadership roles, and international contributions. Chapter 8 provides accounts of policy failures, challenges, and lessons learned. External challenges include politics in the form of values, ideology, and beliefs; politics in the form of powerful corporate and institutional interests; issues of cost and budget; transitions and turnover; and obstacles to successful policy implementation. More personal challenges described include effective communication, scientific and personal integrity, weathering personal attacks, and workload strain. Chapter 9, the final chapter, examines key overarching themes from the previous chapters. The chapter concludes with a set of recommendations for enhancing the future capacity of psychologists to effectively serve the public interest in the social policy arena.

We turn next to an overview of the policy process and a description of the methods and skills used by psychologists to influence that process.

2

Psychologists in the Policy Arena

Policy Process, Use of Research, Vantage Points, Methods, and Skills

> *If you want to influence policy you have to begin with questions that policy-makers either want or should want answers to.*
>
> —T. Vincent, June 7, 2012

This chapter sets the stage for those that follow by providing an overview of the policy process; the use of research within it; and the vantage points, methods, and skills psychologists employ to exert policy influence. The policy process is complex. Having basic knowledge about this complicated process is a precondition for effective policy influence work. An overview of the policy process is the focus of the first section of the chapter, including discussion of the four phases in the policy process where psychologists can exert influence: agenda setting, formulation and adoption, implementation, and evaluation and revision. The use of research by policymakers is not a given in any of these four phases and is of particular importance to the field of psychology. A description of the types of research used and the factors that facilitate and impede their use in the policy process constitutes the focus of the second section of the chapter.

Psychologists seek to influence policy from various **vantage points**, including universities, intermediary organizations, and as policy insiders. The distinctive features of each vantage point are discussed in the third section of the chapter. Across vantage points, psychologists use a variety of methods to influence policy. These methods, presented in the fourth section of the chapter, include serving on policy advisory groups, direct communication with policymakers, courtroom-focused activities, consultation and technical assistance, generation of policy-relevant documents, external advocacy, and use of the media. Some of these methods involve psychologists in direct communication with policymakers and their staff (direct policy pathway), whereas other methods involve psychologists in communication with others (e.g., advocacy groups, media, citizens) who in turn exert influence on policymakers (indirect policy pathway). Furthermore, the methods vary in the extent to which the underlying mechanism of influence relies on education, guidance, persuasion, or pressure.

Regardless of vantage point and method, psychologists employ a core set of skills in their policy influence work. These include relationship building, communication, research, and strategic analysis. These skills are presented in the fifth section of the chapter. You may wonder how to get started in policy work, and this chapter concludes by highlighting some of the ways.

We begin our journey into the policy arena with a brief overview of the policy process.

The Policy Process: An Ecological, Systemic Perspective

There is extensive literature in political science and related disciplines examining the world of social policy through varied lenses. Across theoretical and conceptual models, the policymaking process is described as highly complex, comprising multiple phases, levels, domains, sources of influence, and uses of evidence (e.g., Cochran, 2016; Kraft & Furlong, 2015; Oleszek, Oleszek, Rybicki, & Heniff, 2016; Peters, 2016). Figure 2.1 provides a visual representation of the process. The figure is simplified to focus on elements particularly important to psychologists who seek to influence policy. More comprehensive and contextualized versions can be found elsewhere (e.g., Oleszek, 2016).

Phases of the Policy Process

The four primary phases of the policy cycle are depicted in the center of Figure 2.1, surrounded by key influences and then the stakeholder groups involved. The bottom portion of the figure includes several underlying macro forces and additional contextual factors that exert influence on all aspects of the policy process. The four policy phases are:

- Agenda setting
- Policy formulation and adoption
- Policy implementation
- Policy evaluation and revision

These phases are interactive and iterative, and this dynamic and cyclical nature plays out at interrelated local, state, and national levels.

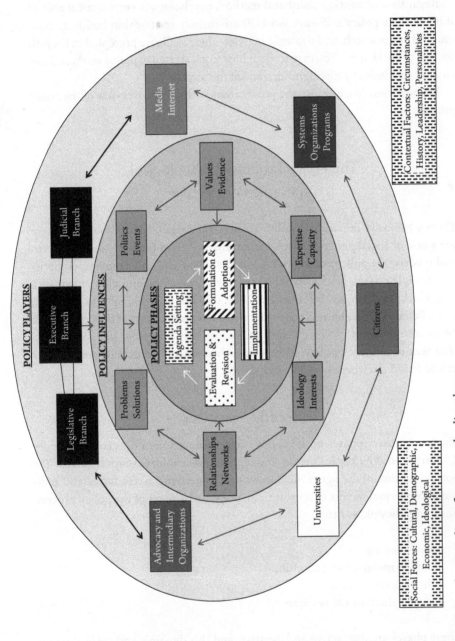

Figure 2.1 Policy players, policy influences, and policy phases.

Phase 1: Agenda Setting

Myriad social issues compete for the attention of policymakers, and very few issues receive serious policy attention at any given point in time (Kingdon, 1984; Kraft & Furlong, 2015). Descriptive models of **agenda setting** underscore the importance of **"policy windows"**—discrete moments when a convergence of factors leads a social problem to rise to the top of the policy agenda. Kingdon (1984) asserts that the convergence of three sets of factors in particular contribute to the opening of a policy window: the problem stream, the policy stream, and the political stream.

- The **problem stream** refers to existing conditions identified as problematic in society.
- The **policy stream** involves policy ideas or solutions that can be applied to various problems.
- The **political stream** refers to political considerations and related macro events that privilege particular problems or solutions.

When two or three of these streams converge, odds are greatly increased that a social issue will make it onto the policy agenda and be addressed by policymakers. For example, in 2015, two South Carolina US senators (one a presidential candidate) and the state's Republican governor called for state legislative action to remove the Confederate flag from the state capitol. This proposal was subsequently approved by the state legislature. This example reflects the convergence of:

- The highly publicized, racially motivated shooting of nine Black churchgoers by a 21-year-old male White supremacist, shown in online images holding a Confederate flag and a gun (problem stream)
- Earlier calls, spanning decades, to remove the Confederate flag from the state capitol (policy stream)
- The 2015–16 competitive Republican presidential primary race and South Carolina's role in it (political stream)

Intrinsic characteristics of a social issue or problem that help attract the attention of policymakers include the particular individuals or groups affected by the issue, the number of people affected, and the nature of the issue's impact (e.g., degree and type of human suffering, economic and social consequences). How the problem is defined and how the evidence is framed are both extremely important. For example, a problem is more likely to rise to the top of the policy agenda if it is shown to be directly related to salient national values (e.g., freedom, justice; Peters, 2016). If feasible means to address a problem are not available, a problem is unlikely to receive consideration by policymakers.

Legislators at the local, state, and national levels have the final say in determining which items will be considered in the form of proposed new legislation. The various stakeholder groups (shown in Figure 2.1) each seek to exert influence with legislators. These groups include the elected officials in the executive branch (president, governors, county executives, mayors), political parties, executive branch agencies, advocacy groups, corporations, the media, human service delivery systems, and citizens.

The policy agendas of elected and appointed executive branch officials are influenced by many of the same groups that influence legislators, as well as by legislators themselves. The **judicial branch** agenda, especially at the highest levels (e.g., appellate and supreme court cases), is less directly affected by the various stakeholder groups given the independence of the judicial branch. Nonetheless, which cases reach the attention of appellate and supreme court justices and are ultimately selected for court action are partly affected by which cases have been brought to lower court levels, which in turn is directly influenced by various stakeholder and interest groups (Howard & Steigerwalt, 2012).

Several types of evidence contribute to agenda setting and problem definition. They include the personal experiences of policymakers, the experiences and perspectives of constituents, statistical data about the extent and nature of problems, social science research findings, and scholarly theory. Sources of evidence related to agenda setting are especially important to elected officials if they pertain to their specific jurisdiction (e.g., their town, city, county, state) and are conveyed by trusted sources (Bogenschneider & Corbett, 2010; Levine, 2009; Tseng, 2012). Trusted sources include individuals and organizations that have established and maintained positive and useful relationships with elected officials. Additional trusted sources include relevant organizations perceived to disseminate quality and politically neutral information.

Phase 2: Policy Formulation and Adoption

Various **policy stakeholders**, including legislative and executive branch officials and each of the nongovernmental groups depicted in Figure 2.1 may directly and indirectly contribute to the policy ideas that take form in a given piece of proposed legislation. Any legislator can submit legislation reflecting potential means to address issues of concern. Bipartisan sponsorship of proposed legislation increases the odds of legislative success. Various forms of evidence, ranging from personal experience to peer-reviewed research findings, may contribute to the proposed legislation.

The policy process includes a number of sequential, yet iterative, steps. What is described here is based on the federal level of government but remains relevant in many cases for state and local policy formulation policy processes as well. Proposed legislation is referred to the appropriate committee by the leader of the chamber. The committee chairs, from the majority party, have great power in deciding if and when a proposed policy will be reviewed by committee members. Extensive policy formulation occurs prior to the time the legislation is formally submitted, and the process continues in committee for the small subset of proposed bills that are taken up. Lobbyists, constituents, and various experts meet with legislators, and especially with their staff, to contribute ideas and perspectives related to possible revisions to the proposed legislation. Hearings may be held where selected experts are asked to testify. Legislators on the committee consider various proposed changes, and, if negotiation is successful and the majority of members vote affirmatively, the proposed legislation moves to the full chamber for discussion and a vote on the floor. If the legislation passes both chambers, with any differences reconciled in a joint committee, it is then up to the chief executive (e.g., president) to sign the legislation into law or to veto it.

Many factors contribute to legislator voting behaviors on a given piece of legislation, including personal values and experiences, evidence related to the legislation's perceived benefits and costs, the position taken on the issue by the legislator's political party, prior deals made to secure support, and how one's vote will be viewed by various stakeholder groups. Constituents and interest groups who contribute money and resources toward re-election are especially important stakeholders (Oleszek, 2016). If research exists that is directly relevant to the proposed legislation, it may be one among many factors that influence how a legislator votes. Research may be especially likely to play an influential role on issues that are relatively noncontroversial, such as aging issues and child welfare. Influential research knowledge often bears directly on key technical issues or contributes compelling evidence, for example, concerning the cost–benefit ratio associated with a particular piece of policy change. Legislation that emerges often differs considerably from that initially submitted due to negotiation and compromise resulting from different perspectives along with cost and feasibility concerns (Oleszek, 2016; Peters, 2016).

The **incrementalism framework** asserts that only small-scale changes tend to occur at a given time in the policy arena. This may be due to resistance to more far-reaching, comprehensive change on the part of stakeholder groups with a vested interest in the current policy (whether related to power, profit, or ideology). Lack of agreement on the nature of the problem and preferred solutions and the inherently paradoxical nature of major social problems (i.e., equally valid but opposing social values or principles at play) require compromises to be made at the expense of more comprehensive or transformative changes. Similarly, the distribution of power between the legislative chambers and between the legislative and executive branches contribute to the norm of incremental rather than transformative policy change (Oleszek, 2016; Peters, 2016).

The **advocacy-coalition framework**, in contrast, provides a perspective on the policy process that accounts for the occasional, far-reaching change that occurs on contentious social issues. According to this perspective, it is the emergence of new coalitions among interest groups, experts, and political parties that allows such far-reaching change. For example, many typically unaligned groups joined forces to support passage of the Affordable Care Act of 2010 (ACA or Obamacare), including liberal progressive groups (e.g., consumer groups, unions, civil rights groups) and varied healthcare stakeholder groups (health insurers, doctors, the pharmaceutical industry, and hospital associations; Kirsch, 2013). According to the advocacy-coalition framework, the current equilibrium is punctuated by such new coalitions. After the significant change has occurred, however, a new status quo emerges, which once again makes fundamental change unlikely until the next transformation in the constitution of the advocacy coalition.

The executive and judicial branches also directly formulate and adopt policy. For example, the president may offer executive orders that do not require Congressional approval, and numerous consequential policy decisions are made by executive branch agencies in specifying how enacted legislation will be implemented. Supreme Court decisions determine the constitutionality of existing legislation and how contested laws are to be interpreted. Supreme Court decisions on social issues such as school desegregation, affirmative action, gender and race discrimination, and gay rights represent major policy changes, both at national and state levels. Advocacy groups and professional organizations often seek to influence court decisions by filing briefs that summarize research and provide interpretative frameworks that are relevant to important court cases (Levine, Wallach, & Levine, 2007).

Phase 3: Policy Implementation

Policy as adopted is distinct from policy as implemented. Implementation is a complicated process involving many actors at many levels. When legislatures pass laws, the implementation of policy typically falls first into the hands of executive branch agencies. These agencies devise the specific rules, regulations, and the many operational details of the laws passed. In many cases, the executive branch selects specific programs to develop and/or fund that ultimately lead to operationalizing the laws. There is extensive literature on implementation challenges that occur within executive branch agencies, including issues of turf, power, ideology, inadequate communication, and bureaucratic ineptitude. In addition, there will likely be multiple levels and layers of executive branch agencies involved spanning a number of departments and various levels of government (e.g., city, county, state, national). One recent and widely known implementation challenge involved the inability of the federal website developed for the ACA to handle millions of users when the website was launched, leading to an ineffective (and politically costly) start to enrollment of the previously uninsured.

Ultimately, in many cases, local education, health, human service, social welfare, and other organizations deliver government-funded or regulated services and programs to citizens with little if any day-to-day oversight from legislative, executive, and judicial branches of government. Thus, these local organizations often make critical policy choices even if they are not explicitly labeled as such (e.g., how a university takes into account applicants' race/ethnicity in deciding who to admit). There is a growing literature detailing the facilitators of and challenges to successful implementation at the level of local organizations and delivery systems (Durlak, 2013; Fixsen, Naoom, Blase, Friedman, & Wallace, 2005; Hall & Hord, 2006; Hodges & Ferreira, 2013; Honig, 2006; Mihalic & Irwin, 2003). Challenges include resistance to change, limited organizational capacity (e.g., resources and staff), insufficient training and supervision, battles over turf and priorities, difficulty adapting new policies and government-funded initiatives to local contexts and populations, and, more generally, failure to obtain "buy-in" and commitment at the local level.

Many case studies have documented implementation problems in major national social policies ranging from school desegregation and the war on poverty to the rollout of the ACA, as noted earlier. Politics, economics, power dynamics, organizational dysfunction, and myriad other factors at multiple levels of complex systems serve as barriers to successful implementation. Given inadequate implementation, it is difficult to determine whether social programs are ineffective because of limitations in the policy solution itself or due to the inadequate implementation. Indeed, the enhanced focus on government funding of evidence-based programs in recent years belies the fact that programs shown to be effective under conditions where they were carefully and fully implemented on a small, local scale may not similarly prove effective when "scaled up" and implemented as part of the local, state, or federal government implementation systems.

Phase 4: Policy Evaluation and Revision

Historically, evaluation of governmental social policies has been based on whether the allocated funds were spent as intended and whether specified activities occurred. In recent decades, there has been greater focus on results accountability, in which outcomes of the policy are examined in some fashion. Data systems and internal data analysis capacities have been enhanced at all levels, ranging from local community agencies to state and federal executive branch agencies. Nonetheless, in many cases, available outcome indicators lack sufficient reliability and validity and cannot be uniquely or definitively linked to policy activities. Indeed, from a social science perspective, it has been difficult to achieve systematic, scientifically valid means to evaluate local, state, and federal policy outcomes. Nonetheless, increasingly in recent decades, there has been funding included in legislation explicitly set aside for systematic evaluation. In particular, funding has been made available for legislation pertaining to discrete social programs serving individuals whose outcomes can be compared to others not receiving the program (McCartney & Weiss, 2007).

Of note, in 2009, building upon newly elected President Barack Obama's commitment to enhanced use of evidence to guide social policy, the federal Office of Management and Budget communicated to all federal agencies that federal policies should include programs that are backed by evidence (Haskins & Margolis, 2014). This commitment has further increased federal funding of social program evaluations and more generally increased focus on evaluation of government social policies and associated discrete social programs.

Although the level of resources devoted to policy and government-funded program evaluations has increased over time, it is not clear to what extent the resulting findings contribute to policy revision or termination. Social policies, once instituted, often develop their own constituencies, including those who carry out the program and receive related resources. Government-funded programs are notoriously difficult to terminate even when findings are negative because constituency groups are often effective at influencing elected officials. The decade of negative findings about the substance use prevention program Drug Abuse Resistance Education (DARE) is often cited as an instance of negative findings proving insufficient to cause governmental program termination. The program's continuance—despite the absence of supportive evidence—was due in part to ardent support for the program from the police departments that implement it and their strong relationships with local politicians (Weiss, Murphy-Graham, & Birkeland, 2005).

Policy revision is much more likely to occur than outright policy termination. Required reauthorizations of existing policies represent a particularly opportune time for stakeholders to reexamine existing programs—to consider whether the policy should remain as is or be revised. Nonetheless, policy revision, even if part of a planned policy reauthorization, is best characterized as simply a new round of policy formulation and adoption. Thus, the full range of actors and forces at work during initial agenda setting, policy formulation, and policy adoption will again be present. Evaluation research findings are only one among many factors that contribute to policy formulation and adoption during the potential revision of existing legislation and related executive branch rules, regulations, and operational details. Furthermore, program evaluations that indicate negative or mixed findings may not necessarily include useful information specifying exactly how a major social policy or government-funded program should be modified.

Executive branch agencies that oversee program selection and funding often contract out evaluations of specific initiatives to social science researchers and research organizations. The limited use of the resulting evaluation findings is part of the larger question about research use in the policymaking process, a topic to which we turn next.

The Use of Research in the Policymaking Process

Research constitutes a key resource that psychologists bring to bear on social policy. As noted earlier, however, research findings are but one of the many sources of input in policy decision-making. Systematic knowledge about the conditions under which research contributes substantively to decisions in the various phases of the policy process does not exist to date. This section delineates several aspects of research use in the policy arena (Bogenschneider & Corbett, 2010; Contantdriopoulos, Lemire, Denis, & Tremblay, 2010; Finnigan & Daly, 2014; National Academy of Sciences, 2012; Nutley, Walter, & Davies, 2007; Weiss & Bucuvalas, 1980).

Types of Research Use

It is helpful to distinguish among several categories of research use, including conceptual, instrumental, and tactical.

Conceptual Research Use

Conceptual research use is also referred to as the "enlightenment" effect. In this type of use, research over time shapes a revised understanding of the nature of a problem and of the value of one or more new approaches to address it. This evolving understanding may occur in multiple stakeholder groups, including policymakers, practitioners, citizens, and the media as research findings and related ideas circulate and become part of the zeitgeist. A prime example of a conceptual research effect is the enhanced acceptance of the importance of early childhood education as a social policy priority for children growing up in poverty and its importance for brain development. As Deborah Phillips, one of the psychologists interviewed (see pp. 117–119) observes, "I don't think anyone at this point can deny that an investment in high-quality, early childhood education is going to be of benefit for children and for society. . . . I think the science is really incontrovertible now, and . . . it's an interdisciplinary science. Developmental science alone, without the marriage with neuroscience and economics, wouldn't have begun to have had the same impact."

Instrumental Research Use

Instrumental research use occurs when findings directly inform and shape specific policy decisions. Research that illustrates and highlights the prevalence and negative effects of a problem may galvanize decision-makers to place the development of policy that addresses the problem high on the policy agenda. Studies that demonstrate the cost-effectiveness of a programmatic approach to address a problem may persuade legislators or executive branch officials to invest substantial funding in the new approach. Executive branch officials responsible for funding research and demonstration projects, for instance, may be persuaded by a new theoretical perspective or a new scientifically derived understanding of the causes of a given problem. A new potential then emerges to develop programs consistent with these new scholarship-based understandings. Findings that show that a current policy or government-funded program does not work may, on occasion, persuade policymakers to terminate the policy or program, or—more likely—to revise it in accordance with the policy evaluation findings. Examples of nurse home visiting programs for new mothers (pp. 64–67) and "housing first" programs for the homeless (pp. 182–185 exemplify areas where empirical findings on impact and cost-effectiveness of programs contributed in an instrumental fashion to policy adoption. As Sam Tsemberis, developer of the "housing first" model (pp. 182–185) observes, "The results from the research combined with the clear and systematic description of the program model and then the demonstrated effectiveness of implementation across a number of different settings and locations by different people drew attention. There were also the voices of key local and national advocates that were spreading the word about the effectiveness, social justice, and cost savings of the model. All that combined added up to eventually influence policy."

Tactical Research Use

Tactical research use occurs when stakeholders use research to justify positions already held, thus advancing courses of action consistent with policymaker interests. The research does not change the policymaker's understanding or policy position, and research that presents alternative perspectives or positions is ignored. Many scholars believe that tactical research use is, unfortunately, the primary mode of research use in the policymaking process. Many legislators, for example, are lawyers. Tactical use in the policymaking arena is fully congruent with the adversarial nature of the courtroom, in which opposing lawyers selectively interpret and contest evidence to make the best case for the position they wish to advance. A number of interviewees for the current volume emphasized the tactical uses of research. For example, Judith Meyers (pp. 126–129) worked as a Congressional Fellow (1982–83) for an influential member of Congress on the House Appropriations Committee. She notes:

> Jane Knitzer's book had just come out [*Unclaimed Children*], a real driving force. . . . That book was an analysis of data about the number of children who have mental health problems and the number who get served or don't get served. . . . I remember being in the Appropriations Committee with the Congressman when we were trying to get money in a line item for children's mental health. . . . I gave him the book. I don't

know that he read it, but he waved it around in the hearing and quoted the key findings.

In other words, the Congressman successfully used research to support his prior position. Meyers goes on to state that the findings "were influential in securing the funding," which suggests that a given set of findings may be used tactically by adherents and yet simultaneously have an instrumental effect on others they are seeking to influence.

Nature of the Policy Issue

The way in which research is used by policymakers may depend on the nature of the policy issue under consideration. For example, highly contested social issues in which personal values, political factors, important vested interests, and/or constituent perspectives are prominent (such as gun control) may leave little room for relevant research to have a persuasive, instrumental impact. On the other extreme, decisions about highly technical, noncontroversial issues free of significant adherents (i.e., food safety) may be especially likely to be influenced by research evidence. A given type of research use, then, may be more likely to occur with some types of policy issues than with others.

Nature of the Research

Research may be more likely to be used instrumentally in policy formulation and adoption when the research is timely, addressing issues under urgent consideration by policymakers at a particular moment. Given the length of time research takes from start to finish, it may be good fortune as much as conscious foresight that produces timely research. Considering how quickly policy issues emerge and then disappear from the agenda—only then to reappear some time later—good fortune indeed seems to be part of the equation. Additionally, foresight, intuition, and an in-depth understanding of policymakers' current and emerging interests and concerns can lead to the selection of research questions to examine that greatly increase the odds of timeliness and applicability of findings.

Research is also more likely to be useful if it supports policy ideas and approaches that are feasible for policymakers to implement. Including strong cost–benefit data is especially important in conservative fiscal times when there is concern about budget deficits and related political resistance to new government spending and to raising taxes. In addition, the quality of the research is important for instrumental use, in part because it must withstand scrutiny by opponents. Quality is also important given the movement in recent years toward selection of **evidence-based programs** for priority funding (e.g., Haskins & Margolis, 2014). Quality may be less important, however, for the tactical use of research. In addition, policymakers may welcome qualitative findings that illustrate constituent experiences and that, together with compelling statistics, serve to engage a broader audience.

Communication of Research Findings

Generally speaking, policymakers appear to assume that intermediary organizations that interpret and translate research, as well as the researchers who produce it, have agendas that guide what they do. Policymakers more willingly accept findings that come from trusted and credible sources. Furthermore, jargon-free, unambiguous, and brief communication of findings is important for busy elected officials and their staff. Brevity may be less important for policymakers who are executive branch content experts and often social scientists themselves.

Nature of Individual, Organizational, and Systemic Decision-Making

The policymaking process from agenda setting through evaluation and revision involves a multitude of individual, organizational, and systems-level decisions. These decisions are made at multiple points in time. Decisions sometimes occur in formal policy decision-making contexts (e.g., a vote) and often in informal contexts (e.g., during a hurried meeting in the hallway). Research can enter into these decision processes in different ways at different times, making it very difficult to generalize about factors that contribute to the effective use of research. In fact, little is known about the dynamics of decision-making across phases and levels of the policy system. Individual policy case studies occasionally describe the use and influence of research on policy. However, it is difficult to generalize from case studies, in the absence of systematic research.

Scholars have increasingly called for enhanced attention to systematic research in this area. For example, a National Academy of Sciences (2012) report emphasized the need for systematic focus on policy argumentation (i.e., what makes for reliable, valid, and compelling arguments), psychological processes in decision-making (e.g., social judgment theory, heuristics and biases, learning and judgment-making teams, naturalistic decision-making), and systems theory (e.g., complex systems, critical systems thinking, activity systems, soft systems). A set of studies of the use of research in educational policymaking at local, state, and national levels revealed that other areas also need further attention. For example, little is known about how non-research types of evidence (e.g., local service system data, anecdotal accounts, personal experience) are integrated with research-based decision-making. More generally, this set of studies revealed that research is primarily used tactically rather than instrumentally. This tactical dominance implies that values, interests, and local circumstances have a major influence on decision-making. Thus, enhanced conceptual and instrumental use of research will require increased levels of trust, capacity, and strong relationships among the varied participants seeking to influence policy and practice (Finnigan & Daly, 2014; Tseng & Nutley, 2014).

Despite the formidable obstacles to research use and the lack of systematic research to guide action, psychologists over the years appear to have made invaluable contributions to policy. This contribution has been achieved from various vantage points, using varied policy influence methods. We turn next to three major vantage points from which psychologists have sought to make a difference in the policy arena.

Vantage Points from Which Psychologists Can Influence Policy

Psychologists can seek to influence policy working for any of the stakeholder groups delineated in Figure 2.1. However, three particular vantage points appear especially common: positions within universities, within advocacy and intermediary organizations, and within government (legislative and executive branches). We start with the university as vantage point for policy influence.

Universities

Academic institutions provide faculty and administrators a unique vantage point through which to influence social policy at local, state, and national levels. In the course of their careers, faculty have the opportunity to develop policy-relevant content expertise, generate specific policy-related findings, promote empirically supported policy ideas and programs, work with professional associations and advocacy organizations, serve as policy advisors and consultants, and take on policy insider roles while on leave. Many major social policy developments have benefitted from the contributions of numerous university faculty members, in ways large and small, directly and indirectly, and often occurring across decades of involvement. Past examples include school desegregation (Pettigrew, 2011), early intervention/child development (Aber, Bishop-Josef, Jones, McLearn, & Phillips, 2007; Culp, 2013), women's rights (Fiske, Bersoff, Borgida, Deaux, & Heilman, 1991), and gay rights (Herek, 2006).

Apart from traditional academic departments, research and policy centers on many campuses serve as catalysts for interdisciplinary policy-relevant research collaborations, influential policy activities, and the training of policy-focused researchers and policy practitioners. Examples include the Center for Law and Social Policy (University of Nebraska), Center on the Developing Child (Harvard University), Institute for Research on Poverty (University of

Wisconsin–Madison), National Center for Children in Poverty (Columbia University), and Rudd Center for Food Policy and Obesity (University of Connecticut). Furthermore, centers explicitly focused on policy training, such as the Bush Centers in Child Development and Social Policy (e.g., Phillips & Styfco, 2007), have made distinct contributions by training both pre- and postdoctoral psychologists who have often proceeded to make important policy contributions (including a number interviewed for this volume).

Furthermore, higher education leaders, who often serve on important governmental advisory boards and become involved in policy-related initiatives, can contribute to enhanced faculty engagement in policy-relevant work (e.g., Cantor, 2012). Universities more generally serve as training grounds for future professionals who serve in various roles in government, in the nonprofit sector, and in service delivery systems. Universities also influence the development of social and civic attitudes and mindsets in our youngest citizens.

This volume highlights the policy work of 50 psychologists who contributed to social policy as university faculty or administrators (Chapters 3, 6, and 7). These examples serve to demonstrate the potential of the university as an important vantage point for efforts to influence social policy.

Policy-Focused Intermediary Organizations

Policy-focused organizations play a major role in the policy process. These organizations include advocacy groups (e.g., Children's Defense Fund); professional membership organizations (e.g., American Psychological Association); think tanks (e.g., Brookings Institution); the National Academies (e.g., National Academy of Science); research, evaluation, and consulting organizations (e.g., Child Trends); foundations (e.g., William T. Grant Foundation); and grassroots community organizations (e.g., People Improving Communities Through Organizing) (Andrews & Evans, 2004; Rich, 2004; Scott, Lubienski, Scott, DeBray, & Jabbar, 2014). Such organizations constitute a source of employment for applied psychologists pursuing policy-related careers, and many offer predoctoral internships and postdoctoral fellowships. Broadly speaking, these organizations can be viewed as intermediary organizations serving as a bridge between university-based researchers and policymakers, between communities of practice and policymakers, and between citizens and policymakers. Four specific types of intermediary organizations that have served as important vantage points for policy influence by psychologists are briefly discussed here: professional membership organizations; the National Academies; research, evaluation, and consulting firms; and foundations.

Professional Membership Organizations

A wide range of professional membership organizations exist in the United States that serve the occupational and/or public service interests of their members through multiple means, including policy advocacy (Ainsworth, 2002; Andrews & Evans, 2004; Loomis, 2011; Maisel & Berry, 2010). For psychologists, the largest is the American Psychological Association (APA), which represents more than 134,000 members (researchers, clinicians, consultants, and students) and employs more than 500 staff, including approximately 50 psychologists. Advocating for key federal policies and legislation is an important goal of APA and one of the key activities of its staff (APA, 2015c). For example, the Government Relations Office at APA employs legislative officers (a number of whom are psychologists) who lobby Congress in the areas of public interest, education, and science. Other professional member organizations that devote resources to policy include the American Psychological Society, numerous specialized professional societies (e.g., Society for Research in Child Development [SRCD], Society for the Psychological Study of Social Issues [SPSSI]), and related coalitions (e.g., Coalition of Social Science Associations).

The National Academies

The National Academies include the National Academy of Sciences, the National Academy of Engineering, the Institute of Medicine, and the National Research Council. The National Academies describe themselves as "private, nonprofit institutions that provide expert advice on some of the most pressing challenges facing the nation and the world" (The National Academies, n.d.). The National Academies do not receive appropriations from Congress, although many of their activities are congressionally mandated. Contracts and grants from federal agencies are the primary source of funding. The private sector, state governments, and foundations also provide funding to address issues of concern. Numerous reports are produced each year by diverse committees of experts in a given area, directed by a full-time study director. The report process involves systematic review and feedback within each academy. Psychologists employed full-time by the National Academies have directed major reports as study directors, and many research psychologists have contributed as project members and chairs. Influential reports include those focused on early child development, health disparities, and prevention and have contributed over time to the development of government-funded initiatives and programs in these and many other areas.

Research, Evaluation, and Consultation Firms

Organizations of varied types, both for-profit and nonprofit, conduct policy-focused research, evaluation, and consultation. Perhaps the most well-known are the large evaluation firms that receive major contracts from federal agencies to conduct such work. A review of the 186 federal Department of Health and Human Services contracts awarded during 2011–12 reveals that approximately three-fifths (105) of such contracts were awarded to 10 well-known research, evaluation, and consulting organizations: Mathematica (25 contracts), Research Triangle

Institute International (RTI; 25), Abt Associates (13), Manpower Development Research Corporation (MDRC; 13), Child Trends (8), RAND (7), IRC/Macro International (5), National Opinion Research Center (NORC, 5), Westat (5), and the Urban Institute (4) (US Department of Health and Human Services, 2012). Systematic literature reviews, major evaluations, and policy consultations provided by experts, including psychologists, in such organizations have contributed to social policy in areas such as welfare reform, manpower training programs, and international development (Haskins, 2006; Haskins & Margolis, 2014). Thus, these organizations represent important employers for psychologists who are interested in helping to shape policy through research, evaluation, and consultation. Furthermore, there are numerous other for-profit and nonprofit organizations of smaller size at the local, state, and federal levels that are involved in policy-related research, evaluation, and consultation.

Foundations

There are thousands of foundations in the United States, and their funding of advocacy and related policy activities has been increasing (Arons, 2007; Coffman, 2008; Ferris, 2009; Philanthropy Roundtable, 2005). Policy and advocacy activities funded by foundations include coalition building, community mobilization, community organizing, litigation, model legislation, media advocacy, public forums, policy analysis/research, policymaker education, and regulatory feedback. Psychologists have played key roles in several foundations focused on social issues, including leadership roles at the Child Fund, the Kellogg Foundation, the McArthur Foundation, and the William T. Grant Foundation. Specific activities supported by such foundations include development of the Congressional Fellowship programs of APA, SRCD, and SPSSI; support for the Bush Centers in Child Development and Social Policy; and funding for scores of policy-relevant research projects.

Working full-time within each of the four types of intermediary organizations (professional membership organizations; the National Academies; research, evaluation, and consulting firms; and foundations) provides psychologists the opportunity for focused effort to influence social policy. Furthermore, graduate students may find many opportunities for involvement as interns within the numerous intermediary organizations that address child and family issues, poverty, discrimination, health, education, violence, and many other social problems. Chapter 4 illustrates the policy issues addressed by 14 psychologists working for intermediary organizations and the policy influence methods and skills they employed.

Policy Insiders: Working Within Government

Psychologists who work within government possess a unique vantage point from which to influence policy. They work as policy insiders in both legislative (e.g., as a Congressional staffer) and executive (e.g., as an executive agency official) branches at the local, state, and federal levels. These policy insider roles may be attained through multiple means, including appointment by an elected official, obtaining civil service employment within an executive branch agency, and successfully running for elected office.

Legislative Branch

Within the **legislative branch**, the most common role is staff member for a legislator or legislative committee. The highest level position within a Congressional office is chief of staff, a position that has been held by a number of psychologists; the most well-known is Patrick DeLeon, who was chief of staff for the late US Senator Daniel Inouye (D-Hawaii) for decades, during which time he worked on numerous social issues. Legislative director and policy advisor positions within Congressional offices have also been held by a number of psychologists over the decades. Committee staff, especially those who serve on committees for extended periods of time, develop expertise in the broad content area of the committee and thus can play important roles in developing legislation.

Executive Branch

Many psychologists have worked in **executive branch** agencies, in departments ranging from mental health to education and child welfare, at all levels of government. Perhaps the most well-known is Edward Zigler, who, as noted in Chapter 1, took leave from Yale University to serve as the first Director of the Office of Child Development and went on to develop the national Head Start Program (Zigler & Styfco, 2010). At the federal level, the **Department of Health and Human Services** (HHS) (an administrative agency) and the **National Institutes of Health** (NIH) (a research-funding agency) employ large numbers of psychologists, as do many other executive agencies. Within HHS, psychologists are especially likely to hold high-level leadership positions within the **Administration for Children and Families** (ACF) and the **Substance Abuse and Mental Health Services Administration** (SAMHSA). In these and related positions, at state and local levels as well as nationally, psychologists have made important contributions to the development and implementation of federal and state policies.

Although psychologists generally do not run for elected office, there are notable exceptions. Most well-known is Ted Strickland (D-OH), who was the first psychologist elected to Congress, specifically to the House of Representatives, in 1992. In 2002, five psychologists, including Strickland, were elected to the House (Thomas, 2004), and currently there are three psychologists in the House. At the state level, in 2002, 16 psychologists won elections to serve on their state legislatures, with 13 elected in 2006 (more recent data are not available). Of special note, in 2006, Strickland was elected governor of Ohio.

Serving as a policy insider provides the unique opportunity to directly shape policy. Chapter 5 illustrates the wide range of policy issues addressed by 14 psychologists serving in policy insider roles and highlights the policy influence methods and skills they used.

Policy Influence Methods

Psychologists employ a wide variety of methods to exert policy influence. These methods vary on numerous dimensions, including policy target (e.g., legislative, executive, judicial branch), pathway (e.g., direct, indirect), and mechanism (e.g., education, guidance, persuasion, pressure). As noted earlier, direct pathways involve communication between psychologists and policymakers (or their staff). Indirect pathways involve communication between psychologists and others (e.g., advocacy groups, media, citizens) who exert influence on the policymaking process. When the primary purpose of communication is to provide policy-relevant information (e.g., the results of research), the mechanism of influence is education; the role of educator is a familiar and comfortable one for academic psychologists. When the primary purpose of communication is to influence decision-making, guidance and/or persuasion will likely be involved as mechanisms of influence as well, involving psychologists in the roles of consultant and advocate, respectively. The use of pressure as a mechanism of influence, involving, for example, mobilization of influential stakeholders, constituents, and public opinion, may not be a familiar or comfortable activity for many psychologists, except those working for advocacy organizations or as political insiders.

Seven policy influence methods used by psychologists are described in Table 2.1. The first two methods are **policy advisory groups** (e.g., boards, commissions, committees, councils, and task forces) and **direct communication** with policymakers (e.g., meetings, hearings, seminars, briefings, conferences). These two methods directly target legislative and executive branch officials and rely on education and persuasion as the primary mechanisms of influence.

The third method, **courtroom-focused influence** (e.g., amicus briefs, expert testimony, expert reports) targets the judiciary branch, involves a direct pathway of influence, and relies mainly on persuasion.

The fourth and fifth methods, **consultation** and **written documents**, primarily target legislative and executive branch officials and are commonly used as part of both direct and indirect pathways of influence. Consultation relies primarily on guidance as a mechanism of influence, whereas written policy-relevant documents rely on education and/or persuasion.

The final two methods, **external advocacy** and **media**, constitute indirect pathways. External advocacy generally targets legislators and elected executive branch officials, using pressure as a means of influence. Media, in the form of news

Table 2.1 **Policy Influence Methods: Pathway Type, Branch of Government Targeted, and Mechanism of Influence**

Activity	Pathway Type	Branch of Government Targeted	Mechanism of Influence
Policy Advisory Groups: Boards, commissions, committees, councils, task forces	Direct	Legislative, Executive	Persuasion, Education
Direct Communication: Face-to-face meetings, seminars, hearings, briefings, conferences	Direct	Legislative, Executive	Persuasion, Education
Courtroom: Amicus briefs, court testimony, expert reports	Direct	Judicial	Persuasion
Consultative Roles: Consultative relationships, technical assistance	Direct, Indirect	Legislative, Executive	Guidance
Documents and Products: Reports, policy & research briefs, fact sheets, publications, tools	Direct, Indirect	Legislative, Executive	Education, Persuasion
External Advocacy: Political pressure, community organizing, social movements	Indirect	Legislative, Executive	Pressure
Media: News coverage, op-eds, letters to the editor, media interviews, news conferences, press releases, social media, websites	Indirect	Legislative, Executive, Judicial	Education, Persuasion, Pressure

coverage, op-eds, letters to the editor, interviews, conferences, press releases, and social media can be used to target any of the three branches of government and involve education, persuasion, and/or pressure as the mechanism of influence. Each method is described further below.

Policy Advisory Groups: Boards, Commissions, Committees, Councils, and Task Forces

It is common practice for policymakers to convene advisory groups composed of content experts to help guide policy planning and decision-making. Such groups vary greatly in mission, scope, size, composition, and type of evidence gathered and reviewed, as well as in the timeframe of their efforts. They may generate and analyze a set of policy options or make specific policy recommendations, and they generally produce policy reports, including policy "white papers" (concise, authoritative reports that set out government positions). Invitations to professionals such as psychologists to serve as members or to chair policy advisory groups may be based on numerous factors, including content expertise in the given policy area, reputation (both for knowledge and for work reliability and quality), and connections. Advisory groups represent a direct strategy for policy influence, drawing upon expert knowledge and skills to generate new policy options and examine existing ones with the end goal of providing actionable policy options and/ or persuasive policy recommendations. For example, the federal Administration on Children, Youth and Families relied on three important advisory panels in the early 1990s to shape an expanded role for research in program planning for Head Start, with a focus on integrating programmatic questions, research, and program improvement (Love, Chazan-Cohen, & Raikes, 2007).

Many of the psychologists interviewed for this volume have served on one or more governmental advisory groups, with seven of these psychologists indicating that their greatest policy success resulted from an advisory group on which they served or chaired. Five of these seven individuals were university faculty. These advisory groups were convened by legislators or elected officials (governors, mayors) or were appointed by executive agency administrators. The two advisory groups created by legislators were the Civil Commitment Standards Task Force of the Virginia Commission on Mental Health Reform (see pp. 209–211) and the Family with Services Needs Advisory Board to the Connecticut General Assembly (pp. 68–70). The three convened by elected executive branch officials included the Governor's Blue Ribbon Commission on Mental Health in Connecticut (pp. 126–129), the Governor's Council on Community Services for Youth and Families in Virginia (pp. 172–174), and the Mayor's Commission for Economic Opportunity in New York City (pp. 77–78). Finally, the two psychologists whose positions were created by appointed executive branch administrators served on the Research Advisory Board of the New York City Department of Homeless Services (pp. 182–185), and the Science Advisory Council for the Office of Justice Programs, US Department of Justice (pp. 213–215).

Direct Communication: Face-to-Face Meetings, Hearings, Seminars, Briefings, and Conferences

One important route to policy influence is through direct communication with policymakers or their staff. Such communication may occur in a variety of venues, including face-to-face meetings, hearings, seminars, briefings, and conferences. The opportunities to communicate may be initiated by the policymaker, by an individual psychologist, or by an advocacy or intermediary organization. When the focus of the conversations relates directly to policy decisions on proposed legislation or executive branch rules and regulations, such communication represents a direct strategy with the major goal of persuasion. Ten of the psychologists interviewed for the current volume highlight direct communication with legislators as an integral part of their greatest policy success, achieved utilizing one or more of the following methods.

Face-to-Face Meetings

In the role of constituent, psychologists can meet with their elected representatives to share their research or practice expertise as it relates to a current social issue or piece of legislation (APA, 2010; Lee, DeLeon, Wedding, & Nordal, 1994). In the role of research or practice expert, psychologists can further meet with the specific legislators and executive branch officials directly responsible for policy decisions in the psychologist's area of expertise. Meetings can be initiated by the psychologist, by the policymaker, or by an advocacy or intermediary group that is coordinating education or advocacy campaigns on a given issue. Concerning the latter, for example, APA routinely arranges advocacy training and "Hill visits" for psychologists to meet with their elected representatives as part of efforts to influence Congress on specific pieces of legislation (e.g., ACA, APA, 2010*a*; also see pp. 101–104). Finally, in the role of certified lobbyist employed by a membership organization (e.g., APA, pp. 106–109) or advocacy organization (e.g., Center on Budget and Policy Priorities), psychologists work to influence legislators on issues of central concern for their employer.

The direct sharing of ideas, findings, experience, and perspectives in a face-to-face meeting has a number of critical advantages over more indirect forms of communication. These advantages include the opportunity for relationship- and trust-building and enhanced learning through discussion and asking and responding to questions. Written materials such as policy briefs and fact sheets (described later) are often left with the policymaker or staff, as well as personal contact information to follow up on subsequent actions.

Seminars for Legislators

Seminars specifically arranged for policymakers provide focused settings for the presentation of research ideas and interactive dialogue between policymakers, sometimes on opposing sides of the aisle. The most well-known state policymaker seminars are convened by universities affiliated with the Family Impact Seminars (Bogenschneider & Corbett, 2010; Wilcox, Weisz, & Miller, 2005). Legislators select topics of current or pending legislative concern prior to the seminar thereby enhancing the opportunity for research use. A number of instances of new legislation in states around the country have been attributed directly to the seminars (pp. 70–72). Examples include a state children's health insurance program in Nebraska, a refundable child care tax credit in Oregon, and a bill addressing truancy in Virginia.

Congressional Hearings

Legislative committees regularly arrange **Congressional hearings** to pursue topics in their assigned areas. The topics are discussed across policy phases, from agenda setting to policy evaluation and revision. Participants in these Congressional hearings are selected by committee legislators of both parties. During the hearing, participants will have a set amount of time to present information and the opportunity to respond to questions. The participants provide a written version of their testimony, and these become part of the public record; one or more face-to-face meetings with legislators or their staff may precede the hearing. The extant case study literature presents examples of psychologists who have testified before legislatures as well as guidelines for such testimony (e.g., Francis & Turnbull, 2013; Jason & Fricano, 1999; McCartney & Phillips, 1993). Several of the psychologists interviewed for this volume describe experiences in Congressional hearings as important aspects of their policy contributions, such as in the areas of children's TV (pp. 229–231) and home visiting (pp. 65–66).

Congressional Briefings

Intermediary organizations regularly arrange opportunities for a panel of content experts to share emerging findings and perspectives on important social issues (Melton, 1995). These **Congressional briefings** are sponsored by a member of Congress, approved by a Congressional planning committee, and generally cost several thousand dollars (Research Caucus, n.d.). The briefing opens up for questions following presentations by the panelists. Elected officials are unlikely to attend; instead, staff members usually attend to become informed on the issue at hand. Several psychologists interviewed for this volume either organized or presented at Congressional briefings. For example, while serving as a Congressional fellow, one psychologist picked up an idea at a briefing that she shared with her legislative boss, a Congressperson. The idea called for a technical adjustment to existing requirements for free and reduced lunch eligibility, which resulted in millions of additional low-income children becoming eligible for the program (pp. 149–151).

Policy Conferences and Meetings

An additional means to influence executive branch administrators and employees is through presentation of research findings and policy ideas at policy conferences and meetings for policymakers. These venues are attended by executive branch officials, administrators, research experts, and staff. For example, the Council for

Juvenile Correctional Administrators, composed of directors of the juvenile correctional systems in all 50 states, holds annual professional meetings and invites experts to make presentations and share emerging findings and ideas. Various opportunities where psychologists shared ideas and policy-relevant research findings in the presence of executive branch officials are described within this volume (e.g., see pp. 192–194 and 213–215).

Courtroom-Focused: Amicus Briefs, Court Testimony, and Expert Reports

Key policy influence methods unique to the judicial arena include submitting amicus curiae briefs to state and federal appellate and supreme courts and providing expert evidence or reports (Borgida & Fiske, 2008). Amicus curiae ("friend of the court") briefs are documents submitted by persons or groups who are not parties in the case and are intended to inform the court about their perspectives or knowledge related to the issues involved. Expert evidence is provided by psychologists who meet legal definitions of "experts." In cases when scientific evidence is to be presented, that evidence must be determined "scientifically valid" by the judge (Levine et al., 2007). A written report of evidence (e.g., research findings) can also be shared with attorneys and introduced as documentary evidence, without the expert serving as a witness. Amicus briefs, testimonies, and reports represent direct strategies to influence policymakers. Such information is presented with the goal of helping to persuade judges to make decisions that are supported by extant research evidence and frameworks (Erickson & Simon, 1998).

The historic amicus brief developed by psychologist Kenneth Clark and colleagues is widely attributed to having played an important role in the US Supreme Court decision outlawing school segregation (Pettigrew, 2011). In the years following that decision, a number of psychologists served as expert witnesses in the court cases addressing issues that arose during implementation of the desegregation decision (Pettigrew, 2011). Ten of the psychologists interviewed for this book provide examples of contributions to social policy through courtroom-based methods including amicus briefs, expert witness testimony, and/or court reports. These contributions include research cited in court decisions in the areas of adolescent development and juvenile justice (pp. 93–95 and 132–134), affirmative action (pp. 197–198), eyewitness accounts of children (pp. 91–93), gender discrimination (pp. 86–87, 88–89, and 234–236), rights of the mentally ill (pp. 211–213), and same-sex marriage (pp. 89–90 and pp. 109–111).

Consultation: Consultative Relationships and Technical Assistance

Consultation represents another means of policy influence, one brought to bear both in direct and indirect pathways of policy influence depending on the

consultee and intentions of the initiative. As a direct pathway, many consultative and technical assistance relationships occur with executive branch agencies
in need of content experts to provide guidance, training, and input on a wide
range of issues under their jurisdiction. Activities may include policy analysis,
evaluation of policies and programs or delivery systems, literature reviews, and
guidance on implementation of government-funded programs. Consultative relationships with policymakers can be paid or unpaid, formal or informal, short-
term or ongoing, at any level of government. Consultation relies on guidance as
a primary mechanism of policy influence. Hadley Cantril is a historic example
of a psychologist who consulted with a US president. He was a frequent advisor
to President Franklin Roosevelt on a range of issues based on information from
early national surveys of American public opinion (Pettigrew, 2011). The psychologists interviewed for this volume describe a wide range of consultative and
technical assistance relationships including much ongoing involvement within
both federal and state agencies, as well as with elected officials. Nine of the psychologists interviewed describe such activities as an integral part of their greatest
policy successes, including providing consultation and/or technical assistance to
city, state, or federal departments of child welfare (see pp. 186–187), education
(see pp. 79–80), health and human services (see pp. 126–129), homelessness (see
pp. 182–185), juvenile justice (see pp. 192–194), mental health (see pp. 172–174),
social and health services (see pp. 207–209), and as advisors to mayors (see pp.
77–78 and 243–245).

   As an indirect pathway of influence, psychologists in university settings develop
consultative and technical assistance relationships with a wide range of advocacy and
intermediary organizations working in their areas of expertise and interest. These relationships vary greatly in their nature, scope, and duration. They can be initiated by the
psychologist or by the intermediary organization. Guidance about the extant research
literature or the importance of one's specific research findings or ideas can inform the
advocacy or educational campaigns of the intermediary organization. Thirteen of the
psychologists interviewed report that working with intermediary organizations to influence social policy was an integral part of their greatest policy success. The intermediary organizations included the American Psychological Association (pp. 112–113,
113–114, 114–116), the National Academies (pp. 117–119, 119–121), advocacy organizations (PICO National Network, pp. 83–84; Community Anti-Drug Coalitions of
America, 124–126; Education Trust, 152–154; New York Immigration Coalition, pp.
201–203; Chronic Fatigue Immune Dysfunction Syndrome Association, pp. 203–
205), and the MacArthur Foundation (pp. 209–211).

Policy-Relevant Documents and Products: Reports, Briefs, Fact Sheets, Publications, and Tools

A range of policy-relevant documents and products are developed regularly to influence policymakers. These include reports, briefs, fact sheets, publications, and

tools (practical aids). They can influence policy via a direct pathway when disseminated directly by their authors to policymakers or their staff and indirectly when used by various groups to inform policy narratives, develop coalitions, conduct advocacy campaigns, and influence the media. When policy-relevant documents and products support a given policy position or perspective, the primary mechanism of influence is persuasion. When their primary focus is to present information, the mechanism of influence is educational.

Policy Reports

A wide range of reports are generated regularly by various groups with the intention of influencing policymakers. Some reports are commissioned by government, including the products of the advisory groups discussed earlier. Others are generated by intermediary organizations or university policy and research centers, often based on research findings and offering policy perspectives, guidelines, and recommendations. The intentions of policy and policy-relevant research reports include raising awareness about an emerging issue, redefining how a population or social issue is defined and conceptualized, promoting new approaches for addressing social issues, and demonstrating the value or lack of value of extant policies and government-funded social programs. On occasion, reports are widely disseminated, groundbreaking, and influence governmental officials. Examples of influential reports in which psychologists played central roles include *Unclaimed Children* (Knitzer, 1982), published by the Children's Defense Fund; *Five Million Children,* from the National Center for Children in Poverty (1990); and *Neurons to Neighborhoods* (Shonkoff & Phillips, 2000), published by the National Academy of Sciences. Three of the psychologists interviewed for the current volume point to influential reports as an integral part of their greatest policy success, in the areas of ethnic and cultural influences on mental health (pp. 81–82), early childhood (pp. 117–119), and health disparities (pp. 119–121).

Policy Briefs, Research Briefs, and Fact Sheets

The preparation of concise documents is widely recommended for effective communication of information and viewpoints to busy policymakers and their staff (e.g., Bishop-Josef & Dodgen, 2013). Such documents can be provided to legislators and/or interested other parties. They can also be included on the websites of intermediary organizations or university policy centers.

- *Policy briefs* often take a position on a given issue, and briefly summarize supporting evidence (for a sample, see American Psychological Association, 2004).
- *Research briefs* summarize a body of literature related to a policy issue without taking a specific position (for a sample, see MacArthur Foundation Research Network on Adolescent Development and Juvenile Justice, n.d.).

• *Fact sheets* provide statistical data related to a social problem.

Many of the psychologists interviewed have written or contributed to policy briefs or fact sheets. A number of them have done so on a regular basis as part of their work in an intermediary organization or policy research center. One of the psychologists interviewed indicated that one of her intermediary organization's greatest policy successes was a widely disseminated fact sheet on teenage pregnancy rates distributed annually over the course of decades at national, state, and local levels (for a sample, see Child Trends, 2011; also see pp. 122–124).

Publications

Although publication in peer-reviewed journals is highly valued in academia, such scholarly products are unlikely to be read by busy policymakers or their staff who prefer more accessible, immediately actionable, and succinct accounts (Rothbaum, Martland, & Bishop-Josef, 2007; Shonkoff, 2000; Shonkoff & Bales, 2011). Nonetheless, policy-relevant findings and policy-relevant concepts published in peer-reviewed publications that are effectively promoted and reach the attention of important advocacy groups and intermediary organizations ultimately can enter into policy discussions. Furthermore, on occasion, scholarly books on pressing social topics can attract the attention of policymakers and their staff as well as citizens and thus contribute to the national dialogue. Examples include Gordon Allport's 1954 book, *The Nature of Prejudice* and William Julius Wilson's 1987 volume, *The Truly Disadvantaged.* The vast majority of the academic faculty interviewed for this book provided examples of the direct or indirect policy influence of empirical findings and generative concepts, both their own and those of others. These research findings and concepts were initially published for an academic audience and then effectively framed, translated, disseminated, and promoted through various means including advocacy and intermediary organizations.

Tools

Policy tools include practical aids and heuristic devices for use by delivery systems in implementing social policies. When developed by experts in a content area, such tools contribute to the evidence-based implementation of policies and practices, helping administrators and staff perform their work in an efficient, standardized, and effective manner. Examples include assessment measures, curricula, and manuals that guide agency delivery of services and programs. Three of the psychologists interviewed for this volume report such tools as integral to their greatest policy influence. These tools include a mental health screening instrument for use in detention centers (pp. 216–218) and heuristic guides for agency administrators and staff to guide, respectively, juvenile justice system program selection (pp. 192–194) and the implementation of evidence-based teenage pregnancy prevention programs (pp. 218–220).

External Advocacy

External advocacy constitutes an indirect pathway to influence policy by placing constituent or political pressure on elected officials (Cigler & Loomis, 2012; Jansson, 2010; Nownes, 2013). Advocacy is often spearheaded by advocacy organizations. It may involve raising public awareness about an issue or a piece of legislation, mobilizing resources, and garnering experts in the field to support the campaign. Advocacy work may also require extensive networking and coalition building among citizens, powerful individuals, and stakeholder groups; extensive use of media; and citizen advocacy (grassroots lobbying) of policymakers. Different strategies and tactics may be employed depending on the issue at hand, the political context, the level (e.g., local, state, federal), and the resources available. Locality-based advocacy efforts may involve community organizing, in which trained organizers mobilize citizens to take actions of various sorts that pressure officials to respond (Shragge, 2012; Speer et al., 2003). Large-scale social movements represent a particularly impactful form of external advocacy in which citizens around the nation mobilize to challenge and seek change in existing governmental policies, as was the case in the civil rights, women's rights, and disability rights movements (e.g., Graham, 1990).

Some psychologists work closely with advocacy organizations in their policy influence work (e.g., Jason, 2013; Knitzer, 2005). This work may involve sharing of research findings, authorship of organization-sponsored reports, serving on organizational advisory boards and task forces, and working full- or part-time for the organization. Relationships between psychologists and advocacy organizations may be initiated by the organization, for example when research experts are sought on a given issue. Relationships can also be sought out by psychologists looking to help ensure that their research findings and ideas are put to use in the policy arena.

Nine of the psychologists interviewed for this volume describe work with advocacy organizations, citizen groups, and the media as an integral part of their greatest policy success. This work included external advocacy in the areas of abandoned housing (pp. 83–84), campaign ethics (pp. 258–260), early childhood education (pp. 134–136), health and health disparities (pp. 119–121, pp. 129–131, pp. 203–205), prevention (pp. 124–126), and sex education policy (pp. 252–254).

Media

Media of various kinds make up the major distributors of information related to cultural, economic, political, and social life. As such, media inform the entire range of stakeholder groups, from constituents to elected officials, about events and emerging developments relevant to specific stakeholders and to the larger society. Media are a potent shaper of public attitudes, beliefs, and knowledge (Lee et al., 1994; Rozell & Mayer, 2008; Zigler & Hall, 2000). Specifically, print media, social media, and the Internet are important resources for mobilizing citizen and stakeholder group involvement to help advance policy agenda setting, formulation, and adoption. Media can be used strategically in grassroots advocacy campaigns. The media similarly influence policy implementation, evaluation, and revision, in part based on news coverage of implementation processes and outcomes including accomplishments, challenges, and failures. Politicians and their staff are regular consumers of the news. Groups attempting to influence the news cycle and the framing of social issues and potential policy solutions more generally utilize a range of media-related techniques. These techniques include media interviews, op-eds, letters to the editor or open letters to policymakers, news announcements, press releases, websites, and use of social media (Bishop-Josef & Dodgen, 2013; Kanter & Fine, 2010; Obar, Zube, & Lampe, 2012; Rothbaum et al., 2007).

Media interviews may be with newspaper, magazine, television, or radio reporters or hosts. They may be recorded or conducted live (television, radio, or social media). Tips for conducting successful media interviews are widely available, including the key advice of conveying and sticking to one or two talking points and speaking clearly and succinctly. Gaining the desired quality and quantity of media coverage is enhanced through the cultivation of relationships with individual reporters or commentators. Additional techniques to enhance the dissemination of policy-relevant information, products, and ideas include press releases, news announcements, and, increasingly, the effective use of social media and the Internet, including blogs and websites. Public relations (PR) offices and staff are present within larger government agencies, advocacy, and intermediary organizations, and research and policy centers on university campuses, as well as within colleges and universities more generally. The expertise, experience, and connections of PR offices and staff can enhance the quality and frequency of communications between psychologists (and others) who work in these settings and the media.

A unique tool that seeks to influence policy is the op-ed, an essay form that expresses the opinion of a writer not employed by the newspaper or magazine in which it is published (e.g., see Brownell, 1994). Op-eds appear on the page opposite to the editorial page and have the potential to bring attention to a given viewpoint on a social issue or policy and thus to influence public and policy-maker views. Op-eds or letters to the editor published in major local, state, or national newspapers or magazines are especially effective. Advocacy campaigns often circulate sample op-eds or letters to the editor through the Internet for use by affiliated citizens and groups as part of systematic attempts to influence policymakers and public opinion.

Psychologists have increasingly focused on the importance of strategic media influence, including careful framing of research findings and related policy ideas, to create a compelling policy narrative (Gruendel & Aber, 2007; Thompson & Nelson, 2001). Nine of the psychologists interviewed for this volume report that effective use of media and the framing of findings were an integral part of their greatest policy success. These techniques include an extensive media campaign with carefully cultivated media interviews (pp. 93–95), meetings with editorial boards focused on state school board policy (pp. 252–254), news coverage in the widely circulated magazine *Consumer Reports* (pp. 232–233), op-eds about emerging policy ideas in the *New York Times* and other leading newspapers (pp. 72–74, 147, and 254), consequential national (pp. 114–116) and local newspaper coverage (pp. 252–254), and use of press releases and radio programming (pp. 258–260). The importance of the effective framing of policy narratives, in particular, is well illustrated in the case of enhanced government investment during the past 15 years in early childhood programs. One central aspect of the policy narrative communicated through the media is that provision of government-funded early childhood experiences for low-income children is cost-effective, contributing directly to healthy brain development and school readiness (e.g., pp. 117–119).

Several of the methods just described are primarily, although not exclusively, used by psychologists who are policy outsiders, working in academia or intermediary organizations (e.g., courtroom-focused, external advocacy). Others are part of the policy arsenal commonly used by psychologists working both inside and outside of government (e.g., direct communication, written documents, media). Several methods are unique to the policy insider role.

Policy Insiders: Working Inside Government

Psychologists working inside government have the opportunity for direct involvement in activities related to policy agenda setting, formulation and adoption, implementation, and evaluation and revision. The extent and nature of the contribution depends, at least in part, on the position held. Existing literature, including case study accounts (several by psychologists), detail the various activities and methods used by policy insiders in pursuing their agendas and carrying out their assigned responsibilities (Haskins, 2006; Lombardi, 2003; Nye, 2008; Oleszek, 2016; Zigler & Styfco, 2010). Psychologists in the roles of Congressional staffers or executive branch officials, for example, routinely participate in a vast array of activities ranging from the seeking and receiving of information to the preparing and adopting of legislation to the overseeing of policy implementation.

Seeking and Receiving Information from Policy Networks and Sources

Policy insiders learn about social issues, legislative possibilities, and related evidence from every group listed in Figure 2.1. These groups include fellow policymakers in various branches and levels of government, advocacy and intermediary organizations, university faculty, service delivery organizations, and citizens (constituents). In essence, psychologists working as policy insiders tend to be on the receiving end of information and ideas communicated via the methods described in the preceding section. As policy insiders, psychologists may, at times, explicitly seek information and ideas from other psychologists with expertise related to a given policy issue; they will also, at times, be the recipients of outreach initiated by psychologists in universities and intermediary organizations. The Congressional staffer who helped to draft the 2010 Maternal, Infant, and Early Childhood Home Visiting legislation both sought out and was approached by psychologists knowledgeable in the area of home visiting (see pp. 66–67).

Preparing and Adopting Legislation

Policy insiders working for legislators and legislative committees contribute in various ways to the preparation of legislation. This may include direct involvement in the formulation and writing of legislation, supervision of others so involved, development of political strategies to build support and to disempower opponents, meetings with constituents and lobbyists, and work with external groups and the media to mobilize external support and advocacy pressure. Specific skills include policy analysis, document review, political strategy development, *research translation*, constituent and lobbyist liaison work, and the arts of negotiation and compromise (Maton, Humphreys, Jason, & Shinn, in press). Seven of the psychologists interviewed describe their greatest policy success as their contributions to the preparation and adoption of legislation as policy insiders. The areas addressed include education (pp. 152–154), healthcare reform (pp. 156–158), homelessness (pp. 159–160), home visiting programs (pp. 66–67), mental health parity (pp. 147–148), and welfare reform (pp. 154–156).

Policy Work in the Executive Branch

Executive branch agencies oversee policy implementation and evaluation through multiple, diverse activities. One important policy role is writing rules and regulations, which typically include a process of obtaining input and feedback from multiple stakeholders and experts. Another responsibility, one placed in the hands of those in higher level positions, is shaping implementation and evaluation priorities, including appropriation of staff and funding resources. Such work will involve sensitivity to and involvement with political staff, on one hand, and hands-on, content-focused work with policy and professional experts including fellow psychologists, on the other. Another major activity is the development, implementation, and oversight of grants and contracts, which staff at all levels contribute to in various ways. Depending on the office and executive agency, such grants and activities may involve implementation of social policies and programs, contract-focused research and evaluation studies, or funding research through traditional granting mechanisms (the latter in research-focused agencies and units). Skills necessary for effective executive branch work include political acumen, leadership and management ability, capacity to work as a team player, and content expertise in one's area of responsibility. Seven of the psychologists interviewed describe their greatest policy success as involving work within the executive branch. Areas of focus include healthcare reform (pp. 162–164), juvenile justice (pp. 170–172), mental health system reform (pp. 172–174), policy implementation (pp. 164–167), substance abuse prevention (pp. 168–170), and teenage pregnancy prevention (pp. 164–167).

Policy Influence Skills

As noted at the outset, the policy system is extraordinarily complex and multifaceted, and psychologists seek to exert policy influence from multiple vantage points and employ multiple methods. Each vantage point, method, and role requires, to some extent, specialized skills. Nonetheless, there are some overarching skills that appear central to effective policy influence work across vantage points, methods, and roles. These skills are relationship building, communication, research, and strategic analysis. Although these skills will take distinctive forms in different policy contexts and additional skills will be essential for activities in a particular context, these four skills appear to represent underlying foundations for effective policy work by psychologists (Maton, Humphreys, Jason, & Shinn, in press).

Relationship-Building Skills

Relationships are critical for policy influence (Bogenschneider & Corbett, 2010; DeLeon, Loftis, Ball, & Sullivan, 2006; Dodgen & Portwood, 1995; Shinn, 2007; Tseng & Nutley, 2014; Vincent, 1990). Given many potential sources of information, decision-makers are especially likely to take into account policy ideas and research evidence when they come from trusted sources. Developing trusted working relationships often involves a considerable investment of time, including face-to-face meetings and network development. It also involves *mutuality*— a willingness to provide, in a timely manner, information or other resources of value to the policymakers—as well as an understanding of confidentiality surrounding sensitive information. Relationships happen on the policymaker's turf; psychologists must proactively bring information to policymakers and not wait for them to seek it out. Furthermore, psychologists need to respond when called upon. Relationship development skills are central to the full gamut of policy influence methods and activities noted earlier.

Communication Skills

Communication skills, both oral and written, are essential to policy influence (Bogenschneider & Corbett, 2010; Wilcox et al., 2005). Since policymakers must consider a large array of issues in a limited amount of time, the ability to communicate clearly and succinctly (e.g., in a 5-minute face-to-face verbal briefing or a 500-word newspaper op-ed) is a critical policy influence skill. Demands of time and attention similarly explain the need for many written policy products to be concise (one- or two-page briefs or fact sheets), although length may be less critical for some executive branch officials or selected legislative staff who may be highly trained specialists in their given content areas.

Two critical aspects of oral and written communication are policy framing and research translation. **Policy framing** involves tailoring policy ideas and research-based findings to maximize leverage within the current policy debate, ideally providing a compelling, practical, and politically acceptable contributions to the policy issue (Gruendel & Aber, 2007; Shonkoff & Bales, 2011). **Research translation** refers to the ability to communicate complicated research findings in a digestible and useful form to non-researchers (Portwood & Dodgen, 2005). Research translation commonly involves summarizing the main findings of research in a clear and concise manner without use of jargon.

Research Skills

Research skills, along with substantive research expertise in a policy-relevant content area, represent critical assets psychologists bring to the policy arena (Jason, 2013; Miles & Howe, 2010; Levine et al., 2007; National Academy of Science, 2012; Phillips, 2000; Shinn, 2007; Speer et al., 2003). The generation of policy-relevant, high-quality research findings and scholarship in a policy-relevant area contributes to the status as "research expert" and enhances the possibility of cultivating productive relationships with policymakers. This expertise may lead to invitations to speak at legislative hearings, to serve on executive branch advisory committees, or to contribute to amicus briefs and provide expert testimony in court cases.

Two specific research skills of note are **research synthesis** and **critical analysis**. Research synthesis skills are important, given that the integration of accumulated findings provides a more reliable basis for policy advice than does a single, unrepli-cated study. The capacity to critically appraise research is of special importance for those in translational research roles who, on the one hand, can select high-quality research studies to communicate to policymakers, and, on the other, critique any low-quality studies cited by advocates on the opposite side of the policy issue.

Strategic Analysis

A fourth overarching skill can be termed **strategic analysis**, which is the ability of the psychologist to critically evaluate social problems and potential solutions and to formulate a plan of action to achieve a policy goal. Strategic analysis encom-passes both **policy analysis** and **strategy development** (Burton, 2013; Phillips, 2000; Speer et al., 2003). Policy analysis encompasses a multitude of activities, including generating novel policy approaches for a given social issue, contrasting the benefits and limitations of various approaches, exploring systemic and un-intended consequences of proposed policies, and evaluating the implementation and impact of current policy initiatives (Kraft & Furlong, 2015). Policy decisions must often be made when evidence is murky.

Strategy analysis also covers a range of strategy development skills that vary de-pending on the policy domain and context (Olson, Viola, & Fromm-Reed, 2011). One such skill is formulating the means to gain access to and influence the opin-ion of a single decisionmaker concerning a specific piece of legislation. Another is generating a large-scale, multiyear advocacy campaign to thrust a new social policy approach onto the policy agenda. Yet another skill is political strategy-making on the part of policy insiders. Thus, skills vary in purpose and complexity. Strategy analysis is often a collaborative process, and it may involve contributions from a range of individuals with different expertise and perspectives.

Getting Started in Policy Work

Readers who are not yet involved in policy work, including graduate students and early-career psychologists, may wonder how they can become involved. Based on the personal experiences and the advice of the psychologists interviewed for this volume, here are practical suggestions for entering into and engaging with the policy world:

- *Participate* in the policy committee of your professional society (e.g., division of APA). Many policy committees actively seek out and desire the help of graduate students interested both in general policy work and specific policy initiatives.

- *Volunteer* for or join a policy-oriented organization (e.g., an advocacy organization) related to your research or personal experience.
- *Seek out* faculty, university research and policy institutes or centers, and practitioners actively involved in policy work, and *ask* about ways to get involved in
  specific policy-relevant projects.
- *Apply* for APA, SPSSI, or SRCD Congressional fellowship programs, or policy
  internships in your specific area of interest.
- *Learn to ask policy-relevant questions* through exposure to:
  - policy-relevant coursework in psychology and other disciplines
  - ecological and systemic theories
  - the policy focus and products (i.e., briefs and reports) of advocacy organiza-
    tions and policymakers in your area(s) of interest
- *Invite input* from policy-informed faculty and/or policy practitioners on how
  to increase the policy relevance of your research projects (master's thesis, dissertation, grant proposals) early on in the planning process.
- *Gain experience* working in the settings and with the populations of interest to
  you to understand first-hand the contextual realities that policy must consider.

Summary

The policy process is complex, with many stakeholders and their interests and ideologies involved at each stage: agenda setting, policy formulation and adoption,
implementation, and evaluation and revision. This process leaves much room for
psychologists to get involved through research and action. Psychologists in university settings, in intermediary organizations, and as policy insiders each employ
a myriad of tools and methods to design, conduct, evaluate, compile, and communicate research to influence the policy process. They may choose to directly
involve themselves in the process or work more indirectly by informing others
and contributing behind the scenes. Psychologists may seek only to educate and
provide guidance or, in addition, seek to actively persuade and contribute to external pressure for change. Each role, method, and specific approach has many
advantages and disadvantages. What all of the psychologists interviewed have in
common, however, is their use of relationship building, communication, and research and strategic analysis skills to exert policy influence. These are skills that
students can develop during their graduate education and strengthen and refine
throughout their careers.

We now turn to concrete, real-world examples of successful efforts by psychologists to influence social policy.

3

University Faculty in the Policy Arena

So much of what I've done has been collaborative, so in terms of my success, it's usually our success.

— J. Herek, January 3, 2013

Academic institutions provide faculty a unique vantage point through which to influence social policy. In the course of their careers, faculty members have the opportunity to develop expertise on important populations and topics, generate specific policy-related findings, and promote empirically supported policy ideas. If these findings and ideas are to actually *influence* policy, communication with policymakers is required. This knowledge transfer can occur in multiple ways, with the most effective method likely occurring through ongoing relationships with policymakers. Other possibilities include serving on key advisory boards or exerting indirect influence through relationships established with intermediary organizations, the media, and other channels. Unfortunately, most psychologists in academia do not seem inclined to leverage their content expertise, findings, and ideas into meaningful involvement and influence in the policy arena. This lack of psychologist involvement is partly due to lack of knowledge about how to conduct policy work, discomfort about the influence of power and partisan politics in the policy arena, and lack of incentives for investment of time in policy endeavors. Additionally, the successes that *do* occur are too rarely known within academia.

The purpose of this chapter is to depict the policy influence methods and skills used by university faculty. This is illustrated primarily through 12 case examples of successful policy influence. The case examples vary in a number of ways, including policy issue addressed, branch of government targeted, type of research conducted, policy method and pathway used (direct vs. indirect), and mechanism of influence (education, guidance, persuasion, pressure). Throughout the case examples, use of the core policy skills of relationship building, communication, research, and strategic analysis is demonstrated. Taken together, the examples illustrate the range of policy influence methods available to faculty. They show the potential of these tools to make a discernable difference in the policy arena—as used in the hands of committed, skilled, and persistent faculty members.

The brief case examples are organized by branch of government targeted: *legislative, executive,* and *judicial.* The examples encompass local, state, and national levels of influence. After presentation of the case examples, the chapter concludes by assessing the advantages and disadvantages of academia as a vantage point from which to influence policy.

Legislative Branch Influence

When we think of influencing policy, the legislative branch of government most likely comes to mind. After all, the legislature is empowered to make the laws that govern us and to appropriate funds for programs and services. Given the constant drum of national news coverage on how Congress is gridlocked and how legislative decision-making is driven by partisan politics, money, special interests, and lobbyists, there is good reason to wonder if empirical research and researchers can make much of a difference. In spite of these obstacles, 12 of the faculty members interviewed for this book describe a contribution in the legislative arena as their greatest policy success. The interviewees highlight several specific policy influence methods: serving on legislative advisory boards, taking part in congressional hearings, meeting with individual legislators or their staff, and working with intermediary organizations. Other methods described include disseminating policy ideas through media, involvement in campus-based policy centers, using an Internet legislative bill tracking tool, coordinating legislative seminars, and obtaining a time-limited position in government (during sabbatical or leave). Each of these approaches provides opportunities for the effective communication of research findings and policy ideas to policymakers. Table 3.1 lists the policy area, faculty member, and primary policy method(s) used.

From these 12 faculty members, four brief case examples are presented here, with the remaining case examples presented elsewhere in this volume. The four selected cases highlight a range of policy issues: home visiting programs, juvenile status offenses, and childhood obesity. Policy influence methods utilized by these psychologists—including participation in face-to-face meetings, in congressional hearings, on a legislative advisory board, and in seminars for legislators—are also discussed. Before each case narrative—to provide context—the psychologist's subfield, institution, year of PhD receipt, and current position are listed.

We begin this section with a national legislation example focused on low-income mothers.

Table 3.1 **Legislative Branch Influence: Policy Area, Faculty Member, Level, and Policy Methods**

Policy Issue (Faculty)	Level	Legislative Advisory Board	Congressional Hearing	Face-to-face Meetings	Intermediary, Media, Policy Center	Other
Home Visiting (Olds)*	US		X	X	Intermediary	
Home Visiting (Brooks Gunn)*	US		X			
Status Offenders (Britner)*	CT	X				
Varied (Bogenschneider)*	WI, Other					Legislator Seminars
Child Obesity (Brownell)*	Multiple				Media, Policy Center	New Bill Tracker
Substance Use Parity (Humphreys)**(5)	US					Policy Insider
College in Prisons (Fine)**(6)	NY			X	Media	
Undocumented Immigrants (Yoshikawa)**(6)	New York City				Intermediary	
Developmental Disability (Ramey)**(6)	WA, US				Intermediary	
Civil Commitment Standards (Monahan)**(6)	VA	X				
Children's TV Regulations (Huston)**(7)	US		X			
Utilities Rate Restructuring (Fawcett)**(8)	Lawrence, KS		X		Policy Center	

* Covered in this chapter.
** (X) = Chapter number where presented as case example.

Maternal, Infant, and Early Childhood Home Visiting Legislation (2010): US Congress

The Maternal, Infant, and Early Childhood Home Visiting (MIECHV) legislation, passed by the US Congress in 2010, committed $1.5 billion over a 5-year period to fund a subset of empirically supported home visiting programs and their evaluation (Pub Law 111-148, Section 2951, 2010). This funding allocation targets programs that support the parenting of low-income parents and in doing so aims to prevent negative child outcomes. The programs funded by MIECHV provide, in different ways and contexts, information, skills, emotional and instrumental support, and linkage to community resources to those served. A major point of contention concerning this legislation was whether it should be limited to the one specific program with empirical evidence from multiple random controlled trials (Nurse-Family Partnership [NFP]), as apparently intended in the initial proposal by the Obama administration (see Haskins & Margolis, 2014, for a detailed history). Congressional discussion centered on whether other programs with evidence established through quasi-experimental designs should be eligible for funding as well (Davis, Bond, & Murray, 2010). Ultimately, the largest amount of money was devoted to the NFP, but a set of additional programs was deemed as meeting the required evidence-based criteria (US Department of Health and Human Services, 2013a). Here, two university faculty members, David Olds and Jeanne Brooks-Gunn, and one psychologist who is a congressional staffer, Jill Hunter-Williams, describe their involvement and perspectives on the MIECHV legislative process.

David Olds

PhD, Human Development, Cornell University, 1976

*Professor of Pediatrics, Psychiatry, and Preventive Medicine,
University of Colorado, Denver*

David Olds, a developmental psychologist, established and conducted multiple evaluations of the well-known NFP program. Three randomized trials conducted over the course of three decades revealed positive short- and long-term outcomes (e.g., fewer childhood injuries, improved school readiness, and increased maternal employment), along with impressive data on cost-effectiveness (Howard & Brooks-Gunn, 2009; Karoly, Kilburn, & Cannon, 2006; Kitzman et al., 1997; Olds et al., 2002; Olds, Henderson, Chamberlin, & Tatelbaum, 1986). The program has been cited in multiple national venues as a leading evidence-based prevention model (Goodman, 2006). Early on, Olds resisted overtures from federal officials to implement NFP on a broad scale, wanting first to firmly establish program effectiveness and the nature of core program components and to retain some control over the fidelity of program implementation. In 2003, a national nonprofit NFP organization was established to facilitate development of NFP programs around the country with high levels of fidelity by providing consultation, marketing, and policy-focused activities for interested parties (www.nursefamilypartnership.org).

When describing his greatest success in the policy arena, Olds framed it broadly as contributing to the increased use of rigorous evidence in policymaking. In the excerpt here, Olds describes the Obama administration's initial funding proposal for nurse home visiting and then what happened in Congress as other stakeholders became involved, promoting the idea that other programs should be funded as well by the emerging legislation:

> The Nurse-Family Partnership was promoted by the Obama administration and the president in the beginning of his first term. He sent a budget proposal to Congress to invest in a program of prenatal and infancy home visiting by nurses for low-income mothers having their first babies. He proposed putting something like $8.6 billion into this program over a 10-year period.
>
> It went to Congress and people said, "You can't base policy on a single program. We need to think more broadly. This particular program [NFP] has very high evidentiary standards. Can't we create an option for programs with less evidence to fit into the broader policy?" My own view about this is that, especially in these hard periods of budget deficits, it makes sense for us to put monies where we have really good confidence that they can make a difference. I think that policy needs to be grounded in programs that are really well-developed and have strong evidentiary foundations. We had team members [from NFP] who were educating members of Congress about this. The key was they weren't overstating, but being clear about what the evidence really said. That is the approach, that's the way we do business everywhere.

Jeanne Brooks-Gunn

PhD, Human Development and Learning, University of Pennsylvania, 1975

Professor of Pediatrics, College of Physicians and Surgeons, Columbia University

A second developmental psychologist interviewed, Jeanne Brooks-Gunn, testified at the 2009 congressional hearing about the proposed home visiting (MIECHV) legislation (Hearing, 2009) and whether programs in addition to NFP (e.g., those in which the home visitor is not a nurse) should be funded. Brooks-Gunn believes she was selected to testify for a number of reasons: she had done related early childhood evaluations, had recently written an extensive review of home visiting programs (Howard & Brooks-Gunn, 2009), was not involved with any of the major programs under consideration, and had a reputation of being objective. Brooks-Gunn notes, "I don't see evidence of effectiveness when none is present, though it doesn't always make me popular." In 2009, Brooks-Gunn co-authored a description of the MIECHV legislative process in an article titled "Social Science Rising: A Tale of Evidence Shaping Policy" (Haskins, Paxson, & Brooks-Gunn, 2009).

In the interview excerpt here, she describes her perspective on the legislative debate, the available evidence, and the final 2010 outcome:

> There was a very interesting lobbying effect about what constituted best practices and what constituted evidence. People commissioned papers, interestingly, paying some of the big research firms quite a bit of money to review in great detail the home visiting programs. The commissioned papers pretty much did what we did in our Future of Children piece, which clearly wasn't funded—go through every study with a fine-toothed comb. Our paper really came to the same conclusion [as the others] in terms of the fact that there is a hierarchy of programs that have more or less evidence for efficacy, with David's [Olds' NFP] program being the one that has the most evidence of efficacy. Then some of the other popular programs have less. . . . It's been fascinating to see how people talk about whether or not we have enough evidence to say that home visiting is effective, and how different constituencies see that so differently. My take was home visiting programs, if done well (and the devil is in defining "well"), can make a difference for children's health and development and for parenting. A lot of what people who sat in the testimony said about home visiting, and said to others [in individual meetings] was used in the legislation. I was pretty happy about that.

Jill Hunter-Williams

PhD, Clinical and Community Psychology, University of Illinois, Urbana-Champaign, 2001

Deputy Chief of Staff for Congressman Danny K. Davis of Illinois

United States Representative Danny K. Davis and psychologist Jill Hunter-Williams were involved in a multiyear, bipartisan effort to pass home visiting legislation prior to the Obama Administration's proposal. Representative Davis served on one of the committees of jurisdiction over the MIECHV legislation in the House of Representatives. His office and several congressional colleagues, with the support of highly regarded researchers, asserted that a set of program models—in addition to the NFP—had strong evidence and should be included in the legislation. Here, Hunter-Williams shares her perspective on the legislative process and the outcome:

> The key battle was over how to define a quality program. For Congressman Davis, working with representatives and senators on both sides of the aisle, the definition was not going to be randomized control trials [RCT] only. . . . [Such an approach excluded] program models with strong impact data [based on quasi-experimental designs] that might provide more insight into implementing programs on the ground for broad populations. . . . It is absolutely necessary to have more than simply RCTs to make effective policy, especially policy focused on national implementation. . . . Not only from a research perspective, but also looking at the very practical . . . landscape of there being multiple home visiting groups with strong research behind them represented by a wide array of members of Congress.
>
> To help educate myself . . . and to make this case, I reached out to researcher Deborah Daro from Chapin Hall at the University of Chicago in our legislative district, to Ken Dodge, and to Ed Zigler, who was tremendously helpful. [note: Daro earned her PhD in Social Welfare; Dodge and Zigler are psychologists].
>
> David Olds' research can really be credited with laying the foundation for the justification for the law. David's group has great political contacts. We would not have been as successful without his group's outreach. . . . We and David might have had policy differences at different places, but ultimately we all agreed in terms of making sure we had the money, making sure quality programs are funded, and making sure we're not undermining ourselves in terms of what we're asking the [funded national evaluation] to show.

In this case example, two faculty members built on their content expertise, reputations as scholars, and the results of their research or scholarship to exert influence. The congressional staffer brought to bear consultation and support from equally well-established researchers. Face-to-face meetings with legislators or their staff, lobbying by interested parties including national intermediary organizations, and congressional hearings all appeared to play a role in the outcome. Relatedly, the ability to clearly and effectively communicate the nature and meaning of the extant research evidence to legislators was important, including the delineation of the relative strengths and weaknesses of various types of research designs. The give and take of negotiation among key policy actors was clearly a crucial part of the process, as was the role of social scientists involved in generating research evidence and assessing its value.

In the next example, we move from the federal to the state level and to a different policy influence method—advisory board involvement, specifically, co-chairing an advisory board of a state legislature.

Diverting Status Offenders from the Juvenile Justice System: The State of Connecticut

Preston Britner

PhD, Developmental and Community Psychology,
University of Virginia, 1996

*Professor in Human Development and Family Studies,
University of Connecticut, Storrs*

Upon his arrival at the University of Connecticut, Storrs, in 1997, developmental and community psychologist Preston Britner volunteered to use his research expertise to help the Connecticut Department of Children and Families in any way they felt important. In the ensuing years, Britner conducted various research projects related to efficacy and treatment in foster care and child abuse prevention for the state. He became well known for this work and, in 2006, was asked to co-chair the Family with Services Needs (FWSN) advisory board to the Connecticut General Assembly. The task of the FWSN board was to propose a system by which status offenders (e.g., youth who were truant, beyond control, or runaways) could be diverted from the juvenile justice system and instead receive community-based services (Britner & Stone, 2010; FWSN, 2008). The focus on diversion and prevention was an integral part of a longer term effort to change the juvenile justice system in Connecticut (Mendell, 2013). The FWSN advisory board proposals were passed into legislation in 2007 and required juvenile courts throughout the state to divert high-risk–status offenders to Family Support Centers, which provided various empirically supported interventions (Public Act 07-04, 2007). Independent evaluations of the outcomes have shown very positive results, including elimination of detention placements and reductions in future judicial system involvement for FWSN youth (Ryon, Winokur, & Devers, 2010).

Here, Britner highlights key aspects of the FWSN status offender diversion and prevention policy work:

> I was asked by the President of the Senate to co-chair that board (FWSN). The leader of the House chose my co-chair, Martha Stone, a lawyer and a tireless advocate for kids. The advisory board was to

put something in place and to shepherd this change through. We did a whole lot of research about what was going on nationally. We went places, flew people in, and did all the research. We held public meetings at the state capital, televised on our equivalent of C-SPAN. We worked very hard to create a system that [would] divert some of those youth into services instead of incarceration, and created a network of trauma-informed therapeutic interventions that worked with the schools, including best practices around truancy prevention and engaging kids and their families.

Then we did the hard work of trying to move this forward. In the 2008 legislative session, we asked for millions of new dollars to create community-based support centers that would treat these families instead of kicking [students] out of schools and maybe trying to detain them or start court records. It was really important for us to build those relationships and to get all the stakeholders at the table to talk about how it was going to work, to be data-based and to be doing best practices, and also to recognize that those big huge systems of judicial and child welfare and education don't talk, don't always share data.

Some of the work was with individual legislators, some with executive branch members. We argued that the dollars invested on the therapeutic interventions would, even in the short-term, probably end up costing less than the detention, court costs, and facilities. We had friendly legislators introduce and shepherd through additional legislation to change some of those referral processes and to create additional funding. There was lots of work with judiciary, budget, education, and social services committees of the legislature to bring all this forward.

In the end, we got millions of new dollars allocated—during the recession, mind you—to create and start up these centers. The pipeline from status offense to juvenile delinquent is down. . . . [The program's] now been recognized by OJJDP [US Office of Juvenile Justice and Delinquency Prevention] as a national model. We've then had opportunity to talk to other states about what we did, what has worked, and what questions remain.

Based on his track record of prior work for state government, Britner was asked to co-chair a consequential legislative advisory board. From this position, he devoted an estimated 5,000 hours over many years to devising and implementing a new approach to how status offenders were treated. Persistence is key to successful policy work, as demonstrated in this example. Multiple policy skills, including relationship building, strategic analysis, stakeholder consultation, management, and research together contributed to the legislative success and, importantly, the effective implementation that followed.

Britner attributes his success to in-depth knowledge of the system and access to key policy players in a small state, with the state capitol in close proximity to his university.

The third legislative example also takes place at the state level. Here, the university faculty member plays a boundary-spanning role between research experts and state legislators.

Family Impact Seminars in Wisconsin and Other States

Karen Bogenschneider

PhD, Child and Family Studies, University of Wisconsin–Madison, 1990

Professor of Human Development and Family Studies,
University of Wisconsin–Madison

Since 1992, Karen Bogenschneider has served as executive director of the Wisconsin Family Impact Seminars (wisfamilyimpact.org). One or two times each year, the seminars bring together researchers and state policymakers including legislators, legislative aides, Governor's Office staff, executive agency officials, legislative service agency analysts, and university/Extension faculty. The seminars constitute a series of presentations, discussion sessions, and briefing reports that communicate high-quality research on timely topics identified by state legislators. Recent seminar topics include the science of early brain development, preparing Wisconsin's youth for success in the workplace, and positioning Wisconsin for the jobs of the future. Success in this case required long-term relationship-building with state legislators, an understanding of differences between policy and academic cultures, and a steadfast commitment to an objective, nonpartisan approach.

Until recently, Bogenschneider also directed the Family Impact Institute that recruits and trains university/Extension faculty members to conduct Family Impact Seminars around the country, now operating in 25 states. In-depth discussion of the seminar model, along with its impact and lessons learned, are presented in the books, *Family Policy Matters: How Policymaking Affects Families and What Professionals Can Do* (Bogenschneider, 2014) and *Evidence-Based Policymaking: Insights from Policy-Minded Researchers and Research-Minded Policymakers* (Bogenschneider & Corbett, 2010). Here, Bogenschneider provides a brief description of her work and some of the policy successes, first in Wisconsin and then in other states:

We provide high-quality, objective research on an issue that legislators identify. Everything is built on relationships. I know the legislators. They know me. They know that they can trust that the information I give them is carefully selected to be rigorous research tailored to the issues they are currently debating. . . . I think the timing of the issue is very important as well as addressing topics with unanswered questions for which research can be useful. Also, policy-relevant research needs to be presented in the format that policymakers prefer [oral presentations in accessible language with opportunities for discussion].

[In terms of impact] every once in a while you're in the right place with the right information at the right time. When Wisconsin was debating prescription drug legislation for seniors, we convened two seminars on prescription drugs that featured administrators who had developed and operated prescription drug programs in other states and researchers who were familiar with their execution and evaluation. When we looked at the prescription drug program that subsequently was passed in Wisconsin, four features that we had discussed in the seminars were incorporated into the law. Also, policymakers have told us that our seminars helped them decide how to vote on other issues, such as Wisconsin's welfare reform law and a cigarette tax increase. We had legislators say that seminar information was influential in a long-term care law that was passed. Another legislator reported that the research we provided at a recent seminar was incorporated into a jobs bill they introduced and passed.

Beyond Wisconsin, several states across the country have conducted Family Impact Seminars that have contributed to policy changes. In Oregon, following their first seminar, a refundable child care tax credit was passed. In Nebraska, they convened a seminar on rising health-care costs. The speaker from their unicameral legislature called the seminar director and said, "Can you bring that seminar information over to my office? I need to read it so I'm up to date on this before we vote." The Nebraska Legislature subsequently passed a State Children's Health Insurance Program. In Indiana, following a seminar on middle school violence, a law was enacted to establish school safety specialists. Following Virginia's seminar on dropout prevention, a truancy bill was passed. This evidence-based, family-focused model of communicating research to policymakers has resulted in policy changes on a range of issues in red and blue states across the country with vastly different demographic and political contexts.

In this example, Bogenschneider plays the role of an intermediary. By arranging and conducting seminars focused on current policy issues of interest selected by the legislators, she helps to link legislators from both sides of the aisle to researchers in an environment designed to promote effective communication and discussion of findings. Varied pieces of legislation were reported to have been influenced by the seminars. Key policy skills employed include relationship building and communication. Bogenschneider's goal is to provide neutral, nonpartisan opportunities for legislators to engage in open dialogue, to foster relationships, and find common ground. This is quite different from the persuasion-based advocacy of many other policy players.

The final legislative example highlights a strategic approach to influencing individual legislators and the national policy agenda through the sustained use of media and Internet-based methods. This work also reveals some of the special benefits of a university-based policy center, including interdisciplinary expertise and concerted, sustained efforts to bring research findings to the attention of policymakers.

Childhood Obesity as a Public Health Problem: The Rudd Policy Center

Kelly Brownell

PhD, Clinical Psychology, Rutgers University, 1977

Dean of the Sanford School of Public Policy and Professor of Public Policy, Psychology and Neuroscience, Duke University

Kelly Brownell's work at the Rudd Center for Obesity has contributed to the public framing of childhood obesity as a public health issue—rather than as a medical or personal one. Brownell developed Yale's Rudd Center in 2005 (in 2015 the Center relocated to University of Connecticut, www.uconnruddcenter.org). The center employs a multidisciplinary research faculty along with a marketing director. One of the policy ideas that Brownell has pioneered through articles in public media, popular books, and publications in leading national medical journals is the use of taxes on certain beverages, such as sugared drinks, to reduce consumption and raise money for public health initiatives (e.g., Brownell, 1994; Brownell et al., 2009; Brownell & Frieden, 2009; Brownell & Horgen, 2003; Brownell & Nestle; 2004). For his work advocating for policy changes related to child obesity, *Time Magazine* named Brownell one of the world's 100 most influential persons in 2006, listed among those whose "power, talent or moral example is transforming the world."

Here, Brownell begins by defining the "strategic science" approach to policy influence used in his work and by the Rudd Center (Brownell & Roberto, 2015). He then discusses several policy methods that have contributed to policy influence:

> Strategic science begins with identifying change agents . . . asking who can make the difference with the problem that interests us . . . It can be legislators, the press, legal officials, or others. . . . Next is to work with the change agents to identify key gaps in knowledge and to define the important questions that will best inform the policy process. Specific studies are often realized from this process and can result not only in scientific papers but in policy briefs, fact sheets and other products helpful to policy makers. The last step, which is often overlooked, is communications. How do you get word to the change agents in ways it will be helpful to them? We refer to this as strategic scholarship.
>
> We can use legislators as an example. It can be very helpful to have a person do legislative tracking. Databases [e.g., LexisNexis State Net] exist that will identify legislation that has been introduced at city, state, or federal levels and do so almost in real time. Researchers can then contact legislators who have introduced bills and offer to be a resource. Research papers can be helpful, but synopses of these in forms helpful to legislators are sometimes more valuable. Researchers can testify at hearings, be available for the press, and help legislators know of information on public opinion around an issue, ways of framing issues, etc.
>
> [Concerning] taxes on sugared beverages, I wrote first about this in the professional literature in the early '90s. I wrote an OpEd piece in *The New York Times* in 1994. Legislators became particularly interested in food taxes as a public health measure around 2009 because of the slumping economy and the idea jumped into the limelight. . . . That year I worked with colleagues on two papers proposing a tax on sugared beverages that were published in the *New England Journal of Medicine*. There are now a number of cities and countries that have passed or are considering taxes. This feels like a real victory to me.
>
> Most academics are not trained to carry out and communicate strategic science, and are not reinforced [rewarded] for the time it takes, and hence the link between scientists and change agents can be weak. This minimizes the policy impact of our work and confines communications to other scientists. It would, in my opinion, better link universities to solutions—for pressing world problems—if scholars were able to connect more closely with policy makers, if there was a support infrastructure to help, and if these activities were considered a legitimate use of time.

This example reflects a concerted, sustained effort to influence the public conversation about a policy topic and highlights the role of various policy methods, including use of the media and publication of research in a major national medical journal. By using a "strategic science" approach to influence policy, Brownell promoted the adoption of a public health perspective on child obesity and the related policy option of a tax on sugary beverages. Like Bogenschneider in the previous example, Brownell emphasizes the importance of communicating to policymakers in a form that is meaningful and useful to them. However, in contrast to the nonpartisan, educational approach advocated by Bogenschneider, Brownell embodies a persuasion-focused, advocacy-oriented approach to policy influence.

Summary

The four cases just presented portray a range of policy methods and related skills through which academic researchers have influenced the policy process in varied social policy areas. Each policy-influence effort took place in a unique policy and political context, and the specific policy methods employed varied accordingly. As noted at the outset of this section, many factors can easily trump research evidence and researchers when it comes to influencing policymakers. Nonetheless, these four cases illustrate that faculty members who are well-positioned can, during windows of opportunity, have a discernable influence on legislative policy.

Next, we switch focus to psychologists who have sought to directly influence decisions about policies and practices made by officials in the executive branch.

Executive Branch Influence

Legislators routinely consider and decide on a wide range of policy issues about which they (and their staff) may know relatively little. In contrast, executive agency officials more often are knowledgeable about and trained in their specific area of focus. Communication of findings and policy-relevant ideas for these decision-makers, then, may involve somewhat less of a cultural and knowledge divide for university faculty. Of course, this cultural and knowledge gap will likely remain at the very highest level of the executive branch where the policymakers are politicians, including the president, governors, county executives, and mayors. Furthermore, in some cases, political appointees who directly oversee the different executive branch agencies will lack pertinent content expertise as well.

Eighteen faculty members describe activities contributing to decisions made by executive branch officials as part of their greatest success in the policy arena. The policy methods include participating on executive branch advisory boards and in other formal and informal consultation roles, preparing major reports, and doing external advocacy through work with intermediary organizations and the media. Table 3.2 lists the policy area, faculty member, and primary policy method(s) described by the 18 faculty members as an integral part of their greatest policy success.

Four brief case examples are presented here, selected to highlight effective influence in the executive branch arena as well as the use of a range of policy influence methods and related skills. Through serving on an advisory board, being a consultant, directing a policy research center, and collaborating with advocacy groups for community organizing, these four psychologists have, respectively, impacted a range of issues including welfare policy, standards for social and emotional learning in schools, ethnic and cultural influences on mental health, and vacant housing and crime. We begin with a case example focused on welfare policy in New York City.

Table 3.2 **Executive Branch Influence: Policy Area, Faculty Member, and Policy Methods**

Policy Area (Faculty Member)	Level	Advisory Board Member	Consultant	Other
Poverty/Family Welfare Policy (Aber)*	City	X		
Social & Emotional Learning (Weissberg)*	State		X	
Culture, Ethnicity, Mental Health (Snowden)*	State, National		X	Policy Report
Vacant Housing (Speer)*	City			Intermediary
Homelessness (Shinn)**(6)	Multiple	X		
Foster Care (Chamberlain)**(6)	City		X	

(continued)

Table 3.2 **Continued**

Policy Area (Faculty Member)	Level	Advisory Board Member	Consultant	Other
Juvenile Justice (Lipsey)**(6)	State		X	
Positive Youth Development (Lerner)**(6)	Multiple		X	Scholarship
Undocumented Immigrants (Yoshikawa)**(6)	City		X	Intermediary
Chronic Illness (Jason)**(6)	National	X		Intermediary
Evidence Based, Dept. of Justice (Mulvey)**(6)	National	X		
Mental Health/ Juvenile Detention Center (Grisso)**(6)	Multiple			Assessment Tool
Getting to Outcomes Model (Wandersman)**(6)	Multiple		X	Model Use
Juvenile Justice (Reppucci)**(7)	Multiple		X	Scholarship
Education (Stipeck)**(7)	Multiple			Leadership
Community Development (Cantor)**(7)	City			Engaged University
Sexual Education Programing (Wilcox)**(7)	State			Media Campaign
Early Childhood (Belsky)**(7)	National (England)			Policy Evaluation

* Covered in this chapter.
** (X) = Chapter number where presented as case example.

Conditional Cash Transfer Antipoverty Policy: New York City

Lawrence Aber

PhD, Clinical-Community and Developmental Psychology,
Yale University, 1982

Professor of Applied Psychology and Public Policy, New York University

In 2006, Lawrence Aber, a clinical, community, and developmental psychologist was appointed by the Mayor of New York City to the Commission for Economic Opportunity, which was tasked with generating innovative ideas to help reduce poverty and increase economic opportunity in the city. This appointment was due at least in part to Aber's decade of prior activity as Director of the National Center for Children and Poverty at Columbia University. Stemming from the commission's work, New York City became the first location in the United States to design and test a conditional cash transfer approach to antipoverty policy, an approach that had proved extremely successful in Mexico and other Latin American nations. Conditional cash transfer programs provide cash to parents conditional on engagement in specific activities that contribute to their children's health, education, and well-being (e.g., visits to the pediatrician). Although the initiative, Opportunity NYC/Family Rewards, showed only modest results on child outcomes and was terminated by the Mayor, a refined version of the policy was initiated in six other cities based on lessons learned in New York (Riccio et al., 2013; Wolf, Aber, & Morris, 2013). Here, Aber describes the development of the conditional cash transfer policy in New York:

> The commission included a few academics, a huge number of heads of community-based and nongovernmental organizations and advocacy groups, two people in government, and two people in philanthropy. It was co-chaired by Geoff Canada [Harlem Children's Zone director] and Richard Parsons [AOL/TIME Warner, African American Republican progressive businessman].
>
> On average, conditional cash transfers distribute [provide] somewhere between 15 and 30% of a low-income family's income to a family, conditioned on the family's investments in their kids' human capital. There was a decade of research that suggested that this worked in Latin America, and that philosophically attracted both the Mayor and

the Deputy Mayor. I was able to cite and effectively communicate the evidence base—[that] this might be a thing worth trying. The argument I began to encourage the Deputy Mayor to use was the question about the opportunity costs. The opportunity costs of a low-income mom taking her child to the pediatrician for a high fever (hourly wages lost; might be fired) are much higher than the opportunity costs for me (salaried; won't be fired). What we're trying to do is reduce the disparities in the opportunity costs that low-income parents pay so they can do the things they want to do . . . and don't have to pay as many penalties in doing them. You know, we have a story we can tell. No, it's not bribing the poor.

What also attracted the Mayor and Deputy Mayor, I think, was that it was politically something that progressives could like because it was an increase in transfers to low-income families, and Republicans could like because it was conditioned on personal responsibility of families investing in their kids. It wasn't just the evidence base, it was the evidence base coupled with a political philosophy and a rhetoric that suited this used-to-be democrat, then-was-republican, and is really an independent mayor.

The punch line is that the Mayor turned the City Commission on Economic Opportunity and Poverty Reduction into the Center on Economic Opportunity within the mayor's office. So, from a temporary commission emerged an institutionalized part of the mayor's office for working on economic opportunity and poverty reduction. And the Center applied to the Obama administration's Strategic Investment Fund (SIF) to try out, in other places in the country, six ideas that came out of the poverty commission. Conditional cash transfer was one of those ideas.

This case illustrates the potential instrumental use of evidence in both instituting and revising policies. Aber's use of strategic analysis and policy framing further highlights the need to generate a policy story in a way that can persuade diverse political stakeholders to support it. This example also reveals how political context matters. In fact, New York City was the site of policy focus of 3 of the 20 policy examples in Table 3.2—likely reflecting the uncommon dedication of Mayor Bloomberg and his appointed staff to data-based policy (Gibbs, 2013).

The next example of policy influence involves development of the first statewide set of social and emotional learning standards in the nation.

Statewide Standards for Social and Emotional Learning in Illinois

Roger P. Weissberg

PhD, Clinical-Community Psychology, University of Rochester, 1980

Professor of Psychology, University of Illinois at Chicago

Roger Weissberg, a clinical-community psychologist, served as consultant to the Illinois State Board of Education officials tasked in 2003 with developing social and emotional learning (SEL) standards in the state for kindergarten through 12th grade (Gordon, Ji, Mulhall, Shaw, & Weissberg, 2011; Illinois State Board of Education, n.d.). Weissberg was asked to serve in this role due to his SEL content expertise and long-time involvement in multiple related activities in the state. For example, he served on advisory panels for several state agencies that serve children and youth and was a scientific advisor to a Children's Mental Health Task Force that recommended inclusion of the statewide SEL as one part of larger child mental health legislation. These prior policy involvements are linked, at least in part, to his role as director of the nonprofit organization Collaborative for Academic, Social, and Emotional Learning (CASEL). CASEL champions research, practice, and policy change that contribute to the implementation of evidence-based social and emotional programs in schools (casel.org).

Here, Weissberg describes his role in developing K–12 SEL standards in Illinois. He begins by recounting the prior policy work that resulted in Illinois becoming the first state to mandate SEL learning in schools. Weissberg then depicts several important tactical decisions made in developing the standards themselves:

> In 2001, there was a children's mental health task force to which I was a scientific advisor. That led to the passage of the Children's Mental Health Act of 2003 in Illinois. That highlighted that the Illinois State Board of Education would establish social and emotional learning standards as part of the Illinois Learning Standards. Then I went with about six or seven people from the state government to the Georgetown Mental Health Policy Academy, where they provided training and technical assistance for states that were trying to introduce innovative policies. It was at that meeting with people from different state agencies that we created four committees. One was the School Policy and Standards Committee. I agreed to be the consultant to that committee.

Instead of getting too creative about how to design the standards, we slavishly adhered to all of the standards that Illinois had developed in other areas. We wanted to design SEL standards so it would be easy to go from our committee to be put on the web page of the Illinois State Board of Education (ISBE). There are other education reforms that get "too creative" and don't build on quality work that exists. They're hidden somewhere deep in the recesses. I think we're on the web page, in part, because we followed the formats of the state and partnered effectively with staff from ISBE.

[In developing the standards,] there are certain battles that we did not want to fight because we might lose the standards. [For example,] one of the questions in the standards is "Should you respect the opinions and perspectives of others?" If you look at the learning goals or standards, it doesn't have "respect" or "tolerate." (But if you go down to the level of performance descriptors, it's there). [This is because] there are certain people who say that the state—the government and schools—should not tell kids who they should respect or who they should tolerate [e.g., drug addicts, murderers].... We changed the language to "understand" or "recognize." There were some people very upset [with this change] saying: "We have to fight this because people should be more tolerant and respectful in a civil society." [From my perspective,] it is important to listen respectfully to the opinions of diverse groups and have a long-term perspective ... you can't win everything the first time around.

As in previous examples in this chapter, Weissberg was brought to the policy table due to prior involvement in policy work, including a network of relationships he developed over time with various policy players. Weissberg describes the incremental nature of policy change and the need to compromise with policymakers throughout the process. Through his use of relationship-building and strategic and communication skills, Weissberg's experience reveals how scholarship-based expertise in a content area is directly applicable to the implementation of legislation by the executive branch of government, in this case the state Department of Education.

The following example incorporates two very different policy influence methods. The establishment of long-term consultation relationships with policymakers represents the first policy influence method, whereas the second is the generation of a major, national executive branch policy report.

Center for Health Services Research in California and the US Surgeon General's Report on Ethnicity, Culture, and Mental Health

Lonnie Snowden

PhD, Clinical-Community Psychology, Wayne State University, 1975

Professor of Health Policy and Management, University of California, Berkeley

Lonnie Snowden, a clinical-community psychologist, worked closely with state executive branch policymakers in California for many years in his role as director of a federally funded health services research center. This work focused on decentralization of services and racial disparities in mental health. Based on his work on racial disparities, Snowden was asked to contribute to the landmark Surgeon General's Report on Mental Health, and he directed and wrote the *Supplement on Culture, Race and Ethnicity* (US Department of Health & Human Services, 2001). The report contributed to renewed interest in mental health disparities, leading to key federal initiatives to monitor and decrease racial disparities in mental health treatment and quality, including initiatives in the 2010 Affordable Care Act (Snowden, 2012).

Here, Snowden first recounts the consultative work done through the Health Services Research Center and then describes his contribution to the Surgeon General's report:

> Health services as a perspective was not at all applied to mental health or substance abuse services until 25 or 30 years ago when advocates forced NIMH [National Institute of Mental Health] to do that. NIMH issued a series of announcements for Health Services Research Centers for the Severely and Persistently Mentally Ill. I participated in one of the centers and wound up heading it. The center included sociologists, economists, political scientists, and clinical psychologists. The state director of Mental Health was on the board. As part of our activities, we maintained close relations with the State Department of Mental Health. We did projects for them, as well as NIMH-funded projects. Also, we developed a very close relationship with the Mental Health System of Colorado.
>
> Those experiences were policy work basically. It was policy research and consultation. I also developed some close friendships that really cemented my relationships. We collaborated with policymakers as we did

the work. For example, I met with the director of Diversity and Cultural Competence for California over the years, where I compared research agendas with her. I would say, "Where does this stand for you?" She'd say, "That's important, but here are some other things that are important." Then on the other end when you're reporting back to the various stakeholders, you give them a call and say, "Here are my findings. You might be interested," or they're saying, "We have this problem. Have you found out your results yet?"

I got involved in interdisciplinary networks in state and to some extent federal mental health policy circles. The most important [result] there was the Surgeon General's Report on Mental Health, the first one ever, which I contributed to, and the Supplement on Cultural Ethnicity, which I directed and wrote. I was asked by the Surgeon General's Advisory Board to write it I think because the board included people who do disparity stuff, people I know. They wanted one person who had enough knowledge about disparities across groups not to favor any particular group, and someone who would work hard, as it involved a lot of work. . . . Both of these reports really had a big effect nationally, changing the dialogue about mental health and about disparities in a major way. Concerning the supplement, there was a 10-year follow-up on that, which was published in the *American Psychologist* [Snowden, 2012].

Snowden's example reveals the importance of his center's interdisciplinary collaboration in generating policy-relevant research. This work depended on ongoing consultation, both formal and informal, with policy stakeholders and conducting research of direct relevance to policymakers—in part based on research questions generated by the policymakers themselves. This can be critical to making research policy-relevant. Snowden's example once again demonstrates the central role of relationship-building (including friendship development), leadership skills, and long-term commitment to furthering policy change. Finally, in addition to needed content expertise, the importance of hard work and a reputation for getting things done are key contributors to invitations to serve in important policy roles.

The previous three examples represent policy influence based on collaboration with the executive branch—working within the system to influence policies and practices. The final example in this section, in contrast, involves collaboration with an agent outside of the system—in this case with a grassroots advocacy group providing pressure on the executive branch to respond to their policy demands.

Vacant Housing and Crime in Camden, New Jersey

Paul Speer

PhD, Community Psychology, University of Missouri–Kansas City, 1992

Professor of Human and Organizational Development, Vanderbilt University

Paul Speer, a community psychologist, was Director of Research at the Center for Social and Community Development at Rutgers when a local branch of PICO, a well-known national community organizing group approached him for his help. Specifically, PICO wanted Speer to work with them to conduct research which tested the group's hypothesis that vacant housing was a driver of violent crime. The group felt that Speer's research could help make the case to local politicians, including the mayor, that there was a link between vacant housing and crime in Camden, New Jersey. Previously, the mayor had downplayed PICO's assertion that there was a vital link between vacant housing and crime, and that, in any case, the city did not have the money to address the problem (Speer et al., 2003). Given Speer's dissertation research on a similar grassroots organizing group, choosing to work with PICO was a natural decision. The collaboration proved to be very effective and spawned major media coverage, graphically highlighting Speer's geographic information system (GIS) findings of the vacant housing–crime linkage. In the end, the City of Camden developed a multifaceted initiative, the Camden Community Housing Campaign, and the governor provided millions of dollars in funding to support housing rehabilitation (Speer et al., 2003).

Here, Speer describes his collaboration with PICO and discusses the process leading to their success in influencing executive branch policy and practice:

When the community organizing group PICO in Camden talked to me, they had been doing work around vacant housing and had done about 800 one-on-one conversations with citizens. The thing they heard so many times was that people had vacant houses on their block and that drugs were being sold out of them, there was gunfire, and people were getting beat up. PICO's analysis was that vacant houses were catalysts to crime. I told the PICO group, "I could help you, but I don't think it's going to work out because we'll never get the data from the police. I've been trying to get it for a year and a half." They said, "We'll see what we can do." Literally it was 10 days later I get a package with disaggregated

crime data from the police department that they'd given to PICO.
I couldn't believe it.

Once I had that data, I was able to do an analysis. My grad students and
I started going down on Saturday mornings to [meetings in] a church fellowship hall. There were several months of meetings with PICO, sometimes week after week but sometimes less frequently. We brought an LCD
projector and computer. We would start showing the leadership team stuff
that we'd done. Then different PICO leaders would ask questions. We
were doing analyses on the fly based on their questions. We would talk a
little bit about why correlation wasn't causation and just the different ways
academics think about how to interpret the patterns in the Camden data.
That's when these Tufte ideas [i.e., data visualization; Tufte, 2001] became
important. As researchers we began thinking about how best to communicate magnitudes of differences, and trends and influences across different
variables on some of these outcomes.

The Camden group then had a big public meeting. There were about
1,100 people there. The PICO leaders developed a PowerPoint incorporat-
ing the analyses we developed in collaboration with them and presented
this data to public officials and to local media. It was really impactful.
Leaders presented maps of crimes distributed throughout Camden based
on our use of GIS systems—particularly the physical distribution of violent crimes and drug crimes clustering in proximity to vacant housing.
The ripple of "oh" across that crowd when they saw all these violent crimes
linked to vacant houses, just visually, was powerful and impactful to both
residents and public officials.

The PICO influence process continued. In the end, the governor gave
two million dollars for a housing initiative and intervention to shore up
vacant housing. A year later, using disaggregated data, our evaluation
showed its positive impact.

This case represents a very different pathway to executive branch policy influence. Specifically, close collaboration with an advocacy group proved
critical. Visually effective presentations of research data helped PICO pressure the executive branch from without. The advocacy group achieved
its success through use of multiple policy methods, including a media
campaign, meetings with public officials, and broad citizen participation. The collaborative action research effort, including initial generation
of a research question by the advocacy group based on citizen interviews,
represents an exemplary community-based instance of strategic science
(pp. 72–74).

Summary

The executive branch is a natural point of policy influence for psychology faculty (and their graduate students), given the direct relevance of content expertise to executive agency programs and practices. This influence can contribute to decisions to initiate new evidence-based programs and practices, as well as to the effective implementation of both newly adopted and existing ones. Formal involvement as an advisory board member, various consultative relationships, preparing major policy-relevant reports, and working with advocacy groups represent some of the key policy influence methods highlighted in the examples, each with unique points of entry and associated skills. As with legislative work, successful work in this area requires perseverance, patience, the ability to compromise, and the willingness to operate in an arena where many powerful actors, forces, and interests affect the decisions made and their implementation. Next, we turn to university faculty's policy involvement in the third branch of government, the judicial, with its own distinctive set of actors and policy influence processes.

Judicial Branch Influence

Eight of the faculty members interviewed identify a contribution in the judicial arena as their greatest policy success. Key policy methods used by these faculty members include submitting amicus curiae briefs to appellate courts (e.g., Supreme Court), providing expert evidence in a case, and working with media and an intermediary organization. As noted in Chapter 2, amicus curiae ("friend of the court") briefs are documents submitted by persons or groups who are not parties in the case, but who desire to inform the court about their perspectives or knowledge related to the issues involved. Expert evidence is provided by those who meet legal definitions as experts and, in cases when scientific evidence is to be presented, that evidence must be determined "scientifically valid" by the judge (Levine, Wallach, & Levine, 2007). A written report of evidence (e.g., research findings) can also be shared with lawyers and introduced as documentary evidence, without the researcher serving as a witness. Table 3.3 lists the policy area, faculty member, level of government, and primary policy method(s) described.

To illustrate the influences of faculty on judicial branch policy we turn to four brief case examples. These psychologists demonstrate how it is possible to use social science research to inform cases on a wide variety of issues—from gender discrimination and same-sex marriage to child witness testimony and the treatment of adolescents in the criminal justice system. The methods used include expert testimony, amicus briefs, research initiatives, and media campaigns.

Table 3.3 **Judicial Branch Influence: Policy Area, Faculty Member, Levels, and Policy Methods**

Policy Area (Faculty Member)	Level	Amicus Brief	Expert Evidence	Other
Gender Discrimination (Fiske)*	US Supreme Court	X	Witness	
Gender Discrimination (Deaux)*	Multiple	X	Witness	
Same-Sex Marriage (Herek)*	CA Supreme Court	X	Witness	
Child Witnesses (Goodman)*	Multiple	X	Witness	
Adolescent Development & Juvenile Justice (Steinberg)*	US Supreme Court	X		Intermediary; Media campaign
Affirmative Action (Gurin)**(6)	Federal District Court		Report	
Mental Health System (Tebes)**(6)	IL Class Action		Report	
Gender Discrimination (Borgida)**(7)	Multiple	X	Witness	

* Covered in this chapter.
** (X) = Chapter number where presented as case example.

Gender Discrimination Precedent: *Price Waterhouse v. Hopkins*, US Supreme Court

Susan Fiske

PhD, Social Psychology, Harvard University, 1978

Professor of Psychology and Public Affairs, Princeton University

Susan Fiske, a social psychologist, provided expert testimony that was cited by the US Supreme Court in the *Price Waterhouse v. Hopkins* (1989) case, a landmark decision extending employer liability for gender bias (American Psychological Association, 1988; Fiske, Bersoff, Borgida, Deaux, & Heilman, 1991). Fiske was invited to provide testimony based on her prior published research on gender stereotyping, prejudice, and discrimination. The research evidence included in the amicus brief submitted for the case was prepared collaboratively by a team of social psychologists including Fiske, Eugene Borgida, Kay Deaux, and Madeline Heilman. Since that case, Fiske has provided expert testimony and/or court depositions in a number of other cases, although she has also turned down numerous opportunities, intentionally restricting her involvement to those that are likely to set a precedent.

Fiske first recounts the details of the *Price Waterhouse v. Hopkins* case and how she became involved:

> I got a phone call from an attorney who thought that psychology would provide an explanation for how perfectly reasonable people could discriminate against a very talented female candidate for promotion. She brought in more money than anybody else in her promotion class, but they turned her down because she wasn't feminine enough.
>
> I had to poke around the literature to say, "What do we know about this? What do we know about women who are penalized for not adhering to traditional gender roles?" It turned out there was a bunch of work like that. Then I prepared testimony.
>
> The woman in question brought the lawsuit, so she was the plaintiff. She won it at trial level, but then it was appealed. She won the appeal. Then it went to the Supreme Court because of a [technical legal] issue. When they wrote the opinion they said, "Fiske's testimony is just icing on the cake." It gave them at least an evidence-based excuse for the decision that they made, which was to remand it down to the lower court but requiring a different burden of proof. The plaintiff eventually won.
>
> The Supreme Court established the precedent, which basically revolved around "mixed motive" issues. The idea is if you bring a discrimination lawsuit and say, "I'm not perfect, but if I were a guy they would overlook it," that's a mixed motive. What the Supreme Court decided was that if gender was tainting any of the process of evaluating the person, that's not okay even if the person is imperfect. They didn't have to decide whether she was an obnoxious person or not. The people who felt she was obnoxious were doing that on the basis of gender.
>
> This mixed motive precedent was an important one. People tell me it's in law text books. Certainly there have been law review articles written about it. The key thing was the precedent. And the idea that you could use social science evidence in gender discrimination cases where it had not been used before.

The mechanisms through which a line of research can lead to policy influence are further elaborated by one of Fiske's collaborators in the *Price Waterhouse v. Hopkins* case.

Kay Deaux

PhD, Social Psychology, University of Texas, Austin, 1967

Distinguished Professor Emerita, CUNY Graduate Center

Kay Deaux was one of the social psychologists who worked with Fiske to synthesize the literature on gender discrimination (Fiske et al., 1991). Prior to the case, Deaux had conducted extensive experimental research on stereotypes, gender discrimination, and attributional issues. After *Price Waterhouse v. Hopkins*, Deaux served as an expert witness in a number of gender discrimination cases, applying the findings of social psychological research in varied case-specific contexts. Earlier, Deaux conducted policy-driven research for the Department of Labor on the job experiences of women in the steel industry. This work included an evaluation of the consequences of the consent decree the steel industry had signed to increase the number of women in blue-collar jobs in the industry—a step to avoid being sued by the government for discrimination (Deaux & Ullman, 1983). In addition, as president of the Association for Psychological Science (APS) and later the Society of the Psychological Study of Social Issues (SPSSI), Deaux helped forge increased focus on policy within organized psychology. This work included helping to lay the groundwork for establishment of APS' policy-focused journal *Psychological Science in the Public Interest* and of SPSSI's standing committee on policy, respectively. Deaux explains why she believes she has been able to influence gender discrimination policies through her experimental social psychology research:

> If you set up . . . experimental research so clearly that there are no other alternative explanations . . . and you see this discrimination or differential evaluation taking place, it can be a powerful convincer. Fundamental research that shows, "These are what these stereotypes are. This is how, all else being equal, men and women are not evaluated the same. Their performance is not explained in the same way." . . . The application to cases like Hopkins and Price Waterhouse . . . really did make people understand that gender discrimination can be subtle and go on even if someone isn't screaming in the foreground, "I don't like women working for me."
>
> How those processes operate and the realization that they really are pervasive in all sorts of domains of human endeavor, including jobs and organizational settings, has made a difference in many corporations and organizations. As a result, there are policies in place that wouldn't have been in place and hiring patterns that are different.

The *Price Waterhouse v. Hopkins* case highlights the relevance of a body of research evidence to help provide an analytical framework (i.e., social framework analysis; Walker & Monahan, 1987) for considering the specifics of a case of apparent sexual discrimination. Fiske and Deaux illustrate the utility of both expert testimony and amicus briefs in the judicial system. They also show how success can come from combining relationship skills (working with lawyers), analytic research skills (literature synthesis and framing), and communication skills (clear, compelling presentation of findings) to work effectively in an adversarial legal context. This example further highlights the reality that many different types of research—including theory-based experimental studies—can, in a given context, influence social policy.

The next example involves a more recent legal decision at the state level, involving the historic court decisions affirming same-sex marriage.

Legal Recognition of Same-Sex Marriage: Marriage Cases, California Supreme Court

Gregory M. Herek

PhD, Social Psychology, University of California, Davis, 1983

Professor of Psychology, University of California, Davis

Gregory Herek, a social psychologist, has conducted seminal research related to lesbian-gay-bisexual-transgender (LGBT) issues, provided expert testimony in key court cases involving gay rights, and contributed to numerous amicus briefs prepared by the American Psychological Association (Herek, 2006). The court cases include those focused on state sodomy laws, military policies excluding lesbians and gays, state anti-gay ballot propositions, anti-gay discrimination by the Boy Scouts of America, and laws restricting legal recognition of same-sex relationships. Herek played a pivotal role in the California *In re Marriage Cases* (American Psychological Association, 2007; In re Marriage Cases, 2008). In this case, the California Supreme Court decided that existing state law that limited marriage to opposite-sex couples was a violation of the rights of same-sex couples under the California State constitution. Consequently, the law could not be used to preclude them from marrying.[1] Here, Herek reflects on his contribution to APA brief to the California Supreme Court and concludes with a key lesson learned in bringing research findings into court:

---

[1] This decision was undone later in 2008, when the voters passed Proposition 8 amending the state constitution in order to prohibit same-sex couples from marrying. As discussed later, Proposition 8 was eventually declared unconstitutional by the federal District Court after a trial that included expert testimony by several social scientists, including Herek. More recently, the US Supreme Court ruled in favor of same-sex marriages. The APA amicus brief cited a number of Herek's studies.

So much of what I've done has been collaborative, so in terms of my success, it's usually been our success. One area in which I took the lead in drafting significant portions of an amicus brief was the marriage cases. It began in 2004 with the APA brief for a case challenging the New Jersey marriage law. Then came cases in Oregon, Washington, New York, and other states. With each of those later cases, we started with the New Jersey brief and built upon it, updated it, and revised it as needed.

When we filed a brief to the California Supreme Court, the issues were somewhat different from previous cases in that California already had a very strong domestic partners law, which conferred couples with most of the same rights as marriage—not at the federal level but in California. So we had to address what it was about marriage that made it so special an institution and set it apart from domestic partnerships. I drafted a passage of the brief (others subsequently contributed to it as well) making the point that sexual orientation is defined in basically relational terms—it's fundamentally about relationships, either actual or desired. If the law discriminates against same-sex relationships and couples, it's discriminating on the basis of sexual orientation.

When the California Supreme Court issued its ruling striking down the 2000 law that barred gay people from getting married, the written opinion quoted from a few amicus briefs that had argued in favor of the law in order to rebut them, to knock them down. But the only amicus brief that they quoted in support of their decision was the APA brief, and they quoted that [the above] passage.

One thing I've learned is to focus mainly on the questions we can address with empirical data. If we don't have directly relevant data for an issue, maybe we can offer speculation about it, but we have to make it clear that we're speculating or drawing a parallel from research in some other area. We try to stick close to the data in these briefs, and I try to do that as well in all of my own expert testimony and policy work.

Herek demonstrates how he used his role and skills as a psychologist to influence same-sex marriage policy. His career highlights the possibility of ongoing, cumulative influence over time. Like Fiske and Deaux, Herek illustrates the importance of combining analytic skills with communication skills in order to effectively frame research evidence for use in the judicial system. Herek has also provided expert testimony in a number of related cases. Especially interesting is his nearly 7-hour testimony in the federal trial challenging the constitutionality of California's Proposition 8. A re-enactment of his testimony can be viewed on YouTube (Prop 8 Trial Re-enactment, 2010).

The next case example encompasses multiple levels of the judicial branch and moves from a focus on case law to judicial process, in this instance concerning the role of children as witnesses in child abuse cases.

Children as Witnesses in Child Abuse Cases: Multiple Levels of Government

Gail Goodman

PhD, Developmental Psychology, University of California, Los Angeles, 1977

Professor of Psychology, University of California, Davis

Gail Goodman, a developmental psychologist, conducted some of the earliest research on children's eyewitness memory, specifically in relation to child abuse cases (Goodman, 1984). She was initially discouraged from this line of research by colleagues who indicated the topic of children's memory was "not important." Goodman pursued it nonetheless, in part due to the support received from mentors. As it turned out, this research had direct implications for the involvement of children as witnesses in the legal system. Her early work indicated that children are able to accurately recall events and memories when they feel safe and the questions are appropriate for the developmental level of the child (e.g., Goodman, Aman, & Hirshman, 1987). Goodman also studied child sexual assault victims testifying in criminal court and found that some children were too frightened to answer the attorneys' questions (Goodman et al., 1992). This research was cited in several US Supreme Court decisions, including a decision that allowed children to testify via closed circuit TV (*Maryland v. Craig*, 1990). Her research, and that of others, has continued to influence the way the courts view children as witnesses and the way they are treated within the judicial system. This includes the use of children's advocacy centers where child witnesses in abuse cases are interviewed (Anderson & McMaken, 1990; Walker, 2011).

Here, Goodman describes her involvement as an expert witness in a highly publicized case and reflects on the multiple contributions her research has made to judicial and forensic practice:

> I started conducting this work [research] when very few people were doing it. Then these big preschool cases hit . . . [One was] a very high profile case in Denver. It was a little girl who had been kidnapped and sexually assaulted. The man tried to kill her, but she lived and was found. I worked on that case to see ways that we could bolster obtaining information from

her that was accurate without our being leading. The issue of how to interview children became very controversial and very heated both within the scientific and clinical communities and the legal community, and internationally. . . . I learned that you really have to be very measured and try to consider multiple issues at the same time . . . how to protect the defendant's rights and innocent adults from false accusations while at the same time protecting children from abuse and trauma.

The initial research showing that children could be very accurate pulled the policymakers in one direction, but then other research showing that under other circumstances children could be very inaccurate pulled policymakers in another direction. You could then see the policy fluctuate. It was partly because when you're dealing with children, the courts and legislators don't know what to do. They feel at a loss because, after all, they're not developmentalists. . . .

The research affected forensic practice in terms of how children are interviewed, even before they get to court, by police or social workers. It influenced the development of children's advocacy centers, which are centers where children are interviewed in forensic cases. There are now over 500 of them worldwide. It affected laws regarding the admission of children's evidence in terms of situations in court where children can give testimony. In America for instance, under certain conditions, the US Supreme Court decided you could have children testify via closed-circuit TV [*Maryland v. Craig*, 1990].

In the big picture, the greatest success is bringing out the issue of children as witnesses, particularly in child abuse cases. It's a complex picture of their abilities and needs. People began to realize that children do become involved [as witnesses] in the legal system, that they need to become involved at certain times, and that there are different ways to best promote their accuracy and emotional well-being in the process. We're fortunate as scientists that we can uncover some deeper truths and really find out what children's abilities and needs are in the legal context.

Goodman's narrative underscores the relevance of psychological research to judicial procedures, especially in controversial areas. Her work has helped establish children's capacity to serve as witnesses and has contributed to forensic practices that support and help abused children when they do provide testimony. Whereas Goodman describes her early policy involvement as personally challenging—an experience shared by others working in policy areas where interests and emotions run strong—her case also highlights the influence researchers can have when their studies are some of the first conducted in a new, "hot" policy area. Because the political climate is always changing, psychologists have to take advantage of opportunities to exert policy influence when they unexpectedly arise.

The final example in this section involves an extended, strategic approach to influence the national conversation about treatment of adolescents in the justice system, culminating in part in a successful US Supreme Court decision.

Treatment of Adolescents in the Justice System: National Conversation and the Supreme Court

Laurence Steinberg

PhD, Human Development and Family Studies, Cornell University, 1977

Professor of Psychology, Temple University

Laurence Steinberg, a developmental psychologist, directed the MacArthur Foundation Research Network on Adolescent Development and Juvenile Justice, a well-resourced group of academic researchers, policy individuals, and legal practitioners. Over a number of years, their work helped place the treatment of adolescents in the justice system on the national policy agenda. Among many positive influences of this work, Steinberg indicates his greatest policy success was being cited in the Supreme Court's decision to abolish the juvenile death penalty (American Psychological Association, 2005; *Roper v. Simmons*, 2005). Steinberg emphasizes that the policy influence of the network's research is due in part to their concerted efforts to gain input from policy individuals and legal practitioners as they formulated research questions. The findings obtained would thus be actionable and policy-relevant. Steinberg notes that an additional contributor to policy influence was an extensive media outreach campaign.

Steinberg explains how political winds and current events converged to influence the focus of the MacArthur Research Network:

> Since the crime rate had gone up so much during the early 1990s, there had been this pendulum shift toward very harsh and punitive policies involving juvenile offenders. That was one of the things that motivated MacArthur to start the research network. The network began a series of research projects looking at how kids were different from adults and if they were different in ways that were relevant for our views of their criminal responsibility and culpability.

Steinberg and his colleagues at the MacArthur Research Network then used multiple methods to exert policy influence, actions that culminated with a Supreme Court decision in a juvenile death penalty case:

> My colleagues and I began writing articles saying kids are still kids even if they commit crimes, and we shouldn't be treating them the way that we treat adults even if it's the same kind of crime. We began a campaign to get that message out. We published a lot in academic journals, but my colleagues and I gave a lot of talks to organizations of judges, defense attorneys, district attorneys, and state legislators. We wrote articles for the newsletters and trade magazines that would go out to these practitioners, correctional people, judges, lawyers, legislators, and so on. In addition to that, we adopted a very aggressive strategy of promoting our work in the press. We developed some very good relationships with some key journalists from the main news outlets like *The New York Times*, *The Washington Post*, NPR, and the major television networks. We made sure that our research was getting into the hands of people who were covering juvenile delinquency and crime. Our work began to get a lot of play in the popular press. Clearly, during the time that we were working on the problem, the media coverage of the issue changed. Basically, we were trying to influence the national conversation and found that, in some senses, doing that by influencing the coverage of that in the press was more effective than trying to influence policymakers.
>
> So, before the Supreme Court took the case, we were already doing a lot of commenting in the press about the issue. Elizabeth Scott, who is a law professor at Columbia, and I published a paper in *The American Psychologist* on adolescent development, the juvenile death penalty and so on [Steinberg & Scott, 2003].
>
> When word got around that the Supreme Court would hear the case, we began getting the names of the clerks who worked for the different justices and sending them our stuff. It must have interested them because they read it, and it got into their opinion.

Steinberg's work sums up many of the methods and skills psychologists use to affect policy change in the judicial system. He and his colleagues directly fashioned their research to be policy-relevant and then engaged in extensive efforts to influence public and professional opinion. They published articles in academic journals and in trade journals while also communicating directly to policymakers (and their staff, including Supreme Court clerks) and advocates. Not only were Steinberg's research skills necessary, but equally so his communication skills and his ability to direct and work with a multidisciplinary network that included individuals involved in research, policy, and legal practice.

Summary

The judicial branch of government differs from the legislative and executive branches in that evidence is an explicit foundation for policy decision-making, and clear rules guide its use and contestation by opposing sides. Furthermore, the specifics of the case under consideration help specify exactly what kinds of research evidence and analytical framework are relevant. The four examples presented, taken together, illustrate that both theory- and application-driven psychological research can and do play an important role in precedent-setting decisions. As in the legislative and executive branches, communication of findings to courts most often requires active participation by the researcher and strong communication skills. In addition, the ability to withstand sustained attacks by opposing lawyers or interest groups may sometimes be necessary (see pp. 197–198 and 234–236).

Influencing Policy from the Vantage Point of the University: Benefits and Limitations

The case examples in this chapter and the interviews reported elsewhere in this volume illustrate that psychologists contribute in important ways to social policy in all three branches of government through a range of policy influence methods and activities. There are clear differences in influencing policy in the legislative, executive, and judicial branches. For example, program development and evaluation appear to be a more prominent pathway to influence in the legislative and executive branches where many psychology-related policy decisions are program-based. In contrast, influence in the judicial branch is more likely to stem from expertise in theory-based knowledge about people and their nature and capacities, albeit applied to specific instances.

The factors affecting the decisions of legislators (e.g., partisan politics), executive branch officials (e.g., embedded system practices), and judges (e.g., precedent) can be expected to differ. As a result, the use of evidence and the methods of influence will differ. However, there are also clear commonalities in the pathways, methods, and skills employed by the faculty across branches of government. In each case, foundational elements of influence are present:

- Content expertise
- Policy-relevant research

- Evidence-based policy ideas
- Relationship-building and effective communication of findings and ideas

Finally, the pathways, methods, and skills in each case are accompanied by a number of essential dispositional attributes, including:

- Persistence in taking one's findings and ideas into the policy arena
- Perseverance in the face of obstacles
- Taking advantage of windows of opportunity when they open

The common vantage point for influencing policy in each of the case examples is the university work context. All interviewees were asked what they perceived to be the advantages and limitations of the university as a work context for influencing policy. Psychologists in academia endorsed a number of advantages that the academic setting provides to conduct policy work. Most prominently, the qualities of academia that support the pursuit of policy-relevant research and influence include job security and flexibility, the reputation of science and the university, access to an interdisciplinary intellectual environment, and the enthusiasm and motivation of graduate students. Here, several psychologists interviewed highlight a number of the advantages of the university for policy work.

Irma Serrano-García, an emeritus psychology professor at the University of Puerto Rico, Río Piedras, reflects on how her academic position and the people she is surrounded with allow her to engage in the policy arena:

> It's a position with a lot of flexibility. Doing policy work requires a lot of time to meet with people, attend hearings, or write documents that are not part of your [academic] work. Academia allows you to do that. . . . The other thing is having a cadre of students who are interested, energetic and willing to absorb some of the work as part of their learning. Those are important benefits.

Aletha Huston, an emeritus professor at the University of Texas at Austin shares Serrano-García's perspective. She further adds that the academic context allows for freedom of inquiry:

> You have much more freedom to select the questions you want to ask than in a government agency. You can determine how the questions ought to be framed and investigated, what methods are best to investigate them, how to interpret the data . . . and [can] be sure that the data aren't suppressed. All of those things are problems when you work for a government agency or work on a government contract. The academic freedom of the university really matters.

Flexibility and freedom of inquiry also contribute to access to content expertise across a wide expanse of disciplines in universities. Alan Tomkins, the founding director of the University of Nebraska's Public Policy Center underscores the importance of such access for the work of his center:

> The major benefit is the access to a variety of disciplines and orientations that a university provides. . . . Our [Center's] lens is "What is the problem? What might be different ways that we could address this problem?" Because we are part of a major research institution, invariably there's somebody at the institution itself who can help us.

All of these characteristics of the academic context make it a prime candidate for policy-related work; however, many barriers also exist. When asked about the limitations of the academic context as a site for policy-related work, many interviewees indicated that the reward system of academia does not generally incentivize their involvement in policy. Although this finding varied depending on the type of academic context (i.e., traditional psychology departments tended to provide the least support), interviewees frequently emphasized the need to conduct active policy work on their own time, in addition to the duties (e.g., publishing in academic journals, obtaining grants, teaching) that were more valued in their context. Occasionally, interviewees remarked on bureaucratic and political challenges wherein grant funding was difficult to sustain or controversial work was stalled because of higher level influences in the academic context. Finally, differences between the agendas and timetables of the worlds of policy (generally short term) and academia (generally longer term) were often cited as challenges to conducting policy work as a faculty member in an academic department.

Deborah Phillips, a psychology professor at Georgetown University, notes that although many academics report being praised for their policy work, a lack of tangible rewards can make such efforts difficult:

> Policy work is still not well rewarded in academe, particularly for junior scholars. While institutions of higher education love to brag when their faculty have tangible policy-relevant impacts (for example, appointments, media coverage), they have not translated this into the reward structure that deeply affects young faculty. Prior to tenure, junior faculty really cannot spend the time that it takes to develop the policy relationships that are needed to be a reliable source of research knowledge. The system rewards grants, peer-reviewed publications, and teaching evaluations. This makes it extraordinarily difficult for junior faculty to be able to do the kinds of things that it really takes to have a meaningful influence and keep their toes in the [policy] waters.

Lonnie Snowden, introduced earlier, concurs:

> The culture of academia and its reward system are not aligned with what
> you need to do to be influential in the policy world. . . . When you're
> coming up for review . . . policy reports and related work don't count
> nearly as much as articles in leading journals. . . . You have to do both.
> That's tough.

Finally, the academic and policy arenas can feel like very distinct worlds. Rhona
Weinstein, a Professor of the Graduate School at the University of California,
Berkeley explains:

> The difficulty I think is that we're engaged in all kinds of work—teach-
> ing, research and applied work. Policy work has a very different pace
> that's hard to reconcile. It's very fast and immediate. . . . The writing style
> is very different. . . . You have to get the knowledge of the relevant studies
> in a very wide review and put it in succinct responses. I found the pace of
> it a bit dizzying.

The academic context can provide a unique and impactful setting for policy work,
but it certainly comes with a set of challenges. In the next chapter, we turn to a
different vantage point from which to influence policy, one with its own set of
advantages, limitations and challenges.

4

Psychologists Working in Intermediary Organizations

An intermediary organization . . . bridges science and research with policy and practice. We engage in a variety of activities; all can be understood through the lens of creating change at the policy, systems, and practice levels.
— J. Franks, May 17, 2013

Policy-focused organizations external to government play a major role in the policy process. These include professional membership organizations, think tanks, the National Academies, research and consultation firms, foundations, and advocacy groups (Andrews & Evans, 2004; Rich, 2004). Such organizations employ applied psychologists pursuing policy-related careers. Furthermore, the staff of these organizations work closely with psychologists employed in academia and elsewhere on policy initiatives. Broadly speaking, these organizations can be viewed as intermediary settings because they serve as bridges between policy-makers and policy-interested parties, including citizens, communities of practice or delivery systems (e.g., mental health practitioners; public health system), and university-based researchers.

The purpose of this chapter is to depict the policy influence activities of psychologists who work for intermediary organizations. Fourteen psychologists identified their greatest policy success as occurring through such work. The 14 case examples are organized by type of intermediary organization in which the psychologist worked: professional membership organization; the National Academies; research, evaluation, and consulting organizations; and foundations. The case examples highlight the specific methods and skills employed by individual psychologists in these intermediary organizations. Major differences in policy focus and methods exist across the case narratives in the chapter, in part due to fundamental differences in mission and culture across the four types of intermediary organizations. Nonetheless, although particular applications may differ, the core policy skills of relationship-building, communication, research, and strategic analysis are central to effective policy work in each context.

The first section of the chapter explores an intermediary organization familiar to many in the field of psychology: the American Psychological Association (APA), a professional member organization. The primary focus is on psychologists influencing policy through their work as employees of APA. However, a number of other psychologists interviewed contributed to such work indirectly as academics contributing to APA committees and, in one case, as an APA critic and change agent. The policy work of several of these psychologists is included in the chapter as well.

In the second section of the chapter, we turn to an intermediary organization with a very different mission and culture, the National Academies. Psychologists employed in this setting work with national experts and contribute to policy through the generation and dissemination of policy-relevant reports. The third section of the chapter focuses on psychologists who work in research, evaluation, and consulting organizations, both nonprofit and for-profit. Psychologists in this varied set of intermediary organizations collaborate across multiple disciplines and influence policy through both research and consultation.

The fourth section looks at foundations, those intermediary organizations that provide funding to support the policy-relevant work of grantees. Psychologists in foundations seek to influence policy by funding programs of policy-relevant research and advocacy, supporting the general capacity of policy-focused organizations, and engaging in targeted networking to link research and practice experts with policymakers.

The policy influence methods employed by psychologists within intermediary organizations are in some cases similar to those used by psychologists in academic settings (e.g., meeting with policymakers, serving on advisory boards, preparing policy reports). In other cases, they are quite different because psychologists within intermediary organizations can engage in activities that include formal lobbying; preparing amicus briefs; funding policy-focused research and advocacy; and bringing together academics, practitioners, and policymakers. The examples described in this chapter encompass national, state, and local levels of influence across the three branches of government. Taken together, the case examples illustrate the range of intermediary organizations within which psychologists work and the policy methods and skills individual psychologists use to make a difference in the policy arena. The concluding section of the chapter examines some of the distinct advantages and disadvantages of seeking to influence policy from the vantage point of intermediary organizations.

Psychologists Working for APA

A wide range of professional and membership organizations exist in the United States that serve the occupational and/or public service interests of their members through multiple means including policy advocacy (Ainsworth, 2002;

Table 4.1 **APA Staff: Policy Issue, Psychologist, Government Branch/Level, and Policy Influence Method**

Policy Issue (Psychologist)	Government Branch/ Level	Policy Influence Method
ACA (Garrison)*	Legislative/National	Managing Advocacy Campaign
ACA (Elmore)*	Legislative/National	Coalition-based Lobbying
Military; Science (Kelly)*	Multiple/National	Lobbying
Gay Rights (Anderson)*	Judicial/Multiple	Amicus Briefs

* Covered in this chapter.

Andrews & Evans, 2004; Loomis, 2011; Maisel & Berry, 2010). For psychologists, the largest professional organization is APA. Advocating for key federal policies and legislation is an important goal of APA and one of the key activities of its government relations staff (APA, 2015c). Four case examples of policy influence from full-time APA staff are presented here (see Table 4.1).

The psychologists who work at APA influence policy through the legislative, executive, and judicial branches of government, at national and sometimes state levels. They use a range of techniques that are both educational and persuasive to influence policies that range from healthcare to military and gay rights policies, as well as advocacy for the behavioral sciences in general.

We begin with Ellen Garrison and her coordination role in APA advocacy related to the Affordable Care Act (ACA).

Advocacy for the ACA

Ellen Garrison

PhD, Clinical Psychology, University of Illinois, Urbana–Champaign, 1983

Senior Policy Advisor to APA's Chief Executive Officer

Ellen Garrison, a clinical psychologist has, since 2006, been the senior policy advisor to APA's chief executive officer. In this role, she coordinates various APA policy initiatives and serves as the organization's point person on policy matters. Prior to this involvement, from 1998 to 2006, Garrison served as APA's associate executive director for public interest policy and co-directed the Congressional Fellowship Program. Her areas of special interest include federal policy related to the integration of mental/behavioral healthcare and the needs of special populations such as children and ethnic minorities.

Garrison reports her greatest policy success as coordinating APA's effort to incorporate provisions of importance to psychology in the ACA. Over a period of several years, she worked with the major stakeholders at APA to develop key policy objectives and to coordinate the ensuing advocacy work of the four APA directorates (Practice, Science, Public Interest, and Education) as well as multiple APA offices related to these objectives. The ACA contains numerous provisions directly reflecting the objectives for which APA lobbied: integrated healthcare (5 provisions); prevention and wellness (22 provisions); psychology workforce (9 provisions); enhancing access to mental healthcare and parity in benefit plans (7 provisions); reducing health disparities (7 provisions); promoting psychological research (1 provision); and engaging consumers, families, and caregivers in care (7 provisions; APA, 2010a).

Here, Garrison describes her role coordinating the ACA advocacy effort, including the skills she brought to bear in this work:

> My role was to coordinate the association's ACA advocacy efforts, starting about 2007—three years before the bill was signed into law by President Obama in March of 2010. First, we identified the key objectives that we wanted to achieve through this legislation. My role included working with APA's CEO Norman Anderson, our Board of Directors, key APA divisions, other association leaders and experts, and APA colleagues to determine our association's priorities in healthcare reform.
>
> Important to moving forward were communication skills and having the convening power to bring key people together from across the association. Organizational skills were also critical to coordinate our government relations staff to review this 2,000+ page bill quickly and thoroughly in order to identify provisions of the bill of particular relevance to psychology and to develop and implement an overall advocacy plan.
>
> Negotiating skills were likewise essential to work with other organizations to reach consensus where disagreements arose on specific provisions of mutual interest. For we all were aware that members of Congress and their staff have little patience or tolerance for being confronted with disputes among advocates. There were also times when it was necessary to resolve competing priorities among APA's directorates, which resulted at times in one directorate stepping back in the interest of the association as a whole. Strategic decisions also included determining which congressional offices to approach to champion specific issues of importance to psychology and which Senate and House Committee to focus on for specific provisions.

We fortunately had a significant body of psychological research to draw upon that showed the positive influence of identifying and treating mental health conditions and underlying behaviors (e.g., tobacco and other substance use; unhealthy diet) to improve health outcomes, and the power of prevention. In our advocacy communications, we would always note that our positions (including our briefing sheets) were research-informed and empirically based. Although this approach generally served to strengthen our arguments, some of our congressional interactions were met with a response reminiscent of the old adage, "Don't confuse me with the facts since I've already made up my mind."

Grassroots advocacy was of paramount importance throughout our efforts. Members of Congress are intent on hearing from their constituents regarding key public policy issues. We helped to facilitate this process in part through sponsoring major grassroots advocacy events, such as the APA State Leadership Conference and the Education Leadership Conference, in which hundreds of psychologists come each year to Washington, DC, for a several-day educational program and to participate in coordinated visits on Capitol Hill with their members of Congress to advance psychology's agenda.

We also periodically activated our grassroots computer networks to send information and action alerts to educate our members about key legislative issues. Through these communications channels, we successfully engaged our members in coordinated advocacy campaigns to contact their congressional representatives to make the case for psychology's priorities in healthcare reform.

In addition to grassroots advocacy, the other vital realm of effective influence in the public policy arena is direct involvement by government relations staff in the development of legislation. Such opportunities arise through effecting APA member participation in congressional hearings and briefings and through engaging in close working relationships with key congressional staff and members of Congress in which input is sought/accepted and draft bills are reviewed for comment. That's exactly where you want to be positioned as an advocate. . . . APA experienced significant successes in these domains based on years of active engagement with our members and key congressional offices.

Garrison's role in APA's advocacy for the ACA was primarily strategic and leadership-focused. Strong project management, strategic analysis, negotiation, and organizational skills contributed to her success overseeing this work. Garrison notes that collaborating with grassroots organizations and encouraging direct involvement of APA members in the legislative process allowed APA to successfully influence policy in this case. Unlike the two case examples that follow, Garrison was not directly involved in lobbying. However, her experience as a congressional fellow and her years of advocacy work for the Public Interest Directorate provided a strong foundation for her effective project leadership of APA's lobbying and related advocacy efforts.

Next, we turn to a policy-related success that combined managerial, strategic, and hands-on advocacy work.

The ACA: Geriatric Workforce Education and Training Provisions

Diane Elmore

PhD, Counseling Psychology, University of Houston, 2002

Director of the Policy Program, University of California, Los Angeles/Duke University National Center for Child Traumatic Stress

Diane Elmore worked in the **Public Interest Government Relations Office** (PI-GRO) at APA from 2002 to 2004 and again from 2005 to 2013, serving most recently as associate executive director. PI-GRO's overall mission is "to apply psychology to the fundamental problems of human welfare and the promotion of equitable and just treatment of all segments of society" (APA, 2015d). Elmore's particular areas of expertise include trauma and abuse, military and veterans issues, aging, underserved populations, and healthcare policy. In her role as associate executive director of PI-GRO, Elmore was responsible for coordinating the varied aspects of public interest advocacy related to the ACA (APA, 2010a, 2010b). These activities included working closely with congressional sponsors during drafting of provisions, congressional visits (lobbying), coordinating visits and letters of support to Capitol Hill, coordinating grassroots activities by members, taking part in congressional hearings and forums, and working closely with various coalitions on coordinated advocacy.

Elmore regards one of her greatest personal policy successes as her hands-on contributions to passage of Title V, Section 5305 of the Act, concerning geriatric workforce education and training (Pub Law 111-148, Section 5305, 2010). This work was done in collaboration with the Eldercare Workforce Alliance (eldercareworkforce.org). The adopted provisions expanded and improved geriatric education and training opportunities for health professionals, in part by embracing an interdisciplinary focus. The interdisciplinary approach included making psychologists (and geriatric health professionals from other historically excluded disciplines) eligible for the existing Geriatric Education Centers program and authorizing a new Geriatric Career Incentive Awards program to include psychology graduate students.

Here, Elmore describes PI-GRO's broad advocacy role related to the ACA and her specific hands-on contributions to the geriatric workforce provisions:

> Public Interest took a leadership role on issues including integrated healthcare, prevention, health disparities, and consumer and caregiver issues. We also worked in collaboration with partners in the Education Directorate on issues related to the healthcare workforce. One of the places where we had a particular impact was workforce development issues for health professionals serving vulnerable populations. We do not have enough culturally competent providers in any of the health disciplines to address the needs of our increasingly diverse, aging, population. And psychologists, and other health professionals, weren't fully benefiting from the three existing federal programs focused on geriatric education and training.
>
> We started to develop relationships in a new coalition called the Eldercare Workforce Alliance. The coalition included an interdisciplinary team of nearly 30 organizations representing physicians, nurses, psychologists, social workers, pharmacists, physical therapists, direct-care workers, eldercare employers, family caregivers, and consumers. After months and months of trust-building, relationship-building, rapport-building, and bringing our science to bear, coalition members started to really understand each other. We finally agreed on a strategy to advocate for the expansion of existing geriatric workforce programs to include a much broader group of health professionals. In order for this more inclusive interdisciplinary policy strategy to work, we also had to agree (as a coalition) to collective advocacy in support of increasing overall funding for these programs, so there would be sufficient resources to support currently eligible and newly eligible disciplines.
>
> We engaged in nearly two years of education and advocacy with key congressional offices and federal agencies. We advocated for interdisciplinary science and practice. We returned again and again to key staff who were drafting the health reform bills to help inform the process. As co-chair of the coalition's policy committee, I worked with other coalition leaders and constituents to coordinate and participate in dozens and dozens of policymaker visits. We reached out and worked with members of the Senate Health, Education, Labor and Pensions (HELP) Committee; the House Energy and Commerce Committee; and leaders on the Senate Special Committee on Aging.

We successfully urged the staff and policymakers writing the bills to include language in the legislation that opened these programs to psychology and other disciplines, ultimately strengthening the programs. Some nights, we were communicating with each other and House and Senate staff until midnight to negotiate legislative language. I would get a conference room here at APA and bring the chips and salsa. We'd work for hours. . . . It was exhilarating, a once-in-a-lifetime effort.

Elmore, like Garrison, performed a critical strategic and managerial role overseeing the public interest portion of APA's advocacy work on the ACA. She also was directly involved in hands-on advocacy. In the latter role, Elmore helped to build an effective interdisciplinary coalition, did direct education and lobbying, and contributed to the drafting of legislation. Her colorful description of "bringing the chips and salsa" to late night coalition meetings illustrates both the relationship aspect of advocacy work and the investment of time and energy involved.

The third case example involves an APA psychologist whose work is based in the Science Directorate. Her lobbying work typically focuses on research funding for behavioral science but on occasion extends to social policy issues as well. This was the case in the example provided, one that focused on ending the military's "Don't Ask, Don't Tell" (DADT) policy.

"Don't Ask, Don't Tell": The Art of Lobbying for Science

Heather Kelly

PhD, Clinical Psychology with Specialization in Community Psychology, University of Virginia, 1998

Registered Federal Lobbyist for the Science Government Relations Office, APA

Heather Kelly, a clinical psychologist, is a registered federal lobbyist for the Science Government Relations Office at APA, where she has worked for 17 years. Her advocacy portfolio focuses on funding for behavioral science within the National Science Foundation, the Department of Veterans Affairs, and the Department of Defense. Kelly also directs APA's Executive Branch Science Fellowship Program (apa.org/about/awards/science-fellowship. aspx). Kelly made clear numerous times during her interview that it is difficult to pinpoint specific outcomes from her work because she is only one of numerous sources of influence on legislators and executive agency officials. Nonetheless, Kelly did single out several instances of likely influence. In terms of science policy, Kelly noted the personal satisfaction she derived from her work helping to highlight the importance of Department of Veteran Affairs research on post-traumatic stress disorder and traumatic brain injury. Furthermore, she highlighted several ways she contributed to the APA effort to repeal the Department of Defense DADT policy. In the wake of this repeal, the Department of Defense changed its policy. Its website now reads, "Statements about sexual orientation are no longer a bar to military service" (Department of Defense, 2010).

Here, Kelly highlights several aspects of her advocacy work related to the repeal of DADT:

> There are two ways I felt I had some influence on the repeal of Don't Ask, Don't Tell, though it was a massive, collaborative effort spanning many years. I do lots of DOD-related [Department of Defense] Hill visits every year, mostly about research funding and mental health services, but on every one of those visits to a staffer that year, I added the Don't Ask, Don't Tell piece. By doing so, the message essentially became, "This is important. This has to change—and we have not only human rights on our side, but also empirical data." When someone would say, "Unit cohesion will go down and morale will go down," I could respond, "No, here's what we know does or does not happen from armies around the world." We were received well because of the other work we had collaborated on with those offices in terms of research and mental health. For example, near the time of the actual vote, a conservative Democrat called us and said, "Tell me again why I should vote this way and not that way." My colleague's reply was, "You can disagree on moral grounds but here's what we know empirically." That vote switched to our direction, and it was a really important vote to switch.
>
> Also, I served as liaison to the APA's Joint Military Division-LGBT Division Task Force on Sexual Orientation and Military Service that was formed in 2005. I was there to make sure that the science piece was well represented in the task force work to address how sexual orientation should be addressed by the military [Joint Task Force on Sexual Orientation and Military Service, 2009]. Research evidence just changes the conversation sometimes, in complementary ways to a human rights appeal. The relationship-building between members of those divisions on the task force that followed was an impressive example of psychologists finding common ground, often after coming at the issue from quite different perspectives. That report was even more effective a tool in the policy realm because of the consensus from a typically disparate group of experts.

Kelly proceeds to share her perspective on key components of effective work as a behavioral science lobbyist:

> More generally, day to day, we're chipping away at the idea that science is not important—and behavioral science in particular. It's about persuasion and science. It's a relationship business. Important elements of effective lobbying include:
>
> - *Cultivating a sense of interpersonal trust.* The information we share is always scientifically based. I always disclose what we know and what we don't know so that legislators can trust the information that we give them. The staffers are really looking for people they can go to for information, who will tell the truth from a scientific standpoint.
> - *Immediate relationship-building.* A lot of the staff move around, so developing a relationship with someone quickly is critical. You don't have a lot of time, either in that actual meeting, or however long that person is going to be on the Hill. I know everything I possibly can about someone before I meet him or her, and ideally I know what the best "hooks" are going to be.
> - *Don't forget the small things.* For example, I was meeting with a staffer in a senator's office. He had a brother just back from Afghanistan—turns out the staffer was also a military brat. Making a personal connection, I said I am too, and it shifted the whole conversation. You look to connect, knowing that people are more likely to accept your argument if they already have a shared experience or perspective on something else.
> - *Use all the points of influence at your disposal.* If I can move a legislator an inch, an important inch, I want to be in that meeting, but we try always to have the most effective person deliver the important message at the right time. So that often means bringing in psychologist experts to meet with legislators or staffers—once policymakers see that a psychologist has something to contribute to an issue of importance to the policymaker, that can move things forward even more dramatically. For example, a senator wanted all federal funding for the social sciences to stop—we had many psychologists in the senator's state call and say, "I'm a constituent, a psychological scientist—and here's what my work does for the state and its people."
> - *Maintain relationships.* I will ask for the world from a legislator or staffer but I will do it respectfully and politely. My mantra is "shameless but polite." We may agree to disagree on issues, but we maintain a relationship based on the knowledge that I will get you any information you want, on what you care about, and I will do it within an hour.

Kelly's hands-on work as a lobbyist provides insight into the importance of relationship-building, communication, and generic "people skills" for effective advocacy work. She reads people well, finds ways to connect, and works to provide information of value to maintain relationships and access. Kelly also regularly draws on strategic analysis and persuasion skills and the ability to mobilize constituents. The need for perseverance and appreciation of "small wins" is evident in her reference to moving her lobbying agenda forward "an important inch" at a time. In terms of the work experience, Kelly notes that advocacy work at the federal policy level "can seem like a marathon, but often it's really a long series of daily sprints."

Whereas the policy work of Garrison, Elmore, and Kelly centers on the legislative and executive branches, the work of a fourth APA psychologist focuses primarily on the judicial policy arena.

Advancing the Cause of Gay Rights

Clinton Anderson

PhD, Community and Applied Social Psychology, University of Maryland, Baltimore County, 2006

Director of the Lesbian, Gay, Bisexual, and Transgender Concerns Office, Public Interest Directorate, APA

Clinton Anderson, initially as a master's level psychologist, was APA staff person who fostered APA involvement in gay rights court cases over the past several decades. He did so by bringing research evidence to bear on legal issues affecting LGBT individuals through the use of amicus briefs. Over that time, the **Lesbian, Gay, Bisexual, and Transgender Concerns Office** (LGBTCO) he directs has made the judicial arena a primary point of focus. The mission of LGBTCO is to "advance the creation, communication and application of psychological knowledge on gender identity and sexual orientation to benefit society and improve lesbian, gay, bisexual and transgender people's lives" (http://www.apa.org/pi/lgbt/).

To date, over several decades of work, Anderson's office has submitted 57 amicus briefs related to sexual orientation in the areas of adoption (3 amicus briefs), custody (5), marriage (29), military policies (2), state anti-sodomy laws (8), tests (use, validity, and security of data, 5), and others (5; e.g., anti-gay discrimination by the Boy Scouts of America (APA, 2015*e*).

Anderson's other contributions include working within APA to generate policy position statements on important LGBT issues and contributing to congressional action through advocacy and lobbying (APA, 2015f). These latter efforts contributed, for example, to APA's adoption in 2004 of the statement objecting to the discriminatory nature of DADT (as discussed by Kelly in the previous case) and to the passage of the Hate Crimes Statistics Act, the first federal statute to recognize and name lesbian, gay, and bisexual people.

Here, Anderson describes aspects of his early congressional work and his office's long-standing contributions in the judicial arena:

My first major issue of focus was the Hate Crime Statistic Act, adopted in about 1989. After that, I was one of a handful of people working with the staff of one member of Congress who was taking a lead on the issue of lesbian and gay people in the military. Eventually President Clinton made a commitment to change the policy in '92, but his efforts to follow through on that were not successful in '93 and '94.

Then because of the change in the Congress from Democratic to Republican in '94, at a federal level there was nothing positive going on. So, as the LGBT civil rights legal strategy shifted to state courts, I initiated consideration of APA's entry into state level cases, cases challenging sodomy laws and cases challenging denial of lesbian and gay parents' rights. APA made the decision to move into this arena of law. The role we played with regard to the court was bringing the scientific information to bear on sodomy laws, parents and their children, the military, ballot measure cases, the marriage cases, and the Boy Scouts case. Court judges' decisions are not necessarily very straightforward in terms of saying, "Well, we were influenced by this particular amicus brief." But the lawyers out there keep coming back to us over and over again, wanting us to do these briefs.

My role on that work has been central, but there have been other people in the field, Greg Herek [pp. 89–90] in particular, who has been most important because he has been willing and ready to do the work intellectually that needs to be done. My role of being between lawyers and him has been at times crucial, because they don't always get along. Also, though I usually depend on people in the field to tell me what the recent literature is, I have to stay on top of the literature to some extent, because if I am going to sign off on a brief I have to understand what it is we're saying.

We [APA] normally do some proactive work to clarify an area, like the marriage area. We adopted our policy position statements in that area. It is this work we have done beforehand that provides us a justification, a basis for getting involved in cases. There has to be a substantial body of literature relevant to the legal issues too. The briefs tell in a sense a story about sexual orientation and that story, depending on the emerging scientific research, has been developing over time.

Unlike the work of others interviewed from APA, Anderson's policy activity has primarily focused on the judicial branch, the arena in which pivotal advances in the area of gay rights in recent decades has occurred. As the promoter of APA's work in contributing amicus briefs to major social policy issues, Anderson has successfully utilized skills of coordination, networking, strategic analysis, and leadership on the state and national level. The recent United States Supreme Court decision (*Obergefell v. Hodges*, 2015) in favor of same-sex marriage, for example, represents in part the culmination of decades of work by Anderson (and many others), including the submission of multiple amicus briefs in important state and federal court cases.

Summary

These four case examples provide insight into the varied roles, activities, methods, and skills involved in the pursuit of policy influence through a major professional membership organization like APA. Additionally, important aspects of APA policy work are performed by psychologists who do not work in APA, including university faculty members. Several examples are presented next.

Contributions to APA by University Faculty

Many of the psychologists interviewed for this book have served in various roles in APA (and other professional organizations with a substantive policy focus). Roles include serving on APA council (governing body), committees, and task forces; preparing policy-relevant reports and legal documents (e.g., amicus briefs); providing informal advice and consultation; and contributing to APA grassroots, constituent-focused advocacy efforts. Another important role is to serve as an outside advocate to help bring about needed reforms to APA. To illustrate the nature and range of these contributions, three examples from the university faculty interviewed are described (see Table 4.2). The first two cases are brief, involving psychologists' involvement in ongoing APA efforts to influence governmental policy. The third is more extended, given its uniqueness in involving external advocacy to transform a controversial APA policy position that directly affects governmental policy.

Table 4.2 **Contributions to APA by University Faculty: Policy Issue, Psychologist, Government Branch/Level, and Policy Influence Method**

Policy Issue (Psychologist)	Government Branch/ Level	Policy Influence Method
Socioeconomic Disparities (Bullock)*	Legislative/National	Advocacy
Education (Weinstein)*	Legislative/National	Consultation (legislation)
Psychologists' Involvement in Interrogations (Olson)*	Executive/National	Advocacy

* Covered in this chapter.

APA Reports: APA Committee on Socioeconomic Status

Heather Bullock

PhD, Social Psychology, University of Rhode Island, 1995

Professor of Psychology, University of California, Santa Cruz

Heather Bullock, a social psychologist, contributed to a policy-focused APA report, *Making "Welfare to Work" Really Work* (Task Force, 1998), distributed to all members of the US Congress and state legislators. In addition to being a former APA Congressional Fellow, Bullock was also the first chair (serving for 3 years) of APA Public Interest Committee on Socioeconomic Status. Established in 2007, its core mission includes advocacy for social policy that reduces or alleviates socioeconomic disparities (APA, 2015g). Here, Bullock provides a perspective on the importance of the Committee on Socioeconomic Status and describes how research can inform advocacy work:

> I was on the APA task force on socioeconomic status [SES]. We wrote a report that advocated for the creation of a permanent office and committee that would be housed within the public interest directorate on SES. I was the first chair of the committee. . . . Individual researchers can make a difference, certainly, in a variety of ways, but having a bigger platform through which to do advocacy I think is really important. I think having that office and that committee has created a venue for raising awareness of the issues and a means for advocacy.

APA committee service provides APA members such as Bullock the opportunity to leverage APA resources, staff, and existing congressional connections in working to influence federal policy on important social issues.

APA Committee on Urban Initiatives: No Child Left Behind

Rhona Weinstein

PhD, Clinical-Community Psychology, Yale University, 1973

Professor of the Graduate School, University of California, Berkeley

Rhona Weinstein, a clinical, community, and educational psychologist, served on the Committee on Urban Initiatives of the Public Interest Directorate during the time the No Child Left Behind (NCLB) legislation was being developed in Congress. Weinstein has done extensive work on the power of teacher expectations in educational achievement (e.g., Weinstein, 2002); initiatives to support placement of students in mixed-ability, heterogeneous classes in public schools (i.e., de-tracking); and the development of a model charter school (Weinstein & Worrell, 2016). As part of APA Urban Initiative Committee's work on NCLB, Weinstein (and other committee members) provided ideas and language for key legislative provisions that were then shared with congressional staffers crafting the bill. Here, she recounts her work with the committee on the NCLB legislation:

> I was on the Urban Initiatives Committee of APA from 1999 to 2001. Almost daily we would be sent drafts of the legislation, section by section, and we would be asked to respond in brief, with research-based critiques and suggested principles or language. The turnaround time was unbelievable. You'd get an email to do something that had to be turned back in 24 hours. We were on an email chain where we could see other people's comments and many versions of the No Child Left Behind law. We would prepare material and the APA staff would get it to the [congressional] committee chairs who [would] read our recommendations and send drafts of the policy back to APA. . . . I think our major contribution to the legislation was helping to turn attention to the achievement gap. We failed, however, to get accountability for providing "equal educational opportunity" [i.e., equal instructional resources and educational quality for low-income and minority youth] into the law, a grave omission.

Weinstein and colleagues on the Urban Initiatives Committee were afforded the opportunity to directly contribute to the emerging NCLB legislation. Extensive education content knowledge, along with the ability to navigate the fast-paced policy environment, were critical to this contribution. This opportunity to exert policy influence was likely due to APA's close connection with psychologist Charles Barone, a former APA congressional fellow and key House education committee staffer (see pp. 152–154). In the world of policy, who you know—relationships—matter a great deal.

The guild interests (see p. 4) of professional membership organizations center on the growth and prosperity of the profession. These interests can result in misguided organizational policies and practices that conflict in important ways with the public interest. Concerning APA, when this occurs, it is incumbent upon psychologists to advocate for change in the organization. The next example represents such a policy change effort—in a highly controversial area.

APA Ethical Standards and Psychologists' Involvement in Interrogations

Bradley Olson

PhD, Personality-Social Psychology, University of Iowa, 2000

Assistant Professor of Psychology, National Louis University

While others were working through APA committees to influence social policy, Bradley Olson, a community psychologist, has worked to influence APA policies via an outside advocacy role. This advocacy has focused on psychologists' involvement in national security settings where controversial interrogation techniques have been used to obtain information from captured or detained prisoners of war (enemy combatants). Olson contributed to ongoing efforts, including the use of media, advocacy meetings with APA leadership, and an APA member referendum to pressure APA to change its ethical standards and policy positions in this area (Psychologists for Social Responsibility, 2014). Most recently, in 2015, he helped mobilize support for the near-unanimous vote of APA Council of Representatives (COR) to ban psychologists from involvement in national security interrogations and from work with detainees in any national security settings that violate the US Constitution or international law (APA, 2015h). These varied efforts were spearheaded by the Coalition for an Ethical Psychology, which Olson co-founded, and Psychologists for Social Responsibility (PsySR), of which Olson is a past-president.

After a decade of criticism, including exposés published by *New York Times* reporter James Risen, APA hired David Hoffman, a Chicago attorney at the firm Sidley Austin to conduct an independent investigation. The resulting Hoffman report provided a scathing critique of APA's role in supporting psychologists' involvement in coercive interrogations. This led to the 2015 policy vote by the COR just weeks after the report's release (Hoffman et al., 2015). The Hoffman report revealed that the Ethics Director of APA, supported at times by other APA officials, colluded with important Department of Defense (DoD) officials over an extended period of time.

This collusion, as detailed in the report, resulted in APA ethical guidelines remaining loose enough so that they did not constrain existing DoD interrogation guidelines. The report concludes, "APA's principal motive [with these actions] . . . was to align APA and curry favor with DoD. There were two other important motives: to create a good public-relations response and to keep the growth of psychology unrestrained in this area" (Hoffman et al., 2015, p. 13). The report also detailed years of cover-up of these activities, including manipulation of APA members and processes. In essence, key APA officials were supporting DoD policy through hidden, beyond-the-scenes efforts. Olson and colleagues worked tirelessly to counter this effort in the face of tactics from APA officials to marginalize, discredit, and disempower them (Hoffman et al., 2015).

Olson discusses this work at the intersection of APA ethics, psychologists' involvement in interrogations, and public policy:

> There are many levers and mechanisms [we have used] . . . from open letters that would go to the APA, to contacting APA Council members, to working with newspapers, including the *New York Times*. We had a "withhold dues movement" which was pretty much a boycott of the APA. Some pressure has been important, but we've always [also] tried to use logical arguments, expecting that psychologists will understand those and change their opinions. We were dealing with many of the APA presidents, and working with those military people and CIA people who supported our opinions. There were also many individual meetings with APA where we tried to change the Ethics Code.
>
> There were many barriers. I feel like the APA was very skilled at looking reasonable and handling things in a positive way . . . and always allowing us to speak, which in a lot of ways was good and positive. But the system was set up to slow down when it wanted to, and dissidents in psychology were sharply criticized by other psychologists, simply for asking the organization to look at the evidence more closely.

The community activist Saul Alinsky says to find out an organization's rules and use them against the organization. We've learned to do so with APA. The referendum would be one example of that. If APA council wasn't going to change its policies, we'll get the membership to change the policy. As a result of the referendum we were better able to succeed in changing the Ethics Code Standard 1.02, which essentially had allowed a psychologist to follow the law, governing authority, or regulations rather than the Ethics Code, in cases of conflict. We felt this completely negated the Ethics Code. We were able to change that and toughen that stance. Pretty much each year since 2005 there's been some major policy change.

I think ultimately what brought success was the idea that you just could never do it alone, but having really good thinkers and friends in different cities and [communicating] over email was really what has kept things going.

Over the years, APA policies and policy positions on various controversial issues have changed due to the passionate advocacy of psychologists, sometimes working from within, and sometimes applying pressure from without. The current interrogations example is illustrative in several regards. On the one hand, it starkly illustrates the capacity of membership organizations to lose their way when guild interests take precedence over human rights concerns. On the other hand, the advocacy initiative mounted by Olson and colleagues reveals the countervailing influence that can be brought to bear by a small number of passionate individuals armed with strongly held values, resilience, a long-term time perspective, and an array of influence methods.

Summary

These three examples represent only a few of the ways that university faculty interviewed have contributed to and influenced the policy work of APA (as well as that of the many other professional membership associations to which they belong). These examples span multiple content areas (e.g., education, foreign affairs, socioeconomic status). Through developing connections with policymakers, adapting to fast-paced environments, and using advocacy methods and strategies, the psychologists were able to influence policy through supporting APA's ongoing policy work and challenging APA's policy positions.

Next, we switch focus to a very different type of intermediary organization within which psychologists exert influence, the National Academies.

Table 4.3 **National Academies: Intermediary Organization, Psychologist, Policy Issue, Government Branch/Level and Policy Influence Method**

Intermediary Organization (Psychologist)	Policy Issue	Government Branch/Level	Policy Influence Method (Documents)
National Research Council/Institute of Medicine (Phillips)*	Early Childhood	Multiple/ Multiple	National Research Council Report
Institute of Medicine (Smedley)*	Health Disparities	Multiple/ Multiple	Institute of Medicine Report

* Covered in this chapter.

Psychologists Working as Study Directors in the National Academies

The National Academies include the National Academy of Sciences, the National Academy of Engineering, the Institute of Medicine, and the National Research Council. As described in Chapter 2 (p. 41), numerous National Academies reports are produced each year by diverse committees of experts in a given area, directed by a full–time study director. Among the psychologists interviewed, two were employed as study directors by the National Academies, and each identified a National Academies report as his or her greatest policy success. These two examples are presented here (see Table 4.3).

National Research Council/Institute of Medicine: *Neurons to Neighborhoods* Report

Deborah Phillips

PhD, Developmental Psychology, Yale University, 1981

Professor of Psychology, Georgetown University

Deborah Phillips, a developmental psychologist, was full-time Director of the Board on Children, Youth, and Families at the National Research Council/Institute of Medicine (NRC/IOM) from 1993 to 1998, and then full-time Study Director of the NRC/IOM Committee on Integrating the Science of Early Child Development from 1998 to 2000. In the latter role,

Phillips directed the influential National Academies report, *Neurons to Neighborhoods: The Science of Early Childhood Development* (Shonkoff & Phillips, 2000). This report contributed to the emergence of early childhood as a high priority in the national policy agenda (Institute of Medicine and National Research Council, 2012). In the interview excerpt here, Phillips describes some of the factors that contributed to the successful development and impact of *Neurons to Neighborhoods*:

The fact that it [*Neurons to Neighborhoods*] came out of the National Academy of Sciences [NAS] is critical. It [NAS] really is viewed as the most credible voice for the field of science given all of the procedures, processes, and reviews that every single document that comes out of that place has to go through. It is highly credible. It's a whole group of scientists who have been carefully selected to be diverse both in a disciplinary sense but even in a policy sense. I had this dream team, and it's not that there weren't disagreements within the committee that had to get worked out, but they did [get worked out]. Everybody respected each other so much and everybody wanted this to come out so well.

It [*Neurons to Neighborhoods*] hit the world of policy and practice at a critical moment. We did the report in part because of what was going on out there in the world but it also hit the world at a time when the world was ready to begin thinking about work on early childhood development. I think the reason for the impact of the report is that it really spans the spectrum from pretty highly applied research that's directly policy-relevant to basic neuroscience. We talked about gene environment interaction and we talked about brain development, but we also talked about economics and child care regulation, and made policy recommendations. It really did cover the whole spectrum.

And the fact that the neuron's piece is there makes policymakers and decision-makers feel like they are neurosurgeons. It's like they think, "If I do this, I'm going to affect brains," and they just loved it. It is also so apolitical. There's nothing more apolitical than brain wiring.

I really came to appreciate the importance of communication, every element of communicating science. We really did try to write the report in a way that was highly accessible. Strong English skills and an ability to write very clearly came in handy. And it's the systematic work that the National Scientific Council on the Developing Child did with communication in the aftermath of *Neurons to Neighborhoods*, learning how to talk about the report so that the people who you were talking to could really hear what we were saying. I also have to totally credit Jack [Shonkoff] and the group of people who have worked with him. Their persistence, reliability, working through thick or thin and ups and downs to continue to give that report legs and updating it and so on. That again is a really critical piece.

Phillips employed many personal assets in her role as study director, including her extensive research experience and knowledge of the literature, leadership and management skills, experience in the policy arena, and communication skills. A convergence of many factors contributed to the report's influence. These included the credibility of the National Academies, the breadth and nature of the content, a timely policy window, and the concerted efforts to disseminate and update it over the years.

Next, we move to another National Academies report, this one in a more controversial area.

Institute of Medicine: *Unequal Treatment* Report

Brian Smedley

PhD, Clinical Psychology, University of California, Los Angeles, 1992

Executive Director of the National Collaborative for Health Equity, Washington, DC

From 1997 to 2006, psychologist Brian Smedley served as Senior Program Officer in the Division of Health Sciences Policy of the Institute of Medicine (IOM). In 1999, during Smedley's tenure at IOM, Congress requested that IOM conduct a study to:

- Assess the extent of racial and ethnic differences in healthcare that are not otherwise attributable to known factors such as access to care (e.g., insurance coverage)
- Evaluate potential sources of racial and ethnic disparities in healthcare, including the role of bias, discrimination, and stereotyping at the individual (provider and patient), institutional, and health system levels
- Recommend interventions to eliminate healthcare disparities

Smedley directed the requested study, released in March of 2002, titled *Unequal Treatment: Confronting Racial and Ethnic Disparities in Health Care* (Smedley, Stith, & Nelson, 2003). The report found that racial and ethnic minorities received, on average, a lower quality of healthcare even when differences in factors related to healthcare access were controlled. Furthermore, the report suggested that bias, prejudice, and stereotyping on the part of healthcare providers contributed to the unequal treatment.

Here, Smedley discusses the creation of the *Unequal Treatment* report, as well as related controversies and its (delayed) impact:

> All five of the reports that I worked on [at IOM] had some level of impact in the policy community around minority health and health disparities. The one that received the most notoriety was the report entitled "Unequal Treatment," which was a report that reviewed the evidence regarding racial and ethnic disparities in the quality of healthcare. We put together this 15-member study committee to look at this question. We knew this report would be controversial because any issues involving race and racial inequality typically are.
>
> The finding of the committee that stereotypes and implicit biases may contribute to racial and ethnic healthcare disparities was shocking to many people. There were a number of recommendations on how health systems can operate, including better data collection and monitoring of access equality by patient ethnicity. The report itself got significant news media attention. What was interesting and frustrating to me was that there was no policy action to deal with this for many years. At the time that the report came out in 2002, the Department of Health and Human Services attempted to dismiss the report's findings. For example, in 2003, when the agency for Healthcare Research and Quality released its first National Healthcare Disparities Report, which was mandated by Congress, it attempted to essentially dismiss some of the key findings of the report. There has been a lot more research in this area since 2002 when that report was released.
>
> For many years after that report, there was no policy action. It was striking to me that it was very difficult for Congress, HHS, or other agencies to respond. Finally, in 2010, when the ACA passed, many of the provisions in the law directly attempted to address some of the recommendations in the "Unequal Treatment" Report.
>
> I'm not suggesting that it was that report that shaped those provisions in the law. It was many things coming together. The report certainly helped to raise awareness of the issue and was referenced in the law, which was gratifying to see. Now we certainly still have a long way to go, but I'm impressed that the ACA does include a number of provisions that specifically attempt to get at this question of racial and ethnic healthcare disparities and set the goal of eliminating them. That's something I'm enormously proud of.

This example highlights the reality that it is extremely difficult for research evidence to influence policy when strong ideologies and interests are present. In this case, these barriers likely included ideologies that ruled out physician racism (or prejudice) as a possible cause of disparities and powerful interests that feared that holding health systems culpable would reduce citizen trust and lead to more government regulation. This example also underscores the long-term time perspective necessary in policy work.

Summary

It is difficult to attribute policy influence to a single policy actor or action, such as the release of a policy report. Nonetheless, despite the multitude of influences on policy, seminal reports do, on occasion, have a distinctive influence, perhaps especially when they emerge from well-regarded sources such as the National Academies.

Next, we turn to another set of contributions from psychologists, in this case from those working for intermediary organizations that engage in policy-relevant research, evaluation, and consultation.

Psychologists Working in Research, Evaluation, and Consultation Organizations

Organizations of varied types, both nonprofit and for-profit, conduct policy-relevant research, evaluation, and consultation, as described in Chapter 2 (pp. 41–42). Here, five case examples are presented of policy work done by psychologists employed in these organizations. The organizations vary greatly in size, the level of government that they engage, and their areas of focus (see Table 4.4).

Table 4.4 **Research, Evaluation, and Consulting Organizations: Policy Issue, Psychologist, Government Branch/Level, and Policy Influence Method**

Policy Issue (Psychologist)	Intermediary Organization	Government Branch/Level	Policy Influence Method
Teen Pregnancy (Moore)*	Child Trends	Executive/ Multiple	Policy Briefs Fact Sheets
Substance Use Prevention (Chavis)*	Community Science	Executive/ National	Evaluation Research Consultation

(continued)

Table 4.4 **Continued**

Policy Issue (Psychologist)	Intermediary Organization	Government Branch/Level	Policy Influence Method
Children's Mental Health (Meyers)*	Child Health & Development Institute	Legislative/State	Advisory Boards Consultation
Child-Serving Systems (Franks)*	Child Health & Development Institute	Executive/State	Advisory Boards Consultation
Healthcare Access (Wolff)*	Community Partners	Executive/State	Building Coalitions Technical assistance

* Covered in this chapter.

We begin with Kristin Moore's work at Child Trends.

Child Trends: Teenage Pregnancy

Kristin Moore

PhD, Sociology with a focus in Social Psychology,
University of Michigan, 1975

Senior Scholar and Co-Director of Youth Development, Child Trends,
Bethesda, Maryland

Kristin Moore, a social psychologist, directed Child Trends from 1982 to 2006 and then returned to full-time research at the organization. Child Trends describes itself as a "nonprofit, nonpartisan research center that provides valuable information and insights on the well-being of children and youth" (Child Trends, 2015). It employs more than 100 staff, including more than 30 with doctorates in psychology, public health, sociology, and related fields. Child Trends is located in the Washington, DC, area. It is a well-known and highly regarded source of information for numerous indicators of child health and well-being (e.g., child obesity, teenage pregnancy) reported at city, state, and federal levels.

Over the years, Moore has developed ongoing relationships with numerous federal agencies to whom she provides research consultation. This consultation work includes contributions of constructs and measures to numerous federal surveys, such as the National Survey of Children, the National Survey of Children's Health, and the National Longitudinal Survey of Youth. Moore was a founding member of the Task Force on Effective Programs and Research at the National Campaign to Prevent Teen and Unplanned Pregnancy. She is also a board member of the Family Impact Seminars (pp. 70–72) and served on the National Institute of Child Health and Human Development Advisory Council.

Moore considers the decades-long contribution of fact sheets in the area of teenage births as her greatest policy success (e.g., Child Trends, 2011). Here, she describes Child Trends' overall approach to informing social policy, discusses the teen birth rates fact sheets, and concludes with a perspective on the role of research in today's highly polarized political environment:

> Child Trends tries to inform social policy in a nonpartisan manner. The kinds of things that inform public policy are pretty broad-ranging. We worked on indicators, such as the Federal Interagency report on child and family well-being indicators—making sure that policymakers understand what some of the important and rigorous indicators might be. I've worked on a lot of surveys like the Early Childhood Survey that the Department of Education did. We also summarize, synthesize, and translate work that many academics do. We've done an awful lot of that and currently we are doing evaluation studies.
>
> We now have over 100 people in three offices, including a really good Communications team. We have a website, and we do research briefs and news blasts. We have Twitter, Facebook, and all of the usual things, but with the policy audience that is not sufficient. You really need to have relationships; the staff of elected officials are very important. Also, advocacy groups regularly cite us and our work, for example, The National Campaign to Prevent Teen and Unplanned Pregnancy. We also work closely with foundations, as they initiate a lot of innovative programs and practices.
>
> Before the data were online [Internet], I did a fact sheet called "Facts at a Glance" for 25 years, on teen birthrates, which we sent to people at the state and local level year after year. The fact sheet was really short and readable. It had state-specific information and data on the cities, so that policymakers could see how their city was doing. We shared findings from research that was pertinent and information on teen birthrates in other countries. We tried to address stereotypes that people have misinformation about. I think the fact sheet helped keep this issue in focus.
>
> We have certain continuous themes, for example, the notion of the whole child—to help the federal government in particular to see children and youth as whole people and to better understand the variety of contextual factors that matter. That we try as hard as we humanly can to be objective has helped. I think that research, in this highly polarized political environment, more than anything else, has the potential to create middle ground.

This example demonstrates how intermediary organizations can contribute to the policy narrative around children and youth—the conceptual use of research—by providing policy-relevant consultation and evidence. By establishing multiple pathways to access data (reports, fact sheets, and briefs, as well as social media), Moore was able to provide context-specific data to federal agencies, advocacy groups, foundations, and academic researchers. Child Trends' explicit focus on government activities related to child and youth naturally benefits from the knowledge base and research training of developmental psychologists, along with researchers from other disciplines.

Community Science, to which we turn next, is a much smaller research, evaluation, and consultation organization with an explicit community systems focus. Like Child Trends, it naturally benefits from the contributions of psychologists with a certain knowledge base and related research skills—in this case, community psychologists.

Community Science: Evaluations of Government-Funded Programs Focused on Social Problems

David Chavis

PhD, Community Psychology, Vanderbilt University, 1983

Principal Associate and Director of Community Science, Gaithersburg, Maryland

David Chavis, a community psychologist, directs Community Science, which describes itself as a "research and development organization that works with governments, foundations, and nonprofit organizations on solutions to social problems" (communityscience.com). It employs 16 staff, including seven doctoral-level researchers, five of whom are psychologists. Areas of focus include community and systems change, diversity, health promotion and equity, substance abuse, crime prevention, education, and youth development. Community Science is located in the Washington, DC, metropolitan area.

Chavis has directed a number of Community Science's national evaluations of government-funded programs. Completed projects include evaluation of the Drug-Free Communities Support Program (Office of National Drug Control Policy; Battelle Memorial Institute & ASDC, 2006), Safe Start Demonstration Project (Office of Juvenile Justice and Delinquency Prevention; Association for the Study and Development of Community [ASDC], 2005), and Embedding Prevention in State Government Evaluation (National Crime Prevention Council; ASDC, 2003). Current Community Science government-funded projects include evaluation of the use of volunteers in disaster preparation, response, and recovery (Corporation for National and Community Service) and evaluation of a national technical assistance and training center focused on the prevention and treatment of violence (Substance Abuse and Mental Health Services Administration). Chavis brings a community systems and social environment-change (i.e., ecological) perspective to his work, believing that individually focused policies cannot bring about population-level changes in areas such as substance abuse prevention. Here, he discusses two mechanisms through which program evaluations can influence policymakers, using his evaluations of the Drug-Free Communities Support Program and the Safe Start Demonstration Project as examples. The Drug-Free Communities work included an important partnership with the advocacy group, Community Anti-Drug Coalitions of America (CADCA; http://www.cadca.org).

Policy impact occurs through the evaluation and data collection process as well as through the final reports. The process part involves having to say, "If you're not doing these things, I can't give you those kinds of results." For example, concerning the evaluation of the Drug-Free Communities program for the White House Office of National Drug Control Policy (ONDCP), it was realizing that "If you're going to have a net effect on the population level, if that's your goal, then use a change strategy that reaches the population as a whole." It was making a case for more focus on the environmental factors that contribute to substance abuse. I worked on the inside, providing the facts and the situation to the ONDCP. I think it was appealing to their political self-interests. John Walters was the drug czar at the time.

The training and technical assistance organization for grantees, CADCA, worked from the outside to advocate for improvements in the program. We had a series of meetings with CADCA to figure out how we could both build a case from the inside and provide pressure from the outside. I'd provide them with the information they would need for their technical assistance and training services, information which CADCA could also use as advocates in terms of speaking to the congressional sponsors. CADCA had 5,000 members and a really strong lobbying effort. They were able to mobilize their constituency to put pressure to preserve government funding, which was in doubt. They wisely leveraged the fact that the fear of losing funding was the opportunity to advance the field and have greater impact. They could have just taken on protecting the funding and left everything as it was, but instead they used that as a way to up the bar. The agency changed the RFP [Request for Proposal], collecting more data and providing more training in these environmental prevention areas. We got them all aligned, not perfectly, but better.

Evaluation reports themselves also can have some effect on continuing programs . . . [by promoting program] refinement. For example, there was an evaluation we did called the Safe Start demonstration project, to see if you could get a system of care that would be able to reduce the impact of exposure to violence on children under three. Can you integrate evidence-based programming into adoption in a wide range of communities in different kinds of systems? The results of that showed where future programming could be improved. Because we structured reflective learning sessions where we could process findings and the lessons learned, they did make some significant improvements based on that. I'd say that's the minority of the cases. I don't think most of the evaluations are really read and acted on. It really depends on the integrity of the agency itself.

Chavis' policy work draws on community research and evaluation skills, extensive experience in systems change and capacity building, and the willingness to work assertively both within and outside the system. A number of the psychologists interviewed for this book similarly emphasized the importance of coordinated, sustained influence from both inside and outside government for policy change.

In the next example, we move from the federal level of government to the state level. In this example, two individuals from the same intermediary organization were interviewed to provide multiple perspectives.

The Child Health and Development Institute of Connecticut: Child-Serving Systems Reform

Judith Meyers

PhD, Clinical and Community Psychology, University of Colorado, Boulder, 1976

President and CEO, Children's Fund of Connecticut and Child Health and Development Institute of Connecticut

Robert Franks

PhD, Counseling Psychology, Boston College, 2000

President and CEO, Judge Baker Children's Center, Boston

Judith Meyers, a clinical and community psychologist, directs the Child Health and Development Institute (CHDI) in Connecticut, a nonprofit organization that has partnered with multiple state child-serving systems to bring about reform (http://www.chdi.org). CHDI is the operational arm of the Children's Fund of Connecticut, a foundation that Meyers simultaneously directs. In her 16 years at CHDI, Meyers has served on many policy advisory groups in Connecticut, including the Governor's Blue Ribbon Commission on Mental Health, the Lieutenant Governor's Mental Health Cabinet, the Behavioral Health Partnership Oversight Council, and the Early Childhood Cabinet. Building on these and other advisory roles, she has played an important role in the reform of the state's mental health system (Connecticut Mental Health Report, 2004; Connecticut Department of Children and Families and Department of Social Services, 2001).

Robert Franks, a child psychologist, worked closely with Meyers during his tenure as the vice president of CHDI and director of its Connecticut Center for Effective Practice (CCEP). (Franks left CHDI in July, 2014.) Created in 2001, CCEP seeks to improve and reform Connecticut's mental health and juvenile justice systems. Working in an intermediary organization that seeks to influence state policies, Meyers and Franks see their work directly affecting local Connecticut communities.

Here, Meyers begins by describing the creation of CHDI and her position and work within the organization:

> I have two jobs here and that's part of the uniqueness. I run a foundation called The Children's Fund of Connecticut but was hired originally to run the Child Health and Development Institute, which the Fund created to do its work. I also direct this institute, which is an independent not-for-profit that was created to work in partnership with academia. When I first came here in 1999 to run this institute, the institute staff included me and a half-time administrator. I now have a staff of 27. . . . The notion is that we have two medical schools and children's hospitals in Connecticut. How do we bring their resources to bear to improve health outcomes for kids in our state? My board has people from University of Connecticut and from Yale on it. It's really about how do we bring information, best practice, research, and evidence to policymakers.
>
> One of the first things I had an opportunity to do was a study of the financing of the children's mental health system. We were able to use that study to help recommend how we were going to move from a system that was bleeding money spent on hospitalizations to one focused on community-based interventions. In the last dozen or so years, the state has moved toward that. We've played a major role in building investment in community-based services and more recently investing in early childhood.

Next, Franks provides an overview of CHDI as an intermediary organization and the types of activities it engages in:

> At the core, an intermediary organization is an entity that bridges science and research with policy and practice. We engage in a variety of activities; all can be understood through the lens of creating change at the policy, systems, and practice levels. A key area of work as an intermediary is consultation, where we work with provider organizations, state agencies, or academic institutions, providing technical assistance and consultation. The next area is around best practice model development, with the intent of broader dissemination and systems change. We also sometimes act as a purveyor of established evidence-based practices like Multi-Systemic Therapy (MST) or Trauma-focused Cognitive Behavioral Therapy (TF-CBT). Further, we engage in quality assurance and improvement activities to support the quality and fidelity of model programs. We also conduct outcome evaluation research to measure the impact of programs and services. And to raise awareness about children's mental health, we engage in public awareness and education activities. In order to support and sustain the changes we are working towards, we also focus on policy and systems development and policy change at multiple levels within our state.
>
> At the policy level, the bulk of our work is conducted through our relationships with the Connecticut Department of Children and Families, the Department of Social Services, and the Department of Mental Health and Addiction Services. We also provide legislators, at their request, with information and recommendations that are based on science and best practice.
>
> Our current areas of focus include: building an early childhood system of care, developing a statewide trauma-informed system of care, and extensive work in school-based mental health. Our strategy has always been to partner with systems and provide the necessary consultation and support that's required for systems change.

CHDI serves as an intermediary among the worlds of science, policy, and practice. Franks demonstrates how important it is to meet the needs both of communities and policymakers through consultation and technical assistance (e.g., training in use of evidence-based models, evaluation). He also shows how to shape the public discourse through public education and awareness work. Franks and Meyers contend that equally important to what psychologists do in the policy arena is how they do it. Meyers concludes with the key factors that have contributed to the policy influence of CHDI:

> It's all about relationships. I'm in a small state, so we can work very closely with state government. You really have to be a trusted advisor.

There are underlying values guiding what we do, but our work is based on theory, research, and evaluation findings. That's an important part of our reputation, what we do, the people that work here, and how we're valued. I think that gets us to the table. My staff and I are involved in 30 different work groups, commissions, and task forces. It's really getting yourself to the tables where decisions can be influenced.

Meyers and Franks demonstrate the benefits of building trusting, long-term relationships with executive agencies at the state level. Meyers recalls the beginning of these relationships; upon her arrival in Connecticut, she was introduced by her predecessor to the director of the state budget office. He was impressed by her appreciation of the importance of financing and asked if she would be willing to conduct a mandated financing study of the children's mental health system. Meyers said she would try, generated a team of colleagues to help her—and three months later produced a very influential report that set the stage for her decades-long involvement in reform. By taking advantage of opportunity, and employing diverse skill sets, Meyers and Franks demonstrate how psychologists in intermediary organizations can exert a sustained policy influence.

The final example involves an intermediary organization that differs in substantial ways from the previous ones included in this section. Its primary goal is to establish relationships—among communities, practitioners, and policymakers.

Community Partners: Children's Health Improvement Program in Massachusetts

Thomas Wolff

PhD, Clinical Psychology, University of Rochester, 1968

Director of Tom Wolff and Associates, Amherst, Massachusetts

Thomas Wolff, a clinical community psychologist, founded and directed Community Partners, a nonprofit organization devoted to collaborative solutions to social problems. Community Partners created grassroots, community-based coalitions in multiple regions of Massachusetts and maintained consulting relationships with them over many years. One important part of coalition activities was advocacy (Wolff, 2010, 2013). Wolff describes his greatest policy success as the work of Community Partners, from 1998 to

2002, in facilitating enrollment in the Massachusetts universal insurance coverage program, Massachusetts Child Health Improvement Program (CHIP).

To help implement the new policy, Community Partners served as an intermediary, building on its ongoing work with multiple regional coalitions to connect health outreach workers, a major statewide health advocacy organization, and state health agency administrators. Key activities were the facilitation of regular meetings throughout the state called Health Access Networks—bringing these three groups and other stakeholders together in productive problem-solving sessions—and the organization of individual meetings with state health agency administrators.

Wolff begins by describing the policy-focused activities of the coalitions and securing a line item in the state budget to sustain their activities:

> When we created community coalitions in regions of the state, one of the goals was to influence policy that affected each region. We were often advocating on state policy around housing, homelessness, sex education in schools, or welfare legislation. In the parts of the state where we worked, the legislators adored us because we went into the community, identified the issues, and then told all of the people who were fighting, like the state and local agencies, to stop screwing around, come together, and develop a plan. The legislature went so far as putting $200,000 as a line item in the state budget to give $50,000 to each of the coalitions and $50,000 to my office to keep this coalition-building work going.

Wolff's success in coalition building stems from his ability to bring together diverse local stakeholders so they could singularly—as a coalition—generate a plan of action and related funding requests that their local state legislator could then sponsor. Wolff next describes his work with CHIP:

> We had dealt with the problem of health access frequently in every community coalition. It was a huge problem. We had a very good statewide health advocacy group, Health Care for All, and we worked closely with them. The state passed legislation in 1997 that provided health insurance coverage for all children, the Children's Health Improvement Program, or CHIP [that later became the national program SCHIP, State Children's Health Improvement Program]. When this bill became state law, MassHealth, which is the Medicaid agency, had to figure out how to do outreach, get people enrolled, and make their offices responsive.
>
> We received funding to focus on state-wide enrollment. For 10 months a year in six regions of the state, we had meetings, each with 30 or 40 people. We brought together MassHealth, Health Care for All, and all of the various outreach workers. Slowly but surely, all of the hospitals and health

centers were sending their representatives. MassHealth started to work very closely with the outreach workers, as opposed to it being an adversarial relationship as before.

Each month, Health Care for All would come and present what the advocacy issue was for this month. Following the meeting, our staff would go to a meeting with very high-level people from the state and pass on the feedback, and Health Care for All would take it on and advocate. As a result, rules and regulations were changed. We affected a lot that happened over those years. This was set up totally on advocacy, policy change, and enrollment plans. It was a terrific innovation, and Massachusetts became number two in the country in enrolling children.

Community Partners' successful policy influence stems from its capacity to develop coalitions, to enhance collaboration among various stakeholder groups, and to work with diverse partners. During his career as a community practitioner, Wolff has influenced policy both as an inside consultant and as an external change agent. He personally prefers the latter—seeking to influence policy by employing outside pressure and external advocacy and working to help increase the effectiveness of community-based groups to engage in activism.

Summary

Taken together, these diverse case examples portray a variety of means of policy influence used by psychologists who work in research, evaluation, and consultation organizations. To influence policy, psychologists who work in these organizations need to develop viable working relationships with influential individuals or groups, connect various stakeholders, and contribute research and/or practice expertise. As in other policy contexts, psychologists must bring to bear relationship-building, communication, and strategic analysis skills and commit to long-term engagement in policy areas of focus.

Next, we turn to psychologists who work in a fourth type of intermediary organization: foundations.

Psychologists Who Work in Foundations

Recent volumes have provided diverse examples of foundations that engage in policy-focused activities, describing the benefits and challenges involved (e.g., Arons, 2007; Coffman, 2008). Chapter 2 of this book also describes the unique context of foundations (p. 42). Three case examples of psychologists

Table 4.5 **Foundations: Policy Issue, Psychologist, Intermediary Organization, Government Branch/Level, and Policy Influence Method**

Policy Issue (Psychologist)	Intermediary Organization	Government Branch/Level	Policy Influence Method
Juvenile Justice (Garduque)*	MacArthur Foundation	Multiple/ National	Funding of Research Network
Early Childhood (Petersen)*	Kellogg Foundation	Legislative/ Multiple	Funding of Community-Based Advocacy
Science Policy (Seidman)*	WT Grant Foundation	Executive/ Multiple	Funding of Research; "Matchmaking;" Consultation

* Covered in this chapter.

working for foundations committed to policy influence are presented here, spanning the justice system, early childhood education, and school policy reforms (see Table 4.5).

We begin with Laurie Garduque's work at the MacArthur Foundation.

John and Catherine MacArthur Foundation: Juvenile Justice System Reform

Laurie Garduque

PhD, Educational Psychology, University of California, Los Angeles, 1980

Director of Justice Reform, MacArthur Foundation, Chicago, Illinois

Laurie Garduque, an educational psychologist, has directed major initiatives to reform juvenile justice systems at the John D. and Catherine T. MacArthur Foundation over the past two decades. One major initiative was the Network on Adolescent Development and Juvenile Justice, which, as described in Chapter 3 (pp. 93–95), brought together academic researchers, individuals involved in policy work, and legal practitioners. The primary goal was to generate research and policy change concerning the treatment of adolescents in the justice system. The resulting research was cited in a number of Supreme Court decisions, including *Roper v. Simpson* (2005), which outlawed the death penalty for adolescents, and *Miller v. Alabama* (2012), which banned mandatory sentences of life without parole for juveniles, regardless of the crime.

In 2010, MacArthur, joined by four other major foundations, developed a national initiative to reform juvenile justice systems in states around the country (Peace, 2013). This multiyear effort focuses on diverting youth from the juvenile justice system, including increased use of alternatives to juvenile incarceration. Over the past four years, the campaign has supported policy advocates, strategists, communications professionals, and campaign coordinators in 37 states, achieving success in 31 states to date. Here, Garduque highlights various changes that have occurred in juvenile justice systems in recent years and the contributions the MacArthur Foundation has made to these changes:

> It is in juvenile justice that I feel we've had the most impact. You have seen dramatic changes over the last 15 years in how we think about young people in conflict with the law. The research that MacArthur supported was used in four major Supreme Court decisions.
>
> A couple of years prior to 1996, we did a very systematic survey of the public policy issues of the day related to children, adolescents, and families and what knowledge would be useful in improving public policy. After we looked across all the different areas, it was clear that juvenile justice was suffering from a lack of knowledge and information about adolescents that could be useful in improving policy and practice. In fact, the reforms were going in the opposite direction. They were moving in the direction of treating kids as if they were adults. The problem was that the research in adolescent development didn't map well onto the issues that the legal system needs to contend with. That's when we decided to create the Research Network on Adolescent Development and Juvenile Justice. Larry Steinberg [pp. 93–95] and I worked together in putting together the network.
>
> The synergy among the researchers, policymakers, and practitioners involved has helped raise the visibility of the issues. That has created a body of knowledge, information, and networks of people who then can point to examples of systems reform and policy and practice innovations. The researchers now have relationships with policymakers and practitioners, and vice versa. When it came time to do the amicus briefs in the Supreme Court, MacArthur didn't have to fund that directly. Because of the networks we cultivated over the years, they were in a position to work together to advance this work.
>
> Then we decided to translate it more systematically by working in states to help move them toward what we would consider a model juvenile justice system based on certain principles and values about fairness, effectiveness, and treating kids as kids. Now we're also complementing that with working more directly in the political and legislative process

through a grant we made to the Public Interest Projects to change the juvenile justice systems in different states, through [changing] law and policy.

Garduque views the MacArthur Foundation as unique among foundations in its efforts to bring together researchers, practitioners, and policy individuals over extended periods of time to influence policy. The policy skills she utilizes in this work include strategic analysis, relationship-building, and networking. Garduque emphasizes that her role is not to undertake any of the research or policy work herself, but rather to help conceptualize the multiyear initiatives and then to fund carefully selected teams to do the work. Of note, Garduque's influential work in juvenile justice reform resulted in President Obama appointing her to the Federal Coordinating Council on Juvenile Justice and Delinquency Prevention.

The next case example depicts foundation funding of community-based advocacy. Unlike the previous example, this represents policy influence activity from the bottom up, working directly with citizens and community-based organizations.

W. K. Kellogg Foundation: Early Childhood Education in New Mexico

Anne Petersen

PhD, Measurement, Evaluation, and Statistical Analysis,
University of Chicago, 1973

Research Professor, Center for Human Growth and Development,
University of Michigan

Anne Petersen, an adolescent development researcher, served as Deputy Director and Chief Operating Officer of the National Science Foundation before joining the W. K. Kellogg Foundation. At Kellogg, Petersen was Senior Vice President for Programs from 1996 to 2005. During this time, Kellogg initiated a major program to enhance the capacity of citizens to engage in advocacy in the areas of health, agriculture, and education. As noted in the Kellogg annual reports during that period, an important area of program focus was "increasing community voices in the policy development process" (e.g., W. K. Kellogg Foundation, 2001, p. 32).

However, foundation staff may be wary of funding policy advocacy because they are unsure of the legal status of such support. As a result, guidelines were developed so that foundation staff, as well as grantees, were aware of the difference between advocacy-focused activities that were legally permissible when using foundation funds and those that were not (W. K. Kellogg Foundation, 2002). Petersen explains:

> We built a strong policy component at the Kellogg Foundation while I was there, especially in the health, agriculture, and education areas. Major initiatives supported by Kellogg involved significant amounts of money—tens of millions of dollars—so it was important for the CEO and I to make a strong case to the Board about the evidence base. The Kellogg policy expert [Pat Babcock] had worked in state government with two different governors, one from each party. He had a good sense of how states worked. We educated the program staff about the potential of this policy work as a major approach to achieve sustainability. It was important for staff to know what was permitted legally and what was not, and to help them get past the "We can't do that" perspective. The core of this advocacy approach was people-based, on-the-ground advocates, including parents, businesspeople, and educators—not lobbyists. It was a sophisticated and effective approach.

When asked to discuss one successful advocacy project, Petersen cited Kellogg's support of advocacy for early childhood education policy in New Mexico. More than $5 million was provided by the foundation to support advocacy efforts, with special focus on grassroots advocacy by community groups and citizens. The funding was channeled through two organizations: the New Mexico Community Foundation (see nmcf.org) and New Mexico Voices for Children (see nmvoices.org; Kellogg annual reports, 2000–2006). Of note, the Governor, Lieutenant Governor, and state legislature thereafter developed New Mexico's state-funded pre-kindergarten initiative, New Mexico PreK, in 2005, which has shown positive outcomes in literacy, language, and mathematics (Hustedt, Barnett, Jung, & Goetze, 2010). Petersen describes the early childhood education advocacy in New Mexico:

> One big focus was the education area, especially early childhood. New Mexico was one of the states we focused on because of their diverse population, including people who were Caucasian, Hispanic or more typically Chicano, and Native American from several tribes. The funded community groups represented the ethnicities of the state. In addition, we provided support to local intermediaries and local consultants who would help with the

policy work. We also had grantees at the state level including state executive position holders and people from companies like Intel and the aerospace industry. We were really careful in the funding design to assure that all groups had the necessary funds to accomplish the goals. At the same time, we at Kellogg had to be careful to only operate in a funding capacity and never as advocates ourselves. The advocacy work was engaged by grantees.

The community groups typically wanted consultants who could help them with messaging. They had incredibly effective videos. Often they would just use the kids as their own spokesperson, but parents were very involved, too. It was the most effective advocacy effort I've ever seen in part because the material was so genuine and compelling. We did have data, too—but their compelling stories were key to obtaining state support for early childhood education.

In contrast to the Garduque example, which centered on an evidence-based pathway of influence, Petersen describes a community-based pathway of influence in which community groups were funded to engage citizens in an advocacy campaign. Petersen's ability to leverage foundation resources, train and educate foundation staff, and benefit from close collaboration with a staff member who had extensive experience and expertise in state policy were central to the initiative. Due to her management and administrative skills, Petersen helped the Kellogg Foundation provide grantees with the opportunity to directly—and effectively—advocate for important policy goals.

The final case example centers on the William T. Grant Foundation's (WTGF) funding of policy-relevant research, national research policy, and networking in the areas of education and after-school programs.

William T. Grant Foundation: Improving the Lives of Children and Youth

Edward Seidman

PhD, Clinical Psychology and Medical Behavioral Science,
University of Kentucky, 1969

Professor of Psychology, New York University

Edward Seidman, a community psychologist, served as senior vice president at WTGF from 2004 to 2012. WTGF has a long history of supporting policy-related work ranging from early and continued funding of the Society for Research in

Child Development (SRCD) policy fellowships (SRCD, 2012) to recent funding of the Coalition for Evidence-Based Policy, which conducts advocacy for increased use of evidence as a guide to federal social policy (coalition4evidence.org). W. T. Grant's current mission is to fund research that increases understanding of the programs, policies, and practices that reduce inequality in youth outcomes and how policymakers and practitioners acquire, interpret, and use research evidence (see http://wtgrantfoundation.org/WhoWeAre).

During his years at WTGF, Seidman spearheaded initiatives on setting-level interventions, measurement of settings, and national research policy. He also contributed to the foundation's networking activities, reaching out to connect researchers, policymakers, and practitioners, and supported the foundation's after-school programming initiative, which included an advocacy component. Here, Seidman describes the mission guiding his work at WTGF and several of the foundation's major initiatives:

> The mission was to contribute to better, more salient research, for both practice and policy, by changing the research we funded and by influencing other funders, both federal agencies and foundations. One prime example of the latter was a meeting we stimulated at the US Department of Education's Institute of Education Sciences (IES). IES had previously funded a character development initiative where the requirement was that investigators randomly assign only five Experimental and five Control schools, not recognizing that this would not provide adequate power to detect even main effects. We had a meeting with IES and Spencer Foundation staff to showcase experts Steve Raudenbush and Howard Bloom, who W. T. Grant had supported to develop accurate ways of calculating power in multi-level RCT [randomized control trial] designs. IES then changed their policies so that future studies would require investigators to demonstrate adequate power to detect effects.
>
> Two other important influences the W. T. Grant Foundation had on research occurred on projects, and the accompanying professional development activities, funded through our RFP [Request for Proposals] mechanism. In the first instance, we developed an RFP for social setting intervention research, and in the second, for the measurement of social processes in classrooms and other settings. Since we initiated this work, the concept of social settings has become a more frequent focus for practitioners and scientists to understand and change.
>
> In terms of measurement, enhancing the work of Robert Pianta, Bridget Hamre, and colleagues on the CLASS [Classroom Assessment Scoring System] as a way of teaching teachers how to teach has had a major influence [curry.virginia.edu/research/centers/castl/class]. Bridget Hamre is engaged in most national Head Start and other preschool evaluations,

introducing the CLASS to enhance ways of teaching. We brought Pianta into our network of fundees. We played a role of matchmaking him with some people, including the director of the Council of Great City Schools, who was a WTGF board member [http://www.cgcs.org].

As a secondary activity, Seidman participated in the foundation's after-school programming initiative, encompassing research, networking, capacity-building, dissemination, and advocacy. This initiative included funding for after-school advocacy groups such as the After School Alliance (see http://afterschoolalliance. org/index.cfm; Granger, 2011). Seidman continues:

In California, after Governor Schwarzenegger had a large budget allocation devoted to after-school programming, we brought our after-school grantees to the state. We influenced the interventions and evaluations being conducted by adding socioemotional criteria to the program evaluations that had been previously limited to an academic focus.

Seidman concludes with his perspective on the growing governmental focus on evidence-based policy and the foundation's contributions in that area:

There's a convergence—us helping to upgrade the structure of intervention in social science and the political push for evidence-based [policy]. There are more and more people in the government who are keen on that. We funded Jon Baron in the Coalition for Evidence-Based Policy. We've been one of his sole stable funders, not with big amounts of money, but consistent until recently. Our grantees would go and present in his convenings of federal policymakers. We do a lot of matchmaking because we know influential people in the worlds of policy, practice, and research.

Seidman used the extensive research experience and expertise he developed prior to his position at W. T. Grant to help establish new areas of focus for the foundation. Furthermore, he describes how foundations utilize a distinct form of relationship-building skills—"matchmaking"—to help researchers and policymakers to form mutually beneficial relationships. More broadly, as in the two previous examples, the foundation served both as a funder of policy-relevant work and as a consultant to both grantees and policymakers.

Summary

Psychologists in foundations are in a unique position to influence policy. Through leveraging their substantial resources, they are able to contribute to policy change in multiple ways. These include determining the individuals, organizations, and research projects they fund; the skills they help their grantees to gain; and the relationships they help their grantees to establish with policymakers. Through this work, psychologists in foundations have the potential to influence decision-makers in all three branches of government.

Influencing Policy from the Vantage Point of Intermediary Organizations: Benefits and Limitations

Psychologists are able to influence policy through work in a diverse array of inter-mediary organizations. The four types of intermediary organizations examined here represent an important, although not comprehensive, sampling of nongov-ernmental policy organizations. They differ greatly in their mission, size, policy influence activities, and representation of psychologists in administrative and staff positions. The methods psychologists employ vary across the organizations. These methods range from direct lobbying (APA staff) to preparation of policy-relevant research reports (National Academies study directors). They encompass advisory and consultation roles, coalition-building, dissemination of empirical findings (research, evaluation, and consultation organizations), and funding of policy-relevant research and evidence-based advocacy campaigns (foundations). Although each context calls for particular methods, across all intermediary or-ganizations, psychologists use their relationship-building, communication, re-search, and strategic skills, along with content expertise, to bridge the worlds of research, practice, and policy.

Psychologists do not have to wait until they are well into their careers to get their feet wet in policy advocacy work with intermediary organizations. Many national organizations, including APA, and local organizations offer internships for graduate students and postdoctoral fellowships so that trainees can develop and hone the skills needed for success in this arena.

The strategic location and role of intermediary organizations—connecting the worlds of academia, practice, and policy—provide both advantages and limitations for psychologists working to influence policy. On the one hand, this location provides unique opportunities to serve as a bridge between these worlds as research translator, educator, networker, and catalyst. On the other hand, gaining access to, establishing credibility with, and exerting effective influence on policymakers remain critical challenges for those working in in-termediary settings—no matter how well-established and well-situated the organization.

The specific advantages and limitations enumerated by psychologists working in intermediaries varies greatly across respondents. They depend in part on the type of intermediary and the particulars of a specific organization's mission, culture, funding source, size, structure, and location.

Primary benefits described by those working at APA are the strength of the membership base and the capacity to leverage considerable intellectual and institutional resources to pursue policy influence. Limitations include the "complicated" nature of APA with its multiple, and sometimes competing, constituencies. Diane Elmore explains:

> APA represents a large constituency. The organization is bigger than many others representing health professions. APA has significant resources, and 500-plus staff, including about 20 lobbyists representing the priorities of the four directorates. Some of the other mental health disciplines have only a handful of government relations staff. . . . Some of the challenges though are these. Representing a single discipline can, at times, be limiting. Also, working on public interest issues and on behalf of the needs of underserved populations doesn't always yield the attention it deserves. Another challenge is that sometimes being a big organization can actually work against you. People sometimes like the "mom and pop" perspective of a smaller organization over ours, but overall we have a lot to contribute and are valuable to the policymaking process.

Ellen Garrison also notes that the general perception of intermediary organizations as "biased" institutions with particular agendas may cause others—including academics, policymakers, and community members—to question the legitimacy of the work:

> The potential influence of APA may at times be limited due to the perception of the association by some policymakers as a liberal organization with a liberal bias. Our research might be viewed with some skepticism as a result. This can also tie into our own perceptions as psychologists. . . . For instance, I am aware of my inclination and that of some of my colleagues to initially question research results that run counter to our presumptions, beliefs, and values, such as the potential harmful effects of after-school programs for acting-out youth. . . . Looking back, I occasionally found myself reminding my Public Interest government relations staff that APA is not an advocacy organization dedicated to a cause, like the Children's Defense Fund or the Sierra Club, but rather a professional association that advocates for policies based on the findings of psychological research—not on beliefs or values.

For those working in the National Academies, the central benefits are the opportunity to work with the country's leading experts to address issues of national concern and generate reports for a national policy audience. Limitations include sources of resistance during internal review processes, especially related to findings and policy implications that are politically charged, such as those involving race and class. Brian Smedley observes:

> There was enormous skepticism in some quarters about the evidence base and whether race and ethnicity were relevant in the clinical encounter. Here's where we as a committee had to be careful to overdocument the problem to overcome skepticism and resistance, which is primarily ideological. It may reflect other concerns, but people don't want to believe that there's still persistent racial inequality in this country.

Psychologists working in research, evaluation, and consultation organizations emphasize the opportunity to focus attention on topics of direct relevance to policymakers without the constraints present in academia ("publish or perish"). On the other hand, limitations include the constant need to secure funding and the reality that the agendas of those providing grants and contracts limit the focus and type of policy work possible. Kristin Moore explains:

> I would say that the benefits are our reputation and the fact that there is a lot of [internal] support, both social support as well as logistical support. We have communications people on staff. . . . The challenges are our funding. It is hard to fund this kind of stuff. If you are on the left or on the right, it is much easier to get funding than if you're science—in the middle.

David Chavis concurs with Moore's perspective, detailing how this issue can be further complicated by the types of policy issues addressed by the intermediary organization:

> We're totally money-dependent. We do very little outside of what we're funded to do. We do have a research and development fund we are building up as kind of a buffer, but we're an organization that is dependent on the kindness of strangers . . . for support. We walk this very fine line that we trip on regularly, in terms of promoting social justice and science and still being acceptable to do work for risk-adverse federal agencies, as well as for foundations that are taking positions on controversial issues.

For Judith Meyers, the advantages of the intermediary role outweigh the limitations:

> It is [a] translational role that we play, and we play it pretty flexibly and easily. We're in a small enough state where people know us and we know them. We build those relationships with legislators and state commissioners and deputy commissioners pretty easily. I think we are pretty well positioned to do what it is we do without some of the institutional baggage that we would have if we were within a university or within government.

Finally, those working in foundations emphasize the opportunity to leverage foundation resources to address policy issues receiving insufficient focus. Limitations include the difficulty of achieving influence outside of a limited set of grantees and the reality that, once funding in a project area or a specific project ends, so may the desired impact, given limited institutionalization and sustainability of externally funded social change initiatives. Laurie Garduque comments on the challenge of sustainability:

> I am worried about how many of the organizations and groups we've been working with are going to continue to get funding, because we are going to be reducing our funding in juvenile justice over the next couple of years. It's not like we don't prepare them for that. That is how foundations work.

Summary

Overall, psychologists working in intermediary settings feel they have substantially greater capacity and flexibility to pursue policy influence in a focused manner than do those in academic settings. Nonetheless, they lack insider access to key policy actors and the distinct potential for influence that insider status affords.

We turn next to the experiences and perspectives of psychologists who work within government, seeking to exert policy influence from the vantage point of the policy insider.

5

Psychologists Working as Policy Insiders

You really get to shape things. You're well situated. But it all depends on . . .
—J. Hunter-Williams, May 29, 2013

Psychologists who work within government possess a unique vantage point through which to influence policy. They become policy insiders through (a) appointment by an elected official, (b) civil service employment within an executive branch agency, or, sometimes, (c) by direct election. Policy insider roles are situated at all levels of government, including federal (e.g., Congressional staffer), state (e.g., appointed official), and local (e.g., elected city councilwoman). This chapter depicts a variety of policy insider roles in which psychologists have sought to influence policy, along with the policy influence methods and skills they have used. The chapter describes the greatest policy successes of interviewees working in staff positions for US Senators and US congressional committees, as an elected official, and in executive branch agency positions. The narratives add to existing accounts of policy influence work by well-known psychologists serving as policy insiders, such as Edward Zigler, first director of Head Start (Zigler, 2007); Theodore Strickland, two-term governor of Ohio (e.g., Shullman, Celeste, & Strickland, 2005); and Patrick DeLeon, long-serving aide and chief of staff for former Hawaii Senator Daniel Inouye (DeLeon, Loftis, Ball, & Sullivan, 2006).

Sixteen psychologists who experienced their greatest policy influence when serving in policy insider roles were interviewed for this volume; 14 are included in this chapter. The first portion of the chapter examines policy insider roles for seven psychologists within the legislative branch. We begin with three psychologists working for US senators, next present three psychologists serving in the more specialized role of committee staff in the US House and Senate, and then conclude the legislative portion with an elected official—a city councilwoman. The second portion of the chapter moves to the executive branch, where psychologists serve in positions that entail implementation and evaluation of policies.

These six policy insiders work as policy analysts, advisors, and administrators at the state and federal levels. The chapter concludes with an exploration of the benefits and limitations of working to influence policy as a policy insider.

Staff Positions Working for US Senators

The first three case examples focus on psychologists working for members of the US Senate (Table 5.1). The insider roles at the time of each psychologist's greatest policy success are legislative director, senior policy advisor, and legislative assistant, respectively. The policy issues of focus encompass dropout prevention in schools, mental health parity, and health. The narratives that follow reveal the use of diverse methods and skills. Some are similar to those portrayed in earlier chapters (e.g., relationship-building, communication, strategic analysis), although played out in a more highly charged and political venue. And some

Table 5.1 **Psychologists Working for US Legislators: Policy Issue, Psychologist, Government Branch/Level, Insider Position, and Legislator**

Policy Issue (Psychologist)	Government Branch/Level	Insider Position	Legislator
Dropout Prevention (Vincent)*	Legislative/ National	Legislative Director	Senator Bingaman (D. New Mexico)
Mental Health Parity (Gerrity)*	Legislative/ National	Senior Policy Advisor	Senator Wellstone (D. Minnesota)
Health (Downing)*	Legislative/ National	Legislative Assistant	Senator Brown (D. Ohio)
Education (HBCUs); Nurse Home Visiting (Hunter-Williams)** (3)	Legislative/ National	Deputy Chief of Staff	Representative Davis (D. Chicago)
Child Nutrition (Zuckerman)** (7)	Legislative/ National	Congressional Fellow	Representative Williams (D. 1st District, Montana)

* Covered in this chapter.

** (X) = Chapter number where presented as case example.

are distinct to insider work in the legislative branch, including specific tactics for moving legislation forward and the art of negotiation and compromise.

Legislative Director for Sen. Jeff Bingaman (D-NM): Dropout Prevention Act

Trudy Vincent

PhD, Psychology, University of Maryland, College Park, 1986

Director of the University of Chicago's Office of Federal Relations

During her 26 years on Capitol Hill, clinical-community psychologist Trudy Vincent served as legislative director for three senators: Barbara Mikulski (MD), Bill Bradley (NJ), and Jeff Bingaman (NM). Prior to Sen. Bingaman's retirement in 2012, Vincent served as his Chief of Staff. One of Vincent's many legislative accomplishments was working with Senator Mikulski to establish the Office of Women's Health at the National Institutes of Health (NIH), which helped to ensure an equitable, explicit focus on women in health research protocols (NIH Office of Research on Women's Health, n.d.; NIH Revitalization Act, 1993). Another success noted by Vincent, this one during her tenure as Legislative Director for Senator Bingaman, was passage of the Dropout Prevention Act, Part H of the 2001 No Child Left Behind (NCLB) legislation (US Department of Education, 2013a). The Dropout Prevention Act provided funding (beginning with $125 million in fiscal year 2002) for research-based prevention activities aimed at reducing the number of students dropping out of school in states around the country. It included the Smaller Learning Communities Program, which funded the creation of small learning communities in large high schools serving adolescents from low-income families (US Department of Education, 2013b, 2013c). Vincent presents an insider's perspective on the development of a federal law stimulated initially by concerns about education outcomes in the senator's home state. Here, she describes the initial impetus and some of the ensuing processes that led to the Dropout Prevention Act:

> What triggered our desire was in part some terrible statistics in New Mexico about the dropout rate, particularly among Hispanic students, who make up over 40% of [the state's] population, and also among Native Americans, who make up 10%. For a few years, we worked on

how to put together some [federal] legislation that would get money out to the states, to work on dropout prevention. In this joint [the Senate], it's very hard to get free-standing legislation not attached to a larger bill passed, but what was fortunate was there was a vehicle coming through, No Child Left Behind.

We worked very hard to gather the evidence about what worked in terms of dropout prevention. One of the things that became clear was that there was some variability in what worked in different settings. Thus, we wanted to leave some flexibility, rather than be prescriptive. Also, we did come to understand, based on emerging research, that in large schools there tended to be higher dropout rates; kids got lost and lose motivation. So we also created a program called Small Learning Communities. We got language into No Child Left Behind that created the two programs, and then we had to work with the appropriators to make sure there was money appropriated for both of those programs. We like to believe we made a difference there.

As legislative director, I was the constant sounding board for our staff that are doing the work. On this bill, there were negotiations about funding levels, and I was giving advice about how to work with the Republicans to set these levels. Furthermore, there was talk about folding this program into a larger block grant where it would simply be one possible activity. We had a lot of discussions and strategizing about how to make sure this remained a free-standing program and didn't get diluted as one possible activity among many. I was involved with that negotiation. I would talk with my legislative director counterpart, or the staff director of the overarching committee on my level about why this was important and how this means something to Jeff [Sen. Bingaman] as well as more broadly. There are a million little decisions that go on in the course of a day, in the course of a week, in the course of a proposal.

Vincent used a number of distinctive skills and tactics to move this policy idea into law. First, she drew on extant data and statistics to highlight, in the senator's state, the need for policy reform. She also examined existing research to help generate policy ideas to address the problem. Vincent engages in strategic actions unique to the policy insider context, such as finding a legislative "vehicle" for the policy. Finally, problem-solving and negotiation skills (including decisions about when to compromise and when to stand firm) appear central to success in this case..

Next, we turn to a case example in the mental health policy area.

Senior Mental Health Policy Advisor to Sen. Paul Wellstone (D-MN): Paul Wellstone and Pete Domenici Mental Health Parity and Addiction Equity Act of 2008

Ellen Gerrity

PhD, Environmental Psychology, University of Arizona, 1983

Senior Policy Advisor, University of California, Los Angeles/Duke University National Center for Child Traumatic Stress

Psychologist Ellen Gerrity served as Senior Mental Health Policy advisor to Sen. Paul Wellstone from 1998 to 2002 while "on detail" (i.e., on loan) from the **National Institutes of Mental Health** (NIMH), where she was Associate Director of Aggression and Trauma Research. Gerrity's primary focus throughout her tenure with Senator Wellstone was on legislation to achieve parity in health insurance coverage of mental illness and addiction. Upon Wellstone's death in an airplane accident, Gerrity returned to her position at NIMH and then to a policy position with the National Child Traumatic Stress Network but continued to contribute to efforts to secure passage of the legislation. Passage was finally achieved when the Wellstone-Domenici Mental Health Parity and Addiction Equity Act (MHPAEA) of 2008 became law (Center for Medicaid and Medicare Services, 2013; US Department of Labor, 2013). This legislation served as a key foundation for, and was extended by, the mental health and substance abuse parity provisions in the Affordable Care Act (the ACA; see SAMHSA, 2013). In the excerpt below, Gerrity describes various aspects of her contributions to the development of the MHPAEA, both during the time she worked for Senator Wellstone and after his death. She discusses the importance of both grassroots and "grasstops" efforts. Grasstops refers to activists and advocates who have prominent public and/or professional profiles and thus can increase the public's awareness of an issue as well as influence policymakers through their connections.

> Paul Wellstone was a champion for advancing the effort to make physical and mental health coverage equal. I worked on that the entire time I worked for him. Just about every kind of policy activity was needed for this effort because it was strongly opposed by wealthy and influential organizations and individuals. The policy work included raising awareness through preparing speeches, op-eds, or press releases; commissioning reports; organizing briefings or meetings; or having a financial analysis

done. Grassroots efforts were very important. I worked with many different groups to learn what they felt was needed and what they could do to help make it more visible and public.

There is also reliance on "grasstops," where influence is conveyed by individuals closely connected to those whose views are pivotal in moving something forward. You do the analysis to answer the question, "Who is approachable?" Of course, there are many people who work in lobbying activities who bring forward money to help sway or influence what goes on. I'm not a lobbyist, and that was not my role. You can bring forward stories, science, and idealism. You never know what will drive someone to change one way or another around a policy decision. I think the science and research background that I had was very helpful. Data were essential, showing, for example, that with appropriate levels of managed care (comparable to physical care) you could keep costs reasonable. The research around that was really important.

There were various successes along the way, but the full law did not pass before Senator Wellstone died. In the aftermath of his death, his son, Dave Wellstone, got involved in advocating for the passage of the law. He asked me to help him. The relationships that had been built with different senators and representatives were very important. People could trust me in terms of the information that I was giving them, including my memories about the different kinds of negotiations that had gone on. Paul Wellstone was deeply respected and his memory meant a great deal to a lot of people.

In 2008, the law passed. . . . It became effective in 2010. The establishment of that law became the foundation from which everything else has happened around mental health parity in the Affordable Care Act and many other things.

Gerrity's account illustrates the many policy methods and skills necessary for securing passage of a major piece of legislation. She highlights the importance of relationships and networking and, relatedly, building trust. Strategic analysis also played a central role in the effort to move mental health parity forward: "You do the analysis to answer the question, "Who is approachable?" Gerrity notes the importance, in terms of strategy, of grasstops efforts, in which influential persons are mobilized to influence both the public and policymakers—a key indirect policy influence pathway. Extant research evidence, particularly that related to cost considerations, also appeared critical. Finally, the account underscores the importance of persistence and commitment; the latter evidenced in Gerrity's continued involvement in the policy work when she no longer was paid to do so (following Senator Wellstone's death).

Next, we turn to an example that further highlights the important roles of relationship-building and bipartisan support.

Legislative Assistant for Sen. Sherrod Brown (D-OH): Healthy Start Reauthorization Act of 2007; Comprehensive Tuberculosis Elimination Act of 2008

Roberta Downing

PhD, Social Psychology, University of California, Santa Cruz, 2004

Deputy Director, Office of Federal & Regional Affairs, Executive Office of MayorMuriel E. Bowser, Washington, DC

Social psychologist Roberta Downing worked as a staff-person for two years in the office of Senator Sherrod Brown (D-Ohio). Responsibilities included healthcare, social security, and other policies aimed at benefitting older Americans. During this time, Downing contributed to passage of the Healthy Start Reauthorization Act of 2007 (Public Law 110-339, 2008). This Act reauthorized and substantially increased authorized funding for the Healthy Start Program aimed at reducing racial disparities in infant mortality. Downing also worked on the Comprehensive Tuberculosis Elimination Act of 2008 (Public Law 110-392, 2008), which funded increased research and public health strategies to prevent the spread of drug-resistant tuberculosis outbreaks in the United States. Both bills were passed through the Senate Health Education Labor and Pensions Committee, where Downing had previously worked as an American Psychological Association (APA) congressional fellow for Senator Kennedy (D-MA). Here, she discusses her contributions to the Healthy Start and Comprehensive Tuberculosis Elimination bills and the importance of timing and relationships in policymaking:

> There are two standalone bills that were signed into law when I worked for Senator Brown that felt like big successes for me. One was an infant mortality bill. We got a 20% increase in authorized funding for Healthy Start. The other dealt with protecting our country from tuberculosis (TB) outbreaks. Quite a big success was being able to arrange Republican co-sponsors of the two bills.
>
> One of the ways that I overcame the partisanship barrier was to develop positive relationships with Republican staff. One of the main Republican staffers on the Senate Health Committee used to ride the

train from Baltimore with me. At first she didn't want to talk to me, but I would just keep trying to talk to her and we became friends. That was extremely helpful. I also developed a friendship with another staffer. . . . It's just breaking down the barriers. . . . Also important, Republican Senator Kay Bailey Hutchison, who was our co-sponsor on the TB bill, had had a recent outbreak of TB in her state.

Downing illustrates the importance of legislative timing because windows of opportunity can open and close quickly with breaking events and the media's quick coverage. She goes on to detail the need for relationships to extend beyond government, the importance of research skills, and the art of compromise and negotiation in policymaking:

Another aspect of relationship building is having relationships with the [advocacy] groups. You start to figure out who the advocates are that you can trust the most. You can call them at the last minute and say, "I need this statistic. Can you get it for me because the boss is asking, and he's on the floor?" Or "Can you get your advocates to call Member X because he's wavering on whether or not he wants to co-sponsor this?"

In terms of research, you have disparities between different racial groups in infant mortality. That research was very relevant and useful. For the TB bill, there were tons of news stories about a guy who went on his honeymoon and contracted drug-resistant TB on the plane. We just tried to show how easy it would be to have a major TB outbreak in the United States, based on the global numbers of TB. That kind of data helps make the case. . . . My research training was useful in meeting with researchers from the Cleveland Clinic and major research institutions in Ohio. That was helpful because they could explain their work in more depth and I understood their research methods, statistics, and findings because of my doctoral training.

One strategy that Republican staff would use to weaken provisions in a bill was to cross out the word "shall" and replace it with "may," so that you're suggesting what the Department needs to do more than instructing the Department to do those things. There were some places where we did have to insert "may" instead of "shall" in provisions in order to get a bill passed. The choice was to let the whole thing die and start all over again in the next Congress or make some concessions. One of the problems with not getting the bill done is that news coverage of Americans' susceptibility to drug-resistant TB was part of what made the bill something that could pass at that moment. If you don't have that public knowledge in the next Congress, then you can have a lot harder time getting movement.

Downing's explanation here continues to underscore the importance of relationship-building with both intermediary organizations and policy insiders, including those on both sides of the aisle. Strategic analysis and negotiation skills are also highlighted, involving issues of both timing and scope of the legislation. Moreover, she continues to emphasize the need to take advantage of the timing of news cycles when research findings are most likely to be of interest to the media, the public, and policymakers.

Summary

Vincent, Gerrity, and Downing demonstrate the substantial potential for psychologists to have a strong impact when working for influential members of Congress. Like psychologists in academia and intermediary organizations, these three psychologists draw on strong research, technical, and communication skills in their policy work, and they especially highlight the need for relationship-building and negotiation skills as critical in the policy insider context. Next, we turn to psychologists working for federal House or Senate committees. These congressional committees play a particularly important role in determining the fate of proposed legislation.

Staff Positions Working for Congressional Committees

When legislation is proposed in the US Congress, it is first referred to congressional committee(s) for their consideration. Most proposed bills "die" in committee (i.e., do not make it out of committee for consideration by the full House or Senate). When a bill is passed by a committee and moves to the Senate or House floor, the content of the legislation has most often changed on its way through the committee. This is due to different committee member viewpoints and priorities, leading to various forms of compromise. The committee chair is especially powerful because he or she controls which bills a committee will consider and the timetable of such consideration, including when congressional hearings and committee votes occur. Committee staff, especially those who serve for extended periods of time, develop expertise in the broad content area of the committee (such as education or juvenile justice) and thus can play important roles in the substantive development of legislation.

As featured in this section, three psychologists interviewed indicate that their greatest policy success involved legislation that emerged while serving on a Senate or House committee (see Table 5.2). Psychologists in these positions use

Table 5.2 **Psychologists Working for Congressional Committees: Policy Issue, Psychologist, Government Branch/Level, Insider Position, and Committee**

Policy Issue (Psychologist)	Government Branch/Level	Insider Position	Government Office
Education Reform (Barone)*	Legislative/ National	Deputy Staff Director	House Education & Workforce Committee
Welfare Reform (Haskins)*	Legislative/ National	Majority Staff Director	House Subcommittee on Human Resources
Healthcre Reform (Morrisey)*	Legislative/ National	Health Advisor	Senate Health, Education, Labor and Pensions Committee

* Covered in this chapter.

many of the skills and influence methods highlighted by the staff in congressional offices, but they have the ability to focus their ongoing efforts on committees with specific areas of jurisdiction. The committee positions held by the three psychologists are deputy staff director, majority staff director, and health advisor, respectively. The policy issues of focus encompass three areas of reform: education, welfare, and healthcare. Many strategic skills are brought to bear in these cases.

US House of Representatives Education and Workforce Committee: The NCLB

Charles Barone

PhD, Clinical-Community Psychology, University of Maryland, College Park, 1991

Policy Director, Democrats for Education Reform, Washington, DC

Charles Barone, a clinical-community psychologist, worked for two influential members of Congress during an important 10-year period concerning federal educational policy. From 1994 to 1996, he served as Chief Educational Advisor to Senator Paul Simon (D-IL). One accomplishment during this period, in 1995, was the restoration of more than $9 billion dollars that the Republicans in the House had sought to cut from key Department of Education programs. Then, from 1997 to 2003, Barone championed education and children's issues for Rep. George Miller (D-CA). After Rep. Miller became the ranking Democrat on the committee in 2001, Barone worked for three years as democratic deputy staff director of the House Education and Workforce Committee, in charge of the development of NCLB, which became law in 2002 (US Department of Education, 2013*d*). Barone played an influential role as a lead negotiator for that legislation, working directly with key Republican congressmen (e.g., Rep. John Boehner, later Speaker of the House), the late Senator Edward M. Kennedy (then Chair of the Senate Health, Education, Labor, and Pensions Committee), and, to some extent, with President George W. Bush. Among other provisions, this legislation required states to disaggregate achievement data by ethnicity and race and set goals for closing achievement gaps. Here, Barone first discusses his work in 1995 helping to restore funding to the Department of Education:

> When the Republicans came in in '95, they wanted drastic cuts to education. Senator Paul Simon and I kept trying to work across the aisle. We actually found Senator Olympia Snow (R-ME) interested in rolling back some of the education cuts. We kept throwing up amendments and getting defeated, and [then] we crafted one that was pretty politically hard to argue against; we won 67 to 32. We won back almost ten billion in education cuts.

Barone next describes aspects of his work related to the development and passage of the NCLB:

> But I would say the biggest success was No Child Left Behind. States were required to report whether students were making adequate yearly progress—this was already in the law that was written in '94, but states weren't taking it seriously. Moreover, they weren't required to disaggregate data [to identify gaps across demographic subgroups]. Rep. Miller and I talked a lot about this, and we actually came across the fact that, in Texas, George W. Bush was disaggregating data. So, we started pushing. With my research background, I knew I was on solid ground. We pushed this long before Bush was even a candidate for [for president]. It happened that he became one; and when he won, it was just a natural alliance between Miller and Bush, and Kennedy was pretty much on board with it too. We had some tough negotiations, but we came out with a law that said, "You must disaggregate your data and try to close achievement gaps." And the other thing we did do, very silently, was change the funding for it. So, we swung a lot of money to the top quintile of the highest-priority schools, where 20% of the poorest kids go.

We had a few groups outside arguing for us, mainly the Citizens' Commission on Civil Rights, the Education Trust, and the Business Round Table. Between those three we had a lot of "echo"—then we could get to the editorial boards. We had virtually every editorial board on our side, and we had these advocacy groups . . . it created this groundswell.

I learned how to be a tough negotiator. And, I learned that details matter in legislation, from thinking that we had at least the requirement to disaggregate data in the '94 bill, and then learning that through the regulatory process, that you could finagle it and say that we didn't. I learned that every word mattered, and so I was a stickler for language.

As a key staffer on the House Education and Workforce Committee, Barone was instrumental to the development of the NCLB. His work demonstrates the need for critical negotiation skills to move legislation forward, including, in this case, late night, nail-biting moments of "hard ball" negotiations in which a powerful Republican senator insisted that key provisions of the legislation be dropped. Like the other policy insider cases detailed, Barone's account demonstrates the need for psychologists to take advantage of opportunities when they arise because timing and who is in power are both critical in the passing of legislation. Finally, Barone shows how building relationships and working with intermediary organizations (described in Chapter 4) can greatly aid policy insiders, exerting outside pressure ("echo") that combines with inside work to bring about substantive policy change.

Next, we turn to welfare reform and another example of the importance of congressional committee staff.

US House of Representatives Subcommittee on Human Resources, House Ways and Means Committee: The Personal Responsibility and Work Opportunity Reconciliation Act of 1996

Ron Haskins

PhD, Developmental Psychology, University of North Carolina, Chapel Hill, 1975

Senior Fellow and Co-Director, Center on Children and Families, Brookings Institute, Washington, DC

Developmental psychologist Ron Haskins served in the US House of Representatives for 15 years. From 1986 to 1994, he was Republican staff

Welfare Counsel for the Subcommittee on Human Resources, Ways and Means Committee. From 1995 to 2000, he served as Majority Staff Director for that subcommittee. Haskins played an important role in the development and passage of the welfare reform legislation in 1996, the Personal Responsibility and Work Opportunity Reconciliation Act of 1996 (PRWORA; Public Law 104-193, 1996). Haskins later wrote a book providing a detailed insider's account of the development of this landmark law (Haskins, 2006). This highly controversial legislation represents a fundamental change in the country's approach to welfare, both encouraging and requiring employment among the poor while emphasizing workforce development. Here, Haskins describes some highlights of the process in 1996 that led to passage of the welfare reform legislation:

> I was the staff director of the main committee that had the main jurisdiction over the welfare reform legislation, but many committees had jurisdiction. We formed a staff group from the leadership and from all the committees that were involved. I chaired that staff group. I planned the hearings and all that kind of stuff. There are all kinds of things that happened that are hard to classify, like who's going to get their way and how do you make a strategy. For example, we had to overcome the House Speaker, Newt Gingrich. That took a lot of different steps.
>
> I think a lot of the ideas, especially how to actually implement, were mine. Here's what I mean. Republicans say, "People on welfare have to work." How do you propose to make that happen? I was familiar with the literature. It just so happened at that time that there was a big movement in the states to help welfare mothers work. It was converting the welfare system so that it would focus like a laser on jobs. We were figuring out all those things and, most of all, talking to people at the state level and finding out how they were doing it. This is even truer of child support. All the attention goes to work and the cash welfare program, but we had a fabulous child support provision in that legislation. That was something that I studied forever. I knew all the important people in the country and the best State Directors. I had good relationships with the National Child Support Enforcement Association and so forth. I had ideas of my own, but the thing that I really learned over the years was never to take credit, know the people who are really smart, and know what needs to be done.
>
> Research did play a role. The research on work was of such high quality and so close to the actual policy to be implemented that it really had an impact. You could talk about a sample of about 45,000 people, if you put all the studies together. I made sure that came to the committee's attention. Also, lobbying was very crucial, especially from the National

Governors Association (NGA). The governors were bipartisan before the Congress was. The advocacy was important, but it was an unusual kind of advocacy. I was on a first-name basis with so many people at NGA. There was very careful coordination, especially with them.

Haskins used diverse policy influence methods and skills to help secure the passage of major welfare reform legislation. These include the use of research, leadership, policy analysis, and strategic political skills, as well as meeting with and learning from key individuals—both policymakers inside Congress and content experts in states around the country. Once again, outside advocacy was central; Haskins describes as critical his relationships and collaboration with members of the National Governor's Association. Haskins' work also underscores the many factors (e.g., ideas, time, policymakers, public support, money) that influence the passage of major legislation and the important role a psychologist can play as a staff member of a congressional committee.

Finally, we turn to a psychologist who worked on one of the key Senate committees involved in development of the ACA.

Health Policy Advisor, Senate Committee on Health, Education, Labor, and Pensions: ACA

Taryn Morrissey

PhD, Developmental Psychology, Cornell University, 2008

Assistant Professor of Public Administration and Policy, American University

Taryn Morrissey, a developmental psychologist, served as Health Policy Advisor on the staff of the Senate Health, Education, Labor, and Pensions committee from 2009 to 2010, when the ACA was developed and became law. Morrissey first worked on the Committee under chairperson Edward Kennedy (D-MA) and continued, after his death, working for the new committee chair, Sen. Tom Harkin (D-IA). Her contributions to the legislation focused on child and maternal health and workforce issues. Morrissey had worked as a congressional fellow on the same committee from 2008 to 2009. Here, she describes the committee and several aspects of her work on the ACA:

After my [congressional] fellowship year ended, I was hired on the staff in the Health Office of the Health Committee, Senator Kennedy's office. When Senator Kennedy passed away, I stayed on under Senator Harkin who became the new chairman. The health office was pretty unique in that there were five PhDs, on a staff of maybe eight or nine. People knew about and cared about research; we got *The New England Journal of Medicine* and *Health Affairs*. I certainly remember one particular study about how many people are estimated to die because they don't have health insurance. Something like that was extremely relevant and used immediately.

HELP (the health committee) was one of the two committees in the Senate that had jurisdiction over the bill. Our jurisdiction included public health, safety, and research (CDC FDA, NIH), as well as enhancing quality in healthcare, workforce issues in terms of making sure there are enough doctors and nurses, and a lot of the public health grants that are designed to prevent obesity and encourage healthy lifestyles. It was a wide range, a lot. Because Senator Kennedy represented Massachusetts, the first state to implement health reform, our committee was a proponent of the Massachusetts model, which included insurance exchanges, which are now called marketplaces.

Morrisey used a number of skills in her work on the ACA, skills she views as important for any psychologist working as a policy insider:

Being able to distill information into short digestible issues is an overall skill useful in many capacities; for legislation it's sort of like solving a research problem. It's thinking of a theory or a potential solution and then trying to crack holes in it and think around it in terms of unintended consequences. Then there is this added layer of what the politics of it are, and related processes.

A lot of legislation isn't writing from scratch. I forget where I heard it, but somebody said, "There are no new policy ideas, just recycled policies." The ACA is a grouping of many bills that had been introduced individually in previous years and modified somewhat. I can really only think of two provisions that I wrote from scratch, actually spec'ing it out and working with the legislative office to put it in legislative language. Most of it was essentially borrowed from previous bills, though sometimes things need to be updated or changed. One I wrote from scratch was about developing appropriate curricular materials for healthcare providers based on cultural diversity as well as for individuals with special needs and disability.

Whereas Barone and Haskins, in the two prior examples, held senior committee positions, Morrissey was a relatively junior person on the Health Committee. The skills she gained during her congressional fellowship, including those related to communication and research translation, aided her in refining and updating prior legislative proposals, as well as in writing new legislative language. In this case, strategic analysis skills again emerge as central, including the simultaneous importance of substantive policy content and political realities—and consideration of unanticipated consequences—when translating ideas into legislation.

Summary

The three case examples just presented highlight the roles played by psychologists working on committees responsible for some of the most important social policy reforms in recent decades—in education, welfare, and healthcare, respectively. The psychologists worked on both sides of the legislative aisle, in varied roles, and in both chambers of Congress. Together with the three case examples presented earlier, these examples portray the complex and rich tapestry of policy formulation and adoption; the multiple forces involved; and the roles, methods, and skills psychologists have effectively brought as insiders to the policymaking process.

Elected Officials

A number of psychologists have been elected to office at federal, state, and local levels. As noted in Chapter 2, Ted Strickland (D-Ohio) was, in 1992, the first psychologist elected to Congress, specifically to the House of Representatives. Currently, there are three psychologists in the House, Judy Chu (D-CA), Alan Lowenthal (D-CA), and Tim Murphy (R-PA). At the state level, in 2006, 13 psychologists won elections to serve on their state legislatures. Of special note, in 2006, Strickland was elected governor of Ohio. It is not known how many psychologists have served in elected positions at local levels, although two of those interviewed noted that their greatest policy success occurred while serving as city council member (Starnes, next section), and town meeting representative (Berkowitz, p. 177), respectively (Table 5.3).

Table 5.3 **Elected Officials: Policy Issue, Psychologist, Government Branch/Level, and Government Office**

Policy Issue (Psychologist)	Government Branch/ Level	Government Office
Homelessness (Starnes)*	Legislative/City	Atlanta City Council
Varied (Berkowitz)**	Legislative/Town	Arlington (MA) Town Meeting

* Covered in this chapter.
** In Vantage Point section at end of this chapter.

Atlanta City Councilwomen: Addressing Homelessness

Debi Starnes

PhD, Organizational-Community Psychology, Georgia State University, 1987

President of EMSTAR Research, Inc., Atlanta, Georgia

Debi Starnes, a community psychologist, served three terms on the Atlanta City Council, from 1993 to 2005, and then as Policy Advisor from 2007 to 2010 to Atlanta Mayor Shirley Franklin. While on the City Council, Starnes contributed to many important initiatives, including services for the homeless, neighborhood redevelopment, citizen participation, poverty, and civil rights (Linney, 2004; Starnes, 2004). Starnes identifies her greatest policy success as helping to generate a comprehensive approach to addressing homelessness. This included development of the Regional Commission on Homelessness (Hardin, 2011), innovative means of funding services for the homeless (Bolster, 2011), and a 24/7 central intake and assessment center (gatewayctr.org). Prior to serving on the City Council, Starnes was a member of the city's zoning review board, president of her neighborhood planning unit, and manager of two political campaigns. Here, Starnes first describes her early policy work:

> The city of Atlanta is divided into 24 neighborhood planning units (NPUs). Each NPU serves as the conduit between 4 to 6 neighborhoods and City Hall. When I became chair of the NPU in my area, I started getting more involved with city governance and local politics. Then, when I went to graduate school in '84, there was a synergistic effect between my neighborhood activism and leadership roles, and the influence of studying community psychology. During this time, I managed two political campaigns—a city council person and a state representative. Then I got appointed to the Zoning Review Board for the city. In '93, a few friends and colleagues talked me into running for City Council. I won, then ran and was elected two more times, so I served 12 years.

Starnes then highlights aspects of her city council career, including her work addressing homelessness:

> Having earned a reputation of delving into problems and complicated issues and figuring out creative solutions, I ended up being floor leader for the two mayors that I served with. Then I was chair of the finance committee for several years. The Atlanta City Council is a part-time position, but it consumes a lot of hours. I decided that three terms in elected office were sufficient, but in 2007, I went back to City Hall with Mayor Shirley Franklin as one of her policy advisors.

I have been involved for many years in the area of homelessness. In 1995, I started a group called the Homeless Action Group, which brought together all providers with the business community and faith leaders to try to get everyone organized and focused . . . on studying and then deciding the approaches to take. Mayor Franklin took a personal interest in the topic and she and I overlapped one term.

In 2005, we developed a central intake and assessment facility called the Gateway Center [see Gateway Center, 2015]. That has been a success and is still going. Then in 2006, Mayor Franklin started the Regional Commission on Homelessness—getting seven counties and the city to work together on this topic, voluntarily, and got some high-powered business people and the United Way engaged. Through that effort we raised $30 million in private funds to issue Housing Opportunity Bond funds to develop supportive housing for the homeless. I'm still engaged in the battle against homelessness and on the board of Gateway.

Starnes' political career evolved from her early participation in a neighborhood planning unit, to increasing local political involvement during her graduate studies, to serving as city councilwoman and then advisor to the mayor. She utilized a number of policy influence methods and skills throughout her work, including relationship-building, coalition-building, strategic analysis, problem-solving, and persistence. In her work on the city council, Starnes reports that research findings generally did not play a notable role. When findings did enter the conversation, they were communicated to the council by researchers of known credibility and trustworthiness and frequently included information about cost-effectiveness.

Summary

In the legislative domain, psychologists work on a diverse range of issues, many outside their areas of training and expertise. This is true both for the elected officials, who must make policy decisions across the wide-ranging set of issues under consideration each term, and their staff, who assist them in every way possible. In the next section, we move from the legislative to the executive branch of government, where psychologists, as policy insiders, are much more likely to address issues within their areas of training and expertise.

Executive Branch Agency Positions

Many psychologists work in executive branch agencies, in departments ranging from mental health to education to child welfare, at all levels of government. They serve in senior appointed leadership positions and in positions of middle-level policy analysis, research, and management. Notable examples at the federal level reside within the Department of Health and Human Services (HHS). Such exemplars include Larke Huang, a clinical-community psychologist who serves as the Senior Advisor in the Administrator's Office of Policy Planning and Innovation at the Substance Abuse and Mental Health Services Administration (SAMHSA) and Daniel Dodgen, a child-clinical psychologist who serves as the Director of the Division for At-Risk Individuals, Behavioral Health and Community Resilience in the Office of the Assistant Secretary for Preparedness and Response.

As noted earlier, the most well-known example of a psychologist working at the federal level is Edward Zigler, who took leave from Yale University to serve as the first Director of the Office of Child Development. Not surprisingly, psychologists in high-level positions are most often found in human service-focused departments, whether in federal, state, or local government. For example, prior to serving as long-time Executive Director of Public Interest at APA, Henry Tomes served as Commissioner of Mental Health in Massachusetts. Among those interviewed for this volume, Robert Cohen (pp. 172–174) served as Associate Commissioner in the

Table 5.4 **Policy Insiders Working Within Executive Branch Agencies: Policy Issue, Psychologist, Government Branch/Level, and Government Unit**

Policy Issue (Psychologist)	Government Branch/Level	Government Unit
Substance Abuse Parity (Humphreys)*	Executive/National	Office of National Drug Control Policy
Child and Youth Policy Implementation (Moorehouse)*	Executive/National	Division of Child and Youth Policy, ASPE, Health & Human Services
Teen Pregnancy Prevention (Oberlander)*	Executive/National	Division of Child and Youth Policy, ASPE, Health & Human Services
Substance Abuse Prevention (Emshoff)*	Executive/National	Center for Substance Abuse Prevention
Juvenile Justice (Jenkins)*	Executive/State	Division of Juvenile Justice, North Carolina Department of Public Safety
Child Mental Health System Reform (Cohen)*	Executive/State	Virginia Treatment Center for Children

* Covered in this chapter.

Office of Mental Health for the State of New York, and Judith Meyers (pp. 126–129) served as Commissioner of Child Welfare for the State of Iowa.

In the following section, six case examples are provided of psychologists interviewed who indicate their greatest policy success occurred while serving in executive branch positions at federal or state levels (see Table 5.4). The first involves a psychologist working in the federal government, specifically a White House office. Parity of coverage for substance abuse constitutes the primary policy issue.

Senior Policy Advisor, White House Office of National Drug Control Policy: Substance Use Treatment Parity in the ACA

Keith Humphreys

PhD, Clinical-Community Psychology, University of Illinois
Urbana-Champaign, 1993

Professor of Psychiatry and Behavioral Sciences, Stanford University

Clinical-community psychologist Keith Humphreys served as senior policy advisor at the White House Office of National Drug Control Policy (ONDCP) during the first year of the Obama Administration. He was recruited to the position by psychologist Tom McLellan, whom President Obama had appointed as the deputy director of ONDCP. Humphreys took a leave of absence from Stanford University, allowing him to accept the appointment. Working in close partnership, McLellan and Humphreys sought to secure substance use treatment coverage as an integral part of the ACA legislation that was being developed in Congress. In making their case, they made use of cost-savings data from the state of Washington indicating that expanded substance use disorder treatment coverage resulted in decreased costs to the state due to reduced emergency room and disability costs (Wickizer et al., 2006). The ACA, as passed, includes the largest expansion of insurance coverage for treatment of substance use disorder in decades (SAMHSA, 2010, 2013). The act provides complete parity of coverage in the policies provided by the health insurance exchanges. Substance use (and mental health) services are one of the 10 Essential Health Benefits. Medicaid also provides coverage for substance use disorder treatment and for screening, intervention, and referrals. Other areas of responsibility for Humphreys at ONCDP included serving on the advisory board that oversaw federal HIV/AIDS policy and working to improve community parole/probation systems. Here, Humphreys highlights several aspects of the policy influence efforts made to secure inclusion of substance use parity in the ACA, beginning with the importance of relevant empirical evidence:

> Tom [McLellan] and I had data from Washington State, where the coverage of substance use disorder treatments within Medicaid was dramatically expanded. They have some really good data analysis teams there, including some psychologists. What they showed was that the state made its money back within the same fiscal year, because when they started to treat people, they had such a drop in emergency room admissions and such a drop in disability costs that they came out ahead financially.
>
> Tom took it [these data] over to Peter Orszag who was head of the Office of Management and Budget. I wasn't at that meeting. I think I was just arriving in Washington. Orszag called him back at 11:00 PM that day. He said, "I reworked all your figures. I actually think you're too conservative on it." Orszag is an economist. He totally understands money. He understands health.
>
> Using various connections and strategies, we arranged a number of meetings, including with Tino Cuellar (also a Stanford professor on leave), the head "handler" for current drug policy on the Domestic Policy Council, with Zeke Emanuel, one of the president's principal healthcare advisors, with Nancy-Ann Deparle, who ran the healthcare reform office inside the White House, and with Dora Hughes, the councilor to Secretary Sebelius. All these meetings were basically the same. You say, "Here's the evidence that this would be a productive goal. Here are the cost implications. Here are the human implications, and so on." You can see it generated some buzz inside the administration.
>
> As you're doing that, the advocacy community is doing the same thing. They may not be able to get the same meetings, but they used the data that Tom and I put together. The advocates took it to Congress . . . on their own. It happens all the time.
>
> The other critical thing was that the parity provisions of the ACA were never highlighted as a pro-addict bill because that would have killed them. It was all done very quietly both by the advocacy community and by us.

Humphreys drew on varied policy influence methods and skills in his work at ONDCP, including networking, relationship-building, effective communication of research findings, and strategic analysis (i.e., policy analysis; strategy development). His prior collegial relationship with McLellan, established over the years, led both to his appointment as senior policy advisor and to a good working relationship. Furthermore, Humphreys creatively utilized a diverse set of network contacts from various sectors of his professional and academic life to gain access to and arrange meetings with key policy players. As in several previous cases (e.g., Gerrity, Morrisey), cost-effectiveness research data and the combined, synergistic influence of internal and external advocacy were critical. The strategy of "keeping quiet" about the proposed change so as not to invite likely pushback from powerful quarters is a distinctive aspect of this policy influence effort.

Next, we turn to several psychologists working in the same office in another executive branch agency. Their work focuses on child and youth policy.

Division of Children and Youth Policy, ASPE Office, HHS: Evidence-Based Programs

Martha Moorehouse

PhD, Developmental Psychology, Cornell University, 1985

Senior Advisor, Office of the Assistant Secretary for Planning and Evaluation, US Department of HHS

Sarah Oberlander

PhD, Community and Applied Social Psychology, University of Maryland, Baltimore County, 2008
Social Science Analyst, Office of the Assistant Secretary for Planning and Evaluation, US Department of HHS

Martha Moorehouse, a developmental psychologist, has worked for more than two decades in the **Office of the Assistant Secretary for Planning and Evaluation** (ASPE), US Department of HHS. ASPE's primary purpose is to advise the HHS Secretary on policy development, including strategic planning, coordination, research, evaluation, and economic analysis (http://aspe.hhs.gov/). At the time of the interview, Moorehouse was the Director of the Division of Children and Youth Policy within ASPE and oversaw a wide range of planning, policy, research, and evaluation projects that focus on children, youth, and their families. Content areas included early childhood, youth development, risky behaviors, child welfare, domestic violence, and program effectiveness. As part of her role, Moorehouse has chaired the Interagency Working Group on Youth Programs (12 federal departments and additional agencies) and served as a member of the Interagency Forum on Children and Family Statistics. She has consulted on the development of legislation, including the generation of language defining the well-being of children, as well as contributing to the tiered-evidence guidelines (i.e., more funding for programs with more rigorous evidential base) for teenage pregnancy and home visiting legislation (the latter described in Chapter 3, pp. 64–67; Haskins & Margolis, 2014). An overarching goal of the Division of Children and Youth Policy is the use of research to guide successful implementation of legislation, including the scaling up of evidence-based programs. In 2012, the Division brought together a wide range of research experts and executive branch officials to discuss and distill extant knowledge related to national expansion of evidence-based prevention programs (Blase & Fixsen, 2013; Child Trends, 2013; Durlak, 2013; Embry, Lipsey, Moore, & McCallum, 2013).

Sarah Oberlander, a community psychologist, also conducts social policy work in ASPE. She began working in ASPE as an SRCD Executive Branch Fellow in 2009; in 2011, following, the end of her fellowship, she continued on as a federal employee. Martha Moorehouse has been her supervisor. One of Oberlander's major areas of focus is teen pregnancy prevention. Currently, she serves as one of two project officers overseeing the evidence review for the teen pregnancy prevention evidence-based initiative (Public Law 111-117, Division D, Title II, 2010) administered by the Office of Adolescent Health. The initiative includes an allocation of approximately $175 million of federal funding toward expanding the use of evidence-based teen pregnancy programs and supporting innovative and untested programs to build the evidence base. The evidence reviews inform decisions about which existing programs have sufficient quality research behind them to be deemed evidence-based. These are the programs for which state and local grantees can apply for federal funding to implement (Goesling, Colman, Trenholm, Terzian, & Moore 2013; Haskins & Margolis, 2014; Office of Adolescent Health, 2014).

Another one of Oberlander's major responsibilities has been to develop the youth.gov cross-governmental agency website that translates and consolidates information about youth issues, resources, and programming for the public. Oberlander also works on a cross-agency youth violence prevention initiative centered on the development of comprehensive approaches in cities and communities. The initiative seeks to reduce youth violence by addressing prevention, intervention, enforcement, and re-entry.

Here, Moorehouse and Oberlander describe some of their policy activities within ASPE. We begin with Moorehouse, who provides an overview of the policy work done by her office during the time she served as Division

Director. She also discusses several of her contributions to this work, including the formation of tiered-evidence guidelines for the home visiting and teen pregnancy prevention programs:

> We interact and collaborate extensively across agencies and across issue areas, but the fundamental focus here is on human service policies, including a focus on the work at the Administration for Children and Families. The bulk of policy work is around how implementation goes from the federal to state and community levels, and the extent to which we can bring research to bear. It's an ongoing pursuit to see how you can help inform programs through data, research, and evaluation over time, trying to create that continuous improvement cycle both in the policy structure and the ongoing implementation.
>
> We were involved in the early policy development work that established the tiered-evidence initiatives for home visiting and teen pregnancy prevention. It was a very big process and had significant involvement out of the Office of Management and Budget (OMB).

Oberlander talks in more detail about the development of the teen pregnancy prevention initiative and the evidence review that she co-directs.

> In 2009 and 2010, when the Teen Pregnancy Prevention Initiative was starting, my office and other relevant parties in the Department of Health and Human Services really worked together to try to shape what a teen pregnancy program could look like. . . . There was a big effort to think about how much evaluation there should be, and what should be the amount of evaluation resources to be allocated to replicating evidence-based programs versus innovative approaches.
>
> The legislation said to replicate programs that are proven effective, but nothing more about what that means. It was a policy decision by the US Department of Health and Human Services to create an evidence review rather than use an existing one and to create one that's really tailored to this legislation. Day to day, it seems like it should be simple to say that this is objective science and what passes the bar and what's below the bar, but there are a million tiny decisions that actually shape that, most of which I make with my other project officer and with the agreement of our leadership here in our office and our funding partners.
>
> Also, there was a big emphasis on training and technical assistance to each of the evaluations [of funded programs] to keep them as high quality and rigorous as possible . . . so that at the end of the day, when we look back on what we've learned, we will have the most confidence we

can on those which have been a real success—and from the others, what we nonetheless could learn.

Moorehouse concludes with another aspect of ASPE's efforts, addressing the challenge of program implementation.

> A recent project focuses on what we do know and where the challenges remain about scaling up existing practices, and where we don't have an evidence base to work from, how we best inform that work and begin to build up the knowledge base. We sponsored a forum for researchers from a lot of different prevention fields. We brought leading program officers and directors together. We had a number of people say they had never been a part of the discussion that brought together people from as many different disciplines who had knowledge about working with programs and their evidence, the strengths and limits of it, and questions about scaling up. A big focus of this work, and I think it is underrecognized by some of the spokespersons for the evidence-based policy movement . . . is the tendency to focus on previous impact evidence in determining whether or not a program is going to produce results in a new setting. There has been next to no focus on the role that implementation is going to play, and that we have implementation science literature. We convened that meeting and then developed a set of research briefs out of the meeting.

Moorehouse relies on a network of relationships, strategic analysis, management, and translational research skills to accomplish the planning and evaluation functions of her executive agency office. While on occasion she has had the opportunity to directly inform policy formulation, her office most frequently focuses on generating and disseminating information that contributes to better implementation and functioning of existing child- and youth-focused federal policies. Oberlander brings to bear research, critical analysis, and team-building skills in her varied concept development, contract management, and interagency coordination activities. Most generally, Moorehouse and Oberlander accomplish many of their policy activities through working within government (e.g., interagency meetings) and through grants and contracts provided to intermediary organizations and university faculty. Of note, the implementation of the "scaling up" workshop and policy brief initiative was facilitated by a contract with an intermediary organization, Child Trends, highlighted in Chapter 4 (pp. 122–124).

Next, we move to another example of a psychologist working within an HHS executive branch office (see US Department of Health and Human Services,

2013b, for a full list of HHS offices and programs). In this case, the policy work focuses on research related to substance abuse prevention and, as in several earlier examples, involves a psychologist on leave from his university.

Center for Substance Abuse Prevention: Community-Based Demonstration Projects

James Emshoff

PhD, Community Psychology, Michigan State, 1980

Vice President/Director of Research, EMSTAR Research, Inc., Atlanta, Georgia

James Emshoff, a community psychologist, took a one-year leave of absence from Georgia State University to work at the SAMHSA Center for Substance Abuse Prevention (CSAP). This was arranged through the Intergovernmental Personnel Act mobility program (opm.gov/policy-data-oversight/hiring-authorities/intergovernment-personnel-act/). The mission of CSAP is to "improve behavioral health through evidence-based prevention approaches" (SAMHSA, 2014). Emshoff developed a request for proposals (RFP) for a national CSAP demonstration program to provide prevention, education, and intervention services to pregnant and postpartum women with substance abuse problems and their infants (Eisen, Keyser-Smith, & Sambrano, 2000). He also contributed to the High Risk Youth and Community Partnership demonstration grants. The High Risk Youth initiative focused on the identification of model approaches and best practices for effective substance abuse prevention, including knowledge about related risk and protective factors (Sambrano, Springer, & Herman, 1997). The Community Partnership demonstration grants provided funding for the development of community-based coalitions involving multiple community partners to work together on substance abuse prevention initiatives (Trudeau, Saunders, Andrews, Hersch, & Oros, 1993; Stolberg, 2009). Here, Emshoff describes several aspects of his research policy work at CSAP:

> I took a one-year leave from Georgia State and went to work at CSAP. One of the things I got engaged in was how to craft an RFP [request for proposal]. What people end up doing with that government money is . . . essentially policy work. From the grantee's perspective, a grant is a gift. From the government's perspective, a grant is a mechanism for getting policy implemented. One subject area was pregnant and post-partum

women [using drugs] and their infants. I spent months traveling the country talking to people who were engaged in that work, figuring out their lessons learned and reading the literature. What I was able to do from that was to craft an RFP, which would require people to use what appeared to be best practices, and then evaluate them . . . because not all of them had been very well evaluated. An example was seeking to provide nonpunitive methods of responding to women who are using [street drugs] during pregnancy.

Compared to academic culture, big decisions are often made relatively easily in government settings. An example is that one day I was talking with my boss about High Risk Youth grants. Those grants were, at least for the first few years, three-year grants.

I said, "Three years is a pretty short time to try to get something up, organized, and implemented in some sort of consistent fashion and then to evaluate it and make decisions about it."

He said, "Really? Do you think that's too short?"

I said, "Yes. I think that's too short."

He said, "How long do you think they should be?"

I said, "I think they should be five years."

He said, "Okay. In the next RFP, we'll make them five years" . . . and they were.

Another example of quick action. One day we got a call saying, "The President wants to put millions of dollars into some new drug abuse initiative. What do you have in mind?" Within 48 hours we had to create a plan with what we would do with X number of dollars to spend on substance abuse prevention. One of the outgrowths of that was the development of the Community Partnership Grants, one of the first federal initiatives that really focused on creating a collaborative community-wide approach to a social problem. You wish you would have six months to put together a task force of experts. Instead, there's no money at all for that for 364 days and then on the 365th day there's a bunch of money and you have to figure out what to do with it—now.

In summary, I was trying to infuse all of the discussions and decisions that took place within my setting with community [psychology] perspectives and values. I think it changed where money went, and because it changed where money went, it changed where practice went. . . . My largest effects were not necessarily achieved using data. Furthermore, I often ran into a wall when I would try to use data for an audience that didn't really care about data. The strategies I used were looking for champions in every possible place I could find them and using multiple messages and modalities. If the numbers didn't work, then maybe a story worked. If this person didn't want to hear the story, then maybe another person did.

During his year working at CSAP, Emshoff sought to influence multiple demonstration projects. Policy influence methods and skills that Emshoff employed include seeking out project champions and utilizing available theoretical perspectives (i.e., community psychology based) along with field-based
research and practice knowledge to shape RFPs. This example illustrates how
policy-related decisions need to be made on the available evidence, however
inadequate or incomplete, and sometimes very quickly indeed—even when
completely new initiatives are involved.

Next, the policy work of several psychologists working in executive branch
agencies at the state level is depicted. The first case example involves work in the
state of North Carolina and is focused on juvenile justice.

North Carolina Department of Public Safety: Prohibiting the Jailing of Juvenile Status Offenders

Robin Jenkins

PhD, Human Resource Development and Community Psychology,
North Carolina State University, 1992

*Assistant Professor, Methodist University and Independent
Consultant, North Carolina*

Community psychologist Robin Jenkins served as Chief Operating Officer
of the Department of Juvenile Justice in North Carolina from 2009 through
2011, and as Deputy Director within the Division of Juvenile Justice of the
North Carolina Department of Public Safety from 2011 through 2013. Jenkins
identifies one of his greatest successes as helping lead the effort to change state
law so that juvenile status offenders (e.g., runaways, truants) could no longer
be placed in detention (General Assembly of North Carolina Session, 2011).
Prior to working in state government, Jenkins gained policy experience as
a member of the Governor's Crime Commission and of the State Advisory
Group operating under the Juvenile Justice and Delinquency Prevention Act.
In addition, as chair of the federal Coalition for Juvenile Justice (CJJ) from
2007 to 2009, he and CJJ staff collaboratively co-directed a major advocacy
effort to shape the bill developed in the Senate Judiciary Committee to re-
authorize the Juvenile Justice and Delinquency Prevention Act (Coalition
for Juvenile Justice, 2009; S. 678, 2009). Here, Jenkins describes how he

obtained his position in state government and his contributions to passage of the legislation prohibiting the jailing of status offenders:

> In 2009 I was asked to become the Chief Deputy Secretary of the Department of Juvenile Justice in North Carolina. One of my partners on the North Carolina Governor's Crime Commission and the State Advisory Group was asked to be the Secretary of that department. Her name was Linda Hayes. Linda was the former Chair of the Governor's Crime Commission and the state's Juvenile Justice Advisory Group. Linda and I had developed a very close working relationship. She was pretty integrated into the North Carolina political system, but she didn't really have any formal program or operating background in the stuff that I knew about. She did have an excellent knowledge base, however. When Linda was asked to be the Secretary, she came to me and said, "Look, we have this amazing opportunity. I really need you to be my Chief Deputy."
>
> North Carolina is a funny state in that you're treated as an adult at 16, which is different than 48 other states. For that reason, we were at odds with federal law around how we treat status offenders. It took us a couple of years, but in working with some lobbyists, advocacy organizations, legal experts at the UNC School of Government, my Governor's Crime Commission partners and the governor's office, we were able to get the law changed to make it illegal to lock up status offenders any more. In large measure because of that, we've been able to reduce detention in North Carolina by 22%.
>
> The benefit of being [in state government] is that I've had the opportunity to work at the highest level relative to discussing and maybe influencing policy. The limitation is that being in an executive branch agency there are strict ethics and rule limitations of the type of policy work I can do, and how I do it. Everything needs to be supportive of the current government, for example. That's an opportunity if the governor has certain values and is focused on the policy goals that I also hope to accomplish. On the other hand, if there is diversion from what I'd like to accomplish, it [my goals] can die a quick death.
>
> There are a number of strategies to address that limitation, though. We have a Legislative Affairs Office in my organization. Working along with them, it becomes bigger than me, maybe a larger organizational issue or couched in terms of a budget or efficiency argument versus a sheer policy argument. Also, I can't go down and lobby the legislature, but if asked, I can educate them. And we get invited to a number of state-level meetings where we get updates on what's happening through state and national advocacy groups. In a sense it's an educational approach, iterative and relational. We can educate them and talk about things relative to budget, policy, or

impacts, and build trust as well as a reputation for having the expertise to best inform various issues.

I'm involved in Reclaiming Futures, a national and state-level juvenile justice, substance abuse reform effort. In this case, we haven't been able to effectively make the case for the fiscal, social, and human benefits from the proposed policy—because the research is not there yet. However, like any major systems reform, the theoretical groundwork is there and we're on the way to demonstrating its positive effects on youths and their families impacted by substance use/abuse.

Working in a state-level executive branch, Jenkins utilized several strategies to influence policy formulation concerning youth who had committed status offenses. Prior relationships established by Jenkins with the Governor's Crime Commission were important both in leading to his appointment to government and in effectively influencing legislation. Consistent with several case studies in this chapter, outside advocacy groups are once again singled out as important in helping to achieve the goals of executive branch officials, in this case at the state level. Also of note, Jenkins attributes the lack of policy influence concerning the Reclaiming Futures initiative, at least in part, to the absence of supportive policy-relevant research.

The final example focuses on a psychologist who has worked toward mental health systems reform in multiple states and through multiple vantage points.

Child Mental Health System Reform
in Virginia
Robert Cohen

PhD, Clinical Psychology, Syracuse University, 1968

Clinical Professor, Virginia Commonwealth University and Independent Consultant, Richmond, VA

Robert Cohen, a clinical-community psychologist, has held both policy insider and academic positions during his career. As the Associate Commissioner for Program Development (1978–82) and subsequently for Policy Analysis (1982–84) in the New York State Office of Mental Health, Cohen conducted policy analyses that led to mental health reform. During several decades of work in Virginia as Director of the Virginia Treatment Center for Children (1984–2002), Cohen played various roles contributing to children's mental health systems reform. The Comprehensive Services Act (CSA; csa.virginia.gov), signed into law in 1993, created a collaborative system of services and funding for troubled youth. Cohen's contributions to CSA included an early mental health services study that helped stimulate the decision to reform the system, leadership of a major committee that designed a new mental health service model for the state, and formal and informal advisory roles to help reform the new system over the years. Cohen describes the ways in which their initial service model was compromised by political, economic, and cultural forces—a process he is currently detailing in a book that examines the decades-long process of system-of-care reform in Virginia. Here, Cohen highlights several aspects of his involvement in contributing to the development of the system of care for troubled youth in Virginia:

> I was hired to be the director of the Virginia Treatment Center for Children, which at the time was part of the State Department of Mental Health. It was the flagship child facility. The commissioner said very clearly he was hiring me because he wanted me to be involved at the state level. . . . I spent three months gathering data and doing a mini policy analysis, with a focus on central Virginia and how we could create a better, less fragmented system of care. Based on our model, I was invited to chair a workgroup for the whole state. We came up with a plan which had some concrete recommendations, including doing some pilot programs in the five regions to show better integration and systems of care.
>
> Then the head of Health and Human Resources organized a bigger initiative. It had 145 people. I was invited to chair the group that developed the service model, excluding the financing or the governance. The planning effort, over a multiyear period, defined a system of care for the state.
>
> The bill was submitted to the legislature. Some agencies didn't like giving up power, so they lobbied their localities that this was a bad bill. There was a lot of horse trading and negotiating to take this very idyllic model and translate it into terms that would be acceptable to the body politic.
>
> Once it was implemented, I was called back five years later because it wasn't working the way they wanted it to. They wanted to look into managed care. There was a debate about what kind of managed care. We did a feasibility study and then proposed basically a decision support system, not a hard and fast managed care. That was implemented with assessment models, etc.
>
> Fast-forward another ten years. The new Republican governor hires an orthopedic surgeon to be his health and human services person. I meet him, we hit it off, and I spend two years educating him on what the problems are and what needs to be done. Finally, as my last step, I decided to do a book on these long-term consequences because I'd seen

what happens between the original intent of a policy and then how it evolves given changes in the culture, politics, and finances. Virginia has worked diligently to correct some of the earlier problems. Even after 20 years, large scale policy initiatives can be adjusted to reduce unintended consequences produced by the initial legislation.

Cohen contributed to statewide child mental health system reform in Virginia in various ways over the course of several decades, utilizing systems analysis, relationship-building, management, and consultation skills. His early assessment of problems of fragmentation in the existing mental health system helped to justify the case for reform (in a similar process to that described in Connecticut, pp. 126–129). Cohen chaired several committees as part of the reform process, proposing a new service system model. The model was compromised in significant ways, however, and in later years Cohen consulted informally with those seeking further reform. This case illustrates the complexity and challenges involved in changing systems, including the inevitable unintended consequences and the potential for psychologists to contribute importantly to policy development and reform over an extended period of time.

Summary

The six examples of psychologists at work in the executive branch reveal similarities as well as differences in efforts to influence policy formulation and implementation. The case examples share a number of key direct policy influence methods and skills used, such as networking and relationship-building, management, strategic analysis, and working indirectly through others to influence legislation. Another relatively consistent theme is the importance of direct or indirect connections with intermediaries, including, in some cases, advocacy groups. Of note, working inside executive agencies allows psychologists to utilize content expertise central to their disciplinary background and training.

Influencing Policy from the Vantage Point of Policy Insider: Benefits and Limitations

Most of the policy insiders interviewed, whether in the legislative or executive branch, underscore the importance—and in many cases the excitement—of being close to the action. In fact, the ability to have influence is the most frequently cited benefit of doing policy work within government. There is also near consensus that

although the insider position provides the power to make decisions, it also car-
ries limitations in the ability to speak freely about policy issues. Usually this is
because interviewees feel that they are "beholden to someone else." In addition,
the desire to focus on policy content areas of personal interest or involvement in
activities directly related to one's training (e.g., conducting empirical research or
in-depth reviews of literature) generally takes a back seat to the pressing issues at
hand. For many policy insiders, adaptability and flexibility are the keys to success.
Furthermore, despite the limitations, those interviewed emphasize that as long as
their policy work aligns with their values and the values of their higher-ups, working as a policy insider can be exhilarating.

We close the chapter with six interview excerpts that illustrate the benefits and
the limitations of a policy insider role as the vantage point from which to influence
policy. Although the context differs across interviewees—ranging from national
legislative or executive branch to state-level to local community contexts—many
of those interviewed describe similar benefits and limitations. For those involved
in Congress, for example, one theme that emerges as both a positive and negative feature of working to effect change is the rapid pace of policy work. Taryn
Morrisey describes this as a benefit, "it's so fast and you do have a lot of power of
the pen," but she also notes that this can be a limitation when "decisions have to
be made, whether or not you are the best person to make them." Multiple perspectives related to a policy initiative may not be heard at times because of the speed
with which policy decisions need to be made, and, once a decision is made, there
may be little possibility of follow-up. Jill Hunter-Williams, introduced earlier
(pp. 66–67) explains this latter dynamic:

> The benefits are that you really get to shape things. You're well situated.
> But it all depends on if your boss is on the right committee and if he has
> an avenue by which to affect the legislation. Also, while you can make
> pretty significant changes, you're very limited in terms of follow through.
> And, I deal with 18 million things, whatever is coming at me, and it's very
> hard for me to follow up.

As a result of handling a broad range of issues, interviewees describe the need to
have a generalist knowledge base when working for a member of Congress. In
contrast, Taryn Morrisey discusses the benefit of being focused on a particular
issue when working for a federal agency:

> In Congress, decisions have to be made. You have to do something to
> take action. But often, on the other hand, you're an extension of your
> boss. You can't go too far. Here at HHS you get more of a chance to be
> a little slower, plan more and be more methodical. On a committee in
> the health office, I covered everything from mental health to child and

maternal health to work force issues to environmental health to women's health. Here I'm only covering early childhood. It's much more focused. You do get to go a lot deeper.

Whereas some describe serving as an extension of their boss as a limitation, others describe it as a benefit—especially when their values align with those of the elected official for whom they are working. Roberta Downing notes the benefit of working for an elected official whom you respect:

> I don't know if you're familiar with Senator Brown, but he's just a great guy. He's a genuine person and genuinely cares about poverty and inequality. If I could work on the Hill again for a member that I respected, I would love to. But . . . it would have to be when both my kids are a lot older.

Although many interviewees describe the role of policy insider as rewarding, they also note limitations related to publicly sharing personal beliefs and perspectives. As Ron Haskins describes:

> I wouldn't give up my experience in Congress for anything, but I'm glad I'm ending my career on the outside. In the Congress, you can actually change policy. That's its great advantage. But you can't be public, go your own way, and say what you really think. To me at least, that's a serious limit and a big part of why I eventually left Congress. I'm glad I'm ending my career on the written products (the legacy) you leave behind, but I'm also very thankful that I had a chance to influence the law.

Another major benefit of working as a policy insider is observing firsthand the process of policymaking. Robert Cohen, former Associate Commissioner at the New York State Office of Mental Health, describes his experience learning how policy really worked. He also notes a corresponding limitation of policy insider work emphasized by a number of others:

> The benefit of my work as associate commissioner is that I was right in the middle of things. I was close to the decision-makers and got to understand how things really worked. I refer to it as my . . . boot camp experience. The limitation is you're pretty much limited in what you can say because you work for people who are beholden to political figures. That's gotten worse over time.

Being close to the policy action is cited as a benefit across varied local, state, and national contexts. At the same time, as an elected official, another potential benefit is being connected to communities at the ground level. Bill Berkowitz, professor emeritus University of Massachusetts, Lowell, and Arlington Town Meeting member discusses this advantage:

> The Town Meeting is the legislative body of the town. At the time I ran [1982] it was hard to win a town meeting seat. I campaigned hard and won. I wanted to be more connected with the town just on a personal level, and I liked the grassroots democracy of the Town Meeting system. It seemed like a good, fun, and growing thing for me to do and something that I would enjoy. I've been in Town Meeting ever since. . . . I learned about how local policy is made. I get a chance to use my persuasion skills and policy skills. And over the years, I might have swayed a few decisions. It's been one of the best things I think I've done in my life.

The opportunity to directly and actively contribute to policy represents a major attraction of the policy insider role, whether at the federal, state, or local level. Key limitations include the inability to pursue and publicly share personal ideas and perspectives (for staff) and lack of opportunity to focus in depth over time on a specific topic of interest (both staff and elected officials). These are two important hallmarks of scholarship. In the next chapter, we return to our earlier focus on those who pursue research and scholarship to examine the characteristics of policy-relevant research and scholarship that make a difference in the policy arena.

6

Policy-Relevant Research

Characteristics and Pathways to Policy Influence

> *The university defendants have presented this court with solid evidence regarding the educational benefits that flow from a racially and ethnically diverse student body.*
>
> —Federal District Judge Patrick Duggan,
> cited in US District Court, 2000, p. 21

Among the many assets the discipline of psychology brings to the policy arena, perhaps the most distinctive is our research and scholarship base. The vast magnitude and variety of published research studies provide a potentially rich repository of knowledge with which to influence policymakers. Unfortunately, a major challenge to the use of most psychology research and scholarship is their limited policy relevance. Many factors contribute to this challenge, including:

- A focus on conceptual/theoretical considerations rather than practical/policy implications when designing research
- The difficulty in generalizing from work conducted in tightly controlled situations to real-world contexts and populations
- Threats to internal validity that limit the interpretability of findings when research is conducted in real-world contexts
- The lack of direct applicability of most findings to specific policy decisions because academic researchers rarely consult stakeholders in the social policy arena when they are developing their research questions

In addition, a number of practical matters limit the policy relevance of research, including the lack of timeliness. The policy formulation process often leads policymakers to adopt an "I don't need it perfect, I need it today" perspective. In contrast, academics are rewarded for the quality of research, which often requires in-depth analysis; multiple waves of data; and detailed, multifaceted depiction of both methods and findings. Thus, researchers have a difficult time producing research on a rushed timeline and feel uneasy about sharing "not yet ready" results or conclusions. Furthermore, the sites where research is published (inaccessible academic journals), how research is written (in technical language), and its lengthiness reduce the likelihood that it will be read by busy policymakers or their staff.

These challenges notwithstanding, psychology research actually can (and sometimes does) influence policy. There does not appear, however, to be a predictable or specific type of research or a defined amount of evidence that distinguishes research that influences policy from that which does not. This chapter depicts a wide array of types of research that interviewees report as their greatest policy successes, shedding light on the diverse pathways through which policy influence occurs.

The chapter is organized around four broad classes of scholarship: program evaluation research, research to enhance understanding of phenomena of interest, research on system policies and practices, and research to generate practical aids for implementing agencies. Fourteen brief case examples are presented across these classes of scholarship. We begin with program evaluation research, which in some cases involves psychologists in the joint roles of program developer and evaluator.

Program Evaluation Research

Ron Haskins, a psychologist with a great amount of experience in the policy domain, shared the following observation during our interview: "If you really want to have an impact on policy, you need a program. That's the most direct way. And you have to have the data to show that it can make a difference." In fact, the majority of the 79 individuals interviewed for this book indicate that outcome evaluation studies, and in particular those demonstrating cost-effectiveness, are especially likely to have policy impact. The example of the Nurse Family Partnership prevention program presented in Chapter 3 is one striking instance of such influence.

Program evaluation research takes various forms depending on the purpose of the research, the type of research design, the type of intervention program, and the relationship of the program evaluator to the program. Thirteen of the psychologists interviewed for this volume consider the influence of program evaluation studies they conducted as their greatest policy success (see Table 6.1). Here, five examples are presented. Three cases involve psychologists developing new programs and then conducting controlled trials to evaluate them. The fourth involves a mixed-methods participatory design, and the fifth consists of meta-analysis. The pathways to policy influence are as diverse as the research methods, including involvement on a governmental advisory board, consultation to executive branch agencies, and advocacy. In the first example, a new approach to addressing homelessness was developed, evaluated, and widely disseminated.

Table 6.1 **Program Evaluation Research: Policy Issue, Psychologist, Research Method, Policy Influence, and Policy Influence Method**

Policy Issue (Psychologist)	Research Method (Program Role)	Policy Influence	Policy Influence Method
Homelessness, pathways to housing (Tsemberis; Shinn)*	Controlled trial (program developer)	Adopted throughout country and internationally	Nonprofit Association; NYC Homeless Advisory Board
Foster care, behavior problems (Chamberlain)*	Controlled trials (program developer)	Adopted throughout country and internationally	Consultation with Foster Care Systems
Federal education policy (Slavin)*	Controlled trials (program developer)	Contribution to education reform	Lobbying Activities
College in prison (Fine)*	Quasi-experimental	Support for legislative changes and executive branch pilot program	Consultation with Policymakers and Advocacy Groups
Juvenile justice programs (Lipsey)*	Meta-analysis	Contribution to systems reform	Consultation with Juvenile Justice Systems
Home visiting-nurse family partnership (Olds)**(3)	Controlled trials (program developer)	Supported by national legislation	Affiliated Organization Works with Agencies, Policymakers
Home visiting programs (Brooks Gunn)**(3)	Systematic review of evaluation studies	Support for national legislation	Congressional testimony

(continued)

Table 6.1 **Continued**

Policy Issue (Psychologist)	Research Method (Program Role)	Policy Influence	Policy Influence Method
Social and emotional learning (Weissberg)**(3)	Meta-analysis; Systematic review; Evaluation studies	Illinois SEL legislation and K–12 learning standards	Advisory Board; Consultation
Substance abuse prevention (Chavis)**(4)	Quasi-experimental	RFPs for drug free communities support programs	Consultation; Collaboration with Advocacy Group; Evaluation Report
Unemployment and mental help: Jobs Club (Price)**(7)	Controlled trial (program developer)	Adopted by governments around world	Media; Dissemination; Consultation
Delinquency prevention: Buddy System (O'Donnell)**(7)	Controlled trial (program developer)	Adopted in several states	Consultation with Agencies in Several States
Two-generation program (Chase-Lansdale)**(7)	Controlled trial	(in process)	(in process)
Child and family support: Sure Start (Belsky)**(7)	Quasi-experimental	Changes in national program	Consultation; Report
Prevention of youth violence (Tolan)**(8)	Systematic review of evaluation studies	Support for evidence-based approach	Surgeon General's Report; Blueprints Website

* Covered in this chapter.
** (X) = Chapter number where presented as case example.

Pathways to Housing: A National Model to Address Homelessness

Sam Tsemberis

PhD, Clinical-Community Psychology, New York University, 1985

Executive Director, Pathways to Housing, New York, New York

Marybeth Shinn

PhD, Community and Social Psychology, University of Michigan, 1978

Professor and Chair, Department of Human and Organizational Development, Vanderbilt University

In 1992, clinical-community psychologist Sam Tsemberis designed Pathways to Housing. The New York City program offered homeless individuals living on the streets apartments of their own with private landlords, without prerequisites for sobriety or participation in treatment (Pathways to Housing, 2015; Tsemberis, 2010). This program also offered them control, as consumers, over any services they received. This approach—which emerged from Tsemberis' conversations with homeless individuals about their needs and preferences—directly contrasted with the prevailing philosophy of providing services before housing. Initial outcome data were striking (84% stability in housing for participants vs. 30% for the existing system), but the research was criticized due to design limitations.

Tsemberis approached Marybeth ("Beth") Shinn, a community-social psychologist and homelessness researcher, to aid in the development of a *randomized controlled trial* (a study in which participants are randomly assigned to an experimental or control group). The findings revealed significantly greater stability in housing and much reduced use of supportive housing and services for program participants compared to controls, with associated cost savings (Gulcur, Stefancic, Shinn, Tsemberis, & Fischer, 2003; Tsemberis, Moran, Shinn, Asmussen, & Shern, 2003). Based on these findings, Tsemberis, along with advocacy groups, advocated for enhanced funding. Shinn in turn shared the findings with state and city officials, the latter while serving on the Research Advisory Board of the New York City Department of Homeless Services (Maton, Humphreys, Jason & Shinn, in press). The "Housing First" approach has now been implemented around the country, aided by a strong endorsement from the Federal Interagency Council on Homelessness (US Interagency Council, 2010). Housing First is

believed to account for a 13.5% decline in the number of chronically home-
less people between 2007 and 2011 (one-night count; US Department of
Housing and Urban Development, 2012). Outside the United States, the
Pathways Housing First model has been adopted in Canada, Japan, the
Netherlands, Spain, and Portugal.

Shinn continues to advise the New York City Department of Homeless
Services. Most recently, the City adopted her empirical targeting/screen-
ing model to direct services to individuals at high risk of homelessness
(Shinn, Greer, Bainbridge, Kwon, & Zuiderveen, 2013). Here, Shinn and
Tsemberis highlight their work on Pathways to Housing. Shinn first shares
her perspective on the program's development and the need for a controlled
experiment:

> Sam [Tsemberis] was on the van that went around and pulled people
> off the streets if the temperature dropped too low, and they were
> likely to freeze. He talked to people and asked them why they weren't
> going to the shelters. They told him that they didn't want to be regi-
> mented. They wanted freedom. He worked with consumers to set up
> a consumer-run drop-in center, a self-governing place where people
> could come in out of the cold. Sam asked the consumers what they
> wanted the most. Their overwhelming response was that they wanted
> housing, but they didn't want to go to these housing programs that
> required them to be clean and sober, participate in treatment on the
> program's terms, and take medications. As Sam put it, "We were tell-
> ing them to take the drugs we wanted them to take, but not the drugs
> they wanted to take."
>
> Then he started the Housing First program called Pathways to
> Housing. The initial data indicated that Pathways' consumers were more
> stable than people in more traditional programs, funded by the same
> city-wide program, the New York/New York Agreement. When Sam pre-
> sented the data, the people who ran the more traditional programs said,
> "Your people aren't like our people. Our people could never live in apart-
> ments all by themselves." Sam decided that it was time for an experiment.

Tsemberis continues the narrative:

> We needed people of tremendous credibility and objectivity to do the ex-
> periment. I was already the PI of a grant that was studying the program,
> but I had invented the program, so people would assume bias. I needed
> to separate myself from the evaluation. Beth was a mentor of mine from
> NYU and was keen to do the evaluation piece. I knew that Beth was one

of the most qualified researchers in the country, and with her we would get the best possible design.

Shinn briefly describes the results:

Sam brought me in, and we worked on the experiment that showed that folks randomly assigned to Pathways to Housing, as opposed to randomly assigned to a control group, were much more stably housed. They were housed faster and stayed indoors better. The bottom line was 99 fewer days homeless in the first year. It was a whopping kind of effect. From there, Sam has really built Housing First.

Tsemberis provides his perspective on how that happened:

There are different ways to advocate. I think my strength is in being able to present the mental health housing programs from the perspective of the consumer. This is an eye opener for clinicians, validating for consumers, and intriguing to policymakers. I asked the question: If it doesn't work well, why are we still using this? My goal is to accurately represent the beliefs and values of consumers who are all too seldom invited to give their point of view. While Housing First is an evidence-based intervention, it has a rights-based foundation. We offer housing as a basic human right, not as something that people with mental illness have to earn by proving that they are ready or worthy. We have the evidence that shows Housing First is the effective, smart choice for housing the chronically homeless. The social justice piece tells you it's the more human choice.

Policymakers want to know how the policy will affect tax payers, and Housing First has proven to be more cost-effective than the traditional model. The Canadian national study of Housing First by the Mental Health Commission of Canada changed Canada's federal policy on housing by showing that the Housing First model was more cost-effective. The study showed great outcomes on housing stability, but the most attractive finding for politicians was that for every $3 invested in Housing First, $10 were saved. To end homelessness, we should focus less on treatment compliance and focus more on affordable housing and ending poverty. It is less about Freud and more about Marx.

Changing policy requires teamwork. Changing systems is a complex task and undertaken at many different levels. Those working in the system need to understand the reasons for change from their own perspective. Expert testimony on political panels and in class action suits has helped to educate those in power. Housing First initiatives have recently garnered a fair amount of media coverage. One of the more effective advocates I have worked with is Philip Mangano, who was the Director of the United States Interagency Council, during George W. Bush's administration. Philip is a tremendously effective advocate and had great success in bringing Housing First into the national conversation. He wanted to abolish homelessness and preached that Housing First was the most effective way to do it. I was part of a team Philip assembled for his advocacy work around the country, "the band" we jokingly called ourselves. It included a top researcher, a skilled city administrator, Philip and me. Philip would set up meetings with mayors, governors, or other legislative committees, and we would go together and make the case. I also had success with a local champion in different European countries that was determined and skillful enough to introduce Housing First to their communities. Over time FEANTSA, a European think-tank and advocacy organization endorsed the model and accelerated its adaptation.

There are many different ways to advocate and create change. When it comes to social programs and program dissemination, the most successful approach is to start with a vision for a program and attempting it as a pilot project. You evaluate the pilot to document its effectiveness and then educate relevant policymakers about the results if you want to take it to scale. One of the reasons that we were effective is that we produced studies of the program from the very start, publishing outcomes in peer-reviewed journals. That takes the conversation about your program out of your local city, town, or community, and into the world of research and policy. That's a key bridge between working locally versus working globally.

The development of an innovative and impactful program, combined with a strong case for cost-savings, provided a foundation for successful policy influence. This case highlights that concerted advocacy and collaboration, together with the support of key national advocacy organizations and the contributions of valued research experts, enhance the odds for successful policy influence. Furthermore, Tsemberis notes the importance of disseminating findings early on in order to build and maintain relationships with key stakeholders, including policymakers and practitioners.

The next example highlights a program developed by a research scientist to reform the foster care system. In this case, the primary policy role reported is that of consultant, rather than advocate.

Multidimensional Treatment Foster Care: Controlled Trials, Consultation, and Systems Reform

Patricia Chamberlain

PhD, Educational Psychology, University of Oregon, 1980

Science Director, Oregon Research Learning Center, Eugene, Oregon

Patricia Chamberlain, a clinical psychologist, developed Multidimensional Treatment Foster Care (MTFC), a multifaceted intervention that provides behavior management parent training to foster parents. This training aims to reduce rates of externalizing and mental health problems in foster care children and youth. The case management and therapeutic services typically last 6 to 9 months and require close collaboration among all parties involved in a child's life, including foster parents, birth parents, program supervisor, case worker, and others (e.g., parole or probation officer, teachers). Controlled trials conducted by Chamberlain revealed fewer behavior problems, less recidivism, and lower rates of placement in more restrictive treatment settings for MTFC recipients versus controls (Chamberlain & Reid, 1991, 1998). Based on the positive findings and consultation services that she and colleagues provide, MTFC has been widely adopted within foster care systems around the country and internationally.

To enhance ease of implementation and to fit with local cultural contexts, Chamberlain developed a "cascading intervention" version of MTFC, a community participatory process in which strong partnerships among program developers, service agencies, and service providers are developed (Chamberlain, Price, Reid, & Landsverk, 2008). Those trained earlier on core MTFC components provide training to later cohorts. Most recently, Chamberlain has been working to reframe the role of the foster care caseworker in New York City. In the interview excerpt here, she describes the evolution of her research-based work to bring about change in foster care systems:

> My entree into trying to change systems is promoting research and evidence supported approaches. Then we come to the question of, "Can those really be done in the real world?" I started out working on a pretty complicated intervention, multidimensional treatment foster care

model. It mobilizes resources that exist in the community to keep kids from getting placed in these very high-end institutional settings where they are disconnected more from their communities, families, and schools and good things are not happening.

We can get that [mobilizing resources] to happen, but there are so many moving parts to that intervention—that then influenced me to think more simply about it. What pieces could be taken and more widely disseminated? Then we got started on working with child welfare systems to make foster care more effective in a much simpler, cheaper way. We did a thing called Cascading Implementation. We trained the first cohort of people in the system. Then we had that cohort train the second cohort of people. We did research to examine if we get a decrement in effect. We were looking toward long-term sustainability and figuring out how to let go, keep the intervention effective and keep intervention fidelity going. That's the second initiative.

We've been working most recently with the New York City child welfare system. The project was initiated by Child Welfare System Commissioner Ron Richter. I had worked in New York City in a number of ways implementing the multidimensional treatment foster care model. We had some good success. . . . When they called and asked me to help them figure out how to change their practice, I was delighted. We've been re-conceptualizing the role of the case worker. We've been changing that role to be a much more hands-on, involved role with both the foster parents and biological parents or the after-care resource for the kids in foster care.

In this case example, as in the previous one, an innovative and well-researched cost-effective program became a national model, leading to widespread adoption. The developers modified the MTFC program in order to simplify implementation and enhance sensitivity to local culture and context, changes supported by careful research. Based on trust established in prior work together, new opportunities for policy influence arose initiated by the executive branch officials in one of the country's largest foster care systems.

In the next example, a controlled evaluation trial of an innovative program is again central. However, policy influence in this case goes beyond increases in program funding and widespread dissemination revealing the potential of experimental evaluations to contribute more broadly to federal government adoption of an evidence-based standard.

Success for All: Advocacy and Enhanced Focus on Evidence-Based Policy in Federal Education Policy

Robert Slavin

PhD, Social Relations, Johns Hopkins University, 1975

Director, Center for Research and Reform in Education, Johns Hopkins University

Robert Slavin, an educational psychologist, developed Success for All (SFA) in 1987. SFA is a whole-school reform model for students in prekindergarten through eighth grade with special focus on reading, writing, and oral language skills. The model includes a highly structured curriculum, frequent assessment, teacher learning, shared leadership, and strategies to build teacher buy-in. Key components include tutoring, across-grade ability grouping, and cooperative learning strategies.

Two national, randomly controlled trials revealed positive outcomes in reading (Borman et al., 2007; Quint et al., 2014; What Works Clearinghouse, 2014). The SFA foundation was developed in 1998, contributing to the program's national dissemination (successforall.org). The foundation employs a full-time policy staff person (lobbyist), along with development and dissemination staff. Slavin and the policy staff person advocate for SFA as well as for evidence-based education reform more broadly. Slavin views this advocacy work as contributing to the development of the Investing in Innovation (i3) competition, a US Department of Education initiative to enhance and scale-up evidence-based interventions. Here, Slavin describes his advocacy work in the education reform area:

> If we really wanted to have change [in education programming and policy] take place, there was going to have to be a change in the way evidence was used, with decisions about programs, practices, and policies themselves based on rigorous research. A lot of our policy efforts have been directed to create a policy environment that is conducive to Success for All and other programs that have been found to be effective. We were talking to anybody who would listen but particularly to staffers for the key congressional committees that deal with education and education appropriations. We found them to be very receptive to good information.

You never know whether your involvement was critical or even helpful when something goes right, but an area in which I'm sure it must
have been involved at some level is i3. It's the very first time that evidence of the effectiveness of educational programs mattered at all to
anything like federal policy or serious amounts of money. In order for
i3 to make any sense, there had to be some "lead-pipe cinch" programs
[programs completely certain to fit the requirements] that would be at
the front end of it. The fact that we had our Success for All programs
to offer as a clear example of what was meant by i3 must have made the
people who were making these decisions more comfortable that they
weren't going to have a party and nobody was going to show up at the
top levels of this.

As things turned out, among the programs that did get funded as scale-
ups in the first round, it was Success for All and Reading Recovery. Those
were the two things that really carried that banner saying, "Here are programs that not only have very deep evidence of effectiveness but have also
done some scale-up themselves and obviously are interested in scale-up because they have done it in the past."

In a certain way, in addition to providing some money, having validation or scaling of funding provides a certain federal imprimatur that
there is strong evidence behind your program. I think that's a major leap
forward. Then the i3 development grants are feeding the pipeline. . . .
The concept that there needs to be feeding of the whole pipeline—all
the way from funding a promising idea through to scaling up something
that's proven to work—is exceedingly old hat in medicine or agriculture
but brand-new and rather out there and risky for education.

Slavin's lobbying work began with his own program, SFA, but expanded to
include evidence-based education reform more generally. This broader focus
is in accordance with the advocacy work of many others interviewed for this
volume (e.g., David Olds; Edward Seidman) and in related groups and institutions (e.g., Coalition for Evidence-Based Policy; W. T. Grant Foundation).
Many factors and forces have contributed to the enhanced evidence-based
focus of social policy (Haskins & Margolis, 2014), one of which is the advocacy efforts of psychologists.

In the next example, we move from randomly controlled experimental studies to
a quasi-experimental study, one that emerged from a unique participatory action
collaboration.

College in Prison: A Mixed Methods Participatory Action Evaluation

Michelle Fine

PhD, Social Psychology, Teachers College, Columbia University, 1980

*Professor of Psychology, Women's Studies and Urban Education,
City University of New York*

Michele Fine is a social psychologist who has conducted many participatory action research projects. These projects vary in the degree to which they are intended to influence policymakers (e.g., Torre et al., 2008; Center for Human Environments, 2015). **Participatory action methods** involve in-depth collaboration between the researcher and those who are the focus of study, often in pursuit of change in current practices or policies. One of Fine's participatory action projects involved a multimethod evaluation of a college program in the Bedford Hills Correctional Facility (BHCF), a maximum security prison for women in Westchester County, New York. The program was closed down (along with 350 other college programs) upon passage of the 1994 federal Violent Crime Act, which prohibited federal funding, including Pell Grants, for college coursework in prisons.

Following the closure, a number of women involved in the BHCF program wanted to document its effects. The resulting evaluation, in collaboration with the prisoners, included individual interviews, focus groups, and quantitative examination of post-release outcomes. The sample comprised 274 women who attended college while in BHCF and a comparison group of 2,031 women who did not. The findings revealed markedly lower 36-month post-release recidivism rates for program participants (7.7%) than nonparticipants (29.9%) and included first-hand accounts of program benefits.

The evaluation report, *Changing Minds* (Fine et al., 2001), became a basis of ongoing advocacy work by Fine and others to support the return of college to prisons and helped stimulate additional research in the area (Davis, Bozick, Steele, Saunders, & Miles, 2013). As a result, state legislatures have passed supportive legislation (Gorgol & Sponsler, 2011), and, in 2015, the US Department of Education enacted an experimental pilot program that allows distribution of Pell Grants on a temporary basis to eligible incarcerated prisoners (Federal Register, 2015).

Fine highlights several policy-related aspects of the Changing Minds project:

> Bill Clinton signed the Violent Crime Act and took college out of prison. I had been doing some work at the prison in the college program when

Clinton pulled the plug. The women in the prison said, "We've really got to document the impact of college in prison." Even the correction officers knew that something needed to be done to restore college. A number of incarcerated women at the time, a bunch of my graduate students, and I then began the project, called Changing Minds. It's a quantitative-qualitative analysis of the impact [of college in prison] on children, women, recidivism, public safety, discipline in the prison, and the tax burden—because college reduces recidivism.

We sent a copy of the report to every governor in the country and to every state legislator in New York State. We produced organizing brochures in English and Spanish for community-based organizations. There was a guy named Michael Jacobson who I met at a meeting who works with an organization of state government officials. He brought together a group of folks from the governor's office, the Department of Education, the Department of Criminal Justice in New York State, and some prison advocates, victim-rights advocates, and me.

The struggle was twofold. One was to restore Pell Grants for folks in prison and the other was to support any college in prison, even if it was a private university initiative. Unfortunately, Pell Grants, to this day, have not been restored [by Congress]. However, there is a lot of movement on college in prison. There are universities offering programs within prisons, and post-prison college as re-entry. In some places there is legislation for minor support for college in prison for people who don't have violent records, who are under the age of 25, who don't have prior convictions, and who are going to get out soon. Even conservative legislators and governors have contacted us about getting copies of the report. It's because they're looking at their budgets and realizing that so much has been dedicated to prison, and they're trying to figure out what to do to reduce recidivism.

Quasi-experimental evaluation designs are commonplace. Many, like the current example, occur in contexts where random assignment is not possible. The results—together with ongoing advocacy efforts by multiple groups—have contributed to legislative changes and have helped to keep attention focused on the issue. Researchers who build and sustain relationships with policymakers and intermediary organizations are more likely to see their dissemination efforts result in policy influence than those who do not. The participatory action nature of Fine's evaluation, working in close collaboration with those affected by the issue, accentuates the "policy story" told. When co-authors presenting results are prisoners or prison program alums, the potential to engage audiences who have the power to work toward reform is enhanced.

In the final example, we turn to **meta-analysis**, an analytical approach to summarizing a body of research on program effectiveness. This method, which has become increasingly important, is particularly valuable when there is a substantial body of work that can be considered together to determine effect sizes. Meta-analysis answers the question of not just whether or not a program or approach works, but the size of its effect and what may account for cross-study differences.

Juvenile Justice System Reform: A Meta-analysis Examining Characteristics of Successful Programs

Mark Lipsey

PhD, Psychology, Johns Hopkins University, 1972

Research Professor of Education and Human Development, Vanderbilt University

Mark Lipsey, a psychology researcher who was an early adopter of meta-analysis, has exerted policy influence by using that method to identify characteristics of successful juvenile justice intervention programs (Lipsey, Howell, Kelly, Chapman, & Carver, 2010). Meta-analysis allows systematic analysis of the magnitude of effects of a set of evaluation studies, including analysis of the program characteristics that are linked to positive outcomes (e.g., intervention approach, implementation quality, type of sample, etc.; Lipsey & Wilson, 2001). Lipsey's (2009) meta-analysis of the characteristics of more than 600 juvenile justice interventions generated the following recommendations for juvenile justice systems:

- target high-risk rather than low-risk cases
- use programs with a therapeutic or constructive personal development focus rather than a control philosophy, and adopt the therapeutic programs with the largest effects
- implement the programs with sufficient dosage and quality (Lipsey et al., 2010)

Based on these rather straightforward but empirically well-supported findings, Lipsey developed a standardized program evaluation protocol (SPEP) to guide program selection and improvement. That instrument has served as a basis for consultation work done in multiple states with juvenile justice systems interested in making better use of evidence to improve their intervention programs for juvenile offenders (Lipsey et al., 2010).

Additionally, Lipsey coordinated a National Academy of Sciences report focused on enhancing the quality of program evaluations in the criminal justice area in ways that would produce even stronger evidence about effective practice (National Research Council, 2005). Here, Lipsey describes his meta-analysis and policy influence work in the juvenile justice area:

> I just charged along accumulating and interpreting the research on interventions with juvenile offenders in a largely academic fashion. We were publishing things that were supportive of the advocacy that was emerging for reassessing the potential for rehabilitation, particularly for juveniles, but not exploring the practical implications in much detail. However, that work did stimulate invitations to present some of the results to practitioners and policymakers, for example, at meetings of the National Council of Juvenile and Family Court Judges and the National Institute of Justice's annual research and evaluation conferences. Those meetings bring in a mix of government folks, practitioners, and applied researchers who showed particular interest in the practical implications of our developing meta-analysis results.
>
> Buddy Howell, the Research Director at the federal **Office of Juvenile Justice and Delinquency Prevention** (OJJDP), was very instrumental in helping me find ways to better connect my research to practice. He picked up on my work at an early stage and helped arrange OJJDP funding to support a critical update of the research included in the meta-analysis. When he retired and became more involved in consulting, he brought me along on some of his visits to juvenile justice agencies to tell them what we knew about what worked. Those experiences developed into something that my colleagues and I are now very involved in on a rather large scale. We developed a Standardized Program Evaluation Protocol, or the SPEP, that essentially translated the meta-analysis work we'd done into a data-driven scheme that allows the juvenile justice agencies to rate each of the programs for which there is an evidence base against the profile of what the research says should be most effective. The difference between telling people what works in conferences, papers, and so on and actually giving them an instrument and a scheme they can apply turns out to be huge. The SPEP version of the key findings of our meta-analyses has been of far greater interest and utility for juvenile justice practice than any publications we could have produced.

Lipsey's case highlights the policy influence of meta-analytic research findings that support the efficacy of one type of intervention approach (therapeutic) over another (control) in the area of juvenile justice. He presented his findings in multiple contexts and to multiple audiences (including executive agency officials). His relationship with a key official who understood the world of practice is what drew him into systems reform work. The critical bridge between these worlds was the transformation of the meta-analysis findings into the form of a practical instrument that could be used directly to facilitate agency decision-making. Additional examples of such instruments are presented in the "Practical Aids and Heuristic Guides" section of this chapter.

Summary

In most cases, program evaluation studies appear to have little influence on social policy (Johnson, Greenseid, Toal, King, Lawrenz, & Volkov, 2009). The five case examples just shared highlight instances in which they do. They range from cases in which the program evaluators are also the developers of innovative, cost-effective programs to collaborative action research to development of a practical tool to facilitate adoption of meta-analytic findings. Similar to work highlighted in previous chapters, policy influence is furthered in these five cases by active dissemination of findings to multiple audiences and pursuit of relationships with intermediary organizations and policy insiders over extended periods of time.

Next we turn to more traditional academic research: theory-based studies directed at understanding naturally occurring phenomena of interest.

Understanding Phenomena of Interest

Research that contributes to a theory-based understanding of the nature of phenomena represents the foundation of most scientific disciplines. In psychology, such research encompasses both laboratory and real-world contexts, spanning a massive range of phenomena—from brain function and structure, to cognition and affect, to child development and social behavior, to communities and cultures. Policy is most likely to be fundamentally influenced by research that contributes to novel understandings of populations and social problems—and that generates foundations for new approaches to social problems. Policy is also swayed by studies that dramatically highlight the magnitude (e.g., prevalence) of new or existing social problems.

Twelve of the psychologists interviewed for this volume describe their greatest policy success as research focused on understanding the nature or magnitude of phenomena (see Table 6.2). Here, four examples are presented, including:

- social psychological research on the benefits of a diverse social environment for college students

Table 6.2 **Understanding Phenomena of Interest: Policy Issue, Psychologist, Research Method, Policy Influence, and Policy Influence Method**

Policy Issue (Psychologist)	Research Method	Policy Influence	Policy Influence Method
Affirmative action: college admissions (Gurin)*	Laboratory and survey research	Decision in favor of race-based admission policies	Expert report
Positive youth development (Lerner)*	Youth development studies and conceptual models	Science policy; Federal mentoring initiative	Dissemination Consultation
Chronic fatigue disease/ME (Jason)*	Epidemiology	Change in funding levels, name of disease	HHS Advisory Board; Work with advocacy organization
Undocumented immigrants: adult education (Yoshikawa)*	Ethnography	City Council of New York Adult Education Program	Consultation with advocacy organization and implementing organizations
Child obesity: sugar-sweetened beverage taxes (Brownell)**(3)	Economic modeling Focus groups Meta-analysis survey research	(Legislation proposed in many states and cities)	Media; Legislative tracking and outreach; Work with advocacy organizations
Abandoned housing and crime (Speer)**(3)	Action-research Geographic Information Systems	Camden Community Housing Campaign	Collaboration with grassroots advocacy organization
Gay rights (Herek)**(3)	Prevalence studies Social psychology field research	Federal and state supreme court cases	Expert report Expert witness

(*continued*)

Table 6.2 **Continued**

Policy Issue (Psychologist)	Research Method	Policy Influence	Policy Influence Method
Child witness testimony (Goodman)**(3)	Developmental field research	Supreme court case; Child advocacy centers	Expert witness Expert report
Gender discrimination (Fisk, Borgida, & Deaux)**(3, 7)	Experimental studies	*Price v. Waterhouse* supreme court and other court cases	Expert witness Expert report
Youth legal competence (Steinberg; Grisso; Reppucci; Woolard)**(3,7)	Developmental research	*Roper v. Simmons*	Extensive media and advocacy work
Children's TV: regulation (Huston)**(7)	Developmental research	Children's Television Act	Congressional testimony Consultation
Utilities rate restructuring (Fawcett) (**8)	Survey research	Utilities rate restructuring ordinance	Presentation to Lawrence (KS) City Commission

* Covered in this chapter.

** (X) = Chapter number where presented as case example.

- developmental research espousing a positive youth development perspective
- a community-based ethnographic study of undocumented immigrant parents and their children
- an epidemiological study examining the prevalence of chronic fatigue syndrome/myalgic encephalomyelitis

Once again, the pathways to policy influence are varied, encompassing diverse policy influence methods and all three branches of government.

In the first example, social psychological (and other) research is applied to a major affirmative action lawsuit.

Affirmative Action Lawsuit at University of Michigan: Social Psychological Research

Patricia Gurin

PhD, Social Psychology, University of Michigan, 1964

Professor Emerita of Psychology and Women's Studies, University of Michigan

Patricia Gurin, a social psychologist, prepared one of the expert witness reports for the *Gratz v. Bollinger* affirmative action lawsuit against the University of Michigan. The lawsuit asserted that the admissions system of the university, which automatically awarded points toward admission for students of color, was unconstitutional. Gurin's report included a review of available studies, as well as the results from analyses she performed on survey data from University of Michigan entering freshmen and graduating seniors. The report drew on Gurin's expertise in the area and available research to demonstrate a "compelling state interest" for use of an admissions policy that took into account race/ethnicity when admitting students. Specifically, the report argued that, based on extant research evidence, a diverse student body contributes in critical ways to cognitive development, identity development, and development of citizen skills and sentiments in ways that are essential for a democracy (Gurin, 1999*a*).

Surveys of the student body at University of Michigan indicated that there was an increase in the number of interracial relationships reported by students from prior to college to senior year. This included the development of close friends from another racial group and enhanced quality of interracial interactions. The data also suggested that classroom diversity contributed to an understanding of those different from oneself (Gurin, 1999*b*). The Federal District judge hearing the case ruled in favor of the University of Michigan.

Here, Gurin describes key aspects of her contribution to the affirmative action case:

Nancy Cantor, the provost here [at the time], asked me to be the expert witness to address compelling state interest, the second of two counts:

- *Do you have a compelling university interest which can be a compelling state interest?*
- *Do you use affirmative action to achieve this compelling state interest* (which in our case was diversity)?

We used the (limited) data that were available and crafted an expert report. It took about a year and a half. We submitted it in 1998.

What I tried to do is frame the value of diversity in three ways. One is how students cognitively grow in these post or later adolescent years, and a second is identity. All of the stuff on discontinuity and discrepancy from the cognitive literature became very relevant for how to frame what diversity is for students at Michigan, where 95% of the White students come from homogeneous White environments. What is diversity? It's discontinuous from the home environment. It's a discrepant set of situations. What does that do? At least to some extent, thinking comes from novelty, discrepancy, where you have to pay attention in the environment. That was enormously helpful for giving me a handle on why diversity should create a learning environment for students where they could deal with differences, raising questions and puzzling "what the hell is going on here?" Then the other big goal of higher education, apart from individual learning is, for many institutions, creating citizens. Once the public educational institutions, such as University of Michigan [1817] and University of Virginia [1819] began to be formed . . . a huge goal of most has been to create democratic sentiments and skills. How do you get those if you're going to be in an environment that's made up of all kinds of people and you don't know anything about them or how to deal with them? That literature, especially sociology and political science, but I could also draw from social psychology, was enormously helpful.

The undergraduate case judge was a Reagan appointee and very conservative, but agreed to make a decision or what is called a summary judgment based on the written materials. He ruled in favor of Michigan on both counts, both on narrow tailoring and compelling state interest.

This example illustrates the potential of research, both laboratory and field-based, to contribute to a major social policy decision. As Federal District Court Judge Patrick Duggan wrote in his opinion, "The university defendants have presented this court with solid evidence regarding the educational benefits that flow from a racially and ethnically diverse student body. This court is persuaded, based upon the record before it, that a racially and ethnically diverse student body produces significant educational benefits such that diversity, in the context of higher education, constitutes a compelling governmental interest under strict scrutiny" (US District Court, 2000).

In the next example, we move from an instrumental to a conceptual use of research and from a direct to a primarily indirect pathway of policy influence.

Strengths-based Positive Youth Development Perspective: Applied Developmental Psychology

Richard M. Lerner

PhD, Developmental Psychology, City University of New York, 1971

Professor and Chair, Applied Development Science, Tufts University

Richard M. Lerner, an applied developmental psychologist, has helped to promote a positive youth development perspective to guide research, practice, and policy focused on our nation's youth. Such a perspective emphasizes the strengths rather than the deficits in youth and champions after-school youth programming and civic engagement as critical practice and policy approaches. Lerner's policy-relevant scholarship in this area encompasses numerous empirical studies, book chapters, and edited volumes (e.g., Lerner & Benson, 2003; Lerner, Boyd, Kiely, Napolitano, & Schmid, 2010; Lerner & Galambos, 1998; Lerner, Lerner, von Eye, & Lewin-Bizan, 2009).

Lerner is the first to acknowledge that he has focused his energies on scholarship rather than on direct policy work, but believes his scholarship (and that of other researchers) has indirectly impacted policy through its influence on important leaders and funders in the area of youth-based research and programs. For example, government officials in the Office of Juvenile Justice and Delinquency Prevention (OJJDP) asked Lerner to consult on how to infuse a positive youth development perspective into their federal youth mentoring initiative.

Here, Lerner describes his work in positive youth development and its direct and indirect policy influences:

> I think my greatest [policy related] success is that my scholarship has changed the way the leadership of youth programs in this nation approach young people, including leaders of programs like the National 4-H Council, Boy Scouts of America, and major funders both in government and the private sector. They take a strength-based, positive development promotion approach as well as a problem-prevention approach, so I think my scholarship has been important. It's not the only source of this change, certainly. There are Peter Benson, Bill Damon, Reed Larson, Jacque Eccles, Jean Rhodes, and Jeanne Brooks-Gunn and I could go on and on. There are other people who have done more and better than me certainly, but I think I contributed to what has really been a sea- change

in the way people in leadership roles think about how we develop action strategies for young people.

I have worked with OJJDP to help them bring a positive youth-development perspective to the mentoring initiatives that they're charged with promoting across the nation. I've done that through being a scholar and not through being someone who identifies himself as a policymaker. We tried to help them think through what taking a Positive Youth Development perspective to mentoring programs would look like. How can you use the strengths of that young person to promote the positive goals that they have as opposed to just working to reduce the negative aspects of their behavior? They issued a RFP [Request for Proposals] to create sort of a national mentoring center that would be involved with evaluation and training precisely along these lines.

I have both authored and edited books on the role of policies and programs in youth development. I participate in symposiums at conferences. For instance, I finished in 2013 editing an issue of *Future of Children* on military children and families. I worked with Colonel (Ret.) Steve Cozza, of the Uniformed Services University of the Health Sciences, and Ron Haskins of Brookings Institution to author a policy brief, which served as a basis for a conference at Brookings on October 1, 2013. There were people from the military and the government talking about the implications of the scholarship about children, their parents, and military settings for policies and programs. That's how I approach it.

The case example reflects the policy-influence potential of scholarship that promotes a new way of looking at a population. Specifically, this developmental research focuses on the strengths and positive development of all youth, including at-risk or troubled youth. Such scholarship appears especially likely to reach the attention of policymakers when it is associated with feasible and cost-effective ways of addressing the population, in this case positive youth development programs (e.g., mentoring). Lerner's work is widely disseminated through multiple means. This is likely due, in part, to the dissemination efforts of national youth organization leaders and related groups that positive youth development scholarship has influenced.

In the next example, the focus moves to a rarely used methodology in psychology: ethnography.

Adult Education for Undocumented Immigrants: Contributions of Ethnographic Research

Hirokazu Yoshikawa

PhD, Clinical Psychology, New York University, 1998

Professor of Globalization and Education, New York University

Hirokazu Yoshikawa, a clinical-community psychologist, produced a book-length ethnographic study, *Immigrants Raising Children: Undocumented Parents and Their Young Children* (Yoshikawa, 2011). **Ethnographic research** generates in-depth description of a culture, population, or setting based on systematic observation and interviewing (Hess, 1999). Yoshikawa's research team studied Chinese, Mexican, and Dominican undocumented immigrant parents of newborns; the latter, born in New York City, were US citizens. The team used qualitative methods, including semi-structured interviews—conversational interviews with a flexible list of questions—and participant observation methods. The study aimed to detail the daily lives of the parents who worked in very low-wage jobs with low access to benefits and few opportunities to learn new skills. Due to the undocumented status and relative isolation of their parents, the children had little access to preschool, child care centers, and schools, with negative effects for early childhood learning and development.

Yoshikawa shared his findings with the New York Immigration Coalition (NYIC) (http://www.thenyic.org/) and developed an ongoing relationship with them. The coalition successfully lobbied the New York City Council. New York thus became the first US city to fund adult education for undocumented parents (New York City Council, 2013). Due to his knowledge of the daily lives of the families he studied, the Coalition asked Yoshikawa to contribute to policy implementation by consulting with local sites to develop strategies for outreach to the undocumented parents.

Here, he highlights aspects of his policy influence work:

Policy debates around immigration reform are not considering the fact that parents are a huge chunk of the undocumented—and the resulting consequences for the next generation. New York City has been the first city in the country to address this issue. It set aside $14 million specifically for this population, essentially doubling the number of city-funded adult education slots. The policy was a terrific achievement led by the

New York Immigration Coalition [NYIC], which is the umbrella organization for 220 immigrant-serving organizations in New York City.

My relationship with the organization started when I contacted them right after my book came out. I didn't want the book just to be sitting on a shelf. I wanted it to actually have some use. The book was based on ethnographic research that examined parental undocumented status, and its effect on kids. I did some follow-up work for the Migration Policy Institute drafting a report, and then shared it with Melanie Reyes, Manager of Education Advocacy, NYIC, to get her feedback. I incorporated her information, that undocumented parents might be under-applying to the pathway to citizenship program, and put it into the policy report. Then, like a good advocacy organization, they turned around and used that report to advocate for the [undocumented immigrant parent education] legislation. A woman in the leadership at this organization was essentially the one working with city agencies and the city council to craft this legislation.

My study provided descriptive, ethnographic texture of what families deal with day to day. It was a very comprehensive ethnography of these families' lives. Various parts of the study are relevant now to policy implementation because they're talking about how you craft outreach. The daily routines of undocumented parents are relevant to that, many of whom have incredibly punishing work schedules.

Since then, it's continued to be a reciprocal relationship. I hooked them [NYIC] up with the folks who are doing the best work with national estimates on the characteristics of the undocumented population and helped them run numbers for New York City to inform the policy implementation. As this gets rolled out, there's going to be a lot of learning about what kinds of outreach actually works for this population to essentially begin integrating them into US society.

... Furthermore, as the first book on the topic of undocumented parents of US citizen children, *Immigrants Raising Citizens* provided part of the knowledge base to support Obama's current executive action. The intermediary in some of this influence was the Migration Policy Institute (MPI), which was the key player to bring data to the development of the Executive Action. One offshoot of the book was my report for MPI on undocumented parents [Yoshikawa & Kholoptseva, 2013].

Ethnography is a marginalized research method in psychology. This example reveals its potential policy value, in this case its textured and detailed documentation of the lives and needs of undocumented immigrant parents and their children. Yoshikawa's work also demonstrates the importance of reaching out to—and having sustained relationships with—members of well-positioned advocacy organizations and other intermediary organizations to use research to further policy initiatives. More generally, the example broadens our understanding of the different types of research and forms of influence that are possible when the conditions are right. Specifically, Yoshikawa's case shows the potential of narratives, through ethnographic methods, in making the case for policy change.

The fourth example involves a type of research, *epidemiology*, that is more typically associated with influencing policy, especially agenda setting. Several particulars of the research context in this case, however, are unique.

Chronic Fatigue Syndrome/Myalgic Encephalomyelitis: The Impact of Epidemiology Research

Leonard Jason

PhD, Clinical/Community Psychology, University of Rochester, 1975

Professor of Psychology, DePaul University

In 1989, community psychologist Leonard Jason developed a debilitating illness that left him gravely ill and physically incapacitated. The illness was ultimately diagnosed as Chronic Fatigue Syndrome (CFS). CFS was widely believed at the time to be relatively rare, to be caused by psychological factors, and to affect primarily upper income, White individuals (thus the derogatory characterization as "yuppie flu"). **Centers for Disease Control and Prevention** (CDC) research, based on physician referrals, concluded that only 20,000 individuals in the United States suffered from CFS (Reyes et al., 1997). Jason believed the actual prevalence rate to be much greater and conducted a community-based study of 28,673 randomly selected individuals. Those who reported having several CFS symptoms received a full medical and psychiatric assessment. The results: an estimated prevalence rate of more than 800,000 cases, with higher rates among ethnic minority than White individuals and no evidence of greater prevalence rates for persons from higher socioeconomic status (SES) backgrounds (Jason et al., 1999). A later CDC-funded study supported the higher prevalence rate (Reyes et al., 2003).

Jason and key intermediary groups used these findings, along with other research, to lobby for change. Jason worked with the largest patient advocacy organization for the disease (Chronic Fatigue Immune Dysfunction Syndrome Association), the professional association of researchers and healthcare professionals (International Association of CFS/ME), and a CFS advisory group to the Secretary of Health and Human Services to which he had been appointed. These efforts ultimately led to revisions in the definition and name of the illness (to CFS/ME—chronic fatigue syndrome/myalgic encephalomyelitis), as well as more attention to the need for increased re-search funding (see Jason, 2013).

Here, Jason highlights aspects of his epidemiological work and the factors that led to policy change:

Initially, I focused on one particular project, doing epidemiology, trying to find out why the CDC was suggesting that less than 20,000 people had this illness. If there is an illness that's very rare, then it's not going to get a lot of public attention or resources. What the CDC had done was to ask physicians in four cities to nominate patients to be evaluated. But if the patients weren't identified because the physicians didn't believe the ill-ness existed, or if the patients weren't involved in the healthcare system because they were too poor, they wouldn't get counted.

Judy Richman and I put a team together, and we went after grant money. We did a community-based study, from 1995 to 1998, interviewing a random sample of people in the community. The people who we thought might have symptoms were assessed medically and psychiatrically. Our estimates suggested that it probably was closer to about 1 million people who had this illness.

That one study changed a lot of people's perceptions of this illness. Most of the people identified were minorities rather than Caucasians. That study catapulted me into a national forum, where I got connected not only with the top scientists in the US and around the world, but also the patient groups. And the federal officials put me on a coordinating committee that was put together to advise the Secretary of Health and Human Services on this illness. Also, the CDC later replicated the study that we did in Chicago.

I was elected to the Board of Directors and later became the vice pres-ident of the International Association of Chronic Fatigue Syndrome. That group used these and other findings to push for change. The policy change was that this illness was taken more seriously, efforts were [made] to change the name, and activists and advocates were provided support-ive data to support their contention that this was an illness that needed to get more federal attention and resources.

Several aspects of this example are noteworthy. Jason's strong intuition that official prevalence rates were discrepant from reality was informed by first-hand knowledge of the number of members populating existing member CFS advocacy organizations. Furthermore, he pursued policy influence through multiple, potentially contradictory roles, including researcher, pa-tient with CFS/ME, advocate, and consultant to both government and ad-vocacy organizations. The policy influence work was set against a powerful and resistant official within the CDC and involved a great amount of persis-tence and additional research to achieve success (see Jason, 2013). Of note, an Institute of Medicine expert panel in 2015 recommended a redefinition of the disease and changed diagnostic criteria, along with another name change (systemic exertion intolerance disease) that reflects its physical, rather than psychological nature (Committee on the Diagnostic Criteria for Myalgic Encephalomyelitis/Chronic Fatigue Syndrome, 2015). The name selected, however, is receiving mixed reactions (e.g., Jason, 2015).

Summary

Taken together, these four examples reflect a range of research questions, research methods, and pathways of policy influence. The research conducted became policy relevant in part due to challenging existing conceptions of a problem or population and in part due to active efforts at dissemination, including efforts to develop and sustain relationships with influential groups. The likelihood that any given research study or area will ultimately influence policymakers cannot be known in advance, given the many vagaries of the policy process, politics, events, and the nature of the research findings. The four examples, along with the larger set of studies listed in Table 6.2, reveal the potential for research focused on understanding phenomena of interest to achieve policy influence when the necessary conditions are present.

Next, we move to research that explicitly addresses current system policies and practices within the domain of a given executive branch agency.

System Policies and Practices Research

Research that directly addresses or has clear relevance to existing policies and practices of service delivery systems is likely to be directly relevant to policy-makers. Such research can address any government-regulated or -funded service system, including child care, child and family welfare, corrections, education, health, mental health, and juvenile justice. Policies and practices that guide the operation of service delivery systems include, but are not limited to, those that determine who is eligible to be served and how they are selected, the nature and quality of services provided, the adequacy of financing, and the quality of governance. In different disciplines, system policies and practice research goes by different names, such as educational policy research, healthcare systems research, and mental health services research. Such research is often multidisciplinary in nature and appears less likely to focus on specific programs than on broader policies and practices (although, technically speaking, evaluation of existing programs can be viewed as a subset of system policies and practices research).

Eight of the psychologists interviewed for this volume conducted system policies and practices research that they viewed as their greatest policy success (see Table 6.3). Four examples are presented here. These cases span institutional practices for

Table 6.3 **Research on System Policies and Practices: Policy Issue, Psychologist, Research Method, Policy Influence, and Policy Influence Method**

Policy Issue (Psychologist)	Research Method	Policy Influence	Policy Influence Method
Children with severe disabilities: institutional treatment and placement (Ramey)*	Experimental; Review of records	State of Washington: Deinstitutionalization	Consultation; Extended meetings with advocacy groups
Civil commitment: mental hospitals (Monahan)*	Survey of judges Economic analysis	State of Virginia: New civic commitment standards	Virginia Commission on Mental Health Reform
Mentally ill in intermediate care nursing homes: civil rights (Tebes)*	Interviews, assessment, review of medical records	Court victory; Illinois: Developing community placements for residents	Expert report in ACLU class action suit
Serious juvenile offenders: adjudication (Mulvey)*	Longitudinal tracking	State of Arizona: Legislation re: Adjudication of juvenile sexual offenders to adult corrections	Meetings with state legislators
Racial disparities in mental health system (Snowden)**(3)	System operations research	National conversation about cultural disparities; State mental health departments	Surgeon General's report on mental health (racial disparities); Consultation
Mental health services for children (Meyers)**(4)	System financing study	State of Connecticut: Movement to community-based system of care	Governor's blue ribbon commission on mental health; Lieutenant governor's mental health cabinet
Mental health services for children (Cohen)**(5)	System operations study	State of Virginia: Comprehensive Services Act for At-Risk Children and Families	Chair of two state advisory committees
Juveniles within adult corrections (Woolard)**(7)	Legal and policy analysis	Advocacy organization sharing with state legislators	Shared with advocacy organizations

* Covered in this chapter.
** (X) = Chapter number where presented as case example.

people with severe mental health problems, civic commitment guidelines in the mental health system, civil rights of people with mental illness housed in intermediate care nursing homes, and the adjudication of convicted juvenile offenders.

We start with a doctoral dissertation that challenged the prevailing practices concerning treatment of children with severe disabilities in state institutions.

Changing the View of the Capacity of Children with Severe Disabilities: A Behavioral Study and Associated Systems Research

Sharon Landesman Ramey

PhD, Developmental Psychology, University of Washington, 1974

Professor and Research Scholar of Human Development, Virginia Polytechnic Institute and State University

The results of developmental psychologist Sharon Landesman Ramey's dissertation led to immediate policy influence. Although it is not common for a dissertation to have such far-reaching and immediate impacts, Ramey's findings, timing, and her outreach and communication skills contributed to such influence. The dissertation, completed in 1974, revealed that, contrary to the prevailing view at the time, nonambulatory children with severe disabilities housed in state institutions could achieve behavior change (Landesman-Dwyer, 1974). The research involved eight experimental and eight control participants; it included baseline measurement, a playpen and peer intervention, and follow-up assessment. Positive changes emerged on a variety of outcome measures for the children receiving the intervention. Ramey immediately shared her dissertation findings with agency officials in Washington State, who invited her to conduct additional, follow-up research examining conditions and treatment protocols for individuals housed in state institutions. Ramey shared these findings in multiple extended meetings with parent advocacy groups, who in turn lobbied for change.

Over the ensuing decades, Ramey has continued to conduct policy-relevant research and policy activities with high-level agency officials, including a focus on preventive intervention (e.g., Ramey & Ramey, 1992; Ramey, Ramey, & Lanzi, 2006) and early childhood/preschool education (e.g., Ramey, 1999; Ramey & Ramey, 2010). Here, Ramey first discusses her dissertation findings and then describes follow-up research and policy activity:

My dissertation research showed that children with severe disabilities have more capacity to learn, to change, than historically had been

recognized. The day I defended, a member of the committee, director of the Child Development and Mental Retardation Center at the
university, said, "If tomorrow you don't call the people in DSHS
[Department of Social and Health Services] in Olympia to let them
know what you've learned, your research will have been for naught."
The next day I called the director of DSHS. I said, "I've made some
important discoveries about children who were thought to be hopeless
and couldn't learn. It's not true. I want you to know about it so everyone in your department can be doing what's helpful." He invited me to
come talk to him.

There were a lot of children who had no treatment plans because they
were considered incapable of benefiting from treatment. . . . [As a result
of the research, the authorities] had to say, "We can't have anyone without a treatment plan." That was a policy change—based on research,
rather than legal mandate. Then, within six months, we created six full-
time research positions in DSHS so that more scientists could work at
the University of Washington and for the department to help do research
on treatment techniques for many other patient populations as well.

Washington State then asked me to do a total population study, all
5,000 plus individuals in their seven institutions [housing persons with
intellectual disabilities]. Our findings showed that some people were
still being neglected. Many people were in favor of moving residents out
of institutions to the community, but then my research on the ecology
of community settings showed that some of the community settings
were worse than the terrible institutions. I then went back to the advocacy groups and was very direct about the facts, but let them decide
on future recommendations. There were many get-togethers per month
over many sustained months. The advocacy groups then went to the
legislature.

Nationally, when the landmark Education for all Handicapped
Children Act was reauthorized, they kept adding additional policies and
tried whenever possible to ground them in evidence. I began to serve on
some of the policy committees of the scientific and professional associations, and sometimes chaired those policy committees, making sure
the research findings on those topics were getting funneled to the people
writing the legislation.

Ramey's dissertation research fundamentally called into question the
system practices of the day. She initiated contact with the state Department
of Social and Health Services to share her findings; proactive outreach has
proved important in many of the other policy influence initiatives (e.g.,
Steinberg, pp. 93–95). Ramey's follow-up research provided additional

data on the need for system-wide change, information that she shared with parent advocates. The combination of directly relevant systems research and relationship development both inside (i.e., with government officials) and outside (i.e., with parent advocates) the system occurred at a critical juncture in the history of care for individuals with developmental disabilities. The "policy window" was opening in this area nationally, and Ramey contributed in a significant way.

Next, we turn to a situation in which a galvanizing event made possible the application of system policies and practices research, in this case focused on mental health law related to civil commitment.

New Civil Commitment Standards in the Wake of the Virginia Tech Tragedy: Research on Violence and Mental Health Law

John Monahan

PhD, Clinical Psychology, University of Indiana, 1972

Professor of Law, University of Virginia

John Monahan, a clinical psychologist, served on the Civil Commitment Standards Task Force of the Virginia Commission on Mental Health Reform (Commonwealth of Virginia, 2007). He brought his extensive expertise on violence and mental health law to this work, in part due to serving as director of two relevant MacArthur Foundation research networks (macarthur.virginia. edu/mentalhome.html; macarthur.virginia.edu/researchnetwork.html). The new civil commitment standards proposed were informed in part by prior research Monahan had conducted, including a study that assessed judges' views of the probability of violence needed to justify involuntary commitment to an inpatient treatment facility (Monahan & Silver, 2003).

In 2007, a massacre took place at Virginia Polytechnic Institute and State University (Virginia Tech). Dozens of individuals were murdered or injured on the campus by a young gunman with severe mental illness. Due in large part to this tragedy, the commission's work received widespread public and political attention, and the proposed civil commitment standards were signed into law (Commonwealth of Virginia, 2007; Cohen, Bonnie, & Monahan, 2009). Monahan attributes his influence on the task force to his knowledge of the literature, understanding of financial and system realities, and ability to remain impartial in the face of strong advocacy from groups with opposing perspectives.

Here, Monahan highlights several aspects of his contributions to the new Virginia civil commitment standards:

Richard Bonnie, a law professor and colleague, asked me if I would be involved in the Virginia Commission on Mental Health Reform. He chaired the commission at the request of the Chief Justice of the Virginia Supreme Court, who had a great personal interest in mental health law reform. The commission was created, with many task forces. I was on a task force on civil commitment standards. As these things often go, there were a lot of constituencies, and progress was pretty slow, until the event that took place at Virginia Tech in 2007. All of a sudden, there were television cameras and reporters at open commission meetings. It was clear that what the commission recommended was going to be taken very seriously by the legislature.

I had been involved in mental health law for a long time. I had directed a MacArthur Foundation research network from 1988 to 1998 on mental health and the law, and from 2001 to 2011 a research network on mandated community treatment. The issues I've researched, like risk assessment of violence and civil commitment, were of benefit to me in the policy context. I knew exactly the positions people had taken in the past and the empirical basis on which they took those positions. From the research on mandated community treatments, I knew the cost and benefits of outpatient commitment [involuntary treatment of people with mental illness who reside in the community, rather than detained in a hospital] as well. Also relevant was a study by myself and sociologist Eric Silver. When courts talk about the term "dangerousness" in civil commitment, as in someone must be mentally disordered and dangerous to self or others, what do they mean by "dangerous"? We did a survey of state and federal judges and asked them to quantify the likelihood of future harm that they interpreted the word dangerous to imply. Most judges, it turned out, would civilly commit someone for a brief period if their odds of committing a serious violent act in the future were greater than one in four. As the statute and commentary to the statute were being drafted, the commentary that suggested dangerousness be defined in these terms came to be adopted.

I thought that my prior experience suited me well for the task of offering advice. The new civil commitment standard for Virginia, which I was involved in writing along with my colleague, Richard Bonnie, is the one in existence today. I think these civil commitment standards are the best in the country and are influencing policy developments in many other states.

Monahan was the right person at the right place at the right time. A distinguished scholar in the area of mental health and the law, his expertise and relationships within the law school at the University of Virginia led to an advisory appointment on a state commission when the committee's work was particularly salient. Monahan combined his research knowledge with his systems knowledge to make sound policy recommendations. Strong interpersonal skills allowed him to then receive testimony from and respond impartially to advocacy groups on opposing sides of the issue, leading to research-based policy influence—new civil commitment standards.

In the next example, mental illness is again the focus but in this case the research was narrowly tailored to address a question at the heart of a class action lawsuit.

Civil Rights of Residents with Mental Illness in Nursing Homes: Research Designed for a Class Action Lawsuit

Jacob Tebes

PhD, Clinical/Community Psychology, State University
of New York at Buffalo, 1984

Director, Yale Consultation Center, New Haven, Connecticut

Clinical-community psychologist Jacob Tebes was asked by American Civil Liberties Union (ACLU) attorneys to conduct an empirical evaluation to determine whether the state of Illinois was denying the civil rights of residents with mental illness in intermediate care nursing homes. Specifically, the court order defined plaintiffs as Illinois residents who "(a) have a mental illness; (b) are institutionalized in a privately owned Institution for Mental Diseases; and, (c) with appropriate supports and services may be able to live in an integrated community." The right for individuals with a disability to live in an integrated community that includes individuals without disabilities was established in 1990 by the Americans with Disabilities Act (ADA) and then affirmed in subsequent court decisions. Tebes and colleagues used a stratified sampling procedure to generate a sample of 121 participants (stratified by geographic region and size of facility). The participants resided in 8 of 26 nursing homes designated by federal law as Institutions of Mental Diseases (IMDs) that house and treat individuals with mental illness (Tebes, Amble, & Baranoski, 2008). Data from interviews, standardized assessments, and medical records were collected and analyzed. Results indicated that the vast majority of the residents had the capacity for independent living (given typically available supports in Illinois, including integrated housing programs) and that they were not currently physically, socially, or psychologically integrated into the community. Based in part on these findings, the court decided in favor of the plaintiffs.

Here, Tebes describes the systems research he conducted for the ACLU class action suit:

> I got a call from the Illinois ACLU about a class action suit they were pursuing concerning Illinois nursing homes, called Institutions for Mental Disease (IMDs). The state had about 5,000 individuals who had diagnoses of mental illness in these settings. Most of those people were technically living in the community but were not actually interacting with people who did not have a disability. Thus, the suit claimed the IMDs were in violation of the Americans with Disabilities Act.
>
> I was asked to collect empirical evidence related to the case, and invited a forensic psychologist and a forensic psychiatrist to join me in this work. We designed an evaluation that was scientifically informed and consistent with clinical and forensic evaluations that combined in-depth interviews with clients and record reviews. Our evaluation was fairly and rigorously designed, and we decided to let the chips fall where they may in terms of what we would find. In my view, despite being retained by an advocacy organization such as the ACLU, you have to tell the truth. That stance appeared to worry some members of the legal team . . . but the ACLU lead attorney who invited me trusted that our work would be fair.
>
> We interviewed well over 100 people across the state individually and looked at their records and their histories. We found that more than 85% could live in community-based settings, with appropriate services and supports. That finding became an important empirical foundation for our report as testifying experts. Along with other reports from experts as well as legal briefs from advocacy groups, [it] led the state to accept a consent decree to move most of the 5,000 residents of IMDs to integrated community settings over a period of five years.
>
> There is now a court-appointed master that monitors the transfer of individuals from those institutions to integrated community settings. I feel a sense of satisfaction about that work because we were able to be scientists and yet our values helped create a rigorous and fair-minded evaluation. We were also able to use our expertise to adopt a strengths-based framework to guide our design to evaluate whether people in IMDs could live in integrated community settings.

The systems research in this example was explicitly designed to answer a policy question. The findings, as it turned out, supported the strengths-based perspective of the investigator and led to appropriate changes in system practices. Tebes acknowledges some implicit pressure from individuals on the legal team about how to proceed, but he did not yield to it. The resulting change in system practices parallels, in some regards, Ramey's case, in that research evidence about unacceptable conditions led to policy change. However, in Tebes' case, the policy influence pathway involved the judiciary, rather than the executive and legislative branches.

The final example in this section is based on **longitudinal research,** an investigation method that involves repeated measurement of the same variables in the same set of participants over time. This research tracked the lives of juveniles who had committed serious offenses.

Adjudication of Serious Juvenile Offenders: Seven-Year Trajectories Following Court Conviction

Edward Mulvey

PhD, Clinical Psychology, University of Virginia, 1982

Professor of Psychiatry, University of Pittsburgh

Community/clinical psychologist Edward Mulvey directs a team of researchers working on the Pathways to Desistance study, an examination of the trajectories of 1,354 serious juvenile offenders in Phoenix and Philadelphia (http://www.pathwaysstudy.pitt.edu/index.html). Following their court conviction, the youth were followed for seven years, into late adolescence and early adulthood. Some of the key findings to date include the relative lack of effectiveness of longer term juvenile incarceration in terms of decreased recidivism and, in contrast, the relative effectiveness of community-based supervision and substance abuse treatment, the latter related to reductions both in substance use and offending (Mulvey & Schubert, 2012; Mulvey, Schubert, & Chung, 2007; Mulvey et al., 2010). Using these findings as a springboard, Mulvey and colleagues worked with Arizona state legislators and advocates who changed the law so that juvenile sex offenders are no longer placed in adult corrections facilities (Arizona Revised Statutes § 8-350.01, 2011). Later, following an overview presentation of study findings to US Attorney General Eric Holder, Mulvey was invited by Holder to serve on the Science Advisory Board for the Office of Justice Programs, US **Department of Justice** (DOJ). (http://ojp.gov/sabrelease.htm; http://ojp.gov/docs/sabcharter.pdf).

Here, Mulvey discusses the Pathways to Desistance Project and concludes with general observations about the group's efforts to influence policy:

> We had been doing this large study for about 10 years of these serious offending kids. Since we had done half the study in Philadelphia and half of it in Phoenix, we made a concerted effort to go back to stakeholders in Philadelphia and stakeholders in Phoenix, talk about results with them, and have them give us ways to think about the data (or how not to think about it) and do analyses. We then brought the results back to them and shared with the people in both sites. The results are relevant, for example, to the relative utility of institutional care and the extent of spending on institutional care in locales.
>
> Many advocates have argued for different procedures for reassessing risks of kids over time to determine whether they still need to be in institutions or back in the community. We've worked with some state legislators. Arizona, for instance, had a law about not transferring kids back to the juvenile system. Once they've committed certain enumerated crimes, they go to the adult system and stay there. We worked with advocacy groups out there and presented information to a state senate committee examining this statute. They then changed that law, at least for their sex offender population. Certain groups are now going after the rest of their population, hoping to get the whole law changed.
>
> Just presenting research results in a lot of places gets you kind of known on the circuit. I think the fact that the initial funder for that project was the MacArthur Foundation played a big role. From the outset, they wanted us to get information from the research to the advocacy field and out to the field more generally, to the practitioners and policymakers. That had me working with a number of advocacy groups and providers whom I would not have known otherwise. As a result, this study got a lot of visibility through being known in the practitioner community and within agencies in the Department of Justice. The director of the Office of Justice Programs, Laurie Robinson, had me give a presentation to her and about three or four of her staff. Then about a month and a half later they asked me to give a presentation to Eric Holder, the Attorney General. We briefed him for 45 minutes or an hour. He had several of his staff people there. The next thing was they were putting the Science Advisory Board together and asked me to be on it.
>
> . . . A lot of policy work is really logical and being able to translate the logic of research to policy people, to understand the realities of practitioners, and to tell them what the research means to them—what it would mean to the way they operate is essential. I think the ability to translate is probably the most successful thing I feel I've done in my career.

Through well-designed longitudinal research, Mulvey effectively illustrated systemic issues with current juvenile corrections policies and identified research-supported alternatives. However, as in all of the other cases, strong research alone was not enough for policy influence. Mulvey worked with many stakeholders, translating his research findings to multiple audiences that ranged from policy insiders to advocacy organizations and practitioners. This widespread dissemination and collaboration contributed to policy change and to Mulvey's appointment to an advisory committee within the DOJ aimed at increasing the use of sound science in their programs.

Summary

Taken together, these four examples illustrate a range of research questions, research methods, and pathways of policy influence in the domain of system policies and practices. Additional examples of questions, methods, and pathways are included in Table 6.3. System policies and practices research are distinctly situated to address questions of direct relevance and interest to policymakers. Generally speaking, this research is broader in focus than evaluation of a specific program and less theory-based than research focused on understanding naturally occurring phenomena.

The final class of scholarship is also likely to be of direct relevance and interest to policymakers because it involves providing concrete, practical aids to enhance the quality of work done by implementing agencies.

Practical Aids and Heuristic Guides

Research and scholarship that generate practical aids and heuristic guides for implementing agencies—tools that steer decision-making and practice—represent a fourth area of policy contribution. Such practical tools include research-based assessment instruments, curricula, guidelines for service provision, and program manuals (see Chapter 2). These tools—given their technical nature—are more likely to influence the decisions of government administrators engaged in the particulars of policy implementation than they are to influence elected officials involved in the broad sweep of policy formulation. Four psychologists interviewed included such practical aids and heuristic guides among their greatest policy influences (see Table 6.4). Two examples are presented here: a mental health screening measure used in detention centers and a heuristic model to guide agencies in the selection, implementation, evaluation, improvement, and sustainability of programs.

We begin with development of a mental health screening measure.

Table 6.4 **Practical Aids and Heuristic Guides: Policy Issue, Psychologist, Research Method, Policy Influence, and Policy Influence Method**

Policy Issue (Psychologist)	Research Method	Policy Influence	Policy Influence Method
Mental Health screening in detention centers: Massachusetts Youth Screening Instrument (MAYSI) (Grisso)*	Measure development	Adopted in 40 states	Widespread dissemination; Consultation
Program selection, implementation, evaluation, improvement, sustainability: Getting to Outcomes (GTO) (Wandersman)*	Heuristic model development	Used by CDC	Widespread dissemination; Consultation
Juvenile justice programs: Standardized Program Evaluation Protocol (SPEP) (Lipsey)*	Meta-analysis	Used by juvenile justice systems	Training and consultation
Homeless prevention services for families: Short Screening Model (Shinn)**(6)	Tracking study of families who applied for community-based services to prevent homelessness	Used by New York City Department of Homeless Services	Consultation; NYC Homeless Advisory Board

* Covered in this chapter.
** (X) = Chapter number where presented as case example.

Mental Health Screening Measure for Detention Centers

Thomas Grisso

PhD, Clinical Psychology, University of Arizona, 1969

Emeritus Professor in Psychiatry, University of Massachusetts Medical School

Thomas Grisso, a clinical psychologist, has conducted policy-relevant research related to multiple justice system issues during his career. He describes the development of a mental health screening tool, the Massachusetts Youth

Screening Instrument (MAYSI), as one distinctive contribution. Grisso and a colleague developed the screening tool in the 1990s, anticipating the need for a reliable and valid way for juvenile justice systems to screen youth for mental health needs upon entry into the system, particularly in juvenile detention centers (Grisso, Barnum, Fletcher, Cauffman, & Peuschold, 2001). The measure's purpose is to identify youth who require immediate attention regarding suicide risk and emergent substance use and mental health problems.

The MAYSI-2 includes 52 yes-no items that generate seven scales: alcohol/drug use, angry-irritable, depressed-anxious, somatic complaints, suicide ideation, thought disturbance, and traumatic experiences (http://nysap.us/MAYSI2.html). The screening measure demonstrates strong reliability and validity (Grisso et al., 2012). The MAYSI-2 is the most widely used screening tool in juvenile detention centers in more than 30 states, and there is evidence that mental health screening in detention centers is a valuable activity (Models for Change, 2011). Here, Grisso describes key aspects of his work on the development and dissemination of the MAYSI:

> I had a friend in New York who in 1992 was editing a small book about mental health problems of kids in the juvenile justice system. It was a time when the juvenile justice system was locking up more and more kids for minor offenses. That was when I first got the notion that "It won't be long that people will get so sick of what we're doing to kids and the pendulum will swing." Another friend, a practicing forensic psychiatrist and I started thinking "Maybe [creating a measure to identity these youth's mental health needs] is something we could do together." The W. T. Grant Foundation funded us, and off we went. I believe the research was completed in the middle of 1998. Before it was completely done, we went to two states, California and Pennsylvania, and did a marketing pilot. We got some assurance that, if you do it right, the [juvenile detention center staff] will turn around and say, "This isn't bad."
>
> It was 2000 and MacArthur gave us a grant to get started. I simply called people I knew in the right leadership positions and said, "I want to come talk to your organizations this year." I hit as broad of a range as I could. We got a lot of active cooperation from juvenile advocacy groups. The instrument allowed them to provide to attorneys and juvenile justice systems a way to actually carry out the initiative of trying to do better for kids. Federal agencies had begun saying, "You're locking all of these kids up. You're going to have to attend to their mental health needs as well."
>
> In a large number of states, the juvenile detention centers are county run. There are other states in which the state has control over the detention centers. We work with both. We have a five-day-a-week, eight-hours-a-day help line.

Our validation research was absolutely essential. Being able to say, "We did the studies. It's validated. Here's how it's validated," has been extremely important. It has gotten even more important in the last five or six years when the words "evidence based" have become the first words that a juvenile justice administrator says as they get out of bed in the morning.

Grisso and his colleague anticipated that the "pendulum would swing" toward more humane treatment of youth in the juvenile justice system and accordingly developed a psychometrically sound mental health screening tool in the mid-1990s. Similar to other cases highlighted in this chapter, the development and validation of this instrument was not enough; Grisso's use of relationship and communication skills allowed him to launch a concerted effort to inform stakeholders of the screening instrument, including practitioners, advocacy organizations, and government decision-makers. Providing ample access to consultation services was the final step in helping to ensure the widespread adoption of this measure.

Tools such as screening instruments enhance the effectiveness of programs and policies through increasing the quality of programming delivered by individual staff. The final case described in this chapter highlights the development of a heuristic aid that is designed to enhance the quality and effectiveness of programming at the organizational level.

Heuristic Guide for Program Selection, Implementation, and Sustainability

Abraham Wandersman

PhD, Personality, Social, Environmental, and Ecological Psychology, Cornell University, 1976

Professor of Psychology, University of South Carolina

Community psychologist Abraham Wandersman has devoted his career to bridging science and practice, including a focus on the development of practical guides to enhance the effective implementation, evaluation, improvement, and sustainability of health and human service programs and policies. One of these efforts was the development of *Getting to Outcomes* (GTO), a 10-step, practical heuristic to guide program selection, implementation, evaluation, continuous improvement, and sustainability by community-based agencies, schools, and coalitions (Chinman, Imm, & Wandersman, 2004; Wandersman, 2014; Wandersman, Imm, Chinman, & Kaftarian, 2000). GTO manuals have been downloaded more than 100,000 times and used in a wide range of areas, including early intervention, home visiting programs, and prevention of substance use and teenage pregnancy (RAND Corporation, 2015).

As part of the President's Teen Pregnancy Prevention Initiative (TPPI), GTO is being employed by the Centers for Disease Control and Prevention (CDC) in partnership with the federal **Office of the Assistant Secretary for Health** (OASH) in a major national initiative to reduce teenage pregnancy and address disparities in teen pregnancy and birth rates (cdc.gov/TeenPregnancy/PreventTeenPreg.htm). Specifically, grantees (funded local agencies) are trained to use the GTO model to guide program planning, implementation, and evaluation (cdc.gov/TeenPregnancy/National-Orgs.html#n1). The use of GTO in an earlier, related teenage pregnancy prevention program initiated by the CDC was found to be successful (Lewis et al., 2012) and formed the basis for the current initiative. Building on GTO, Wandersman developed an Interactive Systems Framework for Dissemination and Implementation (ISF) to guide funders, practitioners, and researchers in bridging science and practice (Wandersman, Chien, & Katz, 2012).

Here, Wandersman describes GTO and how it is being used in a number of different contexts by governmental agencies including the CDC, the Substance Abuse and Mental Health Services Administration (SAMHSA), and several state and local governmental agencies (Hannah, Ray, Wandersman, & Chien, 2010):

> The first couple of steps of Getting to Outcomes are about getting people to pick what to implement and the strategy to implement it in their own jurisdiction, whether we're talking about the school or organization, community, state, or national level. This is a part of strategic planning. Then, once you have your plan, it's implementing it with quality. And then evaluating whether it works and moving into continuous quality improvement and sustainability.
>
> One of the places GTO is being used is in a large, teen-pregnancy prevention project co-funded by the CDC and the Office of Adolescent Health. GTO is the major, strategic process for preventing teen-pregnancy in the $75 million initiative. Each of the sites, among other things, is required to use Getting to Outcomes in how they strategically plan what [programs] they're going to look at, implement, evaluate, and conduct continuous quality improvement [on]. We were involved in a collaborative process to develop a GTO manual related

to teen-pregnancy prevention. Then there were trainings involved, and then technical assistance.

. . . One of the current uses of GTO is for environmental strategies that relate to underage-drinking prevention, such as keg registration, graduated driver's license laws, social host laws, etc. SAMHSA did community forums around the country on environmental strategies for underage drinking prevention and used GTO.

Also, we have done several applications of GTO with outcome-based contracting. . . . The Philadelphia Department of Behavioral Health and Intellectual Disabilities issued a Request for Proposals for Substance Use Partial Hospitalization Services [for co-occurring mental health and substance abuse clients]. The RFP uses GTO to frame their outcome-based contract and build people's capacity to achieve those outcomes. It's a way of helping funders and providers achieve accountability, a key focus of policy.

The idea to develop Getting to Outcomes emerged from a desire to enhance the accountability of agencies when implementing programs paid for by government dollars. As a heuristic aid, GTO addresses many of the challenges to effective program planning, implementation, and sustainability—challenges revealed by decades of empirical research and experience in the field. In addition to developing and disseminating GTO, the consulting and technical assistance provided by Wandersman and colleagues have helped to spur widespread adoption by governmental agencies.

Summary

In some regards, practical aids and heuristic guides represent a contribution to changing system practices and policies, research reviewed in the previous section. The major difference between the two is that practical aids and heuristic guides constitute concrete tools that directly enhance the quality of work done by implementing agencies, whereas the influence of system practices and policies research is more indirect, providing information to guide the policy decisions of higher level officials.

Policy-Relevant Research and Policy Influence

The characteristics of effective and useful policy-relevant research described by interviewees cannot easily be summarized. As revealed in the specific examples and more generally in the full range of studies listed in Tables 6.1, there is no single type of research design or particular type of research question that can be singled out as especially likely to influence policy. Studies that clearly demonstrate the effectiveness and viability of new program or policy ideas, and especially their cost-effectiveness, have proved important. Research that reveals new ways of looking at populations or social problems, with associated implications for practice, also has potential to make a difference. Alternatively, studies that seek to answer questions of importance to policymakers or that anticipate which questions will be important a few years hence have enhanced potential to be of use. Regardless of the type of research study, publication of findings in academic journals will not, in and of itself, lead to policy influence.

As revealed in the case examples, it is the strategic dissemination of policy-relevant and research-based ideas that leads to policy change. Research-based pathways of influence can take many forms:

- meetings with policymakers
- serving on advisory boards
- contributing to court proceedings
- writing major reports
- working with powerful advocacy organizations

Beyond these, determined effort and strategic relationship-building are generally required on the part of psychologists who desire to see their research findings have an impact in the policy arena. This includes seeking out relevant ties and making sure that key stakeholders are aware of the research and its policy implications.

For many psychologists who successfully influence policy, a sustained, career-long effort—not an occasional activity—is required. In the next chapter, we examine distinctive career themes among psychologists who have devoted substantial portions of their career to policy-relevant work.

7

Policy Journeys

Multiple Involvements, Distinctive Aspects, and Influences

> *When considering what you can do, and what policies research might inform, ... [multiple] audiences need to be considered. I move back and forth between teachers and federal policymakers and many levels in between.*
> —D. Stipek, March 26, 2013

This chapter sheds light on the nature of the policy journeys undertaken by psychologists during the course of their careers. Previous chapters have focused on particular ways to influence policy to achieve a given policy success. A primary focus of this chapter, however, is to examine psychologists' career-long policy journeys, an understanding of which can inform graduate students and early career psychologists of the wide variety of pathways through which *they* might influence policy. Multiple policy involvements via multiple avenues may be pursued in the course of one's career. For those considering a potential career in policy or how to position their research and practice to achieve policy influence, examining the careers of similar psychologists may suggest applicable training and experiences to seek out.

A secondary focus of this chapter is to explore the background context of psychologists' career journeys, specifically the array of familial, cultural, and educational influences that psychologists felt contributed to their policy interests and involvement. These influences are presented in the summary section following the description of each case and serve to further demonstrate how earlier experiences contribute to later stages in the policy journey. One guiding question is whether there are any common background factors that predispose psychologists to pursue a career in policy; a preliminary answer to this question is provided at the conclusion of the chapter.

The chapter is divided into two parts. The first centers on psychologists' multiple policy involvements during the course of their careers, with specific focus on the nature of these multiple involvements. Six characteristics of these involvements are described:

1. using multiple policy influence methods
2. collaborating with multiple intermediary organizations

3. becoming involved in multiple substantive policy areas
4. working in multiple policy-related jobs
5. conducting multiple types of research and
6. participating in multiple policy initiatives at the local level.

Each is illustrated with one case example.

The second portion of the chapter focuses on three distinctive aspects of a policy career that interviewees highlight as particularly important for the field moving forward. The importance of these aspects resides in their respective contributions to expanding the quality, effectiveness, and scope of policy influence. The three distinctive aspects are:

- *Interdisciplinary*[1] *collaboration,* facilitated in many cases by positions in multidisciplinary departments or policy centers
- **Policy-related leadership positions**, within academic, intermediary, and government settings
- **International policy involvement**

Eight case examples are presented related to these distinctive career emphases.

No two career journeys presented in this chapter are alike. Each represents a unique tapestry with its own details and particulars. The goal of the chapter—and the lens through which to view the differing case narratives—is heightened awareness and appreciation of the rich array of pathways available to psychologists interested in policy work.

We turn first to an examination of the most salient distinguishing characteristic of psychologists' career journeys—multiple policy involvements.

Multiple Policy Involvements

The majority of those interviewed report multiple involvements in policy-related work across their careers (see Appendix D, Table D.1).[2] These include considerable variety over time in policy methods utilized, organizations

---

[1] The term "interdisciplinary" is used in this chapter to refer to the broad range of situations in which people from multiple disciplines collaborate on a particular issue. Related terms include "multidisciplinary" and "transdisciplinary." Although distinctions across the terms exist, the terms are often used in nonuniform ways. Thus, "interdisciplinary" is used to encompass them all unless a specific interviewee purposively indicated an alternative term.

[2] Due to the chapter's focus on career involvement rather than individual policy examples, Tables D.1–D.3 in Appendix D contain a synthesis of information across the psychologists interviewed (rather than a listing of individual psychologists).

partnered with, substantive area of focus, employment context, types of research conducted, and local policy involvements. Each of these subpatterns is illustrated with brief case examples of psychologists who have engaged in policy across their careers.

Multiple Policy Influence Methods

Three-quarters of respondents reported using multiple influence methods during their careers, with more than half reporting the use of three or more methods (see Appendix D, Table D.1). This variety is largely attributable to changes over time in the substantive policy area, the branch of government focused on, emerging opportunities and relationships, and evolving interest and capacity. The first case example illustrates the shifting of methods across a long policy-related career addressing prevention and promotion in mental health.

Prevention of Mental Illness and Promotion of Mental Health: Policy Reports, Congressional Testimony, Intermediaries, Advisory Roles, and Media

Richard Price

PhD, Clinical Psychology, University of Illinois, Urbana, 1966

Professor of Psychology and Organizational Studies, University of Michigan

Richard Price, a clinical-organizational-community psychologist, utilized multiple policy methods to help establish prevention as an area of research, practice, and policy for psychology (and related fields) in the 1980s and 1990s. During his career, Price served as Chair of both the first American Psychological Association (APA) Task Force on Promotion, Prevention, and Intervention (1983–88), and the first National Institute of Mental Health (NIMH) Committee on Prevention Research (1993–95). He also was a member of the first Institute of Medicine Committee on the Prevention of Mental Disorders (1992–94). Each of these initiatives generated important policy-relevant products (Mrazek & Haggerty, 1994; Price, Cowen, Lorion, & Ramos-McKay, 1988; Reiss & Price, 1996). Additionally, Price directed one of the five initial NIMH-funded prevention centers, the Michigan Prevention Research Center, which developed, evaluated, and disseminated (both nationally and internationally) the JOBS intervention program (www.isr.umich.edu/src/seh/mprc/jobsupdt.html). JOBS provided recently unemployed individuals support in the search for employment and strove to prevent depressive symptoms (Vinokur, Price, & Schul, 1995).

Throughout his career, Price has contributed to awareness of the importance of preventive interventions in general (Infancy to Adolescence, 1987) and the link between employment and mental health in particular, in part through testimony and media work (e.g., Jones & Barber, 2012). His policy work has also addressed prevention of substance use and HIV/AIDS and promotion of positive youth development through his involvement on scientific and advisory boards of the National Academy of Sciences and the William T. Grant Foundation, respectively. Here, Price describes various policy influence methods he used during the course of his career:

> The move to address policymakers about prevention and mental health that eventuated in the volume *14 Ounces of Prevention* was initiated by APA. In producing the book with 14 exemplary prevention cases, we attracted the attention of a lot of other people, including the House of Representatives Select Committee for Children, Youth and Families, where I testified about the results of that book. Since then, there were a lot of avenues for influence. One of them was the first round of the Institute of Medicine panel on prevention. We spent three years writing the first set of prevention policy agendas related to science policy, which was all about saying, "Where are you going to put your dollars in terms of trying to investigate problems and seek out solutions?"
>
> The National Institutes of Health convened consensus conferences that address major treatment and research policy issues. In the first Clinton administration, I was on one which had to do with the prevention of AIDS. We were given vast amounts of scientific data to read about intervention programs aimed at preventing HIV/AIDS and came together to synthesize it. After three days of essentially being a science jury in which scientists get up and present their findings to you, the panelists stayed up all night writing the report. At 8:00 in the morning, they publish this thing. The entire auditorium is full of legislators, staffers, and the media. These are amazing documents because they get taken seriously in Congress. We had a pretty nice impact in terms of AIDS prevention.
>
> I was on the board of the William T. Grant Foundation for about 13 years. We were always moving back and forth between research on youth and really thinking about how the scientific research on youth and youth development could influence both policy and practice. While foundations are not supposed to be directly lobbying Congress, they're always indirect influencers of policy and what is on the policy agenda at any given time. They're both reactors to and influencers of that agenda.

I also spent a fair amount of time and energy trying to influence, informally and formally, practice guidelines and government policy on issues having to do with workers' health and mental health. Just last year [2012], APA convened a group of people from Congress to hear a number of us, both scientists and practitioners, who were engaged in this area. I did a lot of work publicizing these issues, particularly in the media. They [the media] can be a powerful influence. They keep issues alive, influence people, and help policymakers or lawmakers who have to listen to constituents, hear new information, and know what's being done about it.

Influences and Summary

Price began his career with a strong interest in rigorous research and clinical psychology, the latter as a way to help make the world a better place. Early on, he ran a crisis clinic before he decided, "that wasn't going to make the kind of difference" he wanted to make, and he realized that "prevention seemed . . . to be the perfect marriage of science and public action." Beginning at that point, and continuing throughout his career, Price made use of a wide range of policy methods. He was involved in congressional testimony, established long-term relationships with legislators, conducted media interviews, and provided consultation. Price determined which policy influence methods to use based on the substantive policy focus (e.g., employment, AIDS/HIV, substance use, child and youth promotion) as well as the specific opportunities available. More generally, as with many other psychologists interviewed, his strong commitment to pursue all available means to make a policy impact led him to develop and use a range of skills and capabilities, thus enhancing his potential for policy influence.

Multiple Collaborations

In addition to the use of multiple policy influence methods, the policy work of those interviewed is characterized by collaboration with a variety of intermediary organizations during the course of their careers, with most individuals spontaneously noting collaborations with three or more organizations (see Appendix D, Table D.1). The types of organizations included: professional associations (e.g., APA); research, evaluation, and consultation firms; advocacy organizations; and foundations.

The specific intermediary organization of focus varied depending on the social issue, social networks, and opportunity. The next respondent organized his policy career review based on the different organizations he partnered with over time.

Youth Violence Prevention and Positive Youth Development: Collaboration with Intermediary Organizations

Clifford O'Donnell

PhD, Clinical Psychology, University of Kentucky, 1970

Emeritus Professor, Department of Psychology, University of Hawaii at Manoa

Clifford O'Donnell, a community-cultural psychologist, collaborated over the course of decades with a number of research, action, and advocacy organizations in the areas of violence prevention and positive youth development. These organizations included the Center for Youth Research, an interdisciplinary social science research center at the University of Hawaii (http://www.ssri.hawaii.edu/pages/Youth.html); the Peace Corps; the Consortium on Children, Families, and Law; and the Melissa Institute for Violence Prevention and Treatment (http://www.melissainstitute.org). Activities O'Donnell conducted in concert with these organizations encompassed development, evaluation, and dissemination of a peer mentoring program to prevent delinquency (O'Donnell & Williams, 2013) and passage of legislation in Hawaii that prohibits the sale of semi-automatic assault pistols (O'Donnell, 1995). Additional policy issues include the rights of children, positive youth development, and prevention of violence in school contexts (O'Donnell, 2001). Here, O'Donnell describes his collaborations with a number of the different organizations over the course of his career:

> With the Center for Youth Research, I worked with colleagues and students on a youth mentoring program designed to prevent delinquency known as the Buddy System. A 35-year follow-up on adult criminal offenses was recently published. I have consulted with a number of agencies in different states on the Buddy System and on their youth mentoring programs.
>
> In the late 1980s, I worked with the Center [for Youth Research] on a report detailing firearm injuries and deaths nationally among children and youth. The report led to an invitation for my participation at a policy group formed to make recommendations on firearm regulation to the Hawaii state legislature. The recommendations included a ban on the private possession of handguns. Following a legislative hearing, the legislators asked our group and supporters of the local chapter of the NRA [National Rifle Association] to meet and come to an agreement on the recommendations. We met over the following year and reached an agreement to ban semi-automatic assault pistols, a recommendation that the legislature approved.

O'Donnell went on to work with the Peace Corps, as he describes:

> I was invited to Palau in Micronesia to conduct in-service training for Peace Corps volunteers on youth programs. On the first of several trips, we identified the issue of most concern to the leaders in Micronesia: the estrangement of youth from their elders and from traditional culture. To address this issue, we organized the volunteers to form teams in their villages on all the many islands of Micronesia to plan and implement projects for youth [O'Donnell, Tharp, & Wilson, 1993].

In addition to grassroots intervention efforts, O'Donnell collaborated with and provided subject expertise and technical assistance to the Consortium on Children, Families and the Law (Melton, 1995):

> With the support of APA, I have presented briefings through the consortium on many topics. For example, I presented on the rights of children [at the UN Convention on that topic], firearm injuries and deaths among children and youth, the relationships of child maltreatment to delinquency, violence, disabilities and mental illness. I also testified on the overrepresentation of minorities in the juvenile justice system.

Later in his career, O'Donnell began a collaboration with the Melissa Institute for Violence Prevention and Treatment when an opportunity arose to get involved:

> The Institute was created to honor Melissa Aptman, who was tragically murdered at the age of 19. I was invited to join their Scientific Board to help advise the Institute on research findings that could contribute to violence reduction. Their website is now one of the most accessed on violence prevention in the world. In my role on the Board, I presented at their conferences, authored reviews of prevention programs, and represented the Institute in the Not One More task force to reduce gun violence in the Miami area. Currently, I'm working with the Institute on advocating legislation to reduce gun violence in the wake of the Newtown killings.

Influences and Summary

When asked about what influenced his initial entry and ongoing involvement in the policy arena, O'Donnell recounted growing up in a family that discussed social issues regularly; he remembered often discussing political events with his father. As a young person, he was very impressed with the Kennedy administration, and he became involved in the 1960s with both the civil rights and anti-war movements. As an undergraduate, he thought that perhaps "knowledge in psychology could be used to resolve conflicts among groups in communities." Over decades as a community psychology professor, O'Donnell partnered with many intermediary organizations—from research centers and governmental service organizations to advocacy organizations and a consortium of policy centers. The varied organizational collaborations resulted from emerging connections, opportunities, and an evolving substantive policy focus. Similar to Price, O'Donnell used various policy influence methods throughout his career, each of which necessitated clear communication and research translation skills, relationship-building, and technical knowledge.

Multiple Substantive Areas

Most of the individuals interviewed, as was the case with Price and O'Donnell, worked in more than one policy area during the course of their careers, with more than two-fifths working within three or more areas (see Appendix D, Table D.1). The psychologists detail diverse reasons for becoming involved in new substantive policy areas, including:

- changes in the nature of social issues emerging as important in society
- related funding streams
- developments in the field
- naturally occurring opportunities
- evolving personal interests

The next case example depicts how involvement in multiple substantive areas of focus is an integral aspect of a career focused on enhancing, through policy means, the well-being of children and youth.

Children and Media, Child Care Effects, Work-Based Welfare, and Early Childhood Programs

Aletha Huston

PhD, Developmental Psychology, University of Minnesota, 1965

Emeritus Professor, Department of Human Development and Family Sciences, University of Texas at Austin

Aletha Huston, a developmental psychologist, conducted policy-relevant research and directly sought to influence policy in three primary areas during the course of her career:

- the effect of television on children (e.g., Huston, Watkins, & Kunkel, 1989; Murray, 1996)
- childcare use by families and its effects (e.g., NICHD Early Child Care Research Network, 2005)
- the effects of welfare reform interventions on children and families, including the New Hope program, which provided a comprehensive set of services to enhance income and employment for low-income families (e.g., Huston et al., 2005)

Furthermore, since her retirement, Huston has taken on the role of grassroots advocate seeking to enhance local government funding for early childhood education. Here, she highlights the different aspects of her career-long contributions to policy:

> In 1969, I was invited and with Lynette Friedrich ultimately accepted the invitation to submit a proposal for the NIMH program for research on television and social behavior. . . . The Congress in 1990 passed the Children's Television Act (CTA). The CTA is one of the few pieces of legislation that's ever been passed in this country to regulate television content. It was a big triumph. We testified to the hearing about the effects of educational and prosocial television. The research many of us had done had an effect on that act.
>
> In the mid-1980s, I did an internal sabbatical in the political science department at the University of Kansas studying policy analysis, after being inspired by Ed Zigler. Subsequently, I organized an interdisciplinary study group on the topic of children and poverty. I also became involved in the longitudinal, national study of childcare that started around the same time [NICHD Early Child Care Research Network].
>
> In the '90s, I was invited to be part of the MacArthur Network on Successful Pathways through Middle Childhood. Bob Granger, from Manpower Development Research Corporation [MDRC], was a member of that network. Through Bob, I got involved in a long series of studies examining the effects on children and families of the MDRC experiment testing different features of welfare and employment policy. One of them was the New Hope Project in Milwaukee, a community-initiated test of a policy to support work as a pathway out of poverty. It had policymakers on the board who were involved in making decisions. Most of the studies were conducted by government entities. We'd go to Washington and do presentations often interfacing with the federal Administration for Children and Families. They essentially told the states, "If you want to change your welfare system, you have to do a high-quality study to determine what effects it will have before we'll let you do it." We did some other studies trying to put together the results from a number of different experiments summarizing the effects on children.

I testified to congressional committees on many of these topics. . . . If you want to be taken seriously, you have to be really careful about what you have data to support. You're not telling people what they ought to do. You're saying, "Here's what we know about how this might work or what works." I don't think one can be neutral, but you try to be honest about where you have social science evidence and where you don't.

Since I'm retired now, I've gotten much more active locally in out-and-out advocacy, mostly for early childhood programs. I'm involved with United Way and the Early Childhood Council. We go to city council members, county commissioners, and local heads of health and human service and tell them regularly why we want them to invest more in programs for kids. The legislature is in session right now, so we've been testifying there too.

Influences and Summary

Huston's multiple areas of policy-relevant work were driven by her interests, external influence, opportunity, and changing social issues of prominence. She traces the origins of her interest in policy-related work to her parents, who were strong New Deal Democrats (her father, a protégé of Illinois Senator Paul Douglas, ran for Congress twice). Huston recalled that hearing Edward Zigler's talk at the APA convention about the research–policy interface inspired her to spend her ensuing sabbatical year learning about political science and policy and then increasingly engaging in policy-relevant work. Following her retirement, Huston began yet another chapter in her policy-focused career, in this case a change from education-focused presentation of social science research to "out-and-out" advocacy.

Multiple Policy-Related Jobs

Among those individuals interviewed who were primarily employed outside of academia, the vast majority worked in more than one employment context during their careers, with nearly one-third working in three or more government and/or intermediary positions (Appendix D, Table D.1). Many of these individuals moved at some point from working inside government to working in the intermediary sector because the connections and skills they developed as policy insiders were highly valued in policy-focused intermediary organizations. The next example illustrates the common theme of movement among legislative branch, executive branch, and finally intermediary organization work contexts.

Positions in Multiple Branches of Government and Intermediary Organizations

Diana Zuckerman

PhD, Clinical Psychology, Ohio State University, 1977

President, National Center for Health Research, Washington, DC

Diana Zuckerman, a clinical psychologist who also has training in social psychology, has held a variety of positions during the course of her policy-focused career. Following a year as a public health post-doctoral fellow, several years in academia, and one year as a congressional fellow, Zuckerman secured policy-related positions at APA, in a House oversight subcommittee, the Senate Veteran Affairs Committee, the Department of Health and Human Services, and as a senior policy advisor in the Clinton administration. Zuckerman subsequently worked for 19 years in the nonprofit sector, most recently directing the National Center for Health Research (NCHR; http://center4research.org/about-us/). Her policy contributions while in Congress include an amendment to the Child Nutrition Act, which allowed children of parents who received Medicaid to become automatically eligible for free school meals, and directing a congressional oversight investigation. The latter resulted in the US **Food and Drug Administration** (FDA) requiring breast implant manufacturers to submit safety studies for the first time in 1991 and then banning the use of most silicone implants in 1992 until safety studies were completed (FDA Medical Devices, 2014).

As president of NCHR, Zuckerman has testified on numerous occasions to Congress, executive branch agencies, and advisory committees, with special focus on the need for clinical trials to test the effectiveness of medical devices (Metcalf, 2012; Zuckerman, Brown, & Nissen, 2011). Here, she provides a brief tour of her career history:

> Early in my [academic] career, I co-authored some books and presented at conferences. I loved doing research but it soon became clear to me that there were not many opportunities in psychology for someone with my interests [in social change]. I had a friend who applied for the APA Congressional Science Fellowship. She loved it and told me about it. It sounded like a dream come true. I applied and was accepted. That was it for me. I've been in Washington ever since.
>
> After my fellowship year, I worked at APA . . . on committees in the House and Senate . . . at HHS . . . and then in the Clinton White House for a little over a year, which I was very excited about.

Since then, I've been working for the last 19 years in the nonprofit sector on policy issues, mainly health and social policy. I've spent a fair amount of time trying to bring the perspective of a researcher to policymakers.

The National Center for Health Research, which I direct, is an evidence-based research and advocacy organization. We do a lot of work with the FDA. A big part of what we have focused on has been the fact that although prescription drugs have to be proven safe and effective in clinical trials, medical devices don't have to be. That includes most implants and even many cardiac devices. Many medical devices are approved on the basis of laboratory bioengineering data which don't even measure safety or effectiveness. We've tried to bring the perspective that research matters and that if you really want to know what a safe medical product is, it should be tested on human beings in scientific, well-designed clinical trials. Amazingly, it had never been brought up before and nobody was talking about it. It's still very controversial.

When I was employed within government, I was very fortunate. I always worked for people who I thought very highly of and working for them was a pleasure. The advantage of being in the nonprofit sector, though, is that I'm the one saying what I think rather trying to figure out what my boss thinks and how he or she would want to say it. There is a certain freedom of being your own person in the nonprofit sector that you don't get when you work in Congress or the White House.

Influences and Summary

When asked how she originally became involved in policy, Zuckerman indicated that she did not know anyone in college involved in social policy. However, when she graduated in 1972, it was "a time of social change" and she was very interested in "making the world a better place." Zuckerman began a doctoral program in social psychology because of her interest in social change but switched to clinical psychology, doing her thesis on the impact of a new phenomenon called Public Access Cable TV and her dissertation on determinants of women's life goals. She began a career as an assistant professor at Vassar and then as a researcher at Yale and Harvard, but then decided, "that was not a way to make a difference in a big way." That's when she entered the world of policy through a congressional science fellowship. Like many congressional fellows interviewed, Zuckerman moved between the insider world of Congress and the executive branch to intermediary organizations. Her transition between contexts reflected a search for new vantage points from which to make a difference and the need to change due to political transitions in the party in control of government.

Multiple Types of Research

The majority of academic psychologists highlighted in this book conducted multiple types of research across their careers in order to influence policy (see Appendix D, Table D.1). For current purposes, type of research encompasses five distinct categories (see Chapter 6 for a more detailed discussion):

- evaluation research
- theory-based understanding of phenomena research
- problem-based, context-specific understanding of phenomena research
- systems policies and practices research
- other (e.g., tool or measure development, policy influence method focused)

The interviewees moved from one research type to another due to multiple factors. These included developments in the discipline, funding streams, opportunity, and how best to answer the research question under consideration. In the next case example, both theory-based (experimental) and problem-focused, context-specific (survey) research about phenomena of interest were employed over the course of a career in social psychology.

Theory- and Policy-Focused Research: Social Psychology and the Law

Eugene Borgida

PhD, Social Psychology, University of Michigan, 1976

Professor of Psychology and Law, University of Minnesota

Eugene Borgida, a social psychologist, conducted various types of studies in his career, primarily addressing social psychology and the law. His research methods included both basic laboratory studies that had policy-relevant implications and context-specific research focused on particular policy topics. Basic laboratory studies included research on gender stereotyping. Policy-specific research encompassed examination of admissible evidence in rape and sexual assault cases and public attitudes to government regulatory activities. Based on his research findings, Borgida has provided expert testimony, depositions, and consultations on 20 law cases over the course of several decades (Borgida, 1980; Borgida, Hunt, & Kim, 2005). He contributed to the amicus brief submitted to the *Price v. Waterhouse* US Supreme Court case and provided consultation both to the US Economic Opportunity Commission and to fellow psychologists providing expert witness testimony in major court cases (Fiske, Bersoff, Borgida, Deaux, & Heilman, 1991).

Since 1985, Borgida has taught in the University of Minnesota law school and has contributed scholarship on the use of research evidence in court cases (e.g., Borgida & Fiske, 2008). One of his applied research projects focused on understanding consumer perceptions of the health risks associated with various tobacco products, a program of research developed explicitly to address key regulatory questions of concern to the US FDA (Borgida, Kim, Stark, & Miller, 2008). Here, Borgida highlights the varied types of research he has conducted and the associated contributions to policy:

> I think the approach has been to conduct research that is either from the very beginning set up to be directly relevant to the policy questions, or else set out in a more theory-driven way [but having] policy implications. The first projects that I did and the very first grant I got was looking at the psychological assumptions that were built into the law regarding what kind of evidence is admissible in rape and sexual assault cases.
>
> Then, in the late '80s, based on basic gender stereotyping research conducted since I was in graduate school, I was involved in the Price Waterhouse case, to persuade the Supreme Court of the United States that the social science Susan Fiske had entered in at trial had scientific standing. The next thing I knew, I was getting a phone call from some lawyers in Minneapolis and got involved as the expert witness in the very first class action sexual harassment and sexual discrimination case in the country involving a group of women miners in the taconite mining industry in Eveleth, Minnesota.
>
> Since the Price Waterhouse and Eveleth cases, I have written a lot mostly with Susan Fiske on the way in which the science has been used in employment discrimination cases. I think it's been successful in terms of really showing people in the field that you can take the social science and social psychology and put it into the context of a social framework that educates fact finders and bring that perspective to bear on important matters, namely allegations about discrimination. It has been introduced in a lot of cases, and I think has been influential in a lot of cases.
>
> I worked with the **Equal Employment Opportunity Commission** (EEOC) in Washington for three years and helped them evaluate the ways in which social science could influence some of their cases. I troubleshot for them in a number of instances where they had cases in which they tried to introduce social science and ran into problems. I've also worked with the EEOC in a number of cases as an expert witness.
>
> There are other social scientists who have called me for advice, including Jon Krosnick when he was involved in the *Exxon Valdez* case and Claude Steele, before he had a 10-hour deposition in the Grutter and Gratz University of Michigan affirmative action cases in 2003 [pp. 197–198]. Concerning the latter, Claude called me and I spoke to him for many hours about how he could present the work on stereotype threat.

I have also been involved recently in other work, for example a series of studies that have looked at public attitudes toward regulation and what drives FDA regulatory attitudes toward tobacco regulation. That research was driven by the way the policymakers were rolling out the question. . . . I've had different strategies on different projects.

Influences and Summary

Borgida's research—and specifically his translation of research findings for multiple branches of government and the public—has led to significant policy impacts. When describing his path into policy, Borgida indicated that he grew up in a very political household. His mother was a labor organizer in Brooklyn, New York. His father, of Hungarian nationality, was trained as a lawyer and a journalist and served as the first executive producer of the Voice of America, the US government's international broadcasting agency. Borgida has a vivid childhood memory of his mother's labor union commitment and political activism. "I remember going to Giant Foods as a kid. . . . Some person was about to select Hunts ketchup. . . . I still remember the shock in this woman's face . . . my mother was talking about Lamar Hunt, his connections to the John Birch Society [radical conservative group] and how you had to boycott these products." As a graduate student in social psychology at University of Michigan, Borgida took courses in law and political science and was drawn to involvement in the Society for the Psychological Study of Social Issues (SPSSI). Like many of the academic researchers interviewed, during the course of his career Borgida has been involved in some projects that were primarily theory-driven (e.g., laboratory studies of gender stereotyping) and others that were primarily policy-driven (e.g., attitudes toward federal regulation of tobacco products). To answer very different questions, researchers need to conduct different types of studies. Research driven by practical concerns to policymakers may more likely be viewed as of direct, instrumental use. Studies driven by the need to understand phenomena, however, may turn out to be policy-relevant as well, as was the case for the many court cases on gender stereotyping.

Multiple Involvements at the Local Level

Many of the psychologists interviewed for this volume report their primary policy involvements as occurring at the national and state levels. A number, however, have sought to affect policy in the communities in which they live and work (see Appendix D, Table D.1). Many of these local policy-relevant involvements, described in earlier chapters, derive from work roles, including consultation to local policymakers, evaluation of local government programs, or action-focused research projects intended to change local policies and practices. Michelle Fine's ongoing engagement with New York City youth in action research to influence both practice and policy is an example (pp. 190–191). For others, ongoing locality-based policy work is based in their involvement as a citizen, including civic roles such as serving on the local school board (e.g., Tom Wolff, pp. 129–131), taking part in town or city advocacy efforts (e.g., Aletha Huston, pp. 229–231), or involvement in local politics/political campaigns (e.g., Brad Olson, pp. 114–116). In the cases of Debi Starnes (pp. 159–160) and Bill Berkowitz (p. 177), such policy work included election to city and town councils, respectively. Finally, for some psychologists, as in the next case example, professional, volunteer, and citizen roles all come into play over time.

Various Policy Advocacy Roles in Tacoma, Washington

Allen Ratcliffe

PhD, Clinical Psychology, Louisiana State University, 1964

Semi-retired Practitioner, Assessment and Consulting Practice

Allen Ratcliffe is a clinical-community psychologist living in Tacoma, Washington. Ratcliffe first moved to the Tacoma area in 1969 to direct the community mental health center. Over the course of decades, Ratcliffe has taken on various local advocacy roles ranging from testifying at hearings to serving on agency boards to volunteering for policy-relevant causes. These varied efforts in part reflect the relationships and expertise Ratcliffe developed related to his role as mental health center director and in part due to his commitment as a citizen to contribute to his local community.

Here, Ratcliffe details his work in a variety of policy roles during his long career:

> I got acquainted with a lot of people over a period of time and would sometimes be consulted by local politicians or state legislators around policy issues. There were times when I was a consultant to Region 10 of NIMH and helped develop a big workshop on how to bring in and integrate the Vietnamese refugees into the northwest area. There was involvement in the model cities program. In one case as mental health center director [I testified] before the Tacoma Human Rights Commission. I noticed on the agenda to that meeting that two items down was going to be a review of the city's antidiscrimination ordinance. I knew that the antidiscrimination ordinance did not protect handicapped folks against discrimination in housing. Basically I just stayed. When that topic came up and it was time

for people to comment, I raised my hand, pointed that out and asked if they would fix it. They did. We had the first ordinance in the state of Washington that protected handicapped folks against housing discrimination.

Sometimes my policy contributions were in my then-official role as Mental Health Director. Sometimes it was essentially as a citizen. Often it was as a volunteer. I have had some things along the way where I got paid, but I often have done things on a volunteer basis. For instance, at one point I was appointed to the Tacoma Landmarks Preservation Commission. At the present time, I'm a member of the City Human Services Commission that advises the council on what nonprofit organizations and services they should fund.

I was for a while a member of the county's Mental Health Advisory Board when the county operated this system and then gave it up because the state wouldn't fund it. I am now a member of the Mental Health Advisory Board for the for-profit organization that has eventually taken it over and is doing very good stuff.

I'm working with the Housing Homeless Continuum of Care that is a HUD [**Department of Housing and Urban Development**]-mandated body that's here in the county. What I'm working on right now is essentially laying groundwork for an effort to eliminate the discharge of homeless people back to the streets after they've been in the hospital or jail.

Just now I picked up an issue that involves getting the Department of Labor and Industry to cover law enforcement and emergency response personnel that happen to develop PTSD. At this point they're not covered unless they're physically injured.

Stuff has come up. I just do it.

Influences and Summary

Interestingly, Ratcliffe was never a stranger to local policy and politics. His mother was a local precinct council member during his youth in southern Indiana (she later was elected to the city council and became Deputy Mayor). Ratcliffe's first policy involvement coincided with assuming leadership of the comprehensive mental health center in Tacoma, which was in serious financial trouble. Ratcliffe noticed that the state did not cover Medicaid patients, and, to save the center from bankruptcy, he successfully forced the state to begin paying Medicaid for community mental health services. He notes that he learned little about policy in his professional training in clinical psychology, but instead learned "by doing it." Ratcliffe believes that community-based policy work, as is the case with community practice in general, is centered in relationship development and establishment of partnerships with stakeholders on shared issues of concern.

Summary

While some psychologists only become involved in policy work for a short while, many maintain their involvement across their lifetimes. Through their perseverance, psychologists have made significant policy impacts at the local and national levels across all branches of government and in a variety of settings. The careers described are not fixed or stagnant; rather, these psychologists flexibly change their collaborations, policy issues, employment contexts, research methods, and personal roles. Many changes in these various aspects of policy involvement appear to be interrelated—for example, a change in employment context from policy insider to intermediary organization staff person necessitates a change in policy influence methods. The reality that multiple aspects of individuals' policy involvements jointly change over time (e.g., substantive policy area, branch of government, organizational partners, policy method) reflects the multifaceted ecology of policy involvements over the policy career lifespan.

These psychologists' career paths remind us that we should consider the policy issues of greatest concern to us, our current skills, and our desired roles in order to determine in which contexts we would be most effective and with whom we should collaborate. However, we must also recognize the external factors that will push us in particular directions—funding, public concern, current events, and political changes, to name a few—so that we are attuned to and take advantage of opportunities to impact policy.

Distinctive Aspects of a Policy Career

Beyond multiple policy involvements, other aspects of psychologists' career journeys are distinctive and worthy of note. Three are examined below:

- interdisciplinary collaborations
- leadership positions
- international policy work

These three areas of career emphasis appear particularly important for the field moving forward in terms of the quality, effectiveness, and scope of policy influence. We begin with interdisciplinary policy collaborations among university faculty.

Interdisciplinary Collaborations: University Faculty

Policy-relevant collaborations with scholars from other disciplines characterize the work of most of the 50 university faculty interviewed. Three-fifths are members (or directors) of interdisciplinary centers, research groups or research networks, and more than two-fifths hold primary appointments in interdisciplinary departments, schools, or centers (Appendix D, Table D.2). Co-authors on policy-relevant publications are from a wide range of disciplines, including economics, education, law, sociology, political science, medicine, psychiatry, public health, and public policy (Appendix D, Table D-2). Interdisciplinary collaboration sometimes involved a single scholar from another discipline, but also involved scholars from multiple disciplines in many cases, especially in initiatives generated by interdisciplinary centers.

Here, three case examples are presented that highlight interdisciplinary collaborations among scholars. The first encompasses both multidisciplinary research and teaching.

A Multidisciplinary Career Focused on the Intersection of Research, Policies and Programs for Children, Youth, and Families

P. Lindsay Chase-Lansdale

PhD, Developmental Psychology, University of Michigan, 1981

Associate Provost and Professor of Human Development and Social Policy, Northwestern University

P. Lindsay Chase-Lansdale, a developmental psychologist, has collaborated with scholars from multiple disciplines in her policy-relevant research and teaching throughout her career. This work occurred in interdisciplinary work settings, including the Chapin Hall Center for Children and the Irving B. Harris School of Public Policy, both at the University of Chicago, and the School of Education and Policy and the Institute for Policy Research, both at Northwestern University. Research collaborators include historian Maris Vinovskis (Chase-Lansdale & Vinovskis, 1987), sociologists Frank Furstenberg and Andrew Cherlin (Chase-Lansdale, Cherlin, & Kiernan, 1995; Furstenberg, Brooks-Gunn, & Chase-Lansdale, 1989), and economists Greg Duncan, Robert Michael, and Robert Moffitt (Chase-Lansdale & Duncan, 2001; Chase-Lansdale et al, 2003; Desai, Chase-Lansdale, & Michael, 1989).

Currently, Chase-Lansdale is working with fellow development psychologists Jeanne Brooks–Gunn (pp. xx–xx) and Hiro Yoshikawa (pp. xx-xx), public policy professor Teresa Eeckrich Sommer, and economist Christopher King to examine two-generation human capital interventions as a promising means to address poverty (Sommer et al., 2012; Chase-Lansdale &

Brooks-Gunn, 2014). Here, Chase-Lansdale provides an overview of her multidisciplinary policy collaborations:

I was associate director of SRCD's [Society for Research in Child Development's] Washington office for three years. This was my first job after serving as an SRCD/AAAS Congressional Science Fellow in 1981–82, working for then Congressman Paul Simon. In both positions, I interacted extensively with staff from the Washington offices of many professional organizations, such as the American Psychological Association, the American Economics Association, and the American Sociological Association, in addition to Congressional and Federal staff. As part of my position with SRCD's Washington Office, I organized and conducted research and policy seminars on the Hill on current pressing topics related to children and families. It was a very dynamic period, and the policy positions in DC showed me that addressing any social problem required knowledgeable input from multiple disciplines.

I decided that I wanted to go back into research after serving as a knowledge broker between science and policy in Washington, DC, and I was fortunate to be selected as a three-year postdoctoral fellow in the new NIMH Research Consortium on Families. In that capacity, I benefited from the mentoring [received from] 12 leading family research professors, such as E. Mavis Hetherington, David Reiss, and Philip and Carolyn Cowan. During that same period, Jeanne Brooks-Gunn served as an inspirational postdoctoral mentor, and we developed a multidisciplinary collaboration with Frank F. Furstenberg, Jr. on family strengths among young, multigenerational, African American families (grandmothers, young mothers, and preschoolers) in poverty. I also launched a multidisciplinary collaboration with economist Robert Michael and sociologist Sondale Desai on the influence of maternal employment on child development, publishing one of the first child-focused research articles from the National Longitudinal Survey of Youth and introducing that data set to developmentalists.

My expertise in policy and research was deepened when Harold Richman, former dean of the School of Social Service Administration at the University of Chicago and Director of the Chapin Hall Center for Children, hired me to work at Chapin Hall. I was one of the first developmentalists in this interdisciplinary think tank. Robert Michael, the founding dean of the Harris School of Public Policy Studies, invited me to co-teach with him on child and family policy. The Public Policy students loved how the course interwove economics and psychology in order to address policy issues. I later joined the School as an assistant professor and in 1994 was the first developmental psychologist to be tenured in a public policy school in the United States. If I hadn't had the extensive policy experience in Congress and the

SRCD Washington Office, I would have found it very difficult to function and teach in a public policy school. I was stimulated and challenged to highlight my identity and expertise as a developmental psychologist, to become more knowledgeable about theory and empirics in other disciplines, and to combine these perspectives in scholarship and teaching.

Currently, I lead an ambitious, collaborative, multidisciplinary action research program to study two-generation education interventions. I've been thinking and writing about this topic for a long time, but I am now evaluating two model programs that are administered by the Community Action Program in Tulsa (CAP-Tulsa). These involve linking education and job training for parents who have enrolled their children in CAP-Tulsa's Head Start programs. We have funding from the Administration on Children and Families, as well as the Kellogg Foundation and the Foundation for Child Development. The central question is whether two-generation programs have stronger, positive impacts on child development than early childhood education alone.

Influences and Summary

Chase-Lansdale attributes her interest in social policy to many factors, beginning with her parents' values and her early religious and community experiences. As she notes, "I grew up as an Episcopalian and was influenced by the emphasis on social justice. I also attended Quaker meetings . . . and learned about conscientious objectors. . . . The Quakers in my hometown had freed their slaves before the Civil War and had given them land for farming and for their own church. . . . My father was one of the few people who would hire African Americans, at the time, in his mill, which serviced all of the farms in the area (now long gone to DC urban sprawl), and my parents were key role models for me." Chase-Lansdale was also influenced by the various social movements in the 1960s and, in graduate school, by Howard Stevenson. Stevenson initiated the involvement of SRCD in social policy and also established the Bush Program in Child Development and Social Policy at the University of Michigan. Like other psychologists situated within interdisciplinary work settings, Chase-Lansdale has had numerous opportunities to conduct research and teach with colleagues from other disciplines. Such work is especially useful in the policy arena, given the inherently multifaceted and multilevel nature of challenging social issues.

The work of the next psychologist also occurs in an interdisciplinary work context, in this case involving policy consultation and related research across a spectrum of topics.

Interdisciplinary Consultation and Research Center

Alan Tomkins

PhD, Social Psychology, JD, Law, Washington University, 1984

Professor of Psychology and Law, University of Nebraska-Lincoln Acting Division Director, Social and Economic Sciences, National Science Foundation

Alan Tomkins, a social psychologist also trained in law, is founding direc- tor of the interdisciplinary University of Nebraska Public Policy Center. The Public Policy Center (http://ppc.unl.edu/) provides consultation to and conducts research for officials in all three branches of government. An early legislative Center initiative involved forging compromise among conflicting stakeholder groups to develop a statewide, centralized system of child sup- port collection and disbursement (Shank & Tomkins, 1999). In one contri- bution to the judicial branch, the Center took a lead role in developing the Nebraska Minority and Justice Task Force to address racial justice disparities in the state. One specific initiative used reminders to racial minority youth to reduce missed court appearances (Bornstein, Tomkins, Neeley, Herian, & Hamm, 2013). In terms of the executive branch, at the local level, a five- year collaboration between the Center and the city of Lincoln mayor's office employed multiple methods to obtain citizen input to inform budget priori- ties, in one instance resulting in the mayor's agreement, during the "Great Recession" when tax increases were atypical, to preserve local social services through a tax increase rather than eliminating the services to balance the budget (Tomkins et al., 2012).

Given the broad array of policy topics with which Tomkins has become in- volved, an interdisciplinary staff has proved essential, as has generating access to faculty affiliates and fellows spanning a wide range of disciplines (computer science, law, political science, sociology, and so on). Here, Tomkins highlights his interdisciplinary interests and policy work at the Public Policy Center:

> I've always had this interdisciplinary interest. I've always read sociology, political science and other literatures; there's so much to know. . . . What I wanted to do in graduate school was combine law and psychology. At Washington University the law school and psychology department al- lowed me to create an ad hoc law psychology graduate program.
>
> I started the Public Policy Center in 1998 at the request of the uni- versity. It now has about 15 full-time researchers. Because societal problems are so multidisciplinary and complex, I often find useful in- formation from a variety of disciplines, and not even necessarily where I would think I might find it. We benefit by having graduate students

and faculty from sociology, political science, economics, and natural resources.

We address legislative, executive, and judicial branch interests and desires. We have revenues of around $3.5 million; we have about 50 projects. For the first 10 years of our existence, we received financial support from the university, but in 2008 the university stopped investing in us. Most of our money now comes in behavioral health consulting and services. When we started, I got leading state representatives, including the governor, to agree to serve on the policy center's advisory board. Over the years we have been involved in endeavors ranging from helping disburse federal child support payments, a minority justice initiative, and disaster preparedness and relief (including with tribal communities).

We're in a privileged position to use university-based perspectives to implement policy changes in many different systems. For example, I had a state senator call me this week. He wants to do something in energy. I have no idea about technical issues related to energy, but what we can do is reach back into the university and get him the resources he needs for the issues that he wants to address. It's not like we know everything, but we are part of a public university that has lots of expertise and resources.

We have found that we work really well by only being advocates for information, not advocates for ideological, political, or even academic positions. For example, the Center influences the way that the city of Lincoln does its public processes that provide input into the city's budgeting. The city, even though it has a Democratic administration, tells me that it is helpful to them that we have a reputation of being close to the very conservative Tea-Party-like governor of our state. This enhances our credibility. . . . We found that advocacy is not our best way to pursue policy impact and change. What we try to do is say, "We are led by data and information and best practices or promising practices based on an evidentiary-like basis."

Influences and Summary

Like many others interviewed, Tomkins did not plan to do work in psychology and policy. He describes his trajectory of involvement in this area as "haphazard" and "fortuitous." In terms of early influences, Tomkins notes that his religious heritage and awareness of the Holocaust probably provided "that sense, that as Jews, we had a responsibility to speak up for societal interests." He developed an early interest in law and was fortunate, as an undergraduate, to be presented with an opportunity to take a course on psychology and law, which stimulated his desire to pursue both fields in graduate school. The combination of a doctorate in psychology and a law degree provided him an interdisciplinary vantage point, one that is particularly useful in policy work with the courts and with many legislators.

Tomkin's public policy center work addresses a diversity of topics and draws on the varied expertise of faculty members in the wider university community. Even Tomkins' research on citizen participation, squarely based in his social psychology background, is conducted in collaboration with colleagues from other disciplines.

The third example involves interdisciplinary collaboration in a single area of focus—adolescent competency to stand trial—and involves collaboration among a psychology faculty member, his graduate student (now faculty member), and a legal scholar.

An Interdisciplinary Research Collaboration: Adolescent Competency to Stand Trial

N. Dickon Reppucci

PhD, Clinical Psychology, Harvard University, 1968

Professor of Psychology, University of Virginia

Jennifer Woolard

PhD, Community-Developmental Psychology, University of Virginia, 1998

Associate Professor of Psychology, Georgetown University

N. Dickon Reppucci, a clinical-community-developmental psychologist and one of his graduate students, Jennifer Woolard, a community-developmental psychologist, collaborated with lawyer Elizabeth Scott in the early 1990s to enhance understanding of adolescent competence to stand trial (Scott, Reppucci, & Woolard, 1995). First, they developed a conceptual model that added psychosocial factors to the prevailing framework in use at the time, which was limited to cognitive factors (Reppucci, 1999). Then they developed a measure to assess competence to stand trial and used the measure to demonstrate that adolescent samples differed from adults in critical ways in regard to judicial competence (Woolard, Reppucci, & Scott, 1996; Woolard, 1998). This early interdisciplinary work contributed to the development, in 1996, of the interdisciplinary MacArthur Network on Adolescent Development and

Juvenile Justice. In turn, the work of that network contributed, among other things, to the US Supreme Court overturning the death penalty for adolescents (Chapter 3, pp. 93–95). Reppucci served on one of the working groups of the interdisciplinary network, and Woolard and Scott were long-term core network members.

Interview excerpts from both Reppucci and Woolard are presented here. Reppucci highlights aspects of his interdisciplinary experience at the University of Virginia:

> From the beginning of my time here, I got involved with the Institute for Psychiatry, Law and Public Policy, located in the law school. I was working in collaboration with a law faculty member, Elizabeth Scott, and also Ed Mulvey [pp. 213–215], who had been my student, and then-grad-student Jennifer Woolard. The developmental competence of adolescents in the judicial context struck us as something that was terribly important that the law did not take into account. We examined the question, "Are there developmental differences between youth and adults eighteen and above?"
>
> The work that started from those initial meetings with the four of us led to the interdisciplinary MacArthur Network. Future Network member Tom Grisso [pp. 216–218] was at one of our early meetings. . . . The issue of working with lawyers is that they get an idea and often seem ready to move it to policy immediately, without scientific underpinning. Our job was to make sure we had solid data that could be used to help influence the law. The Network did a great big study of kids and the competence to stand trial that was headed by Tom Grisso. If you read the legal brief that led to the 2005 *Roper v. Simmons* Supreme Court case, the one that outlawed the juvenile death penalty, it's based on a huge amount of work out of the Network.

Jennifer Woolard, in turn, recounts her undergraduate experience and then provides additional details about the interdisciplinary collaborative research:

> At the University of Virginia, I was a psychology and sociology double major, but very much interested in the law. I think what really drew me to policy was thinking about larger social structures. I took Dick Reppucci's class on children, families, and the law. I also had a couple of internships as an undergraduate that related to policy. All of those things kind of came together to really press my interest in policy. I realized that research and policy was a better fit for me than law. I entered the community psychology graduate program. It was such a great fit. Having psychologist John Monahan [pp. 209–211] and lawyer Elizabeth Scott on the Law School faculty, it really was an interdisciplinary interaction.

With the MacArthur Network competency research project, we made sure the age groupings for our sampling mapped onto not only developmental research but also onto state statutes for transfer—so that the research could speak to the law and also be theoretically meaningful. If we weren't thinking about that from the beginning, quite a practical contribution from lawyers on the Network, we could have done that less helpfully to the policy and the law argument. The MacArthur Network had a huge impact.

Influences and Summary

Woolard's interest in psychology and policy was influenced by her work with Reppucci who, in turn, decades earlier, had been inspired by Seymour Sarason. Sarason mentored and greatly affected Reppucci's career trajectory when Reppucci was an assistant/associate professor through their involvement in the Yale Psychoeducational Clinic. (See the Foreword to this book pp. xv–xvi.) Reppucci had been trained in clinical psychology in graduate school at Harvard, where he focused on individual change; but, as he notes, "By the time I left Yale, I was convinced . . . that psychology should be playing a role in the larger world. I really was a Seymour addict." Reppucci took a position at University of Virginia, where he, Woolard, and Scott generated a conceptual framework, an empirical measure, and early research findings that helped set the stage for the MacArthur Network's groundbreaking work on adolescent competency and the legal system. The collaboration between psychologists and a lawyer was ideal for addressing the adolescent competence issue, bringing to bear theory and research methods from developmental psychology with knowledge of the workings of the legal system and current legal practice (Owen-Kostelnik, Reppucci, & Meyer, 2006).

Summary

Working with other disciplines and professions is a relatively common occurrence for the university faculty interviewed as they seek to address multifaceted, complex social issues. Multiple disciplines and professions have interests and specialized knowledge, experiences, and perspectives to share on such issues. For university faculty or graduate students who join (or develop) interdisciplinary research centers, networks, and groups, intermediary collaborations are likely to emerge naturally. For psychologists lacking such interdisciplinary work contexts, collaboration often requires reaching out to or being sought by scholars from other disciplines with overlapping interests in a policy area.

Next, we turn to another distinctive career aspect, movement into policy-relevant leadership roles.

Policy-Relevant Leadership Roles

The expanded opportunity to exert policy influence afforded by leadership positions constitutes a second distinctive aspect of psychologists' career journeys. The nature of leadership positions were quite varied in terms of leadership level and employment context. For current purposes, leadership level is divided into:

- high-level organizational leadership, reflecting overall responsibility for an organization
- medium-level leadership, reflecting responsibility for a major unit within a larger organization

High-level leadership positions were held by 15% of those interviewed, across university (e.g., chancellor, dean), intermediary organization (e.g., president or vice president of an advocacy organization), and governmental (e.g., elected official) employment contexts (Appendix D, Table D.3). Medium-level positions were held by 62% of those interviewed, within universities (e.g., research center or policy center directors), intermediary organizations (e.g., director of the policy office, senior policy advisor at APA), and government (e.g., legislative director or chief of staff for a senator). Here, three case examples of policy-relevant leadership are presented: the first two are high-level organizational leadership positions (dean, chancellor) and the third is medium-level leadership (policy center director). We begin with the leadership role of dean at the Stanford School of Education.

Dean of Education: A Vision to Enhance Policy and Practice Research

Deborah Stipek

PhD, Developmental Psychology, Yale University, 1977

Dean and Professor, Stanford Graduate School of Education

As a developmental psychologist and Dean of the Stanford Graduate School of Education, Deborah Stipek spearheads initiatives to enhance faculty focus on policy- and practice-relevant research. For example, Stipek supported the creation of the Center for Education Policy (CEPA; cepa.stanford.edu). CEPA addresses topics such as California school finance and governance, early childhood education, the impact of the California high school exit examination on school trajectories, and the effects of racial school segregation on the black–white achievement gap. Some of the work is initiated by faculty. The school finance and governance studies (Getting Down to Facts, n.d.) were requested by state policymakers, including the Governor's Committee on Education Excellence and the leadership of the California Senate and Assembly.

Stipek describes the policy-relevant leadership vision she brought to her position as dean and the various activities she has pursued to promote that vision:

When I came to Stanford as dean, my vision for the School of Education was to make its work in the field more visible and to encourage efforts to work collaboratively with practitioners and policymakers. A commitment to doing practically relevant research already existed at Stanford. I just had to nurture those interests and find resources to support the work. I made this kind of work a priority in my fundraising and used whatever persuasive power I had to reinforce its importance.

Deans and department chairs can promote policy-related research by letting faculty who are doing that kind of work know that it is valued, by finding resources to support it, and by getting as much publicity for it as possible. I could give you many examples of ways in which the work of our faculty has had a significant impact on policies. For example, not long ago, California's school finance system was a mess and inequitable. The new finance system that Governor Brown and the legislature recently put in place reflects substantially the study and recommendations made by Stanford faculty. It didn't happen immediately but the research and analysis had an effect on the political conversation, and when the economy and the political context were suitable, its impact was clear.

One strategy for making our work relevant and used in policy and practice is to be visible myself and to develop productive relationships. I am on many nonprofit boards that do education-related work. I've given many talks in Washington on a broad array of education topics. I have also organized many meetings for various groups, including journalists, because one way to influence policymakers is to inform and influence the public.

Education policy is not only made at the federal and state levels. Many of the most important decisions are made at the district or even at the school level. Educational researchers have many audiences, at many levels. When considering what you can do, and what policies research might inform, all of those audiences need to be considered. I move back and forth between teachers and federal policymakers and many levels in between.

Influences and Summary

Deborah Stipek relayed during the interview that it was in graduate school, working with Edward Zigler, that she first became interested in policy work. Then, after completing a congressional fellowship, she accepted a position at University of California, Los Angeles (UCLA) School of Education, where she directed the laboratory elementary school. She then moved to Stanford School of Education as their dean. In her interview, Stipek highlights the importance of program visibility and promotion in order to influence policy. Using the leadership tools of vision, program development, hiring, and support of faculty, along with policy- and practice-related activities in the multilevel "educational policy space," Stipek has been able to move individual faculty and the school of education in general toward enhanced focus on policy-relevant research and activity.

We move next to a career that has encompassed multiple levels of university leadership, in multiple locales.

Provost and Chancellor: Affirmative Action, Engaged Scholarship, and Community Development

Nancy Cantor

PhD, Social Psychology, Stanford University, 1978

Chancellor, Rutgers University-Newark

Social psychologist Nancy Cantor has interfaced with the policy world from multiple administrative positions in higher education, including dean, provost, and, more recently, chancellor (at three universities). As provost, one of her major opportunities to influence policy was to spearhead the effort to defend race-based admissions at the University of Michigan in the *Grutter v. Bollinger* and *Gratz v. Bollinger* court cases. She asked faculty member Patricia Gurin to fashion the empirical case for the compelling state interest of affirmative action and then worked closely with her on the strategic framework adopted (pp. 197–198). More recently, during her years as chancellor at Syracuse University, Cantor pursued her vision of Scholarship in Action. She committed considerable time and resources to a multifaceted collaborative community development initiative in a low-income area of Syracuse, New York, that generated $70 million in public-private (non-university) investment across diverse projects and involved multiple public officials (Cantor, 2010, 2012, 2013). As part of this policy influence work, Cantor mobilized faculty and was personally involved in collaborative meetings and networking with local and state policymakers. Cantor views her policy work as enhancing access to college, and she views higher education as a public good in community-building. Following her years as chancellor at Syracuse University, Cantor moved to Rutgers University–Newark, where she is currently chancellor. Here, Cantor highlights key aspects of her policy involvement as a university provost and chancellor:

Throughout my career, I've been involved in institution-level aspects of higher education, both as a faculty member and as a higher education leader. That naturally draws you into caring about federal, state, and local policy as it affects issues in higher education. There are three large areas.

- *First of all, issues of access, opportunity and diversity. Within that, there were affirmative action issues and, more broadly, how to get diversity in the professoriate and in fields like Science, Technology, Engineering, and Math (STEM) and others, issues that revolved strongly around race, ethnicity, diversity and gender.*
- *For the second area, work started at Michigan, but what I've spent the last 10 years or so doing at Syracuse is focus on the role of higher education as a public good in community-building.*
- *Then the third would be how all of this relates to questions of K–12 and to the pathway up and into higher education.*

I interfaced with the policy world a lot in all three of those. As provost at Michigan and defending the affirmative action lawsuits, I did all the time. As an anchor institution in the city of Syracuse and the region, I co-chaired the Regional Economic Development Council and worked constantly with policymakers. In general, as a university president, I interact regularly with congressional and other delegations.

What we did my first year at Syracuse [was] called Exploring the Soul of Syracuse, a listening and conversation tour on campus and in the city. What came out was a clear sense that there was a history of tremendous suspicion and failure to meet expectations, and at the same time tremendous overlap in expertise and needs. We began forming partnerships, based on real collaboration and engagement. In the ninth poorest census tract in the US, in the west side of Syracuse, we helped create a nonprofit [organization], the Near Westside Initiative. It has mobilized more than $70 million of investment. Resident-owned and resident-run collaborations include entrepreneurship; revitalizing abandoned factories; bringing art, technology, and design deeply into the community; and building on community assets as opposed to gentrifying. The policy partners were the city, the county, and through various grants, the Regional Economic Council, the state and the feds. I was certainly at the table in all of those things, but we also just had a lot of local partners.

Say Yes to Education Syracuse, the K–12 district-wide school reform project, was very much embedded in the neighborhood work. That included legal clinics, health clinics, after-school, summer school, financial aid, and a comprehensive model of school improvement. We had substantial urban-school improvement collaboration with foundations, policymakers, mayors, and with county, state, and federal executives.

Influences and Summary

Cantor grew up in New York City and attributes her interest in diversity, access to education, and gender to several influences. These include her exposure to diverse populations riding the subway to school every day and her social activist parents, including the work her social gerontologist mother did with poor, ethnic, elderly populations. She also highlights the impact of the times in which she grew up, stating "the crucible of the civil rights movement, the women's movement, and the Vietnam War peace movement set the stage for caring about those things." Cantor describes her involvement in policy, and ultimately in leadership positions in higher education, as "flowing naturally from the kind of university work that I've been involved in" and as evolving naturally from her scholarly career as a social psychologist—rather than a deliberate decision.

The final example in this section includes leadership positions explicitly focused on policy work.

Director of Public Policy Center: Child- and Family-Focused Policy

Brian Wilcox

PhD, Community Psychology, University of Texas, 1979

Former Director, Center on Children, Families, and the Law (CCFL) and Emeritus Professor, Department of Psychology, University of Nebraska-Lincoln

Brian Wilcox, a community psychologist, has been involved in leadership roles both at APA as director of the public policy office and, for more than

20 years, as director of the interdisciplinary Center on Children, Families, and the Law (CCFL) at the University of Nebraska, Lincoln (http://ccfl.unl. edu/). While director of CCFL, Wilcox was involved in policy work with state executive branch officials, legislators, and members of the judicial branch on a wide range of child-focused policy (http://ccfl.unl.edu/projects_outreach). Through these involvements, various routes of influence were engaged ranging from state advisory board membership (e.g., Nebraska Commission for the Protection of Children), informal consultation to officials, training of child protective workers, family impact seminars for legislators (Wilcox, Weisz, & Miller, 2005), to media campaigns. Concerning the latter, for example, a policy foray that Wilcox described as "fun, and highly successful" involved sex education in the public schools. Conducted in collaboration with Planned Parenthood and involving op-eds and meetings with newspaper editorial boards, in the early 2000s, this effort led to a reversal of the State School Board of Education policy that limited HIV education in the state's schools to abstinence-only approaches.

An example of a more recent initiative was work to "reinvent" the state's child welfare system. Here, Wilcox recounts aspects of his policy influence work, first as director of policy at APA and then as director of CCFL: After working as an assistant professor and then as an SRCD congressional fellow, I went to work with the American Psychological Association where I spent almost nine years, mostly directing their public policy office.

> I was pretty deeply engaged in federal policymaking with the goal of trying to do high-quality policy analysis and bringing that analysis to bear on policy questions in the public interest.
>
> Here at the University of Nebraska, I head the Center on Children and Families and the Law. The main policy areas have been child welfare, child mental health, adolescent sexual health and reproductive health, juvenile justice, and then to a somewhat lesser extent, education policy. Our center contracts with the government to help the state best design and deliver services to, for example, kids in the child welfare system. A lot of time is spent talking with state agency people, working with them in a variety of contexts. I end up serving on a lot of committees that the state has relating to service to children. For example, as soon as I got to Nebraska, the governor appointed me to the Commission for the Protection of Children, and I've served on that commission for six terms now, under three different governors, providing advice to the leadership in the state around children services. And then there's working with legislators, providing testimony and simply providing advice when they're considering policy actions that affect children. It takes all forms imaginable.

One example of policy influence was in 2002 or so. The State Department of Education here in Nebraska had been essentially taken over by a group of conservative religious-right members who established abstinence-only HIV education for the schools in the state. We wrote op-ed pieces in the main newspapers in the state and then got contacted by the editorial boards and met with them. When it came time for the re-election of the board members, these newspapers opposed re-election of these individuals. All of them were voted out, except one who resigned because it was clear that they were going to lose.

Given that there are some 60 people working here at the center, a lot of the work I do is managing the center. But my principle job is really policy-oriented, so I have a very unusual faculty position. My mission is to keep my colleagues in the university informed about and engaged with policy issues that the state is grappling with and then bringing expertise from the university to bear on those problems and working with the policymakers in that respect. So I am a bridge between the two worlds.

Influences and Summary

Wilcox attributes his early interest in policy to growing up in the '60s and '70s and his involvement as "sort of a political activist" in high school and college. His community psychology graduate program was explicitly geared toward getting students involved in policy. Thus, throughout graduate school Wilcox was required to have a least a quarter-time placement in a policy-related setting, which, along with several courses taken in the Lyndon B. Johnson School of Public Policy, solidified his policy interests. As an assistant professor at University of Virginia, Wilcox taught courses on psychology and policy, during which time he took a leave to deepen his knowledge of policy through an SRCD congressional fellowship. From there, as he notes, he made the decision to "step into the deep end of the pool," committing to a policy-focused career ultimately involving important leadership responsibilities.

Summary

The preceding three case examples illustrate differing ways that leadership positions—obtained during the course of a policy-focused career—present opportunities to exert policy influence. Each psychologist mobilized resources (e.g., funding, faculty, community partners) to help actualize his or her policy-oriented visions and used a range of strategies and methods to influence policy. The three share in common contextual influences related to their openness to pursuing policy work (e.g., growing up in the '60s), but their routes to leadership were tied to their specific work contexts and substantive areas of interest.

More generally, the leadership positions held by those interviewed for this volume are impressive in both their importance and diversity. They reflect the opportunities for psychologists to contribute in meaningful ways to shaping policy as their careers evolve and their influence grows. As illustrated in many of the case examples throughout the volume, leadership affords the opportunity to shape agendas and motivate individuals in academic, intermediary, and government contexts alike to bring to bear psychological expertise and interests to important policy-relevant and policy-focused efforts.

The third distinctive career emphasis examined represents an area of growing emphasis in the field—the international policy arena.

International Policy Focus

This volume focuses on US social policy, and interviewees were selected with this in mind. Thus, the examples of greatest policy success typically focus on policy work in the United States. Nonetheless, a number of interviewees describe an international focus as a growing and important aspect of their policy-related work and of their field's policy mission more generally. International policy involvement in the current context is defined as policy-relevant work taking place outside of the United States by psychologists trained in this country. This work most typically involves travel from the United States to other countries to consult about successful programs that the interviewee had developed in the United States or to collaborate with researchers in other countries on policy-relevant research endeavors. Twelve interviewees report policy-related involvement outside of the United States (Appendix D, Table D.4). In some cases, the work involves interfacing with elected officials, but more often it involves working with nonelected government officials tasked with authorizing and implementing programs. Interestingly, several respondents note that aspects of their policy influence work had proved more successful in countries other than the United States. Two case examples of policy work in international context are presented here, from England and Puerto Rico.[3] We begin with the example in England, one focused on families in disadvantaged neighborhoods and family leave policy.

---

[3] Policy-relevant work in Puerto Rico (and other US territories) is viewed as international in the current context. As a US territory, Puerto Rico differs significantly from US states in language (predominantly Spanish), culture, and governance. Furthermore, citizens in Puerto Rico cannot vote in US presidential elections.

Poverty Prevention and Expanded Family Leave in England

Jay Belsky

PhD, Human Development and Family Studies, Cornell University, 1978

Professor of Human Development, University of California, Davis

Jay Belsky, a developmental psychologist, spent 12 years in London, where he founded and directed the Institute for the Study of Children, Families, and Social Issues, Birkbeck University of London. During this time, he played a central role in the national evaluation of Sure Start, a government-sponsored poverty-prevention intervention focused on families living in disadvantaged neighborhoods. The early evaluation results were mixed, including negative effects on the children and families most at risk (Belsky et al., 2006). Belsky and collaborators shared the mixed findings in a set of meetings with government officials. Belsky was surprised that, in the end, these results provided some of the basis for the government's decision to revamp the program. Follow-up evaluation revealed more positive findings in the revised program (Belsky, Melhuish, & Barnes, 2008). Independent of this work, Belsky met with interested officials about the mixed findings of US-based research on infant daycare, including his own work in the area (e.g., Belsky, 1988, 2009). Policymakers ultimately moved to expand family leave, which appeared at least in part to be based on the US research literature.

Here, Belsky begins by noting differences in receptiveness to research evidence in the United States and England, and he shares aspects of his policy influence work related to Sure Start and infant daycare/family leave, respectively:

I spent 12 years in London. One of the interesting things for me was the policy contrast with the US. England is a smaller country and the government, at least while I was there, wanted its social programs to be, as much as possible, evidence-based. The barriers to such an approach were actually the same as in the USA at the time. Policy-related people, including policy-interested scientists, don't like to hear what they don't like to hear. The barriers just were more powerful in America than they proved to be in London, at least at that point in time—in two different substantive areas.

I led a team that put together a massive proposal to the UK Department for Education and Skills to evaluate Sure Start, a multifaceted intervention program specifically targeting small, disadvantaged, geographic areas, mostly, but not exclusively, in cities. We won it [the evaluation project]. When the results came out, they weren't so good. We had a briefing and the officials didn't know what to do. Next they called in higher-up bureaucrats, and then members of the government and Parliament. They didn't like our findings, which suggested that the program might be having negative effects on the most at-risk kids and families, not big ones but other than what they were looking to see. Eventually, they came around, and said, "We have to modify this program. It's not working like we want it to." They came up with a revised model and radically changed the program they had invested so much time, energy, and money in. I've always wondered whether our data compelled them to revise their strategy. Our research design was limited due to constraints that the government placed on what we could so. But this was a case where had our results come out differently, they would have behaved differently. When our results came out the way they did, they steered the ship in a new direction explicitly. It wasn't just because we found some unanticipated negative effects. It was that coupled with other research findings suggesting a new direction to go in.

In the separate area of daycare, in the US for the most part I remain to be convinced that the millions of dollars spent on a federally sponsored daycare study, the biggest ever conducted, has had much effect on policy. In contrast, in England, the Blair government came in, and crafted and revised policy based upon both American scientific research, including my research, and the British intervention research, suggesting that lots of time spent in daycare early in life potentially makes kids more aggressive. There was a woman who was high up in what we would call the Department of Education who had her own concerns about daycare. She gave me opportunities to brief people in the government in power, including a committee of the Parliament. The research was part of the critical mass that led [the government] to extend paid parental leave and encouraged them to work for more financial support for families, giving [families] choices as to whether or not to use childcare.

Influences and Summary

Belsky attended graduate school in human development at Cornell because the program at the time had a strong applied and policy-related focus. In the early years of his career, however, his research indicating possible negative effects of childcare initiated in the first year of a child's life was not well received (i.e., viewed as anti–child care for young children and anti-women). After relocating to London for 12 years, Belsky found greater receptivity to the results of child care research from studies he and others conducted in the United States and those commissioned by the British government. Meetings with policymakers constituted the primary policy influence method utilized by Belsky, providing him the opportunity to share and discuss findings—including those that were negative.

The final brief example focuses on facilitating the involvement of Puerto Rican psychologists in varied policy initiatives.

Puerto Rico Psychological Association: Facilitating Public Interest Policy Activity Through Establishment of a Policy Committee

Irma Serrano-García

PhD, Social Psychology, University of Michigan, 1978

Psychology Professor Emeritus, University of Puerto Rico, Río Piedras

Irma Serrano-García, a social-community psychologist, has worked in recent years to enhance the involvement of Puerto Rican psychologists in policy-related initiatives. This work has primarily been conducted through the Puerto Rican Psychological Association. In 1983, and again 20 years later in 2003, Serrano-García, with a group of students and colleagues, surveyed Puerto Rican psychologists about their experience in and attitudes toward policy work. In both surveys, she found very limited policy involvement, due to lack of training and the belief that policymakers would not be interested in the input of psychologists (Hernández, Pedraza, & Serrano-García, 2005; Serrano-García, 1983; Serrano-García, Rodríguez, & Pérez, 2005). Serrano-García and her work group initiated an effort to develop a public policy committee within the Puerto Rican Psychological Association, which ultimately was accomplished. To date, major activities of the committee, which Serrano-García is actively involved in, include:

- advocacy
- influencing training programs to include policy in their curricula through faculty training and development of a model syllabus
- ethical guidelines for political campaigns shared both with politicians and the public
- media involvement

Here, Serrano-García discusses several aspects of her policy work in Puerto Rico—where she was born and raised—beginning with her decision to move back to Puerto Rico following her graduate work in the United States:

> Six months before I was done with my PhD at University of Michigan, I had a call from the University of Puerto Rico offering me a tenure track position. I considered staying in the US and doing a post-doc. I didn't stay. I came home.

In 1983, I did a mini-study of Puerto Rican psychologists' involvement in public policy. That study generated responses such as, "We do not participate because we are not prepared to participate and because we don't like politics." In 2003, I repeated the survey with a much larger group of folks. The major result was that somewhat more people were involved in policy work, but [the psychologists surveyed] did not recognize their efforts as such, particularly those who were doing so from the bottom-up, working with community-based organizations to help them get policy established. They saw that as volunteer work, not policy work. Also, the majority of respondents still did not participate—because they were not ready, didn't like politics and, interestingly, because they thought the legislature and executive branches had negative perceptions of psychologists.

We then did a study in 2006 or 2007 in which we interviewed every legislator. We found that they didn't have a bad opinion of psychologists and would very much like us to collaborate. We decided to move the Puerto Rico Psychology Association to create a standing policy committee, which they did not have. That took some doing because the association was very conservative at the time. They thought this was too political. We met with many people and presented our data in various places. Finally, it got approved.

The committee prepared a campaign document for the 2008 election with mental health, violence prevention, and education proposals. Then, after the party platforms were put out, we examined which parties had included our proposals the most, and had a press conference to that effect. Then, last year, an election year, we put together an effort to have politicians focus on issues—instead of personal attacks. We generated a set of ethical principles for the electoral process based on principles from many other countries. We presented them to the candidates, and then to the citizenry so they could use them to evaluate candidates. We also evaluated gubernatorial candidates' debates and put out press releases on whether they were meeting these principles or not.

Influences and Summary

Politics has always been part of Serrano-García's life. As she recounts, "My parents were always politically active. Even from childhood I would go to political rallies. . . . Once I got to university I was pro-independence for Puerto Rico . . . we would organize forums and debates, and also help register people for elections. My . . . husband is very active also in political party stuff. It's always been part of what I've done." Despite this background, Serrano-García did not plan to become involved in policy-related work in Puerto Rico: the precipitant of her involvement was an unexpected invitation to participate in an APA policy task force in the early 1980s. As a result of her involvement, she conducted the previously mentioned 1983 survey of psychologists in Puerto Rico concerning their involvement in policy. Puerto Rican psychologists did not have a history of policy involvement, but there now appears to be increased openness to and involvement in policy initiatives in large part due to Serrano-García's and collaborators' pioneering work in developing a public policy committee within the Puerto Rico Psychological Association.

Summary

The two examples represent very different pathways to international influence: one based on an American researcher conducting policy-relevant research overseas, and another based on an American-trained researcher returning to her home overseas and mobilizing psychologists' involvement in advocacy and education initiatives. Both case examples illustrate the potential of psychologists to contribute to policy in international context, a trend that a number of those interviewed emphasize is becoming increasingly important in their own work and in their subdisciplines. Although these two examples involve US-trained psychologists living overseas, other international policy endeavors (Appendix D, Table D.4) were conducted by US-based psychologists who developed overseas relationships and traveled repeatedly to conduct their international policy work.

Influences: Commonalities and Differences

Interviewees view familial, cultural, and educational background experiences as setting the stage for their career journeys. These background experiences are as varied as the career journeys themselves. Some psychologists describe the political, religious, and/or social values and involvements of their parents (and other family members) as formative influences on their own worldview and values—factors that likely predisposed them to pursue and accept policy-relevant opportunities during the course of their careers. Another key background feature that numerous interviewees emphasize is the culture of the times they grew up in, particularly the tumultuous 1960s, with that decade's emphasis on personal engagement and social change. Still others mention that they were shaped by specific policy-relevant courses, practicum experiences, and mentors during college, graduate school, and/or in postdoctoral or early career settings. Although no one common background factor or profile can be singled out as uniquely linked to future policy involvement, there are a set of familial, cultural, and/or educational experiences that appear to enhance the likelihood of a policy-oriented career.

This chapter traced the varied career journeys of psychologists—people who devoted substantial portions of their careers to influencing policy. These journeys included multiple policy involvements over time, interdisciplinary collaboration, movement into policy-related leadership positions, and an emerging international policy focus. The unfolding sequence of policy involvements, the early influences on policy interest and involvement, and the varied avenues of policy work during the course of a career depict a more textured, developmental and multifaceted view of policy involvement than the more focused policy narratives in previous chapters. Like previous chapters, however, the overarching emphasis again has been on the positive aspects and potential of policy work. In the next chapter, we balance this by examining the failures, defeats, barriers, and challenges that appear to be an inevitable feature of working in the highly political and complex policy arena.

8

Policy Failures and Defeats, Barriers and Challenges, and Lessons Learned

You're going to lose plenty. . . . If you're not interested in failures, definitely don't do this work.

—L. Aber, August 29, 2012

Prior chapters of this book have highlighted policy successes achieved by psychologists and the routes to those successes. However, *there will be more failures than successes, more defeats than victories.* The majority of psychologists interviewed emphasize the inherent difficulty in changing social policy—the barriers and challenges typically present, the mistakes made, and the lessons learned. In this chapter, we first hear from a subset of those interviewed about the different types of failures and defeats they experienced in the policy arena. Next, five major barriers that underlie such failures and defeats are highlighted:

- partisan politics, in the form of ideologies, values, and beliefs
- corporate power, vested interests, and position power
- issues of cost and budget
- transitions and turnover
- implementation, scaling up, and challenges of systems change

The third section of the chapter delineates a number of more personal challenges experienced by those interviewed, including:

- effective communication
- scientific and personal integrity
- weathering personal attacks
- time/work pressure

The chapter concludes with respondents sharing key lessons learned in the face of policy failures, defeats, mistakes, barriers, and personal challenges.

An understanding of the intrinsic difficulty of policy work, the varying nature of policy defeats and failures, and the lessons gleaned from them is essential for sustained, productive work in the policy arena. To illustrate these themes, multiple brief interview excerpts are presented—sometimes set off as individual cases and other times within the text narrative—as opposed to the longer case excerpts depicted in the preceding chapters. For the longer cases, please refer to the previous chapters in which the psychologists were highlighted.

We start with a sampling of policy failures and defeats experienced.

Policy Failures and Defeats

After describing their greatest policy success, interviewees were asked to describe a failure (or mistake) related to their work in the policy arena. They provided many accounts of failures (or mistakes), varying greatly in scope and substance. Several individuals spoke poignantly about their inability to help bring about policy change in a major area of interest during the course of an entire career. More often, individuals reported instances in which a specific policy initiative or activity was thwarted. Still others emphasized later reversals of prior victories by legislatures and the cyclical nature of policy work. Here, a number of examples are presented that highlight these various types of defeats and failures.

It is best to view these experiences in the larger context of the extended period of time required to bring about far-reaching social change. Progress in civil rights, women's rights, and lesbian, gay, bisexual, and transgender (LGBT) rights policy, for example, emerged only after extended periods of struggle involving cyclical ups and downs. At times, it appeared that substantial change was unlikely despite persistent efforts. Although honest in their assessments of failures and defeats in specific policy areas, all of the individuals herein have made important contributions to struggles in difficult policy areas. Furthermore, each recorded his or her own share of policy wins and successes in related (or other) policy areas, as detailed in earlier chapters of the book.

Deborah Phillips (pp. 117–119), over the course of several decades, helped to establish the importance of quality of child care for the well-being of children. Along with her colleagues, she amassed an impressive body of research in this area and worked for and with various intermediary organizations in attempts to influence policymakers to reform the child care system. One policy goal was to improve the working conditions under which child care workers toiled (Whitebook, Howes, & Phillips, 1989, 2014). Phillips speaks poignantly about the lack of progress in the child care system:

> I do take it very personally that we don't have a better child care system in this country. I sometimes feel that I've been very ineffective. . . . Children are still exposed to harmful conditions, and I feel bad about that every day. We did try every which way to reframe how we talked about quality. We've done nationally representative studies. We've done economic studies. We're now linking it to stress and the brainwork. I think at this point it's beyond the science. I think it's a matter of national and political will.

The findings of a clear link between child care quality and child outcomes have been slow to translate into fundamental changes in how child care is funded, staffed, and administered in our country, leaving many children at risk in low-quality child care settings. Although important incremental progress has occurred in various aspects of the child care system (e.g., Raikes, St. Clair, & Plata-Potter, 2013), the system, to date, has proved resistant to more far-reaching change.

Similar to Philips' perspective, Aletha Huston (pp. 229–231) views research and policy influence work supporting the regulation of TV violence over the course of decades of her career to have made little difference. Huston also notes the limited impact of research linking violent content in videogames to negative youth outcomes:

> I don't think we made any progress on TV violence. . . . It's not just my failure. It's everybody's failure. I've tried to do my part. . . . People don't want to believe it [a causal relation] and there are a lot of reasons why they don't. . . . The same questions now are rolling around about violent videogames, after the Connecticut [Sandy Hook] incident. Research isn't going to solve that one.

Huston and many other researchers have contributed high-quality scholarship along with policy efforts in the area of the influence of television content on children, including exposure to violence. More recent scholarship and policy influence work has focused on violent videogames (e.g., Anderson, Gentile, & Buckley, 2007). Children and youth remain continually exposed to violence on TV and in videogames, with large profits accruing to both industries, and thus strong resistance to government-imposed change is present. Although policy influence efforts have yet to gain traction, many researchers and intermediary organizations continue to work hard to bring about change.

Some interviewees highlighted their inability to persuade policymakers to address the underlying, root causes of social problems, rather than individual remediation. Marybeth Shinn (pp. 182–185) provides this perspective in the following example, describing her inability to influence New York City policymakers to adopt a community-level strategy to prevent homelessness:

> Right from the start I've tried, not very successfully, to get policymakers to think about community-based intervention and what you can do around communities. Can you identify the buildings from which people at-risk for homelessness are entering shelters and understand why? Are there rapacious landlords? Can you bring banking services in? Can you try to get employment? Can you do what a settlement house might want done—to try to focus, not just on the individuals at risk but also on the community structures? That's not how it has worked. That's a policy advocacy failure. What they've done instead is provide services, including casework and money, to individuals [who are at risk of becoming homeless].

Providing social services (including supportive housing) to individuals and families struggling with homelessness falls *within* the dominant human services paradigm, whereas community-level systemic change, involving alteration in the distribution of resources and power, does not. The latter involves change across multiple policy sectors and cannot occur without strong political support and will. For the most part, systems-level change has been lacking in our country's approach to homelessness. However, the efforts by Shinn and many others seek to persuade policymakers to adopt a more systemic perspective.

Broad attempts at systemic change aside, many respondents note instances in which their specific policy initiative or activities did not bear fruit. The methods used and the scope of policy change sought varied greatly but, at least in the short run, policy influence was not achieved. This experience is well-captured by Jacob Tebes (pp. 211–213) who notes, "Sometimes we put all this effort into a process and nothing comes of it. . . . We've designed a study or contributed an opinion or developed a policy brief and it gets ignored."

Thomas Wolff (pp. 129–131), who developed community coalitions in several regions of Massachusetts and tried to obtain money to expand to other regions provides one example of a failure to pass legislation:

> We created three coalitions that we ran and had secured funding for. We set them up hand-in-hand with legislators. . . . Then we did trainings for 52 other

communities. There were not 52 teams, since there were teams that covered multiple communities. Maybe we trained another 18 teams, four or five a year, for four years. We trained them and sent them out in their community to develop Healthy Community coalitions. . . . We didn't have money for their ongoing support, so we had much less control. We were riding on a high and thought we were doing great work. So we tried to get a piece of state legislation passed that would take tobacco settlement money and create a Healthy Communities Massachusetts Trust Fund that would fund [the other 18 teams]. . . . We worked with a lot of legislators and put a lot of time into it. It went nowhere. It was a hard failure. You need much bigger constituencies and bigger powers-that-be [bigger than local coalitions] to back this up.

This example, like many others, underscores the reality that policy initiatives and activities do not always result in observable success, at least not in the time period and form expected. Policy initiatives that lack the necessary political constituencies and resources may fall short within any policy area. An alignment of factors and forces, including a powerful policy champion, are generally required for desired legislation to be passed.

Finally, the idea that policy progress is cyclical was expressed by a number of those interviewed. Today's success becomes tomorrow's defeat (and vice versa) due to periodic changes in leadership, political party control, or public opinion. Nancy Cantor (pp. 250–252), for example, who was provost when the University of Michigan succeeded in its affirmative action lawsuit, highlights this cyclical aspect of work in the policy arena: "These things ebb and flow. Obviously we won the affirmative action lawsuit for Michigan, but now it is under constant scrutiny and one day it may get reversed in the Supreme Court." Brian Wilcox (pp. 252–254) similarly reflects on the cyclical nature of policy work, in this case focused on child welfare reform in Nebraska, "With policymaking and the policy world, it's all process. You can win in one round and lose it all the next. We've gone through several efforts to reinvent the child welfare system in the state. I think we're in the middle of something right now that holds a lot of promise . . . "

We opened Chapter 8 with one portion of the next, and final, excerpt in this section, from Lawrence Aber (pp. 77–78). Aber emphasizes the inevitability of policy defeats, a perspective acquired from decades of policy work in the highly politicized area of children and family poverty. "Research for policy utility can't be, in any way, shape, or form, exempted from politics. . . . You're going to lose plenty. You can't let losses keep you from doing it. . . . If you're not interested in failures, definitely don't do this work." In spite of challenges, Aber maintains a positive and persistent focus, working in multiple areas to bring about policy change, a theme we will return to at the end of the chapter.

Summary

The preceding examples depict varied perspectives and experiences of psychologists long involved in the policy arena as they relate to policy failures and defeats. Clearly, the policy successes recounted in earlier chapters are best seen as part of a larger cycle of ongoing policy influence work in which the possibility of failure or defeat is ever present but does not deter the determined pursuit of desired social change. Respondents often emphasize a focus on small wins as central to work in the policy arena and the importance of a long-term time perspective because change may take years to achieve. It is important to remember that every individual who cites policy failures in this section remains actively involved and committed to policy change—and has contributed to important successes in one or more policy areas. That said, these challenges and barriers may be part of the reason why more psychologists are not actively involved in policy.

Why is it so hard to bring about policy change? In the next section, five factors that contribute to policy failures and defeats are described, each reflecting the dominant features of the policy terrain in which change agents tread.

The Policy Landscape: Politics, Power, Budget, Transitions, and Implementation

In discussing both their successes and failures, interviewees identified formidable barriers and challenges that shape the landscape of policy work. This section focuses on the five most frequently mentioned barriers: politics, power, budget, transitions, and implementation. The first highlights the influential role of ideological concerns and their relationship to politics.

Politics, Ideologies, Values, and Beliefs

A number of the social policy issues psychologists feel passionately about are ideologically charged. That is, political parties, individual politicians, their constituents, and well-funded advocacy groups are guided by strongly held values and beliefs related to these issues and associated policy options. Thus, policy formulation and policy adoption related to such issues cannot be separated from politics. The examples here cover a range of controversial social issues and related policy approaches, including juvenile justice, LGBT rights, firearms regulation, and education reform.

Laurence Steinberg, who chaired the MacArthur Network on Adolescent Development and Juvenile Justice (pp. 93–95) worked to change policy so that adolescents who commit serious crimes would be treated differently from adults in the legal system due to adolescents' lower levels of competence in judicially relevant contexts. He explains some of the challenges he and other psychologists face when working on such a controversial issue:

> Every time there was another heinous murder or crime committed by a juvenile, it tended to make people look at our research and say, "Those people don't know what they're doing. They don't live in the real world. If you lived in my constituency and had to face victims here, you wouldn't be talking about whether kids are less competent than adults." I think the biggest hurdle or barrier was that we were studying something that people had very strong opinions about. In some circles, those opinions were not going to be moved by any amount of research.

Crime and punishment are ideologically charged issues; the question of how adolescents who commit terrible crimes are to be treated stirs strong passions. The ideological challenges facing psychologists working in this area are considerable. Given the barriers to change, successful policy initiatives necessitate the use of multiple policy pathways and methods. These include sustained work with legislators, the judicial system, intermediary organizations, and the media. Although some progress has been made, including elimination of the death penalty for adolescents, the barriers to fundamental change remain.

LGBT rights constitute another example of an ideologically charged social issue. In the past decade, substantial progress has been made. Gregory Herek highlights the critical role of public opinion and social norms in this policy area, including their contribution to many defeats over decades of work. Herek has contributed testimony and amicus briefs in many major court cases over the past three decades (pp. 89–90). The 1986 *Bowers v. Hardwick* case, referred to here, involved the legal challenge to anti-sodomy laws in Georgia:

> When I began working in this area, it was a real uphill climb. In 1980, I worked on the campaign for a ballot measure in Davis [California] that simply advised the city council to consider drafting a nondiscrimination law. The voters rejected it by a three to one margin. . . . Public opinion, and social norms that were so harmful toward sexual minorities made it possible for people like Jesse Helms and others to do the damage that they did. . . . We lost many times. There are so many examples. Going back to the *Bowers v. Hardwick* 1986 Supreme Court decision upholding state anti-sodomy laws . . . that was a very disappointing loss.

Seventeen years later, the Supreme Court reversed its 1986 decision, finally prohibiting anti-sodomy laws. Then, in June 2015, the Supreme Court found that prohibiting marriage on the basis of a partner's sex was unconstitutional, thus legalizing same-sex marriage across the United States. Social norms change over time, and their continuing evolution has contributed to numerous court decisions that have supported gay rights in the intervening years—decisions informed in part by research conducted by Herek and others in the face of substantial ideologically based opposition.

Heather Bullock (pp. 112–113), serving as a congressional fellow, was involved in an effort to pass national gun control legislation following a widely publicized gun-related tragedy. She describes her experience following the 1999 Columbine High School shooting in Littleton, Colorado.

> The year I was a congressional fellow, our office worked on a series of initiatives following Columbine. They included gun control, mental health issues, and all kinds of issues related to that really horrible tragedy. I don't think any of our initiatives really went anywhere. For me it was really crushing. What I really underestimated was the power of lobbyists in the process. It was a real lesson about the forces at work and how difficult it can be to make change, even when you feel that it's absolutely right in your heart and you believe that the conditions support such a change.

Strongly held beliefs and a powerful pro-gun lobby similarly thwarted efforts to pass gun control legislation following the 2012 Sandy Hook Elementary School tragedy. As John Monahan (pp. 209–211) notes, "After Sandy Hook many researchers wrote letters, from various kinds of organizations, or gave interviews, or tried to analyze research. . . . Nothing happened. The National Rifle Association proved to be so powerful." It should be noted, however, that some progress has been made at the state level over the years, including policy changes to which psychologists contributed (e.g., banning of semi-automatic assault pistols in Hawaii, pp. 227–229).

Ideologies that impede change are not the sole province of elected officials, but reside as well in appointed officials at all levels of government and implementing agencies. Education researcher Robert Slavin (pp. 188–189) provides a striking example of an educational decision-maker whose preexisting beliefs determine whether research findings are considered "good" or "bad," an extreme illustration of the strategic use of research:

> At an IES [Institute of Education Sciences] conference, they had a very well-regarded, intelligent, and capable superintendent who stood at a podium and told a room full of researchers, without smiling and being deadly serious, that good research is research that confirms his previous beliefs and bad research is research that does not.... It's in school districts, state department offices, and other places of power.... People in the applied world, like the superintendent [discount findings they do not like, making] the assumption that when ... a study favors a given program, practice, or point of view [contrary to their own beliefs], the researcher already believed that in advance and was going to come out with that finding.

Slavin highlights the reality that policymakers may selectively draw on research findings that fit their preconceived beliefs and interests, in part due to ideology and in part due to mistrust of researchers and their perceived ideologies and biases. In such cases, the potential for findings to influence policy may depend on internal policy champions with beliefs and interests that support those of the researcher—and who are effectively informed about the relevant research.

The preceding examples span a range of policy issues and illustrate the role of politics, ideology, values, and beliefs as formidable barriers to social policy change. These factors often work to discount research findings and, at times, to discredit the psychologists conducting and presenting them. At other times, the important work completed by these psychologists serves to set the stage for future social change. As public opinion and pressure better align over time with research, policy often changes. Policy change is not a sprint; it is a long-distance relay race in which psychologists work, sometimes against great odds, to improve the starting position of the next team of change agents. Now, we turn to a parallel barrier that strongly influences the policy process: various forms of power.

Corporate Power, Vested Interests, and Position Power

"Loot and power" have long been viewed as dominant barriers to progressive social change (Rappaport, 1977). A number of respondents described instances in which corporate power (manifest in highly paid lobbyists) and position power (in the form of high-level decision-makers in executive branch agencies) served as roadblocks to their policy influence efforts. There is some overlap between the previous section and the current one given that both focus on the link between power and politics. Here, the source of power is related to the corporate "bottom line" (profits in the private sector) or to "turf" (control over resources in the public sector), rather than to contested ideologies and values. In many cases, interviewees were aware that their research would run up against the financial interests of powerful stakeholders. In several cases, however, including the next one, they were caught by surprise.

Steve Fawcett and colleagues at a university-based policy research center contributed to a "lifeline utilities project," an effort to enable low-income families to pay their utility bills and avoid shutoffs in the city of Lawrence, Kansas. The city commission passed an ordinance following a presentation on the problem. The policy, "lifeline utilities" rate restructuring, involved charging a very small fee, about $5 per month, to subsidize the payments of low-income families. However, this policy success was short-lived, as the public utility company responded with a swift, no-holds-barred repeal campaign. Fawcett recounts his experience:

> We gathered survey research data on public willingness to support cash transfers, a few dollars a month paid by all customers to subsidize low-income households. It passed the progressive city commission. . . . It turned out that utility companies had a national war chest to attack any meddling with the rate structure since rates typically favor utilities by allowing them to pay less per unit of energy consumed. In the print media and public meetings that followed, they discounted the data by denying that utility shutoffs were due to inability to pay. They discredited us, alleging that this was a form of socialism. They went after the commissioners—there was a recall campaign, aimed at those who supported it. Then they substituted a voluntary contribution that people could check off on their utility bills, a program that yielded far fewer resources than what was needed. . . . Eventually I was asked to leave my position at the policy research center by the then director who had ties to opponents of this policy change.

This example underscores the resources and tactics that an opposition will utilize to block policies that threaten their interests. In the current case, this included retribution toward elected officials and political fallout for the university's policy research center and its researchers. As a tenured professor, Fawcett had protections that enabled him to establish another university-based center that promotes community health and development, thus continuing his commitment, through another venue, to bring about social change. The work of this new center includes efforts to effect environmental and policy changes related to health promotion, violence prevention, and other community-determined issues. It has been designated a World Health Organization Collaborating Centre for Community Health and Development and is also home to the Community Tool Box (a free online resource and consultation center for people conducting community research and designing, implementing, and evaluating community programs). Rebounding from an early policy defeat, Fawcett and his colleagues have sustained their social change efforts for more than 40 years (Fawcett, Schultz, Carson, Renault, & Francisco, 2003; Fawcett, Schultz, Holt, Collie-Akers, & Watson-Thompson, 2013; Fawcett, Schultz, Collie-Akers, Holt, & Watson-Thompson, in press).

Organizations with vested interests are not limited to the private sector; they also exist in the public sector. The next example highlights the political power of state executive branch agencies in Virginia to undercut systemic child mental health reform. Specifically, an attempt to enhance local flexibility and control over funding by creating a single, statewide funding pool ran into opposition. The plan would have required consolidation of state funding currently distributed across multiple child-serving state agencies (e.g., social services, education, mental health, health, juvenile justice). It challenged executive agency "turf," the extant control over resources by various stakeholders. Robert Cohen, one of the contributors to the reform effort (pp. 172–174), observes:

> Some [state] agencies didn't like giving up power, so they lobbied their localities that this was a bad bill. The governor ended up weakening the provisions to change the funding structure, which 20 years later came back to bite them. These were the things in the policy that weren't done quite the way they should've, and they ended up eroding the intent of some of the policy.

Established public as well as private entities have the power to effectively resist change and can rally the public as well as policymakers to get behind their efforts with effective framing tactics. Although coming up against such a display of power and resources can certainly prove discouraging, it cannot be repeated too often that shaping policy is a long-term process. Cohen persevered and continued to influence and help improve the children's mental health system in Virginia over the ensuing decades.

Proposed policy changes, including those designed with the best of intentions, will inevitably involve potential winners and losers in terms of resources and power. This can create a difficult environment for creating new policies, sometimes resulting in complete gridlock. Sharon Landesman Ramey (pp. 207–209) describes the nature of one such case of gridlock surrounding early child care policy in North Carolina:

> I became the director of a child development research institute at the University of North Carolina at Chapel Hill and worked a lot with the legislature. There were preschool programs that were known to produce major benefits for children from economically and educationally impoverished families. The legislature was ready to make these more readily available and was going to do it through the schools, but the community providers resisted. The family daycare providers, for whom the evidence showed, on average, the quality of services was really below acceptable standards, didn't want to be unemployed. Both sides stood up and fought to get it all. That fight led to legislation that was delayed almost a full decade.

When finally passed, the legislation incorporated a common set of standards across settings that allowed preschool services to be delivered either in the community or in schools. The decade's delay in achieving such an accord was due to the "winner take all" mentality. During that time, the children in the state lost out on new preschool services. Facilitating compromise and cooperation across competing groups can be quite a challenge and can take an extended period of time.

Whereas the previous two examples highlight barriers involving turf and control of resources at the state level, the final example illustrates a comparable problem at the national level. Leonard Jason (pp. 203–205), a chronic disease researcher, describes the obstructive role played by a Centers for Disease Prevention and Control (CDC) official. For decades, this official was perceived by patient activists as blocking efforts to eliminate the prevailing victim-blaming approach to naming, defining, and researching chronic fatigue syndrome.

> The CDC has the most money in the world to do research in this area. They had about $7 or 8 million a year. Much of their research was focused on psychogenic factors, and patients as well as many scientists were concerned about their terminology, the findings from epidemiology, as well as problems with their case definition. One of the largest barriers [to change],

according to many activists, was the chief person who was overseeing this program of research. . . . He had a tremendous amount of power.

After a concerted, long-term effort to have the CDC official removed from his position, he was finally replaced. Overcoming this formidable barrier required persistence on the part of multiple groups and individuals, including Jason, working together to pressure the government to make the necessary change.

These examples expose the ways in which various forms of power—and lack thereof—create formidable barriers to policy change, potentially leading to defeats or failures. In this way, organizations and officials motivated to retain or increase resources, power, and control often impede policy change. Although these barriers seem daunting, many of the psychologists interviewed eventually succeeded through persistent effort. Similar to ideological barriers, when confronting corporate power, vested interests, and position power, psychologists must work to understand the power dynamics, stay focused on the long-term outcome, and seek to achieve smaller, short-term gains (small wins) in order to sustain momentum and motivation.

We next turn to another major barrier to change, one that appears omnipresent in these times of limited government resources.

Cost and Budget Considerations

Social policies typically require a fair amount of funding. It is not surprising, then, that cost and budget considerations were frequently reported by respondents as impediments to both the passage of social policies and to high-quality, sustained implementation. Relatedly, just as research establishing impressive cost–benefit was cited as important to policy success, the absence of such research was cited as contributing to policy failures or defeats. Apart from money to administer new government-sponsored programs and policies, cost and funding limitations also represent barriers to effective work by intermediaries, both advocacy and research-focused. The examples here illustrate these economic considerations. The first two examples focus on the absence of cost–benefit data as an obstacle to generating support for new legislation.

Preston Britner, who has worked both at the state and federal levels on prevention initiatives in the area of children, youth, and families (pp. 68–70), highlights how the absence of cost–benefit data can limit passage of new prevention policies, including one he contributed to that focused on positive parent screening:

We worked with APA's [American Psychology Association] Public Policy Office to draft some federal legislation. Senator Inouye from Hawaii wound up introducing a bill that would fund demonstration studies to do positive parenting screening work in community health centers. It didn't get a hearing in committee, went nowhere. . . . The research was probably not quite strong enough to make really strong cost–benefit statements. You could write an entire book on our failed investment in what should be effective prevention approaches that don't get passed because . . . the budget is the budget.

No matter how promising a given proposed policy, without clear evidence to demonstrate that the monetary savings of the policy are greater than the cost, the legislation can grind to a halt. The negative outcome in this case notwithstanding, Britner was not deterred from moving forward—quite effectively— on other prevention-focused policy initiatives.

Ellen Garrison provides a similar account in her APA-based effort to enhance levels of funding relevant to psychology within the Affordable Care Act (ACA). Here, Garrison indicates that the absence of data establishing a positive cost–benefit relationship between psychological services and medical outcomes limited psychology's inclusion as a primary care provider in the legislation:

We were not successful in including psychology in some ACA provisions. Part of the reason was that we have not yet been able through research to fully establish some critical cost–benefit relationships. In this regard, it would be incredibly helpful to definitively demonstrate that the provision of psychological services actually reduces medical costs, while increasing quality of and access to care—thereby contributing to the "triple aim" of healthcare reform.

In times of tight budgets and with opposition to "big government" serving as a major political lightning rod, it is especially difficult to generate bipartisan support for spending on new social policies and programs. The comments from Britner, Garrison, and many others underscore how the absence of strong cost–benefit data on proposed new policies is an important obstacle to change. In Garrison's case, the limitations of APA policy influence in some areas of the ACA were balanced, however, by successes in other areas (pp. 101–104), underscoring the benefits of a multipronged policy agenda.

Directly related to budget considerations, estimating the financial cost of various policy alternatives is central to the policy formulation process. During this process, as violence and mental health researcher John Monahan indicates, alternatives that are clearly superior from a policy perspective may be discarded due to cost considerations. Monahan was part of a commission considering reforms to the mental health system in Virginia (pp. 209–211). He describes the inevitable limitations placed on policy options due to considerations of cost:

> For people who are being involuntarily committed, one suggestion the commission came up [with] was that they not be taken by the police in handcuffs but instead transported from a rural area to the hospital by ambulance. The problem, it turned out, was that the police can transport people for no additional cost whereas an ambulance would cost many hundreds or thousands of dollars.

Economic considerations constitute a primary factor in deciding among policy alternatives at all levels of government. The nature of the policy compromises involved may not be clear to academic researchers until they become directly involved in policy analysis and formulation. Indeed, Monahan notes that when he began his work on the commission, he was "insufficiently appreciative" of the tradeoffs that needed to be made due to the costliness of many of the preferred means of addressing involuntary commitment. Nonetheless, limitations aside, Monahan views the new policy as a national model and as an important policy advancement.

Aside from government, cost and budget considerations can be major barriers to the conduct of effective advocacy campaigns and sustained policy-relevant research by intermediary organizations, as illustrated separately by Robin Jenkins and Kristin Moore. Jenkins, who worked on a national advocacy effort to move forward the reauthorization of the Juvenile Justice and Delinquency Prevention Act (pp. 170–172), notes, "When you're doing national level policy work, it takes money and funding to generate the conference calls, organizational infrastructure, research, communications, and products you're developing. There's never enough of it." Moore (pp. 122–124), Director of Child Trends, observes that "Funding has varied, ebbed and waned, so it has been hard to keep focused. I think that has been the main challenge." These observations underscore the reality that intermediary organizations, both those involved in advocacy and those that focus on policy research, are limited in their policy influence efforts by money. Furthermore, the substantial time and energy often devoted to the search for funding may limit the scope and quality of work conducted. Budget concerns may become an important obstacle to the sustainability of long-term policy initiatives.

Cost and budget considerations have become increasingly salient barriers to the adoption of new, innovative, and far-reaching social policies during the past 35 years. The extreme politicization of issues related to the budget, deficits, and government spending has been a major deterrent on social policy development. This reality was reflected, directly or indirectly, in many of the interviews. Nevertheless, by paying great attention to financial realities when conducting policy-relevant research (e.g., cost–benefit analyses) and proposing cost-sensitive and cost-effective policy changes, psychologists have been able to contribute to important new social policies. Next, we turn to another barrier to social policy influence: transitions and turnover.

Transitions and Turnover

Transitions and turnover constitute a fourth obstacle to success. Different aspects of transitions and turnover are reflected in the five interview excerpts here. The first three examples focus on transitions within government, highlighting the reality that when elected officials or appointed executive branch officials leave office, policy agendas can change dramatically. Previous relationships contributing to effective policy influence may be lost during these turnovers. The last two examples shift the focus to changes in the agendas or activities of policy actors outside of government. These latter two examples respectively highlight the problems that can emerge when the agendas of foundations and the activities of university faculty change.

Juvenile justice researcher and systems consultant Mark Lipsey first describes a project at the state level that ended when a key administrator left (pp. 192–194):

> We made a lot of progress moving the juvenile justice system in that first state where Buddy Howell and I worked in an evidence-based practice direction with our pilot version of our SPEP scheme. We had one champion in the organization and some supporters who pushed the process forward quite effectively. However, when she [the policy champion] retired, it was astonishing how quickly the whole enterprise deteriorated. We are back in that state now, helping them rebuild the processes and commitments that atrophied, as the leadership there has come back to the view that the original initiative was a good idea. In our current work, we are much more focused on developing sustainability and building critical procedures into

routine practice with the hope that they will then not disappear so quickly when initial innovators are no longer there as advocates.

People matter a great deal and individual policymakers can make or break a policy, which Lipsey experienced when a key champion stakeholder retired. As Lipsey points out, integrating policy change into ongoing practice represents a strategic means to sustain policy initiatives over the longer term—transitions and turnover notwithstanding.

Another state-level perspective on the challenges of transitions and turnover is provided by Judith Meyers. Through her leadership role in intermediary organizations and close collaboration with state policymakers, Meyers has worked toward reform of several child welfare and child mental health systems in Connecticut (pp. 126–129):

> We work with state government. It's a bureaucracy, and it is very slow. If any of your leadership changes, that's always an issue. Whether it's a key legislator or a governor, things turn over. Sometimes that creates an opportunity. Sometimes it stops one.

When a new administration takes office, when a change in majority control of a legislature occurs, or when key executive branch officials transition in and out of office, policy priorities will change. Meyers usefully points out that, on the one hand, such transitions and turnover can undermine a hard-fought-for policy initiative. And, on the other, these changes can herald new possibilities for policy influence. In the latter case, one period's impenetrable resistance to a given policy initiative then yields to the sudden opening of a new policy window. Throughout the inevitable changes, developing, maintaining, and initiating new relationships with policymakers is critical for those seeking direct policy influence.

The third example shows comparable impacts of government transitions in policy work outside of the United States. Lawrence Aber (pp. 77–78), who has worked on multiple policy projects in other countries, notes the direct, negative impact of a governmental transition in South Africa:

> We tried to mount conditional cash transfers with South Africa. It was during the transition between the Mbeki and the Zuma administrations. The Mbeki administration was in favor of it and the Zuma administration wasn't, so we weren't able to do it. That was years of work lost.

Transitioning from working effectively with one administration to another is bound to present a challenge for psychologists when the two administrations differ widely in perspectives and priorities. When the transition is not smooth, it can result in a major defeat. Working in the policy arena requires flexibility, resilience, and a long-term time perspective, qualities exemplified by the psychologists interviewed.

Parallel to changes in government, transitions and turnover occur in intermediary and university settings as well. Funders such as foundations, for example, can be important players in the policy arena. When their priorities change and funding is retargeted to another area, the sustainability of previously funded policy initiatives is at risk. Laurie Garduque (pp. 132–134) views change in a foundation's focus as a major barrier to the sustainability of previous policy work:

> We exited mental health in 2007, and no one picked up much of the work that we had funded in terms of mental health policy. I'm worried in juvenile justice that there will also not be the continued funding of research in this area once we exit because OJJDP [Office of Juvenile Justice and Delinquency Prevention] and NIJ [National Institute of Justice] have not expressed an interest in this area.

Just as a change in government can present policy challenges and opportunities, the same is true for a change in the policy-relevant priorities of foundations. In the current case, Garduque and the various psychologists and other participants in MacArthur Foundation's juvenile justice policy initiatives will no longer influence policy through that particular venue. It remains to be seen to what extent other funders or government agencies will rise to the occasion to continue the work begun. Of note, Garduque will have the opportunity, as a member of the Federal Coordinating Council on Juvenile Justice and Delinquency Prevention, to attempt to steer the federal government to greater involvement in this area.

Finally, when a psychologist's level of policy involvement declines over a period of time, it may present difficulties for future policy work, as mental health systems researcher Lonnie Snowden observes (pp. 81–82):

> The last three years, I was very university focused because I was on this major committee, which the administration runs at the university. It was very rewarding but everything else kind of got dropped— the [policy] connections and who to talk to about what, what the

issues were, how to develop projects, I didn't do that for three years. I thought, "I'll just pick it all up again." It doesn't quite work that way. The world changes. There is no Department of Mental Health anymore. The long-serving director retired. They reorganized a lot of business because of the budget crisis. It has new actors and is a totally new environment. I don't know those people. They don't know me. That's just for starters.

Even though Snowden is cautiously optimistic that he can re-establish ties, this case excerpt highlights the challenges presented by changes in a psychologist's policy involvement, coupled with governmental transitions and changes. It reveals that even a medium-term withdrawal from active involvement with policy networks can have serious consequences for continued policy influence. To proactively address the potential for disruptions in relationships and contacts during times of transition, psychologists will do well to build a team of collaborators who collectively develop relationships with varied stakeholders in that particular policy domain.

Transitions and turnover are integral to democratic government and closely tied in many cases to the election cycle. Especially problematic is the departure from office of a policy initiative's key champion—the new officeholder may have different policy priorities, along with different networks of trusted advisors and working partners. The influence of transitions underscores the role of timing in policy influence work: a policy initiative may have its best opportunity during a "policy window" when key policy collaborators are in place. It should be noted, though, that when a policy window closes, renewed relationship-building and advocacy by psychologists can contribute to its future reopening.

Next, we turn to how the implementation phase of policy may result in policy defeat.

Implementation, Scaling Up, and Systems Change

Victories in the formulation and passage of policy may turn into defeat if implementation fails. As discussed in Chapter 2, there are many potential barriers to effective implementation (e.g., Fixsen, Naoom, Blase, Friedman, & Wallace, 2005; Mihalic & Irwin, 2003; Peters, 2013). They include:

- resistance to the new policy among key stakeholders
- limited community and organizational capacity
- insufficient resources and effort devoted

- contextual differences between populations and settings in which model programs were developed and those in which they are implemented

Careful attention needs to be paid to these multiple barriers if policy implementation is to succeed. The four examples presented here illustrate a number of these obstacles in different implementation contexts. Specifically, the first two address barriers related to scaling up successful programs, the third to statewide systems reform, and the final one to the importance of sustained contributions by intermediary organizations to the policy implementation process.

David Olds (pp. 64–65), developer and evaluator of the Nurse Family Partnership, focuses on the implementation difficulties he encountered in an early government-funded expansion of the program. Olds also notes lessons he learned and applied in a later, national expansion effort:

> The key thing [early on] is that we underestimated the importance of ensuring organizational and community commitment and capacity to do this work. That led to program closures. As part of our [current] national replication strategy, we have really deepened our efforts to make sure that local and state policymakers and organizational leaders have what it takes to deliver this program well.

Olds addresses the central importance of governmental and organizational capacity to the scaling-up of model programs. Developing a careful implementation and dissemination strategy requires collaboration with multiple stakeholders and sustained capacity building responsive to both their strengths and limitations.

Loss of fidelity of core program components is a common concern when successful model programs are expanded. Michelle Fine (pp. 190–191) provides an example of this aspect of implementation failure:

> In both the small schools and the college-in-prison examples, a lot of people are replicating the work, but failing to realize that central to both was a very participatory process involving educators and students. In both cases, this participatory piece got severed. For example, The Gates Foundation encouraged cities to go forth and multiply; they were encouraged to launch more than 200 small schools in a year without any attention to process. It becomes a thing that people do and not a process, a

collaborative commitment of ongoing participation and reflection. It's like turning complicated, deep ideas into thin, replicable versions—as if that is going to scale, thinning out the complexity of interventions that people worked hard to develop.

Fine illustrates how a participatory process in which both students and educators work with professionals to develop a program can become lost in the effort to widely disseminate the program. It is difficult to maintain program fidelity and efficacy as programs are disseminated and brought to scale by implementing agencies and policymakers. As Olds highlighted in the preceding interview excerpt, expansion of policies and programs requires diligence and care, along with collaboration and capacity building.

Replication and scaling-up involve interventions into existing systems. Indeed, systemic reform is at the heart of many attempts to enhance the well-being of citizens served by the state. Based on his experience as director of the Center for Effective Practice (see pp. 126–129), Robert Franks highlights the many barriers, across levels of analysis, that systems change initiatives face:

> There's resistance to systems change at multiple levels. Learning new practices can be threatening to folks. Organizations often don't have the capacity to support new practices. They have productivity requirements, can't afford to support the necessary infrastructure or supervision, and often don't have the capacity to utilize data. There are challenges at the systemic level in terms of reimbursement for evidence-based practices and the ability to collect and analyze systems level data. Local regions often don't want to use their resources to support statewide system change efforts because they have relationships with local provider organizations and are committed to maintaining the status quo. Sometimes the vision of leaders at the state level isn't congruent with those in local communities. They have other priorities. There can be many barriers to systems change which must be addressed in order to be successful.

Franks also notes some of the conditions necessary for overcoming these barriers:

> In order to effectively change systems and create reform you must either build on the existing priorities of policy makers or create the will for systems to change. Often, systems change must be both organic and opportunistic. The timing must be right, and various factors at the policy, systems,

and practice levels must align. There must also be demonstrated need for change and some urgency that the time for change is now. A psychologist functioning as an intermediary can be sensitive to the needs and priorities that drive change and leverage the necessary resources to create reform.

Franks encountered many barriers to systems reform and, over time, found a number of ways to address them. Long-term commitment and involvement, the ability to leverage resources, and sensitivity to the proper alignment of factors and forces contributed to his success. Such strategies may be necessary to increase the odds of successful policy implementation, given the many obstacles that may arise.

Finally, Roger Weissberg provides an example of some of the challenges involved in maintaining such a long-term focus, in this case concerning implementation of social and emotional learning (SEL) standards throughout Illinois (pp. 79–80):

> As part of the [SEL] legislation, 870 school districts developed social and emotional learning policies at the district level to implement as part of their curriculum. I would have loved to see a sustained commitment on the State's part to support quality implementation in all Illinois schools. There was a time when we [Collaborative for Academic, Social, and Emotional Learning; CASEL] had a great deal of optimism for advancing the work. It still exists. But things have stalled a little bit rather than being as high-profile and widespread.

Devoting sustained attention and resources to policy implementation work for a nationally focused intermediary organization is not an easy feat. New policy opportunities arise, and priorities change. It will be interesting to observe if CASEL returns to high-priority focus in this particular case of school-level implementation. Regardless, Weissberg and CASEL continue to devote substantial, high-profile attention to many other policy initiatives, and SEL policy influence efforts continue to gain traction around the country.

The preceding examples depict various factors that may interfere with the successful implementation of new policies and government-funded programs. The interviews—and the policy and program implementation literature more generally—illustrate barriers at all levels of the policy implementation process and across the entire gamut of substantive policy domains. Of special note, several of those interviewed were concerned that the current focus of government policy on evidence-based policy may falter over time due to an inability to successfully implement evidence-based model policies and programs under real-world conditions. A carefully orchestrated, sustained focus on implementation appears necessary to successfully address the challenges involved, exemplified by the decades-long work of a number of the psychologists interviewed for this volume (e.g., Franks and Meyers, pp. 126–129; Olds, pp. 64–65; Tsemberis, pp. 182–185).

Summary

Partisan politics, power, budget, transitions, and implementation constitute formidable barriers to psychologists working in the policy arena, sometimes leading to failures and defeats. These challenges are not insurmountable, however, as revealed by the successful policy narratives highlighted in earlier chapters. One should approach policy work with an appreciation and understanding of these barriers, but also with the confidence that, over time, the barriers can be overcome. Policy success is especially likely to be achieved when the timing is right, the needed coalitions and policy champions are in place, and policy methods, skills, and efforts are strategically marshaled.

The various policy barriers discussed in this section are, in many cases, deeply embedded in the policy landscape. In the next section of the chapter, we turn to more personal challenges that were noted by many of those interviewed.

Challenges: Effective Communication, Integrity, Attacks, and Strain

The psychologists interviewed voiced a variety of personal challenges experienced in the policy domain, with particulars depending in part on their skills, experience, and the vantage point from which they launched their policy initiatives. Four common challenges are the focus in this section:

- effective communication
- personal and scientific integrity
- attacks from the opposition
- strain due to constraints of time, workload, and the nature of policy work more generally

In many cases, these challenges were spontaneously mentioned during the course of the interviews, highlighting their salience and importance.

Effective Communication

Many respondents noted that the differences in worldview and background between psychologists and policymakers often made it challenging to effectively communicate research findings. In part, the challenge resides in communicating complex and technical findings clearly, succinctly, unambiguously, and in compelling fashion—that is, embedded in a policy-relevant narrative. Challenges of communication are also partly due to limited understanding on the part of psychologists of the worldview and perspectives policymakers utilize when considering research. A somewhat different, ever-present challenge is that research findings, even when clearly articulated, will be inappropriately interpreted and used out of context by opposition groups. Several aspects of the challenges of effective communication are illustrated here.

Keith Humphreys describes mistakes he made early in his career and that he has seen other psychologists make when communicating research findings to policymakers—when the psychologists are not fully cognizant of the differences between academic and policy cultures. Humphreys has worked on substance use and veteran affairs issues with policymakers over the course of several decades, including work as senior policy advisor in the Office of National Drug Control Policy (pp. 162–164), to which he refers here:

> Probably the biggest mistake I made earlier in my career and that lots of people make is they talk to policymakers as if they were talking to other academics. They give tons about theory, use a lot of abstruse terms, and don't get to the point. They hedge and say "maybe this works, but maybe not," "perhaps," and "more research is needed." . . . It's very hard to realize that a few slides is enough, that everything needs to fit on one page, and that you can't start with 18 different caveats of what you don't know because that means basically you shouldn't be listened to. I made those mistakes. . . . They know stuff you don't know, and you know stuff they don't know. It's a cross-cultural experience, and you have to learn that culture.

Communicating research in an accessible way for policymakers, without compromising the integrity of the research, can be a challenge for psychologists working to change policy. Humphrey's comments highlight the need to translate research in a clear and concise way to be influential in the policy arena.

Heather Kelly, a lobbyist for the Science Governmental Relations Office at APA (pp. 106–109), also acknowledges the challenges faced by researchers in communicating effectively to legislators. Kelly comments both on the

differences in worldview (e.g., definition of what constitutes evidence) between the two groups and on the reality that research findings are just one of
many factors that policymakers consider in their decisions:

> Psychologists and lots of academically trained people think: "If I could
> just explain it to a member of Congress or show him my journal article,
> page 37 . . . If he just knew what I know, he would think like I think, change
> his mind, and vote the way I want him to vote." And it's just not the case.
> It's not the case sometimes because a legislator holds a completely different
> worldview, and sometimes because even if that person agrees with you on
> that piece of science, she has 40 things that go into what she votes and we're
> lucky if science is one of them.

Kelly indicates how evidence, in the form of research, is only one of many
factors that influence the decisions of policymakers. In addition to the scientific evidence, policymakers must consider factors such as the worldview
of their constituents, cost–benefit of the policy, and others. Ultimately,
these factors add complexity to the decisions to be made by policymakers,
which poses a challenge for psychologists looking to influence policy with
their research.

One of the best means to address this reality, emphasized by Kelly and
others, is to develop longer term, reciprocal relationships with policymakers
and their staff or to partner with those who do, thus increasing the odds that
when the timing is right, policy influence can be achieved.

Kristin Moore (pp. 122–124), former director of Child Trends, provides a
graphic example of the reality that, even when findings are carefully articulated, the researcher cannot control how they will be used. In this case, findings were used in a negative way, completely apart from their intended use:

> We did a research brief about 10 years ago drawing on the research on family
> structure, concluding that children do thrive best in a two-biological-
> parent family that is low conflict. What we didn't say is that the research
> literature to date hadn't focused on gay couples. That has been taken and
> used again and again. It has been submitted to the Supreme Court for their
> decision on the Defense of Marriage Act. We have repeatedly corrected
> the record, yet it continues to be used. Had I known that 10 years later it
> would be used in that way, we wouldn't have said that. It is a risk of being
> in the policy world . . . [even though] our briefs are all reviewed. We send
> a lot of them out for external review.

Despite the strict external review protocols Child Trends uses for its research briefs, policymakers and others can intentionally and unintentionally misinterpret and misapply the findings. Nevertheless, Moore's case reiterates the importance of carefully framing research by evaluating the potential uses of the findings within the policy realm. If research findings are misused by opponents, Moore emphasizes that repeated portrayals of the appropriate interpretation are necessary. While the misuse of the data did not appear to have a negative effect on the high level of respect afforded to Child Trends over the years, continued vigilance is necessary.

The final example relates to the challenge of effectively framing findings for the intended policy audience. It emphasizes the point—repeatedly made by those interviewed—that if communication of findings is to be effective and persuasive, it must be embedded in a compelling policy narrative that relates directly to the policy issue at hand. Gregory Herek (pp. 89–90) speaks to this issue in the context of a judicial brief to the California Supreme Court in a case related to same-sex marriage.

> A big challenge in the California case—as in so many earlier cases—was getting heterosexual people, including Supreme Court justices, to make that leap and see the parallels and similarities between gay and heterosexual couples. At the heart of it, we were talking about intimate relationships between two people. The psychological qualities and dynamics of those relationships don't differ according to the partners' sexual orientation. As I said, we relied very heavily on the research data, but we also had to provide a compelling narrative that tied it all together. Developing a narrative that would be persuasive to judges has been a challenge.

As Herek's example demonstrates, translating research so it is accessible is only one ingredient necessary for policy influence. In addition, to be effective, research should be conveyed in a compelling, persuasive manner, directly applicable to the policy issue at hand.

The distinct cultures of research and policy have often been emphasized in the literature, along with the resulting challenges for effective communication (Bogenschneider & Corbett, 2010). The previous examples emphasize what skills may be necessary to effectively navigate the policy sphere as a psychologist, including the ability to craft a compelling story from research, translate research into a concise format, and evaluate the potential misuse of research findings prior to sharing them. Beyond challenges to effective communication, the differences in research and policy cultures also raise important challenges to scientific and personal integrity—a set of challenges we turn to next.

Scientific and Personal Integrity

A number of respondents spontaneously discussed challenges related to scientific and personal integrity during the course of the interviews. The challenge most frequently reported was situational pressure to present a specific research finding or a synthesis of a research literature in a certain way, usually to conform to the expectations or goals of governmental funders and policymakers (Miller, in press; Morris, 2008). In some cases, those interviewed note situations in which they perceived colleagues to be influenced by such pressures or, in their view, times when fellow researchers were improperly biased by their personal values and advocacy goals. It should be noted, however, that many of the interviewees who were academics privileged the role of *educator of policymakers* over the role of *advocate for particular legislation*. The researchers felt that as educators they would be seen as neutral scientists and have the potential to influence policymakers with varying views. However, as advocates, they believed they would be seen as biased—and thus only able to influence policymakers who already shared their views.

The five examples that follow illustrate several of these perspectives.

Patrick Tolan describes his involvement in research advisory committees addressing child mental health needs for state policymakers. He points to possible areas of conflict between one's research training and the reality of the policy process:

> When I did testimony and was involved in state committees, I learned the extent to which relationships and personal stories were much more critical than data. Most of us who are good scientists don't have the necessary skills because they require the kind of social engagement, ease with uncertainty, and the willingness to accept things as true about which we would say, "You have to qualify that. It's not quite clear." Or to go along with things that normally we would say, "No, I can't agree with that," because of the way we're trained. I can respect those skills and be helpful to people who have them, but I was kidding myself thinking I myself could do those things.

Tolan found that the academic norm of cautious, qualified interpretation of findings (given inevitable research design limitations) is not well-tailored to the less stringent and more strategic practices he observed in the policy arena. He continues, nonetheless, to draw and share policy implications from his research in the area of positive youth development and youth violence and mental health prevention (e.g., Elliott & Tolan, 1999; Tolan, 2014;

Tolan, Sherrod, Gorman-Smith, & Henry, 2004) in his role as director of the University of Virginia Center to Promote Effective Youth Development.

Keith Humphreys (pp. 162–164), based on his year as senior government advisor within the Office of National Drug Control Policy, provides a national executive branch perspective on pressures to hedge what is being shared with key decision makers:

> The [staff assistant to political higher-ups] would say, "You can't discuss anything substantive with anyone unless you have talking points and a handler who will keep you on message." I think what they are thinking is, "These buffoons don't know anything about how this town really works. They go out there and tell the unvarnished truth, and that causes all these problems." There was a reporter from a national political magazine who came to interview Tom [McLellan]. Afterward he confided, "I'm really worried about Tom's future." I said, "Why?" He said, "Because he talks exactly the same way as he did before he got here. He's going to get in a lot of trouble if he keeps telling the truth." Those kinds of things are there, and that can be challenging.

Although "telling the truth" constitutes an overarching value in the academic context, it can prove a liability at times in highly politicized areas of government. For psychologists working for elected officials, both explicit and implicit pressures can be great to "toe the party line"—for example, not presenting information or perspectives that run counter to positions taken by "higher-ups." Working for officials one respects and obtaining support from like-minded and honest peers can help one maintain high standards of integrity and at the same time achieve critical policy goals.

Laurie Garduque (pp. 132–134) comments more generally about distrust and possible threats to integrity in the policy-focused research networks she helped develop and fund at the MacArthur Foundation:

> In the kind of alliances that I was trying to cultivate, there was skepticism and distrust between researchers, practitioners, policymakers, and advocates. From the non-researchers' perspectives:
>
> - *"The research isn't relevant."*
> - *"They don't understand what's really important."*

- *"They're not concerned about the implications of their findings up front."*
- *"They can do damage."*

From the researchers' perspectives:

- *"The advocates go beyond what the data actually say."*
- *"They distort the research findings."*

> Having them work together and maintain the integrity of the research, but also recognizing at a certain point that the researcher has to let go, is always a challenge.

The different approaches to evidence and decision-making pose a challenge to psychologists collaborating with policymakers and advocates. Garduque's experience highlights the importance of maintaining the integrity of the research on the one hand and being sensitive to the needs and realities of the policymaking process on the other.

The final two examples underscore the challenges to integrity in those situations in which there is pressure, whether explicit or implicit, for government-funded contract research to provide certain findings that support policymakers' perspectives or agendas. Developmental researcher Jay Belsky discusses one such situation involving mixed outcome findings in the initial evaluation of the national Sure Start program in England (pp. 256–257):

> The marriage of science and policy is a problematic one. Scientists are there to find out the answers to questions and test hypotheses and, theoretically at least, let the chips fall where they may. I remember in England being told by one of my collaborators, as well by people inside the government, to tone things down. . . . My opinion is that that's not what I do. That's not what you hired me to do. That's not who I am. If you're going to fire me, you can fire me. There were people who wanted to fire me. As far as I was concerned, my job was to tell it like it was and let them do what they wanted with it.

As Belsky's experience reveals, science and policy can clash because of their different norms and goals. In this particular case, however, in the end, the government officials responded to the findings presented by substantially altering the nature of the Sure Start program.

Jacob Tebes (pp. 211–213) similarly describes situations where findings are not consistent with those expected by a government funder, in this case, at the state agency level:

> When we work with states, because they are paying us, they may wish for a certain result. I've been encountering the tension this creates throughout my entire career. Sometimes you are in a different situation and can play a different [advocacy] role, but I don't recommend trying to be an advocate when you are in the role of a researcher because you risk losing your integrity as a scientist.

Tebes clearly articulates the challenge of resisting pressure from funders and sticking close to research findings when presenting and interpreting them. He notes there may be other opportunities in which a more explicit advocacy role, one moving beyond sharing of information, may be possible. For example, earlier in his career, Tebes served as coordinator of a set of programs that served indigent families, and he and colleagues often did advocacy work at the state capitol to increase funding for the programs.

The vast majority of respondents interviewed for this volume entered psychology—and also the policy arena—in order to make a positive difference in the world. Challenges to scientific and personal integrity are inevitable in policy work, however, given pressures from stakeholders, funders, and colleagues to deliver certain findings or to frame findings in a certain way. Interviewees draw on their commitment to behavioral science and practice norms, their passion to better the lives of vulnerable populations, and support from like-minded others to persist in their policy work while adhering to high levels of personal and professional integrity. They acknowledge, however, the tensions experienced when personal and professional standards are challenged by situational demands from important stakeholders.

As discussed in the next section, being true to one's values and beliefs (and to one's data) can occasionally result in challenges typically *outside* the norms of academic research and professional practice: personal attacks and threats, sometimes followed by far-reaching career consequences.

Public Attacks, Private Threats, and Career Consequences

A subset of respondents described the difficult challenges of pushback that occurred as a result of their policy influence efforts. The experiences varied greatly in their nature and severity. Five examples are included here. The first three occurred in the judicial context, involving public attacks, and the two that follow involve attacks and threats from either industry or government agencies, in the latter instance resulting in serious career consequences.

Psychology and law researcher Eugene Borgida (pp. 234–236) observes that, given the adversarial nature of the judicial arena, public attacks on one's credibility and scholarship are normative—but still difficult to contend with, especially when first encountered:

> One of the obstacles for me was the realization early on that just because you summarize the research accurately, state the implications, and do the right thing because you've been trained to do that, doesn't mean that you'll be perceived that way. In the context of social science and law or social psychology and law, there is a broader advocacy framework. You're going to be attacked for your values, motives, affiliations, and associations as hypotheses as to why your representation of the science is skewed and biased. It's a kind of an eye-opener when you first encounter it.

Borgida's comments highlight how psychologists looking to influence policy from an academic, objective vantage point are at risk of their research findings being viewed as partisan or biased. Preparation for critique and attack is useful—even if neither is forthcoming. Seeking out support if the response is harsh is also important. Borgida's experience clearly rings true in the next example, which is also situated in a legal context.

Public attacks appeared in the media against social psychologist Patricia Gurin, who prepared one of the expert reports in the affirmative action case involving the University of Michigan. Her report drew on extant research to make the case for the value and benefits of diversity on college campuses (pp. 197–198). Gurin recounts the attacks she faced during this time:

> They took after me in op-eds. The one in the *Wall Street Journal* was titled "Lies to the Supreme Court." It charged that I had hidden a document that raised critical questions, had failed to turn that document over and therefore we were lying. . . . That day I said to myself, "I really have to talk to [colleague's name withheld]. His wife, an African American woman, picked up the phone. I said 'I'm just beside myself.' She said, 'Pat, if you didn't have the courage, you shouldn't have become involved. . . . Buck up, lady.' She also said that this is the kind of stuff that African Americans have been dealing with all of their lives, so what else is new? . . . Yes, it was hard, but there were very good people who helped.

The attacks on Gurin underscore the need for psychologists to build support systems when undertaking challenging policy work, particularly in high-profile cases such as this one.

Also working within the judicial context, Gail Goodman (pp. 91–93) describes the difficult tension experienced at the very start of her career. Specifically, she discusses the controversy that arose from her research supporting the potential credibility of eyewitness accounts provided by preschool children who had been sexually abused:

> I was asked to consult on and possibly testify in some of the big preschool cases that were in the news at that time. That became very controversial and very heated both within the scientific and clinical communities and the legal community and internationally. Suddenly I was in the middle of this huge controversy and was still so young and so unprepared for that. It was just a very tense, difficult time.

Borgida, Gurin, and Goodman all experienced attacks in the context of court proceedings. Their cases emphasize how psychologists working in policy, especially in highly controversial policy areas, may face unexpected pushback on their research, perspectives, or stances. These experiences notwithstanding, each of the three psychologists persevered and successfully contributed to policy change.

The final two examples involve threats and attacks in nonjudicial contexts. The first depicts financial inducements, and then threats, from the tobacco industry.

Sharon Landesman Ramey (pp. 207–209) recounts a harrowing experience related to her scholarship supporting the placement of warning labels for pregnant women on cigarettes and alcoholic beverages:

> I was working with a team toward labeling cigarettes and alcoholic beverages with warnings to pregnant women. I wrote, with another person, a review article about the effects of women's smoking during pregnancy on their [unborn] children. I got a call from the tobacco industry the day after publication, offering to have me be a consultant for twice my annual salary because I was "such an amazing scientist" that I could "critique the imperfect research on smoking effects." They wanted someone as "brilliant as I was" to advise them. . . . When I said no, I was barraged with phone calls—they were

going to ruin my reputation by going to the press, showing that [given my area of training] I wasn't competent to write the review article.

Ramey's experience underscores the role of powerful corporate interests as barriers to change—in this case taking the form of cooptation and then threats. This was not the only time Ramey had been threatened. Earlier in her career, when her research showed that some people with developmental disabilities and no legal guardians were being neglected and shuttled into nursing homes, she received threats that "The Mafia [purported to have corporate interests in the nursing homes] . . . might harm me or my family if I published the findings." In each case, the threats did not deter Ramey from proceeding with her policy work.

The final example involves serious career consequences following policy efforts, in this case when the interests of a governmental agency were threatened. Specifically, Thomas Wolff (pp. 129–131) was asked to leave the medical school where he had long held a full-time position after authoring a report critical of the state mental health system:

We issued a report on the lack of coordinated outpatient mental healthcare as experienced by community health workers in the Health Access Network meetings. The commissioner of mental health went berserk and screamed at the vice chancellor of the medical school, who screamed at me. Three days later, I was told that after 18 years working at the Medical School I could choose either to be fired or take a settlement and leave. I left.

Ramey's and Wolff's experiences illustrate the potential repercussions of putting forward reports and scholarship whose policy implications run counter to powerful stakeholder interests. As discussed in the previous section, maintaining personal and scientific integrity can prove a challenge in the policy arena, given the entrenched interests of both private and public sector stakeholders. For Ramey and Wolff, as was the case with the other psychologists interviewed, strongly held values and beliefs provided a clear compass to guide decisions that support the interests of vulnerable populations.

Only a subsample of respondents spontaneously offered accounts of attacks, threats, and, in a few cases, negative career consequences from their policy influence efforts. Since no questions explicitly focused on this particular challenge, it is difficult to know how widespread it is. Nonetheless, when it does occur, it represents a form of challenge that can be especially unnerving: a "thick skin," un-relenting resolve, and reaching out for support are necessary to keep engaged—qualities reflected in each of the interviewees. The final challenge is relatively nor-mative for those working in the policy arena.

Work Load, Time Pressure, and Lack of Incentives

Workload and time pressure can be intense in the policy arena. The pace and de-mands of policy work can be unpredictable; when an agenda item is moving for-ward, the need for analysis, meetings, and information can be immediate, at all hours of the day and night. Preparing court testimony and briefs have their own special workload demands, including extensive review of documents. The lack of work incentives further complicates matters and so does geography, which can curtail policy work if the seat of policymaking is far away. For academic psycholo-gists whose primary "day job" is teaching and research, finding time for hands-on policy work can be a challenge. Most of those interviewed noted the lack of rewards in academia for policy work. For those working in staff positions with Congress, the pay is quite modest and the hours quite long. These challenges not-withstanding, the intrinsic rewards of policy work and the critical importance of policy change more than compensates for the situational demands for the vast majority of those interviewed. A number of these aspects of workload, time pres-sure, and incentives are noted in the examples presented next.

First, Susan Fiske depicts the work pressures related to her policy work in the legal arena, from the vantage point of academia (pp. 86–87):

> I remember being on a class action suit where I had probably 10 or 20 file boxes of materials in my dining room for a year. Just finding the time to read all that stuff wasn't easy. . . . In terms of court cases, what do you say to your kid, "I'm going to be away. I don't know how long for?" That's all a challenge. . . . It was sheer brute effort. That's one reason I stopped doing it. I got worn out. But the opportunities that it created were to think about how these things operate in the real world.

Policy work, though rewarding, can be challenging for work–family life bal-ance. Understanding one's support system and personal strengths—as well as limits—is key to successful and sustained policy work. For Fiske, partici-pation in individual court cases yielded over time to other forms of policy involvement. These included policy-relevant scholarship as well as leadership and/or senior advisory roles in national professional organizations that con-duct advocacy.

Lindsay Chase Lansdale (pp. 240–242), also situated in academia, similarly underscores the limitation of time as a barrier to direct policy involvement. She observes, however, that this limitation can be somewhat mitigated through strategic involvement with an intermediary organization:

> A limitation is time. Because I'm in an academic setting, I'm much more dedicated toward the development of [research] evidence—[limiting the time I can put] into all sorts of policy influence . . . [However,] that's being relieved a bit by a very unusual opportunity to be a part of a leadership and communication [initiative].

As was the case for Chase Lansdale, a number of the psychologists interviewed found working with intermediary organizations a meaningful and time-efficient strategy for leveraging their scholarship in service of policy change. The initiative Chase Lansdale refers to is Ascend, a policy program of the Aspen Institute (aspeninstitute.org/policy-work/ascend). Ascend brings together strategically placed leaders devoted to shifts in policies, practices, and resources for vulnerable families through piloting, replicating, and scaling two-generation approaches to poverty reduction (i.e., approaches simultaneously targeting children and their parents). This policy-focused collaboration with an intermediary organization has assisted with the time constraints associated with Chase Lansdale's academic responsibilities.

The final two examples focus on the work demands on policy insiders. We begin with Roberta Downing (pp. 149–151), who early in her policy career worked as a staffer for a highly respected US Senator. She highlights both the high value she accords that experience and the personal sacrifices involved:

> If I could work on the Hill again for a member that I respected, I would love to. But . . . it would have to be when both my kids are a lot older. You're sacrificing a lot of your time and a lot of your personal life working there.

After a stint working in the intermediary sector, Downing recently accepted another policy position—in the executive rather than the legislative branch of government.

The final example depicts a potential consequence of the intense pressures in a political campaign, in this case involving Bradley Olson (pp. 114–116), who served as chief of policy for a mayoral campaign in Chicago. Olson details the challenges he faced during his involvement:

> The mayoral campaign where I was chief of policy was incredibly difficult. I was going all day and night. I felt like I had to learn everything about Chicago in terms of policy in essentially three months. I knew a lot, but the pressure was overwhelming. One time I was at the campaign office and I just started to get really dizzy, I almost fainted. . . . The lessons learned were basically that not only is it time-consuming, but it can be so absorbing that it's [medically] dangerous. It's a lot of scary pressure. Sometimes I'd say, "Maybe this isn't for me."

Olson's experience as chief of policy in a campaign office has not deterred him from involvement in other policy areas. This includes his long-term advocacy to pressure APA to change its policies concerning psychologists' involvement in national security interrogations.

Workload, time demands and limited incentives represent real challenges for psychologists seeking to influence policy. For academics pursuing policy influence, the rewards in most cases will be intrinsic, rather than those awarded by department chairs. Such rewards have proved sufficient for the vast majority of those interviewed. For policy insiders, perhaps especially the staff of elected officials, family and lifestyle may be challenged by great time demands. These concerns led a number of the Washington policy insiders interviewed to ultimately seek employment in the intermediary sector or within executive agencies where family and lifestyle can more readily be accommodated.

Summary

Effective communication, maintaining integrity, coping with attacks from the opposition, and workload strain constitute personal challenges faced by psychologists actively seeking to impact policy. These challenges were generally responded to well by those interviewed, over the course of time. In several cases, a change in policy focus, method, or position was necessary. Across the board, the psychologists interviewed emphasize that resilience is an essential attribute for work in the policy arena, given the many challenges involved.

At a number of points in the interview, respondents were asked about the lessons they learned from the failures, mistakes, barriers, and personal challenges they experienced during their policy work. The chapter concludes with a recounting of some of these lessons.

Lessons Learned: Multiple Approaches, Time Perspective, and Persistence

Policy involvement by no means ensures policy success; the vast majority of those interviewed could easily identify policy failures, defeats, and mistakes (although sharing them publicly took courage). The various barriers and challenges described earlier notwithstanding, the benefits of work in the policy arena were emphasized in interview after interview, along with the valuable lessons learned. In this final section of the chapter, three key lessons emphasized by respondents are presented:

- use of multiple approaches
- the importance of a long-term time perspective
- persistence

Multiple Approaches

Given the difficulty of achieving policy influence, utilizing multiple policy influence methods is important.

Laurence Steinberg (pp. 93–95) emphasizes the strategic lesson that pursuing multiple approaches can be essential to achieving policy success, given the difficulty of bringing about change:

> It's just hard. I think the main lesson I learned from this is that no one approach works by itself. You've got to do it all. You've got to deal with the press, the legislature directly, and the professional and practitioner communities. It just takes a lot of time and work, and it doesn't always pay off. I think that if there's something to learn about how to do this, it's that you've got to develop a whole suite of skills. There's not just one way to do it.

Steinberg and colleagues effectively employed multiple methods as part of a coordinated, multiyear initiative to influence multiple groups of policy stakeholders. Given the complex forces at play in the policy arena, a multipronged strategy will often be essential to achieve change.

The sequential use of multiple approaches is important when earlier strategies prove ineffective. Diana Zuckerman (pp. 232–233) found it necessary to switch approaches in her policy work seeking regulation of medical devices:

> The initial strategy was to try to change the law. When that was not successful the first time, we thought, "We need more nonprofit organizations to talk about this. . . . We tried that strategy, and that didn't work particularly well. Then we really focused more on media and said, "If we can't get lawmakers to make this change because they're all getting donations from medical device companies to keep the status quo, then maybe the way to influence that is to have the public be incensed about it." That was part of what *Consumer Reports* wanted to do [with the article on medical devices] . . . It did result in about 100,000 emails to members of Congress complaining about the law."

As demonstrated by this example, flexibility in approach is integral to policy influence. This was also evident in Clinton Anderson's switch from a legislative to a judicial strategy in his policy work for gay rights when Congress turned Republican in the 1990s (pp. 109–111).

Strategic use of multiple approaches appears critical to effective policy work. Such work often involves a policy team with diverse talents and connections who collectively can employ multiple methods in concerted fashion as part of an orchestrated policy campaign. At other times, different approaches are employed sequentially as new methods are brought to bear when initial ones do not achieve the desired results.

Time Perspective

Respondent after respondent emphasized the importance of a long-term time perspective when seeking to influence social policy.

Robin Jenkins (pp. 170–172), who worked at both state and federal levels in the area of juvenile justice reform, notes that policy adoption does not happen quickly:

> Trying to ramp up and get a policy change done in a particular legislative cycle or even in a congressional session . . . we have set that in our sights and have failed on that on a couple of occasions. It takes a while to get people to see the importance of it, depending on the policy, and to generate the necessary level of support among their peers in those institutions. A major part of this work is relationship-building, and that takes time.

Many aspects of policy work require time. As Jenkins concludes, this may be especially true for the critical relationship-building aspect of policy change efforts.

The necessity of a long-term perspective is similarly emphasized by Robert Franks (pp. 126–129):

> One thing that I've learned is that systems change work is something that's never completed. You can never stop. It's a continuous process of engagement and education. Systems change takes commitment, dedication and time.

The view that policy change is a process, not an outcome, is shared by a number of those interviewed. Given the complexity of systems, their resistance to change, and the inevitability of unintended consequences when changes are initiated, Franks' view that systems change work is "never completed" rings completely true—as does the need for a long-time perspective for those engaged in such work.

Marybeth Shinn (pp. 182–185) underscores the importance of a realistic, measured perspective:

> If you put things out there, some of them will be taken, and some won't. Some were taken at this time and not at that time. Just try to do what you can and not expect to transform the world with it, as much as you want to.

Shinn's lived experience working for decades to enact change in homelessness policy in New York City forms the basis for her tempered, yet hopeful, advice. Idealism combined with realism, passion girded with persistence, describe the policy perspectives of many of the psychologists whose work is portrayed in these pages.

Richard Price (pp. 224–226) uses the analogy of surfing to place into context the challenges of making a difference and the importance of timing:

> A policy colleague of mine always used to say, "Policy influence is like surfing. You have to wait for the right wave, but if you don't have your

surfboard when it comes, you're in trouble." I think that was always a wise comment. Timing is an absolutely crucial issue here.... Having any influence clearly is influenced substantially by public understanding of what the issues are—where the public concern is at that moment in time.

Price's surfing analogy simultaneously emphasizes the importance of preparation, patience, and discernment. Policy ideas and relevant evidence need to be developed and available. At the same time, continual scanning of the policy horizon for new developments and promising openings is necessary so the next round of policy action is initiated in a timely fashion when promising opportunities arise.

The importance of a longer term time perspective for policy change represents a hard-earned lesson for many of the psychologists interviewed. It facilitates effective strategic planning as well as a means to handle the frustrations and setbacks that accompany policy work. A kindred lesson articulated by the psychologists interviewed is the critical need for persistence.

Persistence

The one constant theme across interviews was the importance of persistence. Policy initiatives typically take a long time to unfold and are fraught with opposition, barriers, challenges, and inevitable ups and downs along the way. The final two examples underscore the importance of persistence in several of its various guises: endurance, resilience, and patience.

Here, Bradley Olson (pp. 114–116), involved in the ongoing advocacy campaign to alter APA's policy related to psychologists' involvement in torture, emphasizes endurance as key:

We never knew that these campaigns . . . were sort of eternal. We thought that they would end, we would win this year, it would be over with. . . . They just continued on and on. Right now, I don't think we ever expect it to end. Pretty much each year since 2005 there's been some APA policy change, always falling short of what we actually wanted, but a significant improvement nevertheless . . . the biggest barrier and challenge is endurance.

Persistence by a small group of determined psychologists, including Olson, was critical to the recent revision of APA policy further prohibiting

psychologists' direct or indirect involvement in situations involving coercive interrogation. Persistence was challenging in the face of sustained
organizational resistance and, in some cases, personal attacks (Hoffman
et al., 2015).

The importance of persistence, and relatedly, resilience, is similarly highlighted by
Kelly Brownell (pp. 72–74), a child obesity researcher and advocate. Interestingly,
as one sign of progress, in 2014 the major beverage companies voluntarily committed themselves to a 20% reduction in the amount of sugar included in their
products (American Beverage Association, 2014). Although an organizational,
not a governmental, policy decision, this decision likely reflects, at least in part,
the work of Brownell and many others who have been working for years to bring
about such change.

Summary

Multiple approaches, a long-term time perspective, and persistence may be universal guidelines for effective action in the world, applicable to most domains of
professional (and life) activity. Given the nature of the barriers and challenges
faced in policy work by the psychologists interviewed, however, they ring true in
this context with a special—and heart-felt—resonance.

Striving for Policy Impact: A Long Journey with Great Possibility

Policy work is not for the weak of heart. Failures and defeats, challenges and
barriers are an integral part of the policy journey. It is important to go into
this work with the knowledge that multiple approaches and skill sets will be
needed, along with a realistic time perspective. Furthermore, building the
social and emotional supports that will contribute to longer term persistence
appears essential. These are hard-earned lessons and advice from psychologists who have achieved significant successes in their policy work about issues
they are passionate about—who have faced, but have not been deterred by,
their share of defeats, barriers, and challenges. Maintaining a positive outlook,
recognizing the critical importance of small wins on the pathway to longer
term policy change, receiving support from like-minded colleagues, and being
persistent are some of the ways psychologists successfully deal with the challenges faced en route to policy impact.

9

Conclusions and Future Directions

*Doing research that's relevant to and tries to influence social policy . . . is . . .
something that graduate training programs should validate. It's . . . the 21st
century way to train people.*

—E. Borgida, November 13, 2012

Psychologists possess considerable potential to influence social policy in the
public interest. To fully realize that potential, focused effort is required. This final
chapter summarizes key themes and findings from the current research. It offers
a number of future directions in the realms of training, research, and action to
increase the policy influence capacity of the field. The chapter contains parting
words from many of those interviewed, providing guidance and inspiration for
those entering and continuing their work in the policy arena. The final quote is
from Seymour Sarason, to whom the book is dedicated.

What Have We Learned?

The brief case examples and personal experiences highlighted in this volume
build upon previous literature. Collectively, the personal experiences of those
interviewed underscore a number of generative themes related to psychologists' involvement in policy influence work in the public interest. The themes
represent what our field can learn from seasoned psychologists who work to enhance our country's social policies. Nine of these themes—lessons learned—are
highlighted here.

Psychologists Make Important Policy Contributions

The psychologists interviewed have made important policy contributions in the
public interest. These policy influences span all three branches of government: legislative, executive, and judicial. They occurred at all levels of government: federal,

state, and local. They contribute to a diverse array of policy content areas, including:

- death penalty prohibition for adolescents
- early childhood education
- gay marriage
- gender discrimination in the workplace
- health and mental healthcare reform
- homelessness
- home visiting programs
- sexually abused child witness treatment
- status offender diversion from the juvenile justice system
- substance abuse prevention

Without their consistent efforts, in concert with others, these policy changes may have never come about.

This book portrays diverse forms of policy influence among a relatively large sample of psychologists. It highlights the nature and importance of the policy contributions that psychologists have made (and are making) and in a more comprehensive fashion than has been done to date. The psychologists came from varied disciplinary backgrounds, largely within the realm of developmental, social, and community psychology, and they encompass diverse interests and areas of focus. Additional research is clearly needed to establish the full nature and extent of the contributions of psychologists to policy in the public interest. Such research will require systematic sampling, multiple levels of analysis, and multiple methods of inquiry. The aim of the current research is much more modest—to describe and highlight the policy contributions of a number of psychologists from several subfields. The book hopefully will encourage greater policy interest and involvement among psychologists and psychology graduate students, and perhaps even psychology undergraduate students, including those with blended interested in psychology and related fields (e.g., political science, sociology). Whatever their disciplinary background or area of study, the goal is to increase the contribution of psychology in service of the public interest.

Getting Started: The Many Pathways into Policy Work

The interviews reveal many different pathways into active policy influence work. The vast majority of respondents did not plan to get involved in policy work at the outset of their graduate and professional careers, although most of those interviewed were committed to applied work that would make a difference in the lives of citizens. That is, they wanted their work to have a meaningful, practical real-world impact. Many academic psychologists describe their initial involvement in policy as an unexpected convergence of content interests and opportunities, unfolding over time, rather than as an explicit decision to pursue such work:

- Several of those interviewed developed programs for specific populations and, when results proved positive, became involved in dissemination and funding efforts that led to increasing levels of direct involvement with policymakers.
- For others, involvement in policy emerged as they became experts in an area, realized the policy implications of their work, and initiated contact with policymakers to pursue related policy ideas.
- For many of the psychologists interviewed, their pathway toward involvement was initiated by mentors, colleagues, administrators, lawyers, or policymakers who encouraged them to get involved in a specific policy influence opportunity, and these opportunities then led to future involvement and contributions over time.

For most academic psychologists interviewed for this text, policy work was only one of many activities they pursued. They interwove their policy work with their busy careers in research, teaching, mentorship, and service, with an eye to influencing specific populations, practitioners, and organizations in their areas of expertise and interest.

Psychologists who pursued careers working in intermediary organizations and/or government also came to this interest at various points in their careers and as a result of various influences, some of them fortuitous. The most common pathway was the decision to pursue a fellowship working in the congressional or executive branch of government in Washington, DC, sponsored by the American Psychological Association (APA), the Society for Research in Child Development, or the Society for the Psychological Study of Social Issues. For some, the decision to apply for the fellowship occurred during their first job search process, as an option that was more appealing than academic or other applied opportunities. For others, the decision to apply for the fellowship followed a period of time working in an academic or applied position, after it became apparent that the position did not seem the perfect fit for their interests, including their desire for more direct impact on social issues. Whatever the impetus for and timing of the decision to apply for the fellowship, the ensuing year-long experience, immersed in the policymaking process in Washington, DC, became the basis for continued pursuit of policy work.

Finally, other psychologists were influenced early on by policy-oriented graduate programs and/or graduate mentors. Some of these individuals selected their graduate program due to the policy focus; indeed, several had policy experience prior to graduate school, whereas others did not. For the latter group, the opportunity to take courses in policy and to become involved in policy-oriented projects inspired them to pursue careers in which at least part of the focus was policy-related.

There are multiple pathways into policy-related work. A confluence of factors, some involving prior preparation and others involving a fortuitous coming to-gether of circumstances, led to entry into the policy arena. After an initial foray in policy, whether sought after or primarily the result of circumstance, those inter-viewed elected to continue such work. Their policy work then became an integral part of their careers as psychologists.

A Variety of Policy Influence Methods and Skills

The methods employed to influence policy varied. One important method was serving as a member or chair of a policy advisory group—the recom-mendations of the advisory group, in these cases, were enacted into law (e.g., Britner, Chapter 3). Another method was to exert influence on policymakers directly, through advocacy and lobbying, usually working with or for inter-mediary organizations. An additional method of influence brought relevant psychological theory and research findings to key court cases through direct testimony and/or preparation of amicus briefs. Other methods included es-tablishing consultative relationships with key policymakers or their staff members, writing National Academy reports, and public education through the media.

Throughout the text, psychologists highlight various skills that helped con-tribute to their successes:

- **Relationship-building skills** are consistently reported as essential. Building relationships is critical. This involves connecting with key legislative and/or executive branch policymakers or their staff members, individuals in interme-diary organizations, media, practitioner groups, and/or researchers in multiple disciplines.
- *Research* skills are crucial for those conducting original research, but also important for those in "translational" roles in intermediary organizations or within government. For the latter group, research skills contribute to the ability to differentiate stronger from weaker research (critical analysis) and to perform integrative reviews of varied research literatures (research synthesis).
- *Communication* skills, although related to relationship-building, stand in their own right as another critical policy-influence skill. Both oral and written com-munication skills are important, as is the ability to generate and communicate a compelling policy narrative.

- *Strategic analysis* involves another distinct set of skills, both in terms of policy analysis and strategy development. Knowledge of the political and policy process is a necessary precondition for effective strategy development.
- Additional skills depend on the specific policy role and project and include close and careful attention to negotiation, team-building, and management.

Given that any individual is unlikely to possess all of the skills necessary for effective policy influence, the full complement of skills typically end up being present in a larger policy influence team, which brings us to the fourth theme.

Policy Influence Is a Relationship-Based, Interdisciplinary, and Collaborative Endeavor

The reported examples of policy influence rarely, if ever, involve psychologists working alone. Building relationships and coalitions is critical to policy work whether from outside government or within. Individuals with different backgrounds bring varied policy strategies and knowledge bases to the work. For relationships in the policy arena to thrive, those involved must respect the dignity, opinions, and needs of a diverse array of policy participants. Respect increases trust among researchers, citizens, policy practitioners, and policymakers, and it helps facilitate an understanding of how each group's strengths or skills can be utilized to achieve mutual goals. The psychologists interviewed became trustworthy partners by:

- providing reliable information
- standing with allies
- keeping confidences
- allowing policy questions to guide research
- showing up, repeatedly, when needed

Psychologist Robert Franks succinctly captures the importance of relationships to policy work: "One of the reasons why I'm as effective as I am is because of the relationships that I've built."

Collaborations often involve individuals from varied disciplinary and professional backgrounds. For policy researchers, working with individuals from multiple disciplines expands the ecological understanding of a social problem and the universe of policy alternatives, extending and deepening theoretical perspectives, levels of analysis, and methodological approaches. For policy practitioners, working with individuals from diverse professional backgrounds constitutes an intrinsic aspect of the policy and applied domains, which is essential to generating sufficient support to influence decisions. Such work often involves building and joining formal and informal coalitions.

Building relationships in the policy domain often means writing policy positions for others to present publicly or to be shared at private meetings, with no glory or line on the vita or resume to show for the effort. There is a relevant saying in public policy circles, usually attributed to US President Harry S. Truman: "It is amazing what you can accomplish when you don't care who gets the credit." This motto underscores the collaborative, behind-the-scenes nature of policy work. Academic psychologists may need to be established in their careers to fully invest the time and energy required for policy influence or carefully select academic settings in which policy work is clearly valued and supported.

Multiple Vantage Points: Universities, Insiders, and Intermediaries

The psychologists interviewed contribute to policy from multiple vantage points, each of which has a distinct and critical role to play. One key vantage point is that of the *university*, where psychologists pursue research careers that generate important ideas and findings that broaden and deepen the universe of policy options. The types of research that contribute to policy success vary greatly, including:

- program evaluation (in some cases of programs the psychologists themselves had developed)
- research enhancing the understanding of policy-relevant phenomena
- research on community-based delivery systems
- research that generates practical tools for administrators and practitioners

At times, specific research findings are instrumental in a policy decision; more generally, conceptual influence occurs in which theories and accumulated findings over the years alter the definition of problems, how populations are viewed, and the universe of possible policy solutions (e.g., early childhood as a critical time for policy intervention). Interdisciplinary policy research, evaluation, and consultation centers are seen as important crucibles for policy influence work involving psychologists, as are leadership positions that provide policy-relevant vision and mission (e.g., the engaged university).

A second key vantage point is that of a policy insider. The psychologists interviewed who hold full-time positions within government view their insider status as a critical source of policy influence, although the nature of the influence varies according to the type of position. Those working in executive branch agencies in their area of content expertise are able to directly apply their psychological content knowledge to issues at hand. Those working as congressional aides or as elected officials usefully draw on the general academic psychology skills of critical thinking, understanding of research, and relationship-building. The potential for direct policy influence on pressing social issues presents psychologists within government an opportunity to contribute directly to policy in ways that generally are not possible for those on the outside.

Intermediary organizations represent a third vantage point, one linking the worlds of research, practice, and policy. Such organizations are increasingly seen as critical for policy influence work. The psychologists interviewed for this volume work in a variety of intermediary organizations that vary tremendously in the extent to which they pursue educational versus advocacy strategies of policy influence and in the resources available to conduct policy work. University-affiliated intermediary organizations help leverage the potential of the university to contribute to policy and enable policy insiders to benefit from the research and content knowledge of the university. Psychologists who work for intermediary organizations play a critical bridging role, with their positions often affording them the opportunity to devote considerable time and effort to policy influence work.

Long-term Involvement in a Particular Context

A multitude of factors influence policy decisions and developments at all levels of government. These include:

- political and economic circumstances
- current events and trends
- unique historical contexts
- the capacity and culture of local delivery systems
- the agendas and personal characteristics of key policy players

The unfolding of any given policy decision is more akin to a unique, context-bound historical event than to a predictable social science regularity. Each policy influence scenario depicted in this volume tells its own story. Thus, generalizations must be drawn cautiously. Many psychologists interviewed note that the next policy influence opportunity will differ in significant ways from the previous one, given the particulars of macro and local historical contexts.

Relationship-building, research, communication, and strategic analysis skills need to be present, but the particulars of how they are applied in each situation vary tremendously across policy narratives. Knowledge and understanding of the general policy process involved is critical, and equally important is the understanding of and strategic positioning regarding the particulars of policy content, politics, players, and personalities. In many cases, long-term involvement in policy influence work will be necessary to effectively exert policy influence. Such longer term involvements provide:

- contextually based content knowledge
- embedded relationship-building and trust

- timely identification of new policy windows
- effective, strategic engagement as opportunities for influence emerge

The success stories in this volume unfolded over years. Many university faculty devoted decades to areas of influence and, relatedly, established long-term relationships with specific intermediary organizations or policymaking groups. Examples include:

- Gregory Herek's research on gay rights and related collaboration with APA's Lesbian Gay, Bisexual, and Transgender Concerns Office
- Marybeth Shinn's research on homelessness and advisory work with the New York City Homelessness Department
- David Old's research on the Nurse Home Visiting Program and related consultative and advocacy work through the national Nurse-Family Partnership organization
- Laurence Steinberg's research on adjudicative competence of adolescents as part of an interdisciplinary research network sponsored by the MacArthur Foundation
- Roger Weissberg's work on social emotional learning and associated leadership of the national Collaborative for Social and Emotional Learning (CASEL)

Long-term patterns of involvement are also found among those whose greatest policy success took place while working within intermediary and governmental sectors. Examples within intermediary organizations include:

- Clinton Anderson and Ellen Garrison's long-term tenures at APA
- Laurie Garduque's decades of policy work at the MacArthur Foundation
- Judith Meyers' leadership at the Child Health and Development Institute
- Kristen Moore's decades-long role as director of Child Trends

Comparable career commitments within government include:

- Trudy Vincent's work in the US Senate
- Charles Barone and Ron Haskins' tenures in the House of Representatives
- Martha Moorehouse's work in the Office of the Assistant Secretary for Planning and Evaluation in the US Department of Health and Human Services

Although downsides may exist for longer term involvement in challenging policy domains and stressful policy work environments, the potential for policy influence is consistently linked to persistence and long-term involvement in a given policy area.

Use of Research and the Limitations of Evidence-Based Policy

Research is one of a multitude of factors that influences policy (Bogenschneider & Corbett, 2010; Contantdriopoulos, Lemire, Denis, & Tremblay, 2010; Finnigan & Daly, 2014; National Academy of Sciences, 2012; Nutley, Walter, & Davies, 2007; Weiss & Bucuvalas, 1980). On some issues, research may play an instrumental role in decisions made, particularly if there is an accumulation of research that points to a particular message or policy action. In many other cases, research will not play a direct role. It is more difficult to assess the indirect (conceptual or "enlightenment") influence of research. Such influences emerge over time as new empirically based perspectives become accepted and contribute to altered perspectives on a social problem, the affected population, and potential policy solutions. Executive branch officials may more likely be directly influenced by research findings than legislators, particularly in more technical, less value-laden areas (e.g., funding of a new program or service delivery approach). Conversely, both in legislative and executive branches, research findings are least likely to influence decisions related to controversial value-based issues (e.g., how to address poverty or abortion). Research that is practical, easy to understand, supports a cost–effect approach, makes the news, and/or is effectively communicated to policymakers or those they trust is most likely to have an impact (Bishop-Josef & Dodgen, 2013).

In recent years, the movement toward evidence-based practice and policy has enhanced the potential for research to influence policy (Haskins & Margolis, 2014). However, most of the psychologists interviewed articulate some disadvantages of the high level of enthusiasm associated with this movement. As Mark Lipsey notes, "The whole enterprise might result in disappointment if unrealistic expectations are not realized. We may then hear policymakers saying, 'We tried evidence-based practice, and it didn't work.'" Most individuals interviewed point to one or more limitations and challenges of an evidence-based approach that might contribute to such disappointment. The limitation most frequently articulated was the wide gap between the ideal conditions that underlie positive findings in randomly controlled trials establishing the viability of a social program and the real-world conditions of bringing such programs to scale in the policy arena. The ideal conditions are not present in the field, and thus little or no positive impact occurs. This outcome may be due to:

- differences in quality of training and supervision
- cultural differences in the population served
- differences in the local delivery system culture and practices

- competing priorities
- lack of "buy-in" (commitment)
- possible built-in bias when evaluations are completed by program developers

A second limitation frequently noted is the clear absence of available evidence-based interventions in many social problem areas. The supply of carefully evaluated programs is small when compared to the vast array of existing problem areas, affected populations, and embedded contexts. A third limitation is the lack of complex, systemic, far-reaching interventions that can make sustainable, population-level differences in many social problems. There are also the challenges of evaluating such far-reaching interventions using randomly controlled methods. As Stephen Fawcett observes, "Randomized controlled trials are grounded in the assumption that one variable, and only one variable, is going to be tested. The evidence is that it takes comprehensive, multicomponent interventions—affecting conditions in multiple sectors—to improve outcomes at the community or population level." A fourth concern is the suppression of new approaches, including those tailored to local contexts, when government officials select a few empirically based approaches as those that will be funded.

A number of interviewees point out that it is not clear that research and evidence should serve as the primary consideration in policy decision-making. In a democracy, policymakers are responsible to those who elect them, and thus decisions should ultimately reflect the desires of citizens, not researchers. Others observe that science is often wrong. Understanding that scientific truths change over time limits the amount of confidence that can be placed on current evidence-based solutions. Finally, some argue that many services provided by government, particularly those focused on populations lacking societal power, should be a right of citizenship, supported by government policy regardless of current scientific proof of their efficacy (e.g., K–12 public education). In summary, although the use of research is viewed as central to psychology's contributions to the policy arena, support for the desirability of evidence-based policy is tempered by the limitations of science and the complexities of the interfaces among science, policy, and democracy. These realities increase the importance of psychology's role in public education, community-based advocacy, and clear communication of the strengths and limitations of current research methods and resulting evidence (Trickett & Beehler, in press).

Community-Based and External Advocacy Approaches to Policy Change

A community-based, advocacy approach to policy change represents an alternative policy influence route to the internal, research expert approach. The external advocacy approach involves making common cause with local citizen and advocacy groups in service of putting pressure on governmental officials to bring about change. University-based psychologists involved in such work may share research findings with advocacy groups and the media, provide training, or link groups to needed resources. Paul Speer's action-research with a faith-based community organization and Brian Wilcox's collaboration with Planned Parenthood to criticize conservative board of education member actions provide examples of such work.

Similarly, psychologists working in intermediary organizations may collaborate on advocacy-focused projects with local community groups, providing expertise, funding, and other resources. Brian Smedley's health disparities media campaigns with local community-based organizations through the Health Policy Institute and Anne Petersen's local citizen-based advocacy in New Mexico through the Kellogg Foundation represent examples in the intermediary sector.

Community-based psychologists can take the lead in community-based advocacy work, exemplified by Thomas Wolff's local coalition-based policy influence efforts and Sam Tsemberis' work promoting Pathways to Action. Finally, as citizens, psychologists can join local organizations to enhance their advocacy work, as Aletha Huston does with local advocacy organizations (Early Childhood Council, United Way) to support early childhood education funding in Austin, Texas.

In addition to direct partnerships with local citizens and community groups, indirect influence can occur through the media and national advocacy organizations. Psychologists can influence public opinion through widespread dissemination of research and scholarship. Examples include:

- the dissemination by developmental psychologists of the potential of early childhood education (Phillips & Styfco, 2007; Raikes, St. Clair, & Plata-Potter, 2013; Shonkoff & Phillips, 2000)
- social psychologists publicizing findings on discrimination and prejudice (Allport, 1954; Pettigrew, 1988)
- community psychologists dissemination of research findings in the area of prevention (e.g., Durlak & Wells, 1997; Price, Cowen, Lorion, & Ramos-McKay, 1988)

Furthermore, working directly with national advocacy organizations can contribute not only to citizen mobilization, but also to formulation of public opinion more generally.

The nature of advocacy organizations and the tactics they use vary greatly. The external advocacy work conducted, including mobilization of constituent voices and media coverage, and ultimately the shaping of public opinion, has proved central to policy influence efforts. Indeed, shaping public opinion may be the only means available to confront powerful opposition groups and entrenched interests. Although many psychologists interviewed in their role as researchers shy away from public affiliation with external advocacy efforts, given the desire to maintain credibility in the policy arena in their role as scientists, most are willing to share their findings with influential organizations. On the other hand, psychologists working in advocacy organizations, as policy insiders within the legislative branches of government, and as community-based practitioners have greater freedom to explicitly contribute to external advocacy efforts.

Determined, Passionate, Resilient, and Proactive

Respondents were forthright about the difficulty of achieving policy change and the barriers to success, their policy influence victories notwithstanding. The challenges faced sometimes appear insurmountable, especially when powerful, opposing interests are involved. Policy is often seen as inextricably intertwined with politics, especially when elected officials are the key decision-makers. This reality runs counter to the desire for social policies to be determined by considerations rooted in the public welfare, rather than those rooted in political partisanship. Influencing policy often takes years, and there are many setbacks, frustrations, reversals, failures, and, sometimes, the receipt of personal attacks. The psychologists interviewed describe determination, passion, and resilience in the face of such challenges as essential to policy work, as well as the importance of being proactive and seizing opportunities to make a difference when they arise.

The sources of the motivation to make a difference and persistence in policy work are diverse and multiple. A number of those interviewed grew up during the turbulent 1960s and internalized values about the importance of addressing social problems and working for social justice. The parents of some pursued lives focused on helping those who were less fortunate, both in terms of careers and volunteer work, thus serving as models or sources of inspiration. Religious perspectives, including "*tikkun olam*" (repairing the world), were an integral part of the lives of some. As undergraduate and graduate students, volunteer or job experiences—in which the problems of poor children, families, and communities were experienced first-hand—influenced a number of the interviewees. Guidance and inspiration from mentors passionate about social issues and social justice and the focus of applied psychology on contributing to a better society also set many of the respondents on a path to policy work.

In addition to personal motivation and perseverance in the face of challenges, interviewees also underscore the importance of being proactive. Rather than waiting for policymakers to contact them, many emphasize the importance of initiating relationships and scanning the local, state, or federal policy and intermediary environments for possible opportunities for involvement. Psychologists also underscore the need to be prepared to seize opportunities that present themselves because the confluence of factors that lead to such opportunities may not repeat themselves.

Deborah Stipek and Laurie Garduque capture several of the themes of this section in their observations. Stipek succinctly provides the following guidance: "Be realistic. Never give up. Don't get discouraged. Doors close. Windows open." Garduque observes, "You make the path that you want to be on. There is no one path. You have to take advantage of opportunities when they present themselves, but you have to be looking for them—because the people who actually change law and policy are likely not looking for you."

Future Directions

Although psychologists working in the public interest have contributed in meaningful ways to social policy over the years, substantial changes in approach are necessary if psychology as a field is to achieve an influence commensurate to its potential. Seven future directions are discussed here:

- graduate training
- policy-relevant research
- research translation and research synthesis
- interdisciplinary collaboration
- transformative social change
- international work
- continued research on influencing social policy

Many of the specific ideas presented emerged during the course of the interviews.

Not surprisingly, however, the ideas and perspectives offered by different psychologists were sometimes at odds:

- "Get directly involved" versus "Work behind the scenes, have others do the hands-on work"
- "Advocate and bear witness" versus "Above all, maintain credibility as a scientist"
- "Begin policy-relevant work early" versus "Wait until you have tenure"

Such varying perspectives likely reflect the reality that there is no one single— or best—way to approach policy work. Choice of roles, pathways, and modes of policy influence will differ depending on many factors, including personal strengths, values, work contexts, and available opportunities.

Career Training in Policy

Graduate programs should begin to emphasize and integrate policy influence as an integral part of work as a psychologist. Programs would ideally include a required policy class to familiarize graduate students with the process, varied vantage points, methods, and skills employed by psychologists who have successfully contributed to social policy. If a required course is not possible, elective courses, including those in other departments (e.g., political science, policy sciences) could allow interested students to become familiar with policy work. Policy courses, or a policy section added to existing courses, could include instruction and practice on communicating to policymakers (policy briefs, op-eds, etc.) and opportunities to meet and learn from psychologists, and others, actively involved in the policy process.[1] Ideally, graduate students, psychology interns, and postdocs should have opportunities to work with organizations involved in policymaking, both intermediaries and governmental—local, state, or national. Activities could include helping with policy analysis, policy evaluation, summarizing and synthesizing policy-relevant research, and preparing research or policy briefs. Intermediary organizations exist for every important policy area, so students currently have the opportunity to work with organizations consistent with their passions and interests. Psychological associations and professional associations offer various opportunities to contribute to such work as well, sometimes paid and often under the guidance of psychologists with policy expertise. Graduate programs should disseminate these training opportunities and encourage students to seek out reputable intermediary organizations that can provide experiences in their content areas.

Finally, graduate students and early career professionals would benefit from the mentorship of faculty and applied psychologists conducting ongoing policy-relevant work. A number of interviewees report involvement in policy-related projects of faculty members as a formative experience. If the faculty in a department or postdoc site are not involved in such work, connections can be made with psychologists located elsewhere who are involved in such activities. More generally, faculty, training directors, administrators, and professional organizations should directly and consistently communicate the intrinsic value of policy-relevant work to students, postdocs, and early career professionals; provide role models and mentors; and include incentives and rewards for such involvements in all levels of the profession.

Policy-Relevant Research and Theory

The field's contributions to social policy would also be enhanced by increasing our capacity to generate policy-relevant research and theory related to a wide variety of policy areas.

---

[1] Textbooks and training materials should be developed for all public interest areas of psychology, to expand on those currently available in the child development, family, and law and psychology areas of policy (e.g., Bogenschneider, 2014; Culp, 2013; Levine, Wallach, & Levine, 2007). Policy-focused texts from other disciplines can usefully be drawn upon as well (e.g., Jansson, 2010). Two sample course syllabi can be found at: www.scra27.org/files/5713/8784/6875/Applied_Psychology_and_Public_Policy.pdf; www.scra27.org/files/1813/8990/6381/Britner_policy_children_syll.pdf

Selection of research questions and methods in collaboration with policymakers, influential intermediary organizations, and other stakeholders (e.g., service providers, citizens) will increase the timeliness and applicability of findings. An in-depth understanding of policymakers' interests and needs will also contribute to increased policy-relevance. Although the development of working partnerships with policymakers and intermediary organizations takes time and concerted effort, the benefits in terms of policy usefulness and impact appear substantial. A variety of research methods and approaches will be necessary, depending on the policy need, including epidemiology, participatory action research, qualitative and mixed method designs, systems research, controlled trials, cost–benefit analyses, and meta analyses. Methodological rigor and creativity will both be needed, the latter being important given the special demands and challenges faced in research in applied settings.

Research that contributes to a new understanding of the causes of social problems, that expands the understanding of the lived experiences of populations in need, and that generates new ideas to address social problems has contributed to policy influence, as reported in many of the examples in the current volume. Applied research is especially likely to have direct relevance to policy analysis and policy development. In addition, basic research that contributes to understanding psychological processes central to social problems may contribute to policy, as is the case in some of the precedent-setting Supreme Court cases covered.

Evaluation research is increasingly being funded and seen as important by policymakers, although its use in policy decisions, even when commissioned by policymakers, is not by any means ensured. Rigorous designs are more likely conducted for programs focused on individuals than for complex, multilevel, and multifaceted policies. Inclusion of cost–benefit and cost-savings analyses, whenever possible, appears especially significant to increase policy 1impact. Since determination of "core components" is critical to implementing delivery systems in "scaling-up" and adapting model programs to the real world, evaluation research should ideally include means to distinguish core components from those that are less critical to be retained in original form. Inclusion of measures to assess the process of implementation in general, and the fidelity and adaptations made of intervention components in particular, will help determine if problems in implementation are behind poor policy outcomes. Finally, inclusion of measures that assess the extent to which intermediate, theory-based variables are impacted can help contribute both to program modification and to further theory development. When initial program developers serve as program evaluators, it is imperative for replications to be done by external investigators (Olds, 2009).

The generation of policy-relevant theory and research is a tall undertaking, requiring considerable resources and incentives. Yet such theory development and testing is necessary if our field is to increase its policy contributions. However, even outstanding theory-based policy-relevant research will not be utilized if policy partnerships are not formed and effective communication of individual and accumulated findings does not take place, which brings us to the next area.

Research Translation and Research Synthesis

Research findings in most cases will not make their way to policymakers on their own, and even when policymakers (or their staff) are interested in research on a topic, findings will not necessarily be understood and interpreted in a veridical fashion. Thus, in the case of both basic and applied research, translational work is crucial. To be effective, psychologists must communicate findings of both individual studies and entire bodies of research in straightforward language that draws out their policy implications. The research translation work can be done by psychologists working in universities, in intermediary organizations, and/or in government. Ideally, psychologists should directly communicate the results of translational work to policymakers, allowing interaction and clarification to aid appropriate interpretation of findings and consideration of their implications. Written reports can take multiple forms, including policy briefs for busy elected officials and their staff or more extended versions for professionals in the executive branch and for judges reviewing evidence in a court of law.

Research syntheses can prove particularly important in the policy arena because they bring together the accumulated findings of multiple studies over an extended period of time. Such work is traditionally done through major literature reviews, sometimes commissioned, but in recent years reliance on statistical meta-analyses has increased. In both cases, research translation for policymaking purposes involves the interpretation of findings, with implications for policy in the forefront. Systematic literature reviews and accompanying policy recommendations can, as is the case for individual research studies, be commissioned by government at all levels, by intermediary organizations, or be initiated by an individual academic or university-based research center. The translation process is best done via direct communication with policymakers or their staff but will likely have maximum impact if widely disseminated by the media or through the Internet and other venues, often by intermediary organizations.

The work of research translation for practice has become increasingly recognized as a high priority in our field, and the need is equally acute for policy. Increased training in such work is critical, as are incentives and the discipline more clearly valuing research translation as a career pathway.

Interdisciplinary Research and Interdisciplinary Policy Centers

Important social problems are inherently multilevel and multisectorial, implicating causal factors and policy solutions that encompass the expertise and focus of multiple disciplines.

Interdisciplinary research collaboration will enhance the likelihood of ecologically valid research, understanding, and policy. In this volume, meaningful interdisciplinary collaborations of those interviewed occurred with scholars from a wide range of disciplines, including anthropology, criminology, economics, education, law, political science, public health, and sociology. The benefits of such work were clearly evident. For example, Steinberg's collaborative research with lawyers revealed that 16- and 17-year-olds displayed lower levels of cognitive competence than adults, findings that directly challenged existing legal standards that treated these adolescents the same as adults (e.g., in terms of the death penalty). The specific age categories selected for research study followed directly from the advice of lawyers—given their relevance to existing legal standards. In Steinberg's case, the interdisciplinary team was an integral part of the MacArthur research network that was tasked with generating policy-relevant research and using the findings to influence policymakers.

Interdisciplinary research centers constitute a primary setting for the development of collaborative research relationships. In some cases, these centers are policy-focused and develop ongoing relationships with state or local policymakers, intermediary organizations, and other diverse stakeholders, often joining existing coalitions or forging new ones. Many of the academic psychologists interviewed for this volume worked within such research and policy centers for at least part of their careers. One example is the Rudd Center for Food Research, which included scholars from psychology, economics, and marketing.

Moving forward, psychologists are likely to make sustained contributions to policy through collaborations with scholars from other disciplines, often through involvement in interdisciplinary research and policy centers. Ideally, such centers would be developed across the entire range of social problems in which psychologists are involved. Funding for such centers can come from governmental and foundation sources, ideally with active encouragement and financial support from university administrators. The University of California, Berkeley, for example, would like policy-relevant research centers to be developed in every sector of the university, geared and ready to respond on almost every policy issue (Weinstein, 2013).

Toward Transformational Change: Direct Policy Influence Is Necessary but Not Sufficient

Our hopes for a more equitable society and world depend on progress in the policy arena. If we ignore direct social policy work and better social policies do not emerge, the prospects for positive social change are limited. However, social policies and social policymaking are constrained by the larger cultural, economic, and political contexts in which they occur. When changes in the larger contexts in which policies are embedded (e.g., a culture of excessive individualism) are not forthcoming, social policies, at best, can only have an incremental impact. Social policy influence is not sufficient in and of itself to bring about the type of societal changes that are necessary to fundamentally improve the quality of life for segments of society who are persistently marginalized and disempowered. In short, direct social policy influence, without larger cultural change, is unlikely to reduce the disparities that underlie our most vexing social problems. Social policies can, over time, contribute in significant ways to changes in the larger societal context. Yet larger community-based and social movement work to bring about shifts in social values and norms—what might be termed indirect social policy work—is critically important as well.

Work bringing about larger cultural, democratic, economic, and political change is even more daunting than that aimed directly at achieving better social policies. But the need for such changes was the subtext, even if not always articulated, of the frustration some respondents voiced about the challenge of making a difference in the policy arena. Far-reaching improvements in our social policies may require, over time, larger changes in our citizenry, communities, and society as a whole. Such changes, while aided by improved social policies, require other means of social influence than direct policy work per se. Such means of influence include public education, citizen mobilization, and social movements.

Taryn Morrissey underscores the importance of public education: "It's . . . a matter of public education. . . . Politicians are voting for what their constituents desire or believe. Unless you change the constituent pressure . . . [it does not] matter how many studies come out on a certain topic." Psychologists can contribute to public education, broadly defined, in multiple ways including:

- individual involvement with citizen groups
- concerted efforts to publicize findings through various means such as print and social media
- collectively working to fashion engaged universities (and intermediaries) that view citizens and communities as primary recipients of academic knowledge and expertise and as partners in their generation

Major social policy changes in controversial areas such as women's rights, civil rights, and gay rights followed from citizen mobilization and social movements as part of ongoing, longer term, community-based, and national advocacy efforts. Although the confluence of forces that lead to citizen mobilization and social movements are beyond the influence of individual psychologists, we can nonetheless be poised to contribute our knowledge to such movements. *The major transformative changes in our lifetime likely benefitted from the research, consultation, and direct action activities of psychologists whose work contributed to the social mobilization efforts of community-based and national advocacy organizations.* For example, the pioneering psychologists who contributed to APA's position statement that homosexuality was not a mental disorder in the 1970s; the coalition-building work of Clinton Anderson in the 1990s; and the consultation, research, and judicial efforts of Gregory Herek can be viewed in this context. Continually focusing one's efforts on major social justice concerns, in concert with similarly motivated others, may be the best means, over the longer term, of positioning our work to be of service to larger social movements when they emerge.

Policy in International Context

In an increasingly interconnected world, psychologists' policy work in international contexts becomes increasingly important. Indeed, a number of psychologists interviewed for this volume have contributed to policy in other countries. For example, Patricia Chamberlain, Gail Goodman, David Olds, Richard Price, and Sam Tsemberis describe ongoing consultation with governmental officials in other nations interested in implementing their evidence-based programs. Hiro Yoshikawa developed partnerships with officials in other countries to evaluate policy initiatives, and Lawrence Aber, Stephen Fawcett, and Cliff O'Donnell have worked with international organizations such as the International Rescue Committee, the World Bank, the World Health Organization, and the Peace Corps, respectively, on policy-relevant initiatives. Furthermore, innovative policy initiatives from other countries have been developed in the United States, in part through the involvement of American psychologists. Finally, psychologists working internationally and in US territories, such as Irma Serrano-García who trained on the mainland, have generated policy work upon return to their native lands.

Psychologists in the United States have the skills and potential to contribute to policies in other countries. Professional organizations often facilitate such work through increasing focus on collaboration with comparable organizations in other nations and with international nongovernmental organizations (NGOs). Psychologists also pursue this work through participation in international research projects and conferences. Forming relationships in this context can facilitate involvement in international policy-related work. Furthermore, graduate programs should include additional focus on work done by psychologists in other countries, including policy-relevant work, to enhance knowledge and interest in the international policy context. Finally, through international organizations such as the United Nations, psychologists can contribute to the development of international agreements to guide basic human rights concerns, including for children and women. As Lawrence Aber noted, "We're becoming an increasingly globalized world, a world in which values can really only be dealt with through normative agreements . . . including charters, treaties, and international laws."

Furthermore, psychologists from other countries can help shape US and international policy. Although all of the psychologists interviewed for this book were from US states and territories, there are a great number of psychologists working in policy across the globe. US psychologists working in international contexts also have the advantage of learning about effective policies and programs that have been developed elsewhere (e.g., pp. 77–78), so they can be considered for adoption and adaptation in this country.

Although this section has focused on international policy work, it should also be noted that an additional pathway of focus is to alter US domestic and foreign policies that inflict damage on other nations and cultures. Examples of such policies include those related to global warming, economic policy, and use of torture (e.g., pp. 114–116).

Future Research on Psychologists' Involvement in Policy

Influencing Social Policy represents a step forward in our understanding of psychologists' active involvement in the policy arena, their contributions to a wide variety of policies, and the range of policy influence methods and skills employed. There are important limitations to the volume, however. First, the sample of psychologists interviewed was limited in several regards. Developmental psychologists, social psychologists, and community psychologists are central contributors to social policy in the public interest, but so are psychologists in many other subdisciplines. Furthermore, within these three subareas of focus, it was not possible to delineate an inclusive population of psychologists actively involved in policy from which to sample. And a number of individuals contacted declined participation, whereas many others were not contacted so as to keep the interviews to a manageable number. It is not known if the sample interviewed is representative of their subfields or if the three subfields are representative of applied psychology more generally. Furthermore, the policy experiences of respondents may be limited in important regards to the specific time periods in which they occurred and may have limited generalizability to other countries and cultures. As with all qualitative research, the reader must determine the utility of this text for his or her particular context.

The interview methodology employed has clear limitations as well:

- The narrative accounting of policy activities and successes was inevitably limited by memory.
- Key details may have been withheld on politically sensitive topics, and what was shared may have been influenced by conscious or unconscious bias.
- Time constraints limited the amount of detail that could be provided.
- Reliance on a single perspective cannot capture the multifaceted, multilevel influences that contribute to the unfolding of policy.
- Funding was not available to obtain corroborating information from other policy actors.

- And, finally, the biases and perspectives of the interviewer likely colored the nature and quality of the information obtained, as well as the selection of themes from the rich array of narrative material.

Future research should improve upon the current effort. Development of a database of psychologists directly involved in the policy arena from across subfields of psychology would allow a representative sample of psychologists to be selected. Studies comparing the policy involvement of psychologists with those in other disciplines would contribute to identification of similarities and differences in the nature and extent of policy influence work.

Diverse methodological approaches are also called for. Longitudinal and observational research would enhance the quality and validity of information obtained. Obtaining the perspectives of the varied policy players involved in a given policy initiative would allow deeper understanding of the role of psychologists viewed from multiple lenses. Survey-based research conducted on representative samples would allow enhanced breadth of focus on psychologists' involvement. It would also provide the ability for hypothesis-testing and comparative analyses of the nature of policy involvement and perceived outcomes across (a) branches and levels of government, (b) methods of influence, and (c) social policy domains. Mixed-methods approaches likely would be most valuable, as well as studies that contribute to theoretical understanding of policy involvement and outcome and that test-specific theory-based hypotheses.

Parting Messages and Advice from Psychologists Involved in Policy Influence Work

This section contains parting messages and advice from a number of the interviewees. Given the perspectives afforded by disciplinary background and policy vantage point, the parting words are presented separately for five subgroups of psychologists. The first three subgroups are developmental, social, and community psychology research faculty. The final two subgroups are psychologists whose greatest policy success occurred while working in intermediary organizations and within government, respectively.

Developmental Psychology Researchers

The developmental psychology researchers interviewed had encouraging—and challenging—parting words for those interested in careers seeking to influence social policy. Their comments encompass—but are not limited to—a focus on science and social justice, the crafting of effective interventions, the need for robust science, and interdisciplinary training.

Put people on a different developmental path, and evaluate the effectiveness . . . in the real world

Being a good scientist and trying to promote social justice are not antithetical. In fact . . . the two are synthetic endeavors. . . . The way to test our theory is . . . to put people on a different developmental path, and evaluate the effectiveness of those actions in the real world. We're not only evaluating an actual or possible policy or program, but we're also elucidating the basic, relational process of human development. (Richard M. Lerner, Tufts University)

Prepar[e] people to think deeply about . . . behavior change

Because this is really hard work, you have to be willing to have a very deep commitment to making a difference. . . . Applied work requires enormous rigor. . . . There is some real value in . . . being able to grapple with the complexities that exist in supporting adaptive behavioral change. Being able to craft interventions that both embrace and understand that complexity . . . is an absolutely essential component. (David Olds, University of Colorado, Denver)

Do we have time in the four years that we're training people to do it all?

I think in the end if you don't [train students to] do good science, then [training in policy] doesn't really matter. The question is do we have time in the four years that we're training people to do it all? I do think that having a course in how policy gets made would be constructive. (Laurence Steinberg, Temple University)

Interdisciplinary training is absolutely essential

Interdisciplinary training is absolutely essential. Getting people into policy schools . . . or doing internships in policy settings. Probably some of the best contributions that SRCD [Society for Research in Child Development] has made to policy are through the people that we've put in these policy settings. (Aletha Huston, University of Texas, Austin)

Social Psychology Researchers

The social psychology researchers interviewed shared a wide range of parting comments directed to those interested in the field's contributions to social policy.

Messages shared include a focus on graduate training, facts versus values, small wins, and transformational values.

The 21st-century way to train ... social psychologists

What I'd like ... is to train more grad students to think in a bigger interdisciplinary way and to get out of the campus lab environment, doing more field and applied work. Doing research that's relevant to and tries to influence social policy ... is ... something that graduate training programs should validate. It's ... the 21st century way to train people as social psychologists. (Eugene Borgida, University of Minnesota)

Address the factual questions

What we can do with science is address the factual questions. . . . What I'd like to emphasize . . . is the importance of really knowing the relevant research literature and, when need be, taking the initiative to conduct new research to address unanswered policy questions. We have to be appropriately conservative about applying the data to policy—careful about saying what we know and not saying more than that. (Gregory Herek, University of California, Davis)

We win small victories all the time

People become easily discouraged when they don't see major transformative change. I don't think that should be discouraging. In all kinds of venues, whether it's local, state, or national, we win small victories all the time and make a difference in work towards social justice. . . . I would like to see us push forward and have even more of an impact. (Heather Bullock, University of California, Santa Cruz)

Transformational work ... infusing a set of principles of justice

Transformational work is important. . . . Can you kick up an interest in inequality gaps in public education rather than just test scores? Can you help a school imagine that by de-tracking [eliminating ability grouping] everybody is elevated? We need theory of the relationship between what is and what could be. The transformation is about ... infusing a set of principles of justice into the institution and denaturalizing the inequities. (Michelle Fine, City University of New York)

Community Psychology Researchers

The community psychology researchers interviewed had various words of advice for those interested in careers seeking to influence social policy. The themes expressed include a focus on power, developing partnerships, passion, and taking risks.

The issue of power ... something we have to bring back into our field

The issue of power and power inequities makes a lot of people nervous . . . We avoid that topic, we don't have training to deal with it. . . . That's probably something we have to bring back into our field. . . . Our students are wanting to understand how we work with power, and how it can be used for good and bad. . . . I think that power's always operating. It's the abuse of power that often we're doing our work to change in the policy arena. (Leonard Jason, DePaul University)

Figure out ways to develop relationships and partnerships at the outset

The mutual interests of psychologists and policy makers will be advanced the second we can figure out ways to develop relationships and partnerships at the outset, rather than simply have psychologists trying to conduct what we think is good policy research and delivering that. . . . Take almost any other work community psychologists do. . . . We do good work by developing relationships and partnerships. (Brian Wilcox, formerly, University of Nebraska, Lincoln)

Do what you love and what you feel passionate about

When I was an assistant professor, many people said, "Do basic research and get lots of publications. . . . Don't get involved with policy because it's time consuming." . . . In contrast, Gary Schwarz said to me "Do what you love and what you feel passionate about, and things have a way of working out." . . . People who want to . . . improve conditions for many people have to get involved in some way with policy. (Roger Weissberg, University of Illinois at Chicago)

Policy work can be fun, exciting, and really gratifying

I think it's important to recognize that this policy work can be frustrating and tedious, but it can also be fun, exciting, and really gratifying. I think it's important to take risks and try to do the translation. Sometimes it will work. Sometimes it will be stuck in committee, but if we don't do it, who's going to do it? If we don't translate our work, someone else will. (Preston Britner, University of Connecticut)

Psychologists Working in Intermediary Organizations

The psychologists whose greatest policy influence occurred from the vantage point of an intermediary organization shared a wide range of parting comments. Their comments encompass, but are not limited to, a focus on the positive potential of their settings to bridge the gap between researchers and policymakers, and the potential of the current generation of graduate students to make distinctive contributions to policy.

Bridging the gap . . . You can influence thousands of individuals. . . .

Psychologists have gravitated toward these roles where we're really bridging the gap between research and practice. . . . You really can influence thousands of individuals through your work at the policy level. To me, it makes it extremely gratifying and something that I wake up every day and look forward to doing. (Robert Franks, formerly, Child Health & Development Institute)

How do you use [research] so that it actually changes something?

Initially, I thought I was going to be able to improve the social condition by doing research. Then I figured out there were plenty of people doing research. The question is how do you use it so that it actually changes something? That's a whole different skill set. . . . You have to be in it for a long time and have to sit in a different place to do that. (Laurie Garduque, MacArthur Foundation)

There are organizations that know how to get it out

It actually can be harmful for individual academics to jump out without knowing the policy world in depth. They should work with translator organizations or intermediaries. I wish more people came to us and said, "Can I do a brief for you?" There are organizations that know how to get it out. (Kristen Moore, Child Trends)

I'm placing all of my bets on the next generation

I'm placing all of my bets on the next generation. . . . They are breathtaking. . . . They're excited about connecting science to policy . . . and they are so sophisticated methodologically. They have energy and optimism. I guess my parting words would just be, "Get as much training as you can and go get 'em." (Deborah Phillips, formerly, National Academies)

Policy Insiders

The policy insiders interviewed had varied parting messages for those seeking to influence social policy. The themes expressed include the conduct of policy-relevant research, getting involved, and the potential for policy influence.

Begin with questions that policymakers ... want answers to

If you want to influence policy you have to begin with questions that policymakers either want or should want answers to. And then, you can't influence policy without understanding the process, being involved in the process. Get involved, even if it's local politics, policy, it's not dirty, it's just the way it works. ... And learn to communicate the results. (Trudy Vincent, former Chief of Staff, Senator Bingaman, D-NM)

Just do it and jump in

Anybody can do this work. ... Just do it and jump in. In the communities, it's just a matter of making a phone call to a congressional office or volunteering on a campaign or with a community group. ... [Also] psychologists have skills that are applicable to the [legislative] work that's being done, whether it's statistics, research, or the understanding of human psychology. (Roberta Downing, former legislative assistant, Sen. Sherrod Brown, D-OH)

Set up research questions that are informative to the government

Psychologists have so much talent, and [yet are not] ... answering critical policy questions. ... [Be sure to] set up research questions that are informative to the government. ... I, as a policymaker, could be so much more effective. (Jill Hunter Williams, legislative director, Rep. Danny K. Thomas D-IL)

It takes patience and time, but it's extremely rewarding work

Psychology and social research can have a huge impact. ... It takes patience and time, but it's extremely rewarding work. I would encourage more folks to do it. (Robin Jenkins, former Deputy Director, North Carolina Department of Juvenile Justice)

Closing Remarks

These closing remarks are from Seymour Sarason, to whom this book is dedicated:

> If I were doing it [my career] all over again I would connect the graduate training program to those who are in the "legislative-administrative-political system": national, state, and local. . . . I would want [students] to become knowledgeable about how legislation and policies arise: where their points of origins are in communities, how and why the issues are posed as they are, and the implicit and explicit criteria by which proposed actions will be judged. The fateful question the student must confront is "What is there in the corpus of writings and research in the field that is relevant to the issues? . . . How, if at all, could it be reflected in legislation and implementation? Can this be done in a way that may allow you to learn more than you already know?" . . . The student would be an agent of the field, not a hired hand of others. That kind of role is not easy, the dangers of cooptation are real, but since when is "easy" a criterion for action? (Sarason, 1995, p. 13)

The policy successes highlighted in this volume constitute resounding, affirmative answers to the "fateful" questions posed by Sarason. Research relevant to contemporary social issues can indeed be identified from the massive corpus of psychology scholarship and usefully brought to the attention of policymakers. When the timing is right, psychologists can help to shape policy formulation and implementation, learning much in the process. Policy-relevant roles of various types can indeed be fashioned in which the psychologist is not simply "a hired hand of others," but rather a proactive agent. True, the work is never easy: structural barriers and personal challenges, including threats to integrity, are present every step of the way. But, over time, many of the barriers and challenges can be addressed and overcome.

Sarason had a genius for asking questions that broaden our field's perspective and modes of action in the world—questions that need to be grappled with and answered by each generation anew. It falls to future generations of psychologists to more fully answer the questions he posed above, building on the seminal policy work depicted in this volume and fashioning an ever more robust and impactful psychology, one increasingly capable of serving the public interest.

Appendix A

INTERVIEWEES BY SUBFIELD

Table A.1 **Interviewees by Subfield**

Subfield	N (%)
Community psychology	31 (39.2%)
Community	14 (17.7%)
Community and clinical	14 (17.7%)
Community and health	1 (1.3%)
Community and law	1 (1.3%)
Community and organizational	1 (1.3%)
Developmental psychology	18 (22.8%)
Developmental	10 (12.7%)
Human development	5 (6.3%)
Educational	3 (3.8%)
Social psychology	13 (16.5%)
Social	9 (11.4%)
Social and law	2 (2.6%)
Social, environmental, and clinical	2 (2.6%)
Developmental, social, community hybrids	7 (8.9%)
Developmental and community	5 (6.3%)
Social and community	2 (2.5%)
Other areas of psychology	10 (12.7%)
Clinical	3 (3.8%)
Clinical and law	3 (3.8%)
Counseling	2 (2.5%)
Measurement, quantitative, evaluation design	2 (2.5%)

Appendix B

ALPHABETICAL LIST OF INTERVIEWEES

Last Name	First Name	Subfield(s)	Year PhD
Aber	Lawrence	Clinical, community, developmental	1982
Anderson	Clinton	Community, applied social	2006
Barone	Charles	Clinical, community	1991
Belsky	Jay	Human development, family studies	1978
Berkowitz	Bill	Experimental, community	1965
Bogenschneider	Karen	Child, family studies	1990
Borgida	Eugene	Social, law	1976
Britner	Preston	Developmental, community	1996
Brooks Gunn	Jeanne	Learning, development	1975
Brownell	Kelly	Clinical	1977
Bullock	Heather	Social	1995
Cantor	Nancy	Social, sociology	1978
Chamberlain	Patricia	Clinical psychology	1980
Chase-Lansdale	Lindsay	Developmental	1981
Chavis	David	Community	1983
Cohen	Robert	Clinical, community	1968
Deaux	Kay	Social	1967
Downing	Roberta	Social	2004
Elmore	Diane	Counseling, public health	2002
Emshoff	James	Ecological, community	1980
Fawcett	Stephen	Human development, community	1974
Fine	Michelle	Social	1980

Fiske	Susan	Social	1978
Franks	Robert	Counseling, community	2000
Garduque	Laurie	Educational psychology	1980
Garrison	Ellen	Clinical, law	1983
Gerrity	Ellen	Environmental, clinical	1983
Goodman	Gail	Developmental	1977
Grisso	Thomas	Clinical, law	1969
Gurin	Patricia	Social	1964
Haskins	Ron	Developmental	1975
Herek	Gregory	Social	1983
Humphreys	Keith	Clinical, community	1993
Hunter-Williams	Jill	Clinical, community	2004
Huston	Aletha	Child development	1965
Jason	Leonard	Clinical, community	1975
Jenkins	Robin	Human relations, community	1992
Kelly	Heather	Clinical, community	1997
Lerner	Richard M.	Developmental	1971
Lipsey	Mark	Psycholinguistics, evaluation	1972
Meyers	Judith	Clinical, community	1976
Monahan	John	Clinical, community, law	1972
Moore	Kristin	Social psychology, sociology	1975
Moorehouse	Martha	Human development	1985
Morrissey	Taryn	Developmental	2008
Mulvey	Edward	Clinical, community, law	1982
Oberlander	Sarah	Community, applied social	2008
O'Donnell	Clifford	Clinical, community	1970
Olds	David	Developmental	1976
Olson	Bradley	Personality, social, community	2000
Petersen	Anne	Measurement, evaluation, statistics	1973
Phillips	Deborah	Developmental	1981
Price	Richard	Clinical, community, organizational	1966
Ramey	Sharon Landesman	Developmental	1974
Ratcliffe	Allen	Clinical, community	1964
Reppucci	N. Dickon	Clinical, community, law	1968

Seidman	Edward	Clinical, community	1969
Serrano-García	Irma	Social, community	1975
Shinn	Marybeth	Social, community	1978
Slavin	Robert	Social relations	1975
Smedley	Brian	Clinical	1992
Snowden	Lonnie	Community, clinical	1975
Speer	Paul	Community	1992
Starnes	Debi	Community, organizational	1987
Steinberg	Laurence	Human development	1977
Stipek	Deborah	Developmental	1977
Tebes	Jacob	Clinical, community	1984
Tolan	Patrick	School, community	1983
Tomkins	Alan	Social, law	1984
Tsemberis	Sam	Clinical, community	1985
Vincent	Trudy	Clinical, community	1985
Wandersman	Abraham	Personality, social, environmental, ecological, community	1976
Weinstein	Rhona	Clinical, community, educational	1973
Weissberg	Roger	Clinical, community	1980
Wilcox	Brian	Community	1979
Wolff	Thomas	Clinical, community	1968
Woolard	Jennifer	Community, developmental	1998
Yoshikawa	Hirokazu	Clinical, developmental, community	1998
Zuckerman	Diana	Clinical, social	1977

Appendix C

INTERVIEW PROTOCOL

Thanks for agreeing to take part in this interview which will focus on your personal experience working to influence social policy. The content of the interview will contribute to a volume, *Influencing Social Policy: Applied Psychology Serving the Public Interest.* Approximately 100 psychologists are being interviewed for this project.

The book will codify current knowledge about the practices applied psychologists employ in their attempts to influence social policy to serve the public interest. Interview questions will encompass career pathways to policy-related work, detailed accounts of policy-related successes, challenges faced and strategies used to address challenges, perceived benefits and limitations of disciplinary background and training and employment context, and suggestions to enhance applied psychology's contributions in the years ahead.

This research project has been approved by the UMBC institutional review board. The interview is expected to take one to one-and-a-half hours and will be audio taped. A transcript of the interview will be made available to you so you can make any desired revisions. Do you have any questions before we begin?

First, please read through the informed consent form, and if you remain willing to take part, sign when you are done. Thanks. Now, are you ready to begin?

I. Becoming Involved in Policy-Related Work

1. When did you first decide to become involved in policy related work?
2. What led to this decision?
3. What are the prior experiences, influences, and events in your life that may have predisposed you to a career focus on policy-related work?

II. Policy Involvement, Greatest Success, Lessons Learned, and Work Context

4. Please indicate the nature and extent of your involvement attempting to influence social policy.
5. What has been your greatest success in influencing a social policy?
    a. Please provide a detailed account of the factors and processes that led to change in this policy area.
    b. What role did policy-relevant research findings play?
    c. What types of advocacy approaches led to your success?
    d. (If not mentioned) What were the barriers and challenges you faced?
    e. What strategies did you use to address these challenges?
6. Do you feel that over time your policy involvement has had an influence on the general perspective adopted by policymakers toward your area(s) of interest? If so, please describe.
7. Some of the most valuable lessons learned in our work come from a failure experience. Is there a failure experience (or mistake made, or difficult choice confronted) that you can share, along with what lessons you learned from it?
8. What are the benefits and limitations of your work context in doing policy-related work?

III. Disciplinary Background and Training

9. What are the benefits and limitations of your disciplinary background and training in doing policy related work?
10. What are the strategies that can be used to effectively address the limitations and related challenges?

IV. Policy-Relevant Research

11. What do you see as the characteristics of effective and useful policy-relevant research?
12. Which of the following types of research have made the greatest impact on policy in your experience?
    a. Studies that effectively highlight or dramatize the magnitude of a social problem? Why so? Specific examples?
    b. Studies that influence how issues are defined and populations viewed by policy makers? Why so? Specific examples?
    c. Studies that generate new policy approaches to difficult social problems? Why so? Specific examples?

    d. Outcome evaluation studies? Why so? Specific examples?

    e. Process evaluation studies? Why so? Specific examples?

    f. Implementation studies? Why so? Specific examples?

13. What do you see as the strengths and weaknesses in terms of the movement toward enhanced focus on evidence-based interventions as a priority for social policy?

V. Policy Influence Skills and Tools

14. Which of the following skills have you found most important in your policy influence work:

    a. Relationship building skills? Why?

    b. Strategic analysis skills? Why?

    c. Generating a policy story skills? Why?

    d. Communication skills? Why?

    e. Negotiation skills? Why?

    f. Research skills? Why?

    g. Others?

15. Which of the following policy influence tools have you found most important:

    a. Meetings with elected officials (or their staff)? Why?

    b. Consultative relationships with executive branch officials? Why?

    c. Congressional hearings? Why?

    d. Policy position statements? Why?

    e. Press releases? Why?

    f. News announcements? Why?

    g. Public interviews? Why?

    h. White papers? Why?

    i. Dissemination through public outlets (including the Internet)? Why?

    j. Coalition-building? Why?

    k. Conferences for policymakers or practitioners? Why?

    l. Amicus briefs? Why?

    m. Expert witness/court testimony? Why?

    n. Others?

VI. Incremental Versus Transformative Policy

16. A distinction is often made between incremental policy change and transformational or systemic policy change.

    a. Which type have you been most involved in, and why?

    b. What types of research and policy-influence efforts are necessary, in your view, for transformative or systemic in contrast to incremental policy change?

VII. Psychology and Policy in the Years Ahead

17. What can be done to enhance [subdiscipline] psychology's contributions in the years ahead?
18. What resources are available to applied psychologists to build their capacity in the social policy arena?
19. Do you have suggestions in particular to enhance the future social policy influence capacity of
    a. Graduate students?
    b. Early career academic researchers?
    c. Early career policy practitioners?
20. Who are important partners for (subdiscipline) psychology to collaborate with in future policy influence work?
21. Three case studies of exemplary policy influence by researchers and three case studies of exemplary policy influence by policy practitioners (non-academics) are to be highlighted in the book? Do you have any suggestions as to who to highlight? Psychologists to interview?

VIII. Additional or Final Points

22. Are there other points you would like to emphasize for the field that I have not asked about? Anything you especially want to emphasize?

Appendix D

CAREER POLICY INVOLVEMENTS: POLICY CHARACTERISTICS, INTERDISCIPLINARY INVOLVEMENTS, LEADERSHIP POSITIONS, AND INTERNATIONAL FOCUS

Table D.1 **Policy Characteristic by Frequency of Policy Involvement**

Policy Characteristic	Frequency over Course of Career		
	One	Two	Three or more
Policy methods (Full sample, $N = 79$)	19 (24.0%)	15 (19.0%)	45 (57.0%)
Collaborations (Full sample, $N = 79$)	15 (19.0%)	23 (29.1%)	41 (51.9%)
Policy areas (Full sample, $N = 79$)	24 (30.4%)	22 (27.8%)	33 (41.8%)
Policy-focused jobs (Subsample, $N = 29$[a])	8 (27.6%)	11 (37.9%)	10 (34.5%)
Types of research (Subsample, $N = 53$[b])	22 (41.5%)	19 (35.9%)	12 (22.6%)
Local policy involvements (Subsample, $N = 38$[c])	16 (42.1%)	11 (28.9%)	11 (28.9%)

[a] Subsample of psychologists whose primary employment has been in governmental and intermediary settings.

[b] Subsample of psychologists who reported policy influence through conduct of policy-relevant research.

[c] Subsample of psychologists who described local (town, city, county) policy involvements.

Table D.2 **Interdisciplinary Involvements of University Faculty: Research Contexts, Publications, and Primary Appointments**

	N	%
Member (or director) of interdisciplinary center, research group, or research network[a]	30	60.0%
At least one co-author from another discipline on a policy-relevant publication[b]	29	58%
Discipline of co-author		
Anthropology	2	4%
Economics	8	16%
Education	5	10%
Human development	2	4%
Law	5	10%
Medicine	3	6%
Other	7	14%
Political science	4	8%
Psychiatry	3	6%
Public health	2	4%
Public policy	3	6%
Sociology	5	10%
Primary appointment in interdisciplinary department, school, or center[a]	22	44%
Department, school, or center		
Education or human development (sometimes with policy in name)	11	22%
Psychiatry/Medicine	6	12%
Independent research or policy center	3	6%
Other (law, social welfare)	2	4%

[a] *N* = Subsample of 50 university faculty.

[b] *N* = Total number of interdisciplinary co-authors (50), with limit of three most frequently counted for any given faculty member.

Table D.3 **Leadership Position Level by Employment Context**

Leadership Position Level	Academic	Intermediary	Governmental	Total
High-level administrator (or elected official)	2 (2.5%)	9 (11.4%)	1 (1.3%)	12 (15.2%)
Director of a center, office, or unit within organization	33 (41.8%)	8 (10.1%)	8 (10.1%)	49 (62.0%)
Neither of the above	15 (19.0%)	0	3 (3.8%)	18 (22.8%)
Total	50	17	12	79 (100%)

Table D.4 **International Focus: Policy Area, Country, and Policy Methods**

Policy Area (Faculty Member)	Country	Policy Methods
Childcare; Family poverty (Belsky)**(7)	England	Consultation Evaluation research Meetings with legislators
Political ethics Public education Issue advocacy (Serrano-García)**(7)	Puerto Rico (US territory)	Advocacy; Media
Unemployment, job search, mental health (Price)**(7)	China, Finland	Program implementation Consultation
Youth and community development (O'Donnell)**(7)	Micronesia	Consultation; Program development
Nurse home visiting (Olds)**(3)	Canada, The Netherlands, England, Scotland, Northern Ireland, Australia	Program implementation Consultation
Child and family poverty reduction; Elementary school intervention (Aber)**(3)	Congo, South Africa	Evaluation research Consultation

(continued)

Table D.4 **Continued**

Policy Area (Faculty Member)	Country	Policy Methods
Mental health system redevelopment	Iraq	Consultation meetings with legislators
Substance use policy (Humphreys)**(5)	England	
Homelessness, pathways to housing (Tsemberis)**(6)	Canada, The Netherlands, Portugal, Denmark, Sweden, Australia.	Consultation
Foster care (Chamberlain)**(6)	Denmark, England, The Netherlands, New Zealand, Norway, Scotland, Sweden	Program implementation Consultation
Education (Slavin)**(6)	Australia, Canada, England, Israel, Mexico	Program implementation Evaluation; Consultation
Pre-school education; Early child development services (Yoshikawa)**(6)	Chile, Cambodia, Mexico	Program evaluation Consultation: Systems research
Community health development (Fawcett)**(8)	Multiple	Consultation

** (X) = Chapter number where presented as case example.

GLOSSARY

Academic Field Influence—efforts to influence fellow academics by communicating findings through venues such as academic journals and professional conferences

Active Policy Influence—efforts to influence the policy process, including communication of ideas and findings directly to policymakers or indirectly through intermediary organizations or media

Advocacy-Coalition Framework—a policy process framework that accounts for the occasional, far-reaching change that occurs on contentious social issues

Agenda Setting—the process by which problems and alternative solutions gain or lose policymaker and/or public attention

Amicus Brief—legal document filed in appellate court cases by individuals or organizations not involved with the lawsuit (nonlitigants) with a strong interest in the subject matter of the case

Communication Skills—within policy, the ability to convey information efficiently and effectively to influence policymakers and the policy process

Community Psychology—branch of psychology that studies the interrelationships between individuals and communities, with an action focus on empowerment, prevention, promotion of well-being, and social justice

Conceptual Research Use—referred to as the "enlightenment" effect, where the use of research over time shapes policymakers' understanding of the nature of a problem and possible solutions

Congressional Briefings—presentations on a specific topic used to communicate information to policymakers in the US Congress

Congressional Hearings—method by which congressional committees collect and analyze information

Courtroom-focused Influence—efforts to influence court cases by communicating relevant evidence and expertise relevant to a case through amicus briefs, expert testimony, and reports

Consultation—within policy, efforts to influence policy by providing guidance to policymakers and policy stakeholders

Critical Analysis—within research and policy, careful analytical evaluation of policy-relevant research studies, including strengths and weaknesses

Developmental Psychology—branch of psychology focused on the psychological processes and stages of growth through the entire life span

Direct Communication—within policy, providing information and perspectives to policymakers and policy stakeholders through direct mechanisms such as individual meetings, hearings, seminars, briefings, and/or conferences

Ecological Systems Theory of Child Development—theory that suggests that individuals exist in multilevel contexts that impact developmental processes and outcomes

Ethnographic Research—a collection of qualitative research methods, including observation and interviews, that focus on the study of individuals and groups in their own locale or context

Evidence-based Programs—approaches or programs that are found to be effective through results of rigorous evaluations

Executive Branch—branch of government that is broadly responsible for implementing, supporting, and enforcing the laws made by the legislative branch and interpreted by the judicial branch

External Advocacy—efforts to persuade or pressure policymakers through mobilization of policy stakeholders, including constituents, influential individuals and organizations, groups of experts, the general public, and the media

Government—the officials who make laws and regulations and who fund services for citizens and organizations in a political jurisdiction

Governmental Policy—set of guidelines developed by government officials that outline expectations for citizens or organizations within a given jurisdiction

Guild Interests—within psychology, efforts to advance or protect the status, power, and resources of psychologists

Incrementalism Framework—asserts that only small-scale changes tend to occur at a given time in the policy arena

Instrumental Research Use—findings that directly inform and shape a specific policy decision

Interdisciplinary Collaboration—collaboration between individuals or groups from diverse academic disciplines or schools of thought

Intermediary Organizations—organizations that serve as a bridge between university-based researchers and policymakers, between communities of practice and policymakers, and between citizens and policymakers

International Policy Involvement—policy-relevant work taking place outside of the US by American-trained psychologists

Jurisdiction—geographic boundaries within which judicial or governmental bodies may legally exercise their power

Judicial Branch—branch of government charged with the interpretation of laws and the administration of justice

Legislative Branch—branch of government with the power to formulate laws and policies

Longitudinal Research—correlational research that involves repeated observations of the same variable(s) over time

Media—the major distributors of information related to cultural, economic, political, and social life. Major source of influence on all phases of the policy process

Meta-analysis—statistical technique used to combine findings from multiple studies

Organizational Policy (also known as Institutional Policy)—expectations by the leaders of an organization for its members

Organizational Practice—refers to behaviors of organizations and their members to help or educate clients, customers, or service recipients

Participatory Action Methods—research methods that emphasize participation by stakeholders in designing and conducting the research and practical use of the findings to bring about change

Policymaker Education—information provided to policymakers to inform or educate

Policy Advisory Groups—boards, commissions, committees, councils, and task forces that seek to advise policy stakeholders

Policy Advocacy—efforts to persuade or pressure a policymaker to take a specific policy action (e.g., vote a certain way on a piece of legislation)

Policy Analysis—determining which policy options will best achieve a given set of policy goals

Policy Framing—tailoring policy ideas and research-based findings to maximize leverage within the current policy debate

Policy Insider—person holding an official position within the government or otherwise employed by the government

Policy-related Leadership Positions—within social policy, leadership positions in organizational, academic, or governmental contexts responsible for policy-related work

Policy Stakeholders—within policy, persons, groups, and organizations directly or indirectly affected by governmental policies

Policy Stream—current policy ideas or solutions that can be applied to various social problems

Policy Windows—discrete moments when a convergence of factors leads a social problem to rise to the top of the policy agenda

Political Stream—political considerations and related macro events that privilege particular social problems or policy solutions

Problem Stream—existing conditions identified as problematic in society

Public Interest—within psychology, activities that aim to address the fundamental problems of human well-being, including the equitable and just treatment of all members of society

Public Policy—encompasses the entire spectrum of laws, regulatory measures, courses of action, and funding priorities enacted by government

Relationship Building Skills—within policy, the ability to develop and maintain good working relationships with key legislative and/or executive branch policymakers or their staff members, individuals in intermediary organizations, media, practitioner groups, and/or researchers in multiple disciplines

Research Synthesis—practice of systematically integrating and condensing findings from a variety of research studies to draw more reliable conclusions about a given issue

Research Translation—within policy, communication of research findings in a digestible and useful form to policymakers and policy stakeholders

Social Policy—governmental laws, regulations, and services that enhance the well-being of citizens

Social Psychology—the scientific field that seeks to understand the nature and causes of individual behavior in social contexts

Strategic Analysis—within policy, critical evaluation of social problems and potential solutions to formulate a plan of action to achieve a policy goal

Strategy Development—within policy, process of defining a plan of action to achieve a particular policy goal

Tactical Research Use—use of research to justify and advance policy positions already held by a policymaker

Vantage Points—the policy influence opportunities available through different settings and associated roles

Written Documents—within policy, includes reports, policy briefs, research briefs, fact sheets, and related documents generated to inform and influence policymakers and policy stakeholders

List of Government Agencies and Professional Associations

Administration for Children and Families (ACF)—a division of the Department of Health and Human Services whose mission is to promote the economic and social well-being of children and families

Administration on Children, Youth, and Families (ACYF)—part of the Administration for Children and Families, under the Department of Health and Human Services. ACYF is divided into two bureaus—the Children's Bureau and the Family and Youth Services Bureau.

American Psychological Association (APA)—the largest scientific and professional organization representing psychology in the United States; its mission is to advance the creation, communication, and application of psychological knowledge to benefit society and improve people's lives

American Psychological Association Public Interest Directorate (APA PI)—fulfills APA's commitment to apply the science and practice of psychology to the fundamental problems of human welfare and the promotion of equitable and just treatment of all segments of society through education, training, and public policy

American Psychology-Law Society (AP-LS)—Division 41 of the American Psychological Association; aims to further the use of basic and applied psychological research within law and legal institutions

Centers for Disease Control and Prevention (CDC)—federal agency under the Department of Health and Human Services, focused on public health and safety

The Children's Bureau (CB)—an office of the Administration of Children and Families, which partners with state, federal, tribal, and local agencies to improve the health and well-being of children and families

Department of Health and Human Services (HHS)—a cabinet-level executive agency of the US federal government with the goal of protecting the health of all Americans and providing essential human services

Department of Housing and Urban Development (HUD)—a cabinet-level executive agency of the US federal government charged with creating equitable, safe, nondiscriminatory, and affordable housing for all

Department of Justice (DOJ)—a cabinet-level executive agency of the US federal government responsible for the enforcement of law

Equal Employment Opportunity Commission (EEOC)—US regulatory body responsible for enforcing federal antidiscrimination laws

Food and Drug Administration (FDA)—US government office under the Department of Health and Human Services tasked with regulating human and veterinary drugs, biological products, medical devices, the US food supply, cosmetics, and products that emit radiation

Lesbian, Gay, Bisexual, and Transgender Concerns Office (LGBTCO)—APA office that works to advance the creation, communication, and application of psychological knowledge on gender identity and sexual orientation to benefit society and improve lesbian, gay, bisexual, and transgender people's lives

National Institutes of Health (NIH)—an agency of the US Department of Health and Human Services made up of 27 institutes and centers focused on various health issues, diseases, and demographics

National Institutes of Mental Health (NIMH)—part of the National Institutes of Health; seeks to transform knowledge and treatment of mental illnesses through research

Office of the Assistant Secretary for Health (OASH)—Within Department of Health and Human Services, oversees 12 core public health offices, including the Office of the Surgeon General, 10 regional health offices, and various Presidential and Secretarial advisory committees

Office of the Assistant Secretary for Planning and Evaluation (ASPE)—advisory office to the Secretary of the US Department Health and Human Services

Office of Juvenile Justice and Delinquency Prevention (OJJDP)—office of the US Department of Justice, focusing on juvenile justice issues

Psychologists for Social Responsibility (PsySR)—independent, nonprofit organization that applies psychological knowledge and expertise to promote peace, social justice, human rights, and sustainability

Public Interest Government Relations Office (PI-GRO)—part of APA's Public Interest Directorate; advocates at the federal level to apply psychology to the fundamental problems of human welfare and the promotion of equitable and just treatment of all segments of society

Society for Child and Family Policy and Practice—Division 37 of the American Psychological Association; a professional society concerned with issues relative to services and service structures for children and youth

Society for Community Research and Action (SCRA)—Division 27 of the American Psychological Association; a professional society that explicitly focuses on collaborative research and action to enhance the quality of life for community residents, including use of methods such as social action, political activism, and policy engagement

Society for the Psychological Study of Ethnic Minority Issues—Division 45 of the American Psychological Association; a professional society for psychologists who conduct research on ethnic minority concerns or who apply psychological knowledge and techniques to ethnic minority issues

Society for the Psychological Study of Lesbian and Gay Issues—Division 44 of the American Psychological Association; a professional society interested in psychological research, education and training, practice, and advocacy on lesbian, gay, bisexual, and transgendered issues and all lesbian women, gay men, bisexual women, bisexual men, transgendered people, and their allies

Society for the Psychological Study of Social Issues (SPSSI)—Division 9 of the American Psychological Association; a professional society that brings research to bear on a wide array of societal problems

Society for Research on Adolescence (SRA)—professional society focused on the theoretical, empirical, and policy research issues of adolescence

Society for Research in Child Development (SRCD)—Division 7 of the American Psychological Association; a professional society with a joint focus on understanding child development and bettering the lives of children

Society for the Study of Peace, Conflict, and Violence—Division 48 of the American Psychological Association; professional society with a focus on peace psychology that deals with the psychological aspects of peace, conflict, violence, and war

Substance Abuse and Mental Health Services Administration (SAMHSA)—agency within the Department of Health and Human Services in charge of public health efforts to promote the country's behavioral health; seeks to reduce the negative impact of substance abuse and mental illness

REFERENCES

Aber, J. L., Bishop-Josef, S. J., Jones, S. M., McLearn, K. T., & Phillips, D. A. (Eds.). (2007). *Child development and social policy: Knowledge for action.* Washington, DC: American Psychological Association.

Aber, L. (2012, August 29). Personal interview.

Achilles, G. M., Barrueco, S., & Bottoms, B. L. (2013). The evolving legacy of the American Psychological Association's Division 37: Bridging research, practice, and policy to benefit children and families. In A. M. Culp (Ed.), *Child and family advocacy: Bridging the gaps between research, practice and policy.* Issues in clinical child psychology (pp. 271–290). New York: Springer.

Ainsworth, S. H. (2002). *Analyzing interest groups: Group influence on people and policies.* New York: W. W. Norton.

Alfaro, J., Sánchez, A., & Zambrano, A. (Eds.). (2012). *Psicología comunitaria y políticas sociales. Reflexiones y experiencias* [Community psychology and social policies: Reflections and experiences.] Buenos Aires: Paidós.

Allport, G. W. (1954). *The nature of prejudice.* Reading, MA: Addison-Wesley.

American Beverage Association. (2014, November 5). *American Beverage Association statement on soda taxes.* Retrieved from http://www.ameribev.org/news-media/news-releases-statements/more/337/News Releases & Statements

American Psychological Association. (1988). Amicus curiae brief in *Price Waterhouse v. Hopkins,* 490 US 288. *American Psychological Association.* Retrieved from http://www.apa.org/about/offices/ogc/amicus/hopkins.pdf

American Psychological Association. (1990). Amicus curiae brief in *Craig v. Maryland,* 497, US 836. *American Psychological Association.* Retrieved from http://www.apa.org/about/offices/ogc/amicus/craig.pdf

American Psychological Association. (2004). *Sexual orientation and military service briefing sheet.* Retrieved from http://www.apa.org/pi/lgbt/resources/military-sexual- orientation.aspx

American Psychological Association. (2005). Amicus curiae brief in *Roper v. Simmons,* 543 US 551. *American Psychological Association.* Retrieved from http://www.apa.org/about/offices/ogc/amicus/roper.pdf

American Psychological Association. (2007). Amicus curiae brief in Marriage Cases, Case No. S147999. 43 Cal.4th 757. *American Psychological Association.* Retrieved from http://www.apa.org/about/offices/ogc/amicus/marriage-cases.pdf

American Psychological Association. (2010). *A psychologist's guide to federal advocacy: Advancing psychology in the public interest.* Washington, DC: American Psychological Association, Public Interest Government Relations Office. Retrieved from http://www.apa.org/about/gr/advocacy/pi-guide.pdf

American Psychological Association. (2010a). *APA health reform matrix: Key provisions by APA priority*. Retrieved from https://www.apa.org/about/gr/issues/health-care/health-reform-matrix.pdf

American Psychological Association. (2010b). *PI-GRO health reform overview*. Retrieved from Apa.org/about/gr/issues/health-care/reform-overview.aspx

American Psychological Association. (2012). *Committee on legal issues 2012 annual report*. Retrieved from http://apa.org/about/offices/ogc/2012-coli.aspx

American Psychological Association. (2015a). *About the public interest directorate*. Retrieved from http://apa.org/pi/about/index.aspx

American Psychological Association. (2015b). *APA history*. Retrieved from https://www.apa.org/about/apa/archives/apa-history.aspx

American Psychological Association. (2015c). *Who we are*. Retrieved from http://www.apa.org/about/apa/index.aspx

American Psychological Association. (2015d). *Advocacy*. Retrieved from http://www.apa.org/about/gr/

American Psychological Association. (2015e). *APA amicus briefs by issue*. Retrieved from http://www.apa.org/about/offices/ogc/amicus/index-issues.aspx

American Psychological Association. (2015f). *APA policy statements on LGBT concerns*. Retrieved from http://www.apa.org/pi/lgbt/resources/policy/index.aspx

American Psychological Association. (2015g). *Committee on socioeconomic status*. Retrieved from http://www.apa.org/pi/ses/committee/index.aspx

American Psychological Association. (2015h). *APA's council bans psychologist participation in national security interrogations*. Retrieved from http://www.apa.org/news/press/releases/2015/08/psychologist-interrogations.aspx

Anderson, A. F., & McMaken, M. E. (1990). Implementing child advocacy: A rationale and a basic blueprint. *Juvenile & Family Court Journal, 41*(2), 1–14.

Anderson, C. A., Gentile, D. A., & Buckley, K. E. (2007). *Violent video game effects on children and adolescents: Theory, research and public policy*. New York, NY: Oxford University Press.

Andrews, K. T., & Evans, B. (2004). Advocacy organizations in the US political process. *Annual Review of Sociology, 30*, 479–506.

Arizona Revised Statutes § 8-350.01. (2011). Title 8 Children Youth Sex Offenders. 8-350.01 (2011). Retrieved from www.azleg.gov/ars/8/00350-01.htm

Arons, D. F. (Ed.). (2007). *Power in policy: A funder's guide to advocacy and civic participation*. St. Paul, MN: Fieldstone Alliance.

Association for the Study and Development of Community (ASDC). (2003). *Embedding prevention in state policy and practice: Second annual evaluation report. Volume I*. Retrieved from http://www.communityscience.com/pdfs/NCPCYear2.pdf

Association for the Study and Development of Community (ASDC). (2005). *Safe Start demonstration project 2005*. Retrieved from http://www.communityscience.com/pdfs/PERF022005.pdf

Battelle Memorial Institute and ASDC. (2007). *Annual findings report 2006. Drug-free communities support program: National evaluation*. Retrieved from communityscience.com/pdfs/DFC%202006%20Annual%20Findings%20Report%2002_12_07%20v9_1.pdf

Belsky, J. (1988). The "effects" of infant day care reconsidered. *Early Childhood Research Quarterly, 3*, 235–272.

Belsky, J. (2009). *Effects of child care on child development: Give parents real choice*. Retrieved from http://www.mpsv.cz/files/clanky/6640/9_Jay_Belsky_EN.pdf

Belsky, J., Melhuish, E., & Barnes, J. (2008). Research and policy in developing an early years initiative: The case of Sure Start. *International Journal of Child Care and Education Policy, 2*, 1–13. Retrieved from file:///C:/Users/maton/Downloads/01.UK(1)2.pdf

Belsky, J., Melhuish, E., Barnes, J., Leyland, A. H., Romaniuk, H., & the NESS Research Team. (2006). Effects of Sure Start local programmes on children and families: Early findings from a quasiexperimental, cross-sectional study. *BMJ, 332*, 1476–1578 (formerly *The*

British Medical Journal; also published at BMJ online: Http://bmj.com/cgi/doi/10.1136/bmj.38853.451748.2F).

Bevan, W. (1980). On getting in bed with a lion. *American Psychologist, 35,* 779–789.

Bishop-Josef, S. J., & Dodgen, D. (2013). Advocating for children, youth, and families in the policymaking process. In A. M. Culp (Ed.), *Child and family advocacy: Bridging the gaps between research, practice and policy* (pp. 11–18). Issues in clinical child psychology. New York: Springer.

Blase, K., & Fixsen, D. (2013). *Core intervention components: Identifying and operationalizing what makes programs work* (Research Brief). Retrieved from aspe.hhs.gov/hsp/13/KeyIssuesforChildrenYouth/CoreIntervention/rb_CoreIntervention.cfm

Bogenschneider, K. (2014). *Family policy matters: How policymaking affects families and what professionals can do* (3rd ed.). Mahwah, NJ: Lawrence Erlbaum Associates.

Bogenschneider, K., & Corbett, T. (2010). *Evidence-based policy making: Insights from policy-minded researchers and research-minded policymakers.* New York: Routledge.

Bolster, P. (2011). *Atlanta's homeless opportunity fund* (Powerpoint Presentation). Retrieved from http://www.supporthousing.org/documents.htm

Bond, M. A., & Haynes, M. C. (2014). Workplace diversity: A social-ecological framework and policy implications. *Social Issues and Policy Review, 8,* 167–201.

Borgida, E. (1980). Evidentiary reform of rape laws: A psycholegal approach. In P. D. Lipsett & B. D. Sales (Eds.), *New directions in psycholegal research* (pp. 171–197). New York: Van Nostrand Reinhold.

Borgida, E. (2012, November 13). Personal interview.

Borgida, E., & Fiske, S. T. (Eds.). (2008). *Beyond common sense: Psychological science in the courtroom.* New York: Wiley-Blackwell.

Borgida, E., Hunt, C., & Kim, A. (2005). On the use of gender stereotyping research in sex discrimination litigation. *Journal of Law and Policy, 8*(3), 613–628.

Borgida, E., Kim, A., Stark, E., & Miller, C. (2008). Educating consumers about "safer" tobacco products: Some lessons from psychology and law. In C. Haugtvedt, P. M. Kardes, & F. R. Herr (Eds.), *Handbook of consumer psychology* (pp. 915–932). Mahwah, NJ: Lawrence Erlbaum.

Borman, G. D., Slavin, R. E., Cheung, A. C. K., Chamberlain, A. M., Madden, N. A., & Chambers, B. (2007). Final reading outcomes of the national randomized field trial of Success for All. *American Educational Research Journal, 44,* 701–731.

Bornstein, B. H., Tomkins, A. J., Neeley, E. M., Herian, M. N., & Hamm, J. A. (2013). Reducing court's failure-to-appear rate by written reminders. *Psychology, Public Policy, and Law, 19,* 70–80.

Brewster-Smith, M. B. (1990). Psychology in the public interest: What have we done? What can we do? *American Psychologist, 45,* 530–536.

Britner, B., & Stone, M. (2010). Testimony of co-chairs of the Families with Service Needs Advisory Board before the Judiciary Committee. Retrieved from http://www.cga.ct.gov/2010/JUDdata/Tmy/2010HB-05148-R000226-Center%20for%20Children's%20Advocacy-%20Martha%20Stone%20and%20Preston%20Britner-TMY.PDF

Bronfenbrenner, U. (1979). *The ecology of human development.* Cambridge, MA: Harvard University Press.

Brownell, K.D. (1994, December 15). Op-Ed; Get slim with higher taxes. *New York Times.* Retrieved from yaleruddcenter.org/resources/upload/docs/press/ruddnews/OpEdNYTimesTaxes1994.pdf

Brownell, K. D., Farley, T., Willett, W. C., Popkin, B. M., Chaloupka, F. J., Thompson, J. W., & Ludwig, D. S. (2009). The public health and economic benefits of taxing sugar-sweetened beverages. *New England Journal of Medicine, 361,* 1599–1605. [NEJM hpr0905723]

Brownell, K. D., & Frieden, T. R. (2009). Ounces of prevention: The public policy case for taxes on sugared beverages. *New England Journal of Medicine, 360,* 1805–1808. [NEJMp0902392]

Brownell, K. D., & Horgen, K. B. (2003). *Food fight: The inside story of the food industry, America's obesity crisis & what we can do about it.* New York, NY: McGraw Hill.

Brownell, K. D., & Nestle, M. (2004, January 23). Op-Ed; The sweet and lowdown on sugar. *New York Times.* nytimes.com/2004/01/23/opinion/the-sweet-and-lowdown-on sugar. html?scp=3&sq=sweet%20and%20lowdown&st=cse

Brownell, K. D., & Roberto, C. A. (2015). Strategic science with policy impact. *The Lancet,* (No. 9986), 2445–2446.

Bullock, H. (2013). *Women and poverty: Psychology, public policy, and social justice.* Malden, MA: Wiley.

Burton, M. (2013). In and against social policy. *Global Journal of Community Psychology Practice,* 4(2). Retrieved July 1, 2013 from http://www.gjcpp.org/

Campbell, D. T. (1969). Reforms as experiments. *American Psychologist, 24,* 409–429.

Campbell, R., Feler-Cabral, G., Pierce, S. J., Sarma, D. B., Bybee, D., Shaw, J., Horsford, S., & Feeney (2015, March). *The Detroit Sexual Assault Kit (SAK) action research project (ARP), Final report.* Retrieved from https://www.ncjrs.gov/pdffiles1/nij/grants/248680.pdf

Cantor, N. (2010). *Scholarship in action and the public mission of universities.* Speech given at Baylor University, December 7, 2010, as part of the Presidential Inaugural Lecture Series. Retrieved from http://www.syr.edu/chancellor/speeches/Baylor_final.pdf

Cantor, N. (2012). *Universities as anchor institutions: Building coalitions and collective expertise.* Invited lecture given under the Kai Juba Lecture Series at the University of Nevada-Las Vegas School of Architecture, September 25, 2012. Retrieved from http://www.syr.edu/chancellor/speeches/UNLV_FINAL.pdf

Cantor, N. (2013). *Scholarship in action and the connected community.* Invited talk presented at the iConference, Fort Worth, Texas, February 12–15, 2013. Retrieved from http://www.syr.edu/chancellor/speeches/iConference_speech.pdf

Center for Human Environments. (2015). *Public science project.* The Graduate Center, CUNY. Retrieved from http://www.gc.cuny.edu/Page-Elements/Academics-Research-Centers-Initiatives/Centers-and-Institutes/Center-for-Human-Environments/Research-Sub-Groups/Public-Science-Project-%28PSP%29

Center for Medicaid and Medicare Services (CMS). (2013). *The Center for Consumer Information and Insurance Oversight: The Mental Health Parity and Substance Abuse Equity Act of 2008.* Retrieved from http://cms.hhs.gov/CCIIO/Programs-and-Initiatives/Other-Insurance-Protections/m hpaea_factsheet.html

Chamberlain, P., Price, J., Reid, J., & Landsverk, J. (2008). Cascading implementation of a foster and kinship parent intervention. *Child Welfare, 87,* 27–48.

Chamberlain, P., & Reid, J. B. (1991). Using a Specialized Foster Care treatment model for children and adolescents leaving the state mental hospital. *Journal of Community Psychology, 19,* 266–276.

Chamberlain, P., & Reid, J. (1998). Comparison of two community alternatives to incarceration for chronic juvenile offenders. *Journal of Consulting and Clinical Psychology, 6*(4), 624–633.

Chase-Lansdale, P. L., & Brooks-Gunn, J. (2014). Two-generation programs in the 21st century. *Future of Children, 24*(1), 13–39.

Chase-Lansdale, P. L., Cherlin, A. J., & Kiernan, K. E. (1995). The long-term effects of parental divorce on the mental health of young adults: A developmental perspective. *Child Development, 66,* 1614–1634.

Chase-Lansdale, P. L., & Duncan, G. J. (2001). Lessons learned. In G. J. Duncan & P. L. Chase-Lansdale (Eds.), *For better and for worse: Welfare reform and the well-being of children and families* (pp. 307–322). New York: Russell Sage Foundation.

Chase-Lansdale, P. L., Moffitt, R. A., Lohman, B. J., Cherlin, A. J., Coley, R. L., Pittman, L. D., . . . Votruba-Drzal, E. (2003). Mothers' transitions from welfare to work and the well-being of preschoolers and adolescents. *Science, 299*(5612), 1548–1552.

Chase-Lansdale, P. L., & Vinovskis, M. A. (1987). Should we discourage teenage marriage? *Public Interest, 87,* 23–37.

Cherry, G., Ellingwood, H., & Castillo, G. (2011). "Cautious courage": SPSSI's connections and reconnections at the United Nations. *Journal of Social Issues, 6,* 165–178.

Chinman, M., Imm, P., & Wandersman, A. (2004). *Getting to outcomes* 2004: *Promoting accountability through methods and tools for planning, implementation, and evaluation.* Santa Monica, CA: RAND Corporation, TR-TR101. Retrieved from http://www.rand.org/publications/TR/TR101/

Child Trends. (2011). *Facts at a glance: A fact sheet reporting national, state, and city trends in teen childbearing* (Publication 2011–10). Retrieved from http://www.childtrends.org/?publications=facts-at-a-glance-2011

Child Trends. (2013). *Key implementation considerations for executing evidence-based programs: Project overview* (Research Brief). Retrieved from aspe.hhs.gov/hsp/13/KeyIssuesforChildrenYouth/KeyImplementation/rb_keyimplement.cfm

Child Trends. (2015). *About us.* Retrieved from http://www.childtrends.org/about-us/

Cigler, A. J., & Loomis, B. A. (2012). *Interest group politics* (8th ed.). Washington, DC: CQ Press.

Coalition for Juvenile Justice. (2009). *Platform position regarding reauthorization of the Juvenile Justice and Delinquency Prevention Act.* Retrieved from http://www.juvjustice.org/sites/default/files/resource-files/resource_146_0.pdf

Cochran, C. E. (2016). *American public policy: An introduction* (11th ed.). Boston, MA: Cengage Learning.

Cocoa, J. J., DePrato, D. K., Phillippi, S.Jr., & Keator, K. J. (2013). Changing juvenile justice policy and practice: Implementing evidence-based practice practices in Louisiana. In A. M. Culp (Ed.), *Child and family advocacy: Bridging the gap between research, practice and policy* (pp. 159–172). Issues in clinical child psychology. New York: Springer.

Coffman, J. (2008). *Foundations and public policy grantmaking.* The James Irvine Foundation. Retrieved from http://irvine.org/assets/pdf/pubs/philanthropy/PublicPolicy_Coffman.pdf

Cohen, B. J., Bonnie, R. J., & Monahan, J. (2009). Understanding and applying Virginia's new statutory civil commitment criteria. *Developments in Mental Health Law, 28,* 127–139.

Cohen, R., & Ventura, A. (in preparation). *Virginia's bold attempt to establish and sustain a comprehensive system of care for at-risk youth.*

Committee on the Diagnostic Criteria for Myalgic Encephalomyelitis/Chronic Fatigue Syndrome (2015). *Beyond Myalgic Encephalomyelitis/Chronic Fatigue Syndrome: Redefining an illness.* Washington, DC: National Academies Press.

Commonwealth of Virginia. (2007). *Report of the task force on civil commitment.* Commission on Mental Health Law Reform. Retrieved from http://www.courts.state.va.us/programs/concluded/cm h/taskforce_workinggroup/reports/2008_0918_tf_rpt_civil_commitment.pdf

Connecticut Department of Children and Families and Department of Social Services. (2001). *Connecticut Community KidCare: A plan to reform the delivery and financing of children's behavioral health services.* A report to the General Assembly pursuant to June special session Public Act 00–2, Section 5. Retrieved from Ct.gov/dcf/lib/dcf/mental_health/pdf/kidcare_2001_legislative_report.pdf

Connecticut Mental Health Cabinet Report. (2004). *Recommendations of the Lieutenant Governor's Mental Health Cabinet.* Retrieved from http://www.fchealth.org/images/pdfs/Connecticut_Mental_HealthKBS2_FINAL.pdf

Contantdriopoulos, D., Lemire, M., Denis, J. L., & Tremblay, E. (2010). Knowledge exchange processes in organizations and policy arenas: A narrative, systematic review of the literature. *Milbank Quarterly, 88,* 444–483.

Cook, S. L., Woolard, J. L., & McCollum, H. M. (2004). The strengths, competence, and resilience of women facing domestic violence: How can research and policy support them? In K. I. Maton, C. J. Schellenbach, B. J. Leadbeater, & A. L. Solarz (Eds.), *Investing in children, youth, families and communities: Strengths-based research and policy* (pp. 97–115). Washington, DC: American Psychological Association.

Costanzo, M. A., & Gerrity, E. (2009). The effects and effectiveness of using torture as an interrogation device: Using research to inform the policy debate. *Social Issues and Policy Review, 3,* 179–210.

Costanzo, M., & Krauss, D. (2012). *Forensic and legal psychology: Psychological science applied to law.* New York: Worth.

Cowen, E. L. (1983). Primary prevention in mental health: Past, present and future. In R. D. Felner, L. A. Jason, J. N. Moritsugu, & S. S. Farber (Eds.), *Preventive psychology: Theory, research, and practice* (pp. 11–25). New York: Pergamon.

Culley, M. R., & Angelique, H. L. (2011). Participation, power, and the role of community psychology in environmental disputes: A tale of two nuclear cities. *American Journal of Community Psychology* (Special Section on Community Psychology and Global Climate Change), 47, 410–426.

Culp, A. M. (Ed.). (2013). *Child and family advocacy: Bridging the gaps between research, practice and policy.* Issues in clinical child psychology. New York: Springer.

Dalton, J. H., Elias, M. J., & Wandersman, A. (2001). *Community psychology: Linking individuals and communities.* Stamford, CT: Wadsworth.

Davis, D. K., Bond, C. S., & Murray, P. (2010, August 17). *Letter to Mary K. Wakefield and Carmen R. Nazario from Rep. Davis and Senators Bond and Murray.*

Davis, L. M., Bozick, R., Steele, J. L., Saunders, J., & Miles, J. N. V. (2013). *Evaluating the effectiveness of correctional education: A meta-analysis of programs that provide education to incarcerated adults.* Santa Monica, CA: RAND Corporation. http://www.rand.org/pubs/research_reports/RR266

Deaux, K., & Ullman, J. C. (1983). *Women of steel: Female blue-collar workers in the basic steel industry.* New York: Praeger.

DeLeon, P. H. (1988). Public policy and public service: Our professional duty. *American Psychologist, 43,* 309–315.

DeLeon, P. H., Loftis, C. W., Ball, V., & Sullivan, M. J. (2006). Navigating politics, policy, and procedure: A firsthand perspective on behalf of the profession. *Professional Psychology: Research and Practice, 37,* 146–153.

Department of Defense. (2010). *Repeal of "Don't ask, don't tell" (DADT): Quick reference guide.* Retrieved from Defense.gov/home/features/2010/0610_dadt/Quick_Reference_Guide_Repeal_of_DADT_APPROVED.pdf

Desai, S., Chase-Lansdale, P. L., & Michael, R. T. (1989). Mother or market? Effects of maternal employment on four-year-olds' intellectual abilities. *Demography, 26,* 545–561.

Dodgen, D. W., & Portwood, S. G. (2005). Influencing policymaking for maltreated children and their families. *Journal of Clinical Child and Adolescent Psychology, 34,* 628–637.

Dovidio, J. F., & Estes, V. M. (2007). Psychological research and public policy: Bridging the gap. *Social Issues and Policy Review, 1,* 5–14.

Durlak, J. (2013). *The importance of quality implementation for research, practice and policy* (Research Brief). Retrieved from http://aspe.hhs.gov/hsp/13/KeyIssuesforChildrenYouth/ImportanceofQuality/rb_QualityImp.cfm

Durlak, J. A., & Wells, A. M. (1997). Primary prevention mental health programs for children and adolescents: A meta-analytic review. *American Journal of Community Psychology, 25,* 115–152.

Dymnicki, A. B., Wandersman, A. H., Osher, D. M., & Pakstis, A. (in press). Bringing interventions to scale. In M. A. Bond, I. Serrano-García, & C. Keys (Editors-in-Chief), *Handbook of community psychology.* Washington, DC: American Psychological Association.

Eisen, M., Keyser-Smith, J., & Sambrano, S. (2000). Evaluation of substance use outcomes in demonstration projects for pregnant and postpartum women and their infants: Findings from a quasi-experiment. *Addictive Behaviors, 25,* 123–129.

Elliot, D., & Tolan, P. H. (1999). Youth violence prevention, intervention, and social policy: An overview. In D. Flannery & R. Hoff (Eds.), *Youth violence: Prevention, intervention, and social policy* (pp. 3–46). Washington, DC: American Psychiatric Association.

Embry, D. D., Lipsey, M., Moore, K. A., & McCallum, D. F. (2013). Best intentions are not enough: Techniques for using research and data to develop new evidence-informed prevention programs (Research Brief). Retrieved from aspe.hhs.gov/hsp/13/KeyIssuesforChildrenYouth/BestIntentions/rb_bestintentions.cfm

Erickson, R. J., & Simon, R. J. (1998). *The use of social science data in Supreme Court decisions.* Urbana: University of Illinois Press.

Fawcett, S. B., Schultz, J. A., Carson, V. L., Renault, V. A., & Francisco, V. T. (2003). Using Internet-based tools to build capacity for community-based participatory research and other efforts to promote community health and development. In M. Minkler & N. Wallerstein (Eds.), *Community-based participatory research for health* (pp. 155–178). San Francisco: Jossey-Bass.

Fawcett, S. B., Schultz, J. A., Holt, C. M., Collie-Akers, V., & Watson-Thompson, J. (2013). Participatory research and capacity building for community health and development. *Journal of Prevention and Intervention in the Community, 41*(3), 139–142.

Fawcett, S. B., Schultz, J., Collie-Akers, V., Holt, C., & Watson-Thompson, J. (2017). Community development for population health and health equity. In P. C. Erwin & R. C. Brownson (Eds.), *Principles of public health practice* (4th ed.) (pp. 443–460). Clifton Park, NY: Delmar Cengage Learning.

FDA Medical Devices. (2014). *Regulatory history of breast plants in the US* Retrieved from http://www.fda.gov/MedicalDevices/ProductsandMedicalProcedures/ImplantsandProsthetics/BreastImplants/ucm064461.htm

Featherman, J., & Vinovskis, M. A. (2001). Growth and use of social and behavioral science in the federal government since World War II. In J. Featherman & M. A. Vinovskis (Eds.), *Social science and policy making: A search for relevance in the twentieth century* (pp. 40–82). Anne Arbor: University of Michigan Press.

Federal Register. (2015). *Notice inviting postsecondary educational institutions to participate in experiments under the Experimental Sites Initiative; Federal Student Financial Assistance Programs Under Title IV of the Higher Education Act of 1965, as Amended.* Retrieved from https://www.federalregister.gov/articles/2015/11/03/2015-28010/notice-inviting-postsecondary-educational-institutions-to-participate-in-experiments-under-the

Ferris, J. M. (Ed). (2009). *Foundations and public policy: Leveraging philanthropic dollars, knowledge, and networks for greater impact.* New York: Foundation Center.

Fine, M., Torre, M. E., Boudin, K., Bowen, I., Clark, J., Hylt, O. N., . . . Upegui, D. (2001). *Changing minds: The impact of college in a maximum security prison.* Retrieved from http://www.prisonpolicy.org/scans/changing_minds.pdf

Finnigan, K. E., & Daly, A. J. (Eds.). (2014). *Using research evidence in education: From the schoolhouse door to Capitol Hill.* Cham, Switzerland: Springer International.

Fischoff, B. (1990). Psychology and public policy: Tool or toolmaker? *American Psychologist, 45,* 647–653.

Fiske, S. T., Bersoff, D. N., Borgida, E., Deaux, K., & Heilman, M. E. (1991). Social science research on trial: The use of sex stereotyping research in Price Waterhouse v. Hopkins. *American Psychologist, 46,* 1049–1060.

Fixsen, D. L., Naoom, S. F., Blase, K. A., Friedman, R. M., & Wallace, F. (2005). *Implementation research: A synthesis of the literature* (Publication No. 231). Tampa: University of South Florida, Florida Mental Health Institute.

Flattau, P. E., & Howell, W. (1996). A renewed need for research on the science of public policy. In R. P. Lorion, I. Iscoe, P. H. DeLeon, & G. R. VandenBos (Eds.), *Psychology and public policy: Balancing public service and professional need* (pp. 117–121). Washington, DC: American Psychological Association.

Foster-Fishman, P. G., & Behrens, T. R. (2007). Systems change reborn: Rethinking our theories, methods, and efforts in human services reform and community-based change. *American Journal of Community Psychology, 39,* 191–196.

Fowler, R. (1996). Foreward: Psychology, public policy, and the congressional fellowship program. In R. P. Lorion, I. Iscoe, P. H. DeLeon, & G. R. VandenBos (Eds.), *Psychology and public policy: Balancing public service and professional need* (pp. ix–xiv). Washington, DC: American Psychological Association.

Francis, G. L., & Turnbull, R. (2013). Lessons from the legislative history of federal special education law: A vignette for advocates. In A. M. Culp (Ed.), *Child and family advocacy: Bridging* the gaps between research, practice and policy (pp. 233–252). Issues in clinical child psychology. New York: Springer.

Frank, R. G., & Callan, J. E. (1996). Public policy: A process with a purpose. In R. P. Lorion, I. Iscoe, P. H. DeLeon, & G. R. VandenBos (Eds.), Psychology and public policy: Balancing public service and professional need (pp. 23–28). Washington, DC: American Psychological Association.

Franks, J. (2013, May 17). Personal interview.

Furstenberg, F. F., Jr., Brooks-Gunn, J., & Chase-Lansdale, P. L. (1989). Teenage pregnancy and childbearing. American Psychologist, 44, 313–320.

FWSN Advisory Board. (2008). Report to the Connecticut General Assembly. Connecticut: Families with Service Needs Advisory Board. Retrieved from http://www.cga.ct.gov/KID/FWSN/Docs/fwsn_report_0208.pdf

Garner, A. S., Shonkoff, J. P., Siegel, B. S., Dobbins, M. I., Earls, M. F., McGuinn, L., Pascoe, J., & Wood, D. L. (2012). Early childhood adversity, toxic stress, and the role of the pediatrician. Pediatrics, 129(1), 224–231.

Gateway Center. (2015). About us. Retrieved from http://www.gatewayctr.org/about/

General Assembly of North Carolina Session. (2011). Session Law 2012–172. House Bill 853. Retrieved from http://www.ncleg.net/sessions/2011/bills/house/pdf/h853v4.pdf

Getting down to facts: A research project examining California's school governance and finance systems (n.d.). Retrieved from http://www.stanford.edu/group/irepp/cgi-bin/joomla/california-school-finance-governance.html

Gibbs, L. (2013, April). Investing in what works The importance of evidence-based policymaking (Discussant comments in Results for America). The Brookings Institute Hamilton Project panel, Washington, DC. Retrieved from http://www.hamiltonproject.org/files/downloads_and_links/TranscriptPanel14–23.pdf

Goesling, B., Colman, S., Trenholm, C., Terzian, M., & Moore, K. (2013). Programs to reduce teen pregnancy, sexually transmitted infections, and associated sexual risk behaviors: A systematic review (ASPE Working Paper). Department of Health and Human Services. Retrieved from http://aspe.hhs.gov/hsp/13/Reduce-TeenPregnancy/rpt_tppevidence.pdf

Goff, P. A., & Kahn, K. B. (2012). Racial bias in policing: Why we know less than we should. Social Issues and Policy Review, 6, 175–207.

Goodman, A. (2006). The story of David Olds and the Nurse Home Visiting Program. The Robert Woods Johnson Foundation. Retrieved from http://www.rwjf.org/en/research- publications/find-rwjf-research/2006/07/the-story-of-david-olds-and-the-nurse-home-visiting-program.html

Goodman, G., Aman, C., & Hirschman, J. (1987). Child sexual and physical abuse: Children's testimony. In S. J. Ceci, M. P. Toglia, & D. F. Ross (Eds.), Children's eyewitness memory (pp. 1–22). New York: Springer-Verlag.

Goodman, G. S., Taub, E. P., Jones, D. P., England, P., Port, L. K., Rudy, L. & Pradlo, L. (1992). Testifying in criminal court: Emotional effects on child sexual assault. Monographs of the Society for Research in Child Development, 57(5), 1–142.

Goodman, G. S. (1984). Children's testimony in historical perspective. Journal of Social Issues, 40(2), 9–32.

Gordon, R., Ji, P. Mulhall, P., Shaw, B., & Weissberg, R. P. (2011). Social and emotional learning for Illinois students: Policy, practice, and progress. The Illinois Report 2011 (pp. 68–83). Institute of Government and Public Affairs, University of Illinois. Retrieved from http://www.casel.org/library/2013/11/8/social-and-emotional-learning-for-illinois-studentspolicy-practice-and-progress

Gorgol, L. E., & Sponsler, B. A. (2011). Unlocking potential: Results of a national survey of postsecondary education in state prisons. Washington, DC: Institute for Higher Education Policy.

Graham, H. D. (1990). The civil rights era: Origins and development of national policy. New York: Oxford University Press.

Granger, R. (2011). *Our work on the quality of after-school programs:* 2003–2011. Retrieved from: http://wtgrantfoundation.org/library/uploads/2016/03/Our-Work-on-the-Quality-of-After-School.pdf

Grisso, T., Barnum, R., Fletcher, K., Cauffman, E., & Peuschold, D. (2001). Massachusetts Youth Screening Instrument for mental health needs of juvenile justice youths. *Journal of the American Academy of Child and Adolescent Psychiatry, 40,* 541–548.

Grisso, T., Fusco, S., Paiva-Salisbury, M., Perrauot, R, Williams, V., & Barnum, R. (2012). *The Massachusetts Youth Screening Instrument-Version 2 (MAYSI-2): Comprehensive research review.* Worcester: University of Massachusetts Medical School. Retrieved from http://nysap.us/MAYSI-2%20Review.pdf http://nysap.us/MAYSI-2%20Review.pdf

Gruendel, J., & Aber, J. L. (2007). Bridging the gap between research and child policy change: The role of strategic communications in policy advocacy. In J. L. Aber, S. J., Bishop-Josef, S. M. Jones, K. T. McLearn, & D. A. Phillips (Eds.), *Child development and social policy: Knowledge for action* (pp. 43–58).Washington, DC: American Psychological Association.

Gulcur, L., Stefancic, A., Shinn, M., Tsemberis, S., & Fischer, S. N. (2003). Housing, hospitalization and cost outcomes for homeless individuals with psychiatric disabilities participating in continuum of care and housing first programmes [Special issue]. *Journal of Community & Applied Social Psychology, 13*(2), 171–186.

Gurin, P. (1999a). Empirical results from the analyses conducted for this litigation. *Expert Report of Patricia Gurin.* Prepared for *Gratz, et al. v. Bollinger, et al., No. 97–75321 Grutter, et al. v. Bollinger, et al., No. 97–75928.* Retrieved from http://www.vpcomm.umich.edu/admissions/legal/expert/empir.html

Gurin, P. (1999b). Appendix E: Classroom and informal interactional diversity at the University of Michigan. *Expert Report of Patricia Gurin.* Prepared for *Gratz, et al. v. Bollinger, et al., No. 97–75321 Grutter, et al. v. Bollinger, et al., No. 97–75928.* Retrieved from http://www.vpcomm.umich.edu/admissions/legal/expert/gurinape.html

Gurin, P., Lehman, J. S., Lewis, E., with Dey, E. L., Gurin, G., & Hurtado, S. (2004). *Defending diversity: Affirmative action at the University of Michigan.* Ann Arbor: University of Michigan Press.

Hall, G. E., & Hord, S. M. (2006). *Implementing change: Patterns, principles and potholes* (2nd ed.). Boston, MA: Allyn and Bacon.

Hammack, P. L., & Windell, E. (2011). Psychology and the politics of same-sex desire in the United States: An analysis of three cases. *History of Psychology, 14,* 220–248.

Hannah, G., Ray, M., Wandersman, A., & Chien, V. (2010). Developing performance-based contracts between agencies and service providers: Results from a Getting to Outcomes support system with social services agencies. *Children and Youth Services Review, 32,* 1430–1436.

Haney, C., & Zimbardo, P. G. (1998). The past and future of US prison policy. Twenty-five years after the Stanford prison experiment. *American Psychologist, 53,* 709–727.

Haney, C. (2006). *Reforming punishment: Psychological limits to the pains of imprisonment.* Washington, DC: American Psychological Association.

Hardin, J. (2011, November 25). We seek to end homelessness. *Atlanta Journal Constitution.* Retrieved from http://www.ajc.com/news/news/opinion/we-seek-to-end-homelessness/nQN2R/

Harris, J. L., Brownell, K. D., & Bargh, J. A. (2009). The food marketing defense model: Integrating psychological research to protect youth and inform public policy. *Social Issues and Policy Review, 3,* 211–271.

Haskins, R. (2005). Child development and child-care policy: Modest impacts. In D. B. Pillemer & S. White (Eds.), *Developmental psychology and social change: Research, history and policy* (pp. 140–172). New York: Cambridge University Press.

Haskins, R. (2006). *Work over welfare: The inside story of the 1996 welfare reform law.* Washington, DC: Brookings Institution.

Haskins, R., & Margolis, G. (2014). *Show me the evidence: Obama's fight for rigor and results in social policy.* Washington, DC: Brookings Institution.

Haskins, R., Paxson, C., & Brooks-Gunn, J. (2009). *Social science rising: A tale of evidence shaping policy* (Policy Brief). The Future of Children. Washington, DC: Brookings Institution.

Hearing before the Subcommittee on Income Security and Family Support of the Committee on Ways and Means, US House of Representatives. One Hundred Eleventh Congress, First Session, June 9, 2009. Serial Number 111-24. Retrieved November 9, from: http://www.gpo.gov/fdsys/pkg/CHRG-111hhrg52502/pdf/CHRG-111hhrg52502.pdf

Herek, G. M. (2006). Legal recognition of same-sex relationships in the United States: A social science perspective. *American Psychologist, 61*(6), 607–621.

Herek, J. (2013, January 3). Personal interview.

Hernández, E. A. L., Pedraza, F. M., & Serrano-García, I. (2005). Que hacer para fomenter la participacion de los psicologos y psicologas en politica publica? Recomendaciones. *Revista Puertorriquena de Psicologia, 16*, 283–297.

Hess, G. A. (1999). Using ethnography to influence public policy. In J. Schensul, et al. (Eds.), *Using ethnographic data: Interventions, public programming, and public policy* (pp. 57–113). Walnut Creek, CA: AltaMair.

Hodges, S., & Ferreira, K. (2013). A multilevel framework for local policy development and implementation. In A. M. Culp (Ed.), *Child and family advocacy: Bridging the gaps between research, practice and policy* (pp. 205–216). Issues in clinical child psychology. New York: Springer.

Hoffman, D. H., Carter, D. J., Viglucci Lopez, C. R., Benzmiller, H. L., Guo, A. X., Latifi, S. Y., & Craig, D. C. (2015). *Independent review relating to APA ethics guidelines, national security interrogations, and torture.* Retrieved from http://www.apa.org/independent-review/APA-FINAL-Report-7.2.15.pdf

Honig, M. (Ed) (2006). *New directions in education policy implementation: Confronting complexity.* Albany: State University of New York.

Howard, S. H., & Brooks-Gunn, J. (2009). The role of home visiting programs in preventing child abuse and neglect. *Future of Children, 19*(2), 119–146.

Howard, R. M., & Steigerwalt, A. (2012). *Judging law and policy: Courts and policy in the American political system.* New York: Routledge.

Huang, L., Stroul, G., Friedman, R., Mrazek, P., Friesen, B., Pires, S., & Mayberg, S. (2005). Transforming mental health care for children and their families. *American Psychologist, 60*, 615–662.

Humphreys (2012). Will the Obama administration implement a more health-oriented approach to drug policy? *Journal of Drug Policy Analysis, 5*(1), 1941–2851.

Hunter-Williams, J. (2013, May 29). Personal interview.

Hustedt, J. T., Barnett, W. S., Jung, K., & Goetze, L. D. (2010). *The New Mexico pre-K evaluation: Results from the initial four years of a new state preschool initiative. Final report.* New Brunswick, NJ: National Institute for Early Education Research, Rutgers University. Retrieved from Nieer.org/pdf/new-mexico-initial-4-years.pdf

Huston, A. C., Duncan, G. J., McLoyd, V. C., Crosby, D. A., Ripke, M. R., Weisner, T. S., & Eldred, C. A. (2005). Impacts on children of a policy to promote employment and reduce poverty for low-income: New hope after five years. *Developmental Psychology, 41*, 902–918.

Huston, A. C., Watkins, B. A., & Kunkel, D. (1989). Public policy and children's television. *American Psychologist, 44*, 424–433.

Illinois State Board of Education. (n.d.). *Illinois Learning Standards: Social and emotional learning.* Retrieved from http://isbe.net/ils/social_emotional/standards.htm

Infancy to Adolescence: Hearing before the Select Committee on Children, Youth, and Families, House of Representatives, 100th Cong. 1. (1987). Retrieved from https://www.ncjrs.gov/pdffiles1/Digitization/112782NCJRS.pdf

Institute of Medicine and National Research Council. (2012). *From neurons to neighborhoods: An update: Workshop summary.* Washington, DC: National Academies Press. Retrieved from http://www.nap.edu/openbook.php?record_id=13119

Jansson, B. S. (2010). *Becoming an effective policy advocate: From policy practice to social justice* (6th ed.). Pacific Grove, CA: Thomson Learning.

Jason, L. (2013). *Principles of social change.* New York: Oxford University Press.

Jason, L. A. (2015). *How disease names can stigmatize.* Oxford University Press blog. Retrieved from http://blog.oup.com/2015/02/disease-name-chronic-fatigue-syndrome-me/

Jason, L. A., & Fricano, G. (1999). Testifying at a congressional hearing on the tobacco settlement. *Professional Psychology: Research and Practice, 30,* 372–377.

Jason, L. A., Richman, J. A., Rademaker, A. W., Jordan, K. M., Plioplys, A. V., Taylor, R. R., , . Plioplys, S. (1999). A community-based study of chronic fatigue syndrome. *Archives of Internal Medicine, 159,* 2129–2137.

Johnson, D. W., Johnson, R. T., & Stevahn, L. (2011). Social interdependence and program evaluation. In M. M. Mark, S. I. Donaldson, & B. Campbell (Eds.), *Social psychology and evaluation* (pp. 288–317). New York, NY: Guilford Press.

Johnson, F. (2011). Education report card. *National Journal Magazine.* Retrieved from http://www.nationaljournal.com/magazine/grading-no-child-left-behind-20111208

Johnson, K., Greenseid, L., Toal, S. A., King, J. A., Lawrenz, F., & Volkov, B. (2009). Evaluation use: A review of the empirical literature from 1986 to 2005. *American Journal of Evaluation, 30,* 377–410.

Joint Task Force on Report on Sexual Orientation & Military Service (2009). *Report of the APA Joint Divisional Task Force on Sexual Orientation & Military Service.* Retrieved from: http://www.apa.org/pi/lgbt/resources/19-44-taskforce-report.pdf

Jones, K., & Barber, J. (2012, January). Help for unemployed Americans. *Monitor on Psychology, 43,* 18. Retrieved from https://www.apa.org/monitor/2012/01/unemployed.aspx

Kanter, B., & Fine, A. (2010). *The networked nonprofit: Connecting with social media to drive change.* San Francisco, CA: Wiley.

Karoly, L. A., Kilburn, M. R., & Cannon, J. (2006). *Early childhood interventions: Proven results, future promises.* Rand Corporation. Retrieved from http://www.rand.org/pubs/monographs/MG341.html

Kiesler, C. A., & Morton, T. L (1988). Psychology and public policy in the health care revolution. *American Psychologist, 43,* 993–1003.

Kimmel, P. (2011). SPSSI and peacebuilding: A participant's perspective. *Journal of Social Issues, 67,* 122–136.

Kingdon, J. W. (1984). *Agendas, alternatives and public policies.* New York: Harper Collins.

Kirsch, R. (2013). The politics of Obamacare: Health care, money, and ideology. *Fordham Law Review, 81,* 1737–1747.

Kitzman, H., Olds, D. L., Henderson, C. R.Jr., Hanks, C., Cole, R., Tatelbaum, R., . . . Barnard, K. (1997). Impact of prenatal and infancy home visitation by nurses on pregnancy outcomes, childhood injuries, and repeated childbearing. *Journal of the American Medical Association, 278,* 644–652.

Knitzer, J. (1982). *Unclaimed children: The failure of public responsibility to children and adolescents in need of mental health services.* Washington, DC: Children's Defense Fund.

Knitzer, J. (2005). Advocacy for children's mental health: A personal journey. *Journal of Clinical Child and Adolescent Psychology, 34,* 638–645.

Kraft, M. E., & Furlong, S. R. (2015). *Public policy: Politics, analysis, and alternatives* (5th ed.). Washington, DC: CQ Press.

Landesman-Dwyer, S. (1974). *A description and modification of the behavior of nonambulatory, profoundly mentally retarded children* (Unpublished doctoral dissertation). University of Washington, Seattle.

Lanning, K. (2012). Social psychology and contemporary immigration policy: An Introduction. *Analyses of Social Issues and Public Policy, 12,* 1–4.

Lee, J. A., DeLeon, P. H., Wedding, D., & Nordal, K. (1994). Psychologists' role in influencing Congress: The process and the players. *Professional Psychology: Research and Practice, 25,* 9–15.

Lerner, R. M., & Benson, P. L. (Eds.). (2003). *Developmental assets and asset-building communities: Implications for research, policy, and practice*. New York: Kluwer Academic.

Lerner, R. M., Boyd, M., J., Kiely, M., K., Napolitano, C. M., & Schmid, K. (2010). Applications of developmental systems theory to benefit human development. In K. E. Hood, C. T. Halpern, G. Greenberg, & R. M. Lerner (Eds.), *Handbook of development systems, behavior, and genetics* (pp. 663–684). Malden, MA: Wiley-Blackwell.

Lerner, R. M., & Galambos, N. (1998). Adolescent development: Challenges and opportunities for research, programs, and policies. In J. T. Spence (Ed.), *Annual review of psychology* (Vol. 49, pp. 413–446). Palo Alto, CA: Annual Reviews.

Lerner, R. M., Lerner J. V., von Eye, A., & Lewin-Bizan, S. (Eds.). (2009). Foundations and functions of thriving in adolescence: Findings from the 4-H study of positive youth development. [Special issue]. *Journal of Applied Developmental Psychology, 30*(5).

Leshner, A. I. (1991). Psychology and public policy: Balancing public service and professional need. *American Psychologist, 46,* 977–979.

Levine, B. J. (2009). *The art of lobbying: Building trust and selling policy*. Washington, DC: CQ Press.

Levine, M., & Levine, A. (1992). *Helping children: A social history*. New York: Oxford University Press.

Levine, M., Wallach, L., & Levine, D. (2007). *Psychological problems, social issues, and law*. Boston: Pearson.

Lewis, K., Lesesne, C., Zahniser, S., Wilson, M., Desiderio, G., Wandersman, A., & Green, D. (2012). Developing a prevention synthesis and translation system to promote science–based approaches to teen pregnancy, HIV and STI prevention. *American Journal of Community Psychology, 50,* 553–571.

Limber, S. P. (2011). Development, evaluation, and future directions of the Olweus Bullying Prevention Program. *Journal of School Violence, 10,* 71–87.

Linney, J. A. (2004). Introduction of Debi Starnes: 2002 recipient of the award for Distinguished Contribution to Practice in Community Psychology. *American Journal of Community Psychology, 33*(1–2), 1.

Lipsey, M. W. (2009). The primary factors that characterize effective interventions with juvenile offenders: A meta-analytic overview. *Victims and Offenders, 4,* 124–147.

Lipsey, M. W., Howell, J. C., Kelly, M. R., Chapman, G., & Carver, D. (2010). Improving the *effectiveness of juvenile justice programs: A new perspective on evidence-based* practice. Center for Juvenile Justice Programs. Retrieved from http://cjjr.georgetown.edu/pdfs/ebp/ebppaper.pdf

Lipsey, M. W., & Wilson, D. B. (2001). *Practical meta-analysis*. Thousand Oaks, CA: Sage.

Lombardi, J. (2003). *Time to care: Redesigning child care to promote education, support families, and build communities*. Philadelphia: Temple University Press.

Loomis, B. (2011). *CQ Press guide to interest groups and lobbying in the United States. America*. Washington, DC: CQ Press.

Lorion, R. P., & Iscoe, I. (1996). Introduction: Reshaping our views of our field. In R. P. Lorion, I. Iscoe, P. H. DeLeon, & G. R. VandenBos (Eds.), *Psychology and public policy: Balancing public service and professional need* (pp. 1–19). Washington, DC: American Psychological Association.

Lorion, R. P., Iscoe, I., DeLeon, P. H., & VandenBos, G. R. (Eds.). (1996). *Psychology and public policy: Balancing public service and professional need*. Washington, DC: American Psychological Association.

Love, J. M., Chazan-Cohen, R., & Raikes, H. (2007). Forty years of research knowledge and use: From Head Start to Early Head Start and beyond. In J. L. Aber, S. J., Bishop-Josef, S. M. Jones, K. T. McLearn, & D. A. Phillips (Eds.), *Child development and social policy: Knowledge for action* (pp. 79–95). Washington, DC: American Psychological Association.

Maccoby, E. E., Kahn, A. J., & Everett, B. A. (1983). The role of psychological research in the formation of policies affecting children. *American Psychologist, 38,* 80–84.

Maisel, L. S., & Berry, J. M. (Eds.). (2010). *The Oxford handbook of American political parties and interest groups*. Oxford: Oxford University Press.

Marriage Cases, 43 Cal.4th 757 *(2008)*.

Maryland v. Craig (89–478), 497 US 836 (1990).

Massey, S. G., & Barreras, R. E. (2013). Introducing "impact validity." *Journal of Social Issues, 69,* 615–632.

Martin, W. E., Jr. (1998). *Brown v. Board of Education: A brief history with documents.* New York: Bedford/St. Martin's.

Maton, K. I., Humphreys, K., Jason, L. A., & Shinn, M. (in press). Community psychology in the policy arena. In M. A. Bond, I. Serrano-García, & C. Keys (Editors-in-Chief), *Handbook of community psychology.* Washington DC: American Psychological Association.

Maton, K. I., Schellenbach, C. J., Leadbeater, B. J., & Solarz, A. L. (Eds.). (2004). *Investing in children, youth, families, and communities: Strengths-based research and policy.* Washington, DC: American Psychological Association.

McCartney, K., & Phillips, D. (Eds.). (1993). *An insider's guide to providing expert testimony before Congress.* Washington, DC: Society for Research in Child Development.

McCartney, K., & Weiss, H. (2007). Data for a democracy: The evolving role of evaluation in policy and program development. In J. L. Aber, S. J. Bishop-Josef, S. M. Jones, K. T. McLearn, & D. A. Phillips (Eds.), *Child development and social policy: Knowledge for action* (pp. 59–76). Washington, DC: American Psychological Association.

McMahon, S. D., & Wolfe, S. M. (in press). Career opportunities for community psychologists. In M. A. Bond, I. Serrano-García, & C. Keys (Editors-in-Chief), *Handbook of community psychology.* Washington, DC: American Psychological Association.

Melton, G. (1995). Bringing psychology to Capitol Hill: Briefings on child and family policy. *American Psychologist, 50,* 766–770.

Melton, G., Thompson, R., & Small, M. (2001). *Toward a child-centered neighborhood-based child protection system.* Westport, CT: Praeger.

Mendell, R. A. (2013). *Juvenile justice reform in Connecticut: How collaboration and commitment have improved public safety and outcomes for youth.* Juvenile Justice Institute. Retrieved from justicepolicy.org/uploads/justicepolicy/documents/jpi_juvenile_justice_reform_in_ct.pdf

Metcalf, N. (2012, May). Dangerous medical devices. *Consumer Reports.* Retrieved from http://www.consumerreports.org/cro/magazine/2012/04/cr-investigates-dangerous-medical-devices/index.htm

Meyers, J. (2013, April 15). Personal interview.

Meyers, J. C. (2011). A community psychologist in the world of philanthropy. *The Community Psychologist, 44*(3), 10–11.

Mihalic, S. F., & Irwin, K. (2003). Blueprints for violence prevention: From research to real-world settings—factors influencing the successful replication of model programs. *Youth Violence and Juvenile Justice, 1,* 307–329.

Miles, J., & Howe, S. (2010). Consulting in public policy. In J. Viola & S. D. McMahon (Eds.), *Consulting and evaluation with nonprofits and community-based organizations* (pp. 283–308). Sudbury, MA: Jones & Bartlett.

Miller, G. A. (1969). Psychology as a means of promoting human welfare. *American Psychologist, 24,* 1063–1075.

Miller, R. (in press). The practice of program evaluation in community psychology: Intersections and opportunities for stimulating social change. In M. A. Bond, I. Serrano-García, & C. Keys (Editors-in-Chief), *Handbook of community psychology.* Washington, DC: American Psychological Association.

Miller, R. L. (2013). Evaluating HIV/AIDS prevention, care and advocacy. Retrieved from http://msutoday.msu.edu/360/2014/robin-lin-miller-evaluating-hiv-aids-prevention-care-and-advocacy/

Miller v. Alabama (2012) No. 10–9646. Retrieved from http://www.supremecourt.gov/opinions/11pdf/10-9646.pdf

Models for Change. (2011). *Knowledge brief: Does mental health screening fulfill its promise?* Retrieved from http://www.modelsforchange.net/publications/316

Monahan, J., & Silver, E. (2003). Judicial decision thresholds for violence risk management. *International Journal of Forensic Mental Health, 2*, 1–6.

Montgomery, A. E., Metraux, S., & Culhane, D. P. (2013). Rethinking homelessness prevention among persons with serious mental illness. *Social Issues and Policy Review, 7*, 57–80.

Morris, M. (2008). *Evaluation Ethics for Best Practice: Cases and Commentaries.* New York, NY: Guilford.

Mrazek, P. J., & Haggerty, R. J. (Eds.). (1994). *Reducing risks for mental disorders: Frontiers for preventive intervention research.* Committee on Prevention of Mental Disorders, Institute of Medicine. Washington, DC: National Academy Press.

Mulvey, E. P., & Schubert, C. A. (2012). Some initial policy implications from the Pathways to Desistance study. *Victims and Offenders, 7*(4), 407–427.

Mulvey, E. P., Schubert, C. A., & Chung, H. L. (2007). Service use after court involvement in a sample of serious adolescent offenders. *Children and Youth Services Review, 29*, 518–544.

Mulvey, E. P., Steinberg, L., Piquero, A. R., Besana, M., Fagan, J., Schubert, C., & Cauffman, B. (2010). Trajectories of desistance and continuity in antisocial behavior following court adjudication among serious adolescent offenders. *Development and Psychopathology, 22*, 453–475.

Murray, J. P. (1996). Aletha Huston. In N. Signorielli (Ed.), *Women in communication: A biographical sourcebook* (pp. 220–227). Westport, CT: Greenwood.

Murray, J. P. (2013). Media violence and children: Applying research to advocacy. In A. M. Culp (Ed.), *Child and family advocacy: Bridging the gap between research, practice and policy* (pp. 149–158). Issues in clinical child psychology. New York: Springer.

National Academies. (1999). *Committee on understanding and eliminating racial and ethnic disparities in health care.* The National Academies. Retrieved from mfdp.med.harvard.edu/fellows_faculty/california_endowment/publications/pdf/National_Academies.pdf

National Academy of Science. (2012). *Using science as evidence in public policy.* Washington, DC: Author.

National Center for Children in Poverty. (1990). *Five million children: A statistical portrait of our poorest young citizens.* New York: Columbia University.

National Research Council. (2005). *Improving evaluation of anticrime programs.* Washington, DC: National Academies Press. Retrieved from http://www.nap.edu/catalog.php?record_id=11337

Newbould, P. (2007). Psychologists as legislators: Results of the 2006 elections. *Professional Psychology: Research and Practice, 38*, 3–6.

Newman, R., & Vincent, T. (1996). Introduction. Balancing expertise with practical realities. In R. P. Lorion, I. Iscoe, P. H. DeLeon, & G. R. VandenBos (Eds.). *Psychology and public policy: Balancing public service and professional need* (pp. 203–206). Washington, DC: American Psychological Association.

New York City Council. (2013). *Press release.* The Council of the City of New York Office of Communications. Release 127–2013. Retrieved from http://council.nyc.gov/html/pr/071713daca.shtml\

NICHD Early Child Care Research Network. (Ed.). (2005). *Child care and child development: Results from the NICHD study of early child care and youth development.* New York: Guilford.

Nicholson, I. (1997). The politics of scientific social reform, 1936–1960: Goodwin Watson and the Society for the Psychological Study of Social Issues. *Journal of the History of the Behavioral Sciences, 33*, 39–60.

NIH Office of Research on Women's Health. (n.d.). *History and mission.* Retrieved from http://orwh.od.nih.gov/about/mission.asp

NIH Revitalization Act. (1993). S.1 - National Institutes of Health Revitalization Act of 1993. Subtitle B--Clinical Research Equity Regarding Women and Minorities. Retrieved from http://orwh.od.nih.gov/about/pdf/NIH-Revitalization-Act-1993.pdf

Nosek, B. A., & Riskind, R. G. (2012). Policy implications of implicit social cognition. *Social Issues and Policy Review, 6*, 113–147.

Nownes, A. (2013). *Interest groups in American politics: Pressure and power.* New York: Routledge.

Nutley, S., Walter, I., & Davies, H. T. O. (2007). *Using evidence: How research can inform public services.* Bristol, UK: Policy Press.

Nye, J. S., Jr. (2008). *The powers to lead.* New York: Oxford University Press.

Obar, J. A., Zube, P., & Lampe, C. (2012). Advocacy 2.0: An analysis of how advocacy groups in the United States perceive and use social media as tools for facilitating civic engagement and collective action. *Journal of Information Policy, 2*, 1–25.

Obergefell v. Hodges, 576 US. (2015). Brief for the American Psychological Association as amicus curiae. Retrieved from http://www.apa.org/about/offices/ogc/amicus/obergefell-supreme-court.pdf

Obergefell v. Hodges (2015). 135 S. Ct. 2584. Retrieved from http://www.supremecourt.gov/opinions/14pdf/14-556_3204.pdf

O'Donnell, C. R. (1995). Firearm deaths among children and youth. *American Psychologist, 50*, 771–776.

O'Donnell, C. R. (2001). School violence: Trends, risk factors, prevention, and recommendations. *Law & Policy, 23*, 409–416.

O'Donnell, C. R., & Tharp, R. G. (2012). Integrating cultural community psychology: Activity settings and the shared meanings of intersubjectivity. *American Journal of Community Psychology, 49(1–2)*, 22–30.

O'Donnell, C. R., Tharp, R. G., & Wilson, K. (1993). Activity settings as the unit of analysis: A theoretical basis for community intervention and development. *American Journal of Community Psychology, 21*, 501–520.

O'Donnell, C. R., & Williams, I. L. (2013). The buddy system: A 35-year follow-up of criminal offenses. *Clinical Psychological Science, 1(1)*, 54–66.

Office of Adolescent Health. (2014). *TPP resource center: Evidence-based programs.* Retrieved from http://www.hhs.gov/ash/oah/oah-initiatives/teen_pregnancy/db/index.html

Olds, D. (2009). In support of disciplined passion. *Journal of Experimental Criminology, 5*, 201–214.

Olds, D. L., Henderson, C. R., Jr., Chamberlin, R., & Tatelbaum, R. (1986). Preventing child abuse and neglect: A randomized trial of nurse home visitation. *Pediatrics, 78*, 65–78.

Olds, D. L., Robinson, J., O'Brien, R., Luckey, D. W., Pettitt, L. M., Henderson, C. R., . . . Talmi, A. (2002). Home visiting by paraprofessionals and by nurses: A randomized, controlled trial. *Pediatrics, 110*, 486–496.

Oleszek, W. J., Oleszek, M. J., Rybicki, E., & Heniff, B. (2016). *Congressional procedures and the policy process* (10th ed.). Washington, DC: CQ Press.

Olson, B., & Soldz, S. (2007). Positive illusions and the necessity of a bright line forbidding psychologist involvement in detainee interrogations. *Analyses of Social Issues and Public Policy, 7*, 45–54.

Olson, B., Viola, J., & Fromm-Reed, S. (2011). A temporal mode of community organizing and direct action. *Peace Review: A Journal of Social Justice, 23*, 52–60.

Owen-Kostelnik, J., Reppucci, N. D., & Meyer, J. R. (2006). Testimony and interrogation of minors: Assumptions about maturity and morality. *American Psychologist, 61*, 286–304.

Pathways to Housing. (2015). *Housing first model.* Retrieved from https://pathwaystohousing.org/housing-first-model

Peace, R. (2013). *The national campaign to reform state juvenile justice systems.* Retrieved from publicinterestprojects.org/general/spotlight-on-the-national-campaign-to-reform-state-juvenile-justice-systems/

Peters, B. G. (2016). *American public policy: Promise and performance* (10th ed.). Washington, DC: CQ Press.

Pettigrew, T. F. (1988). Influencing policy with social psychology. *Journal of Social Issues, 44*, 205–219.

Pettigrew, T. F. (2011). SPSSI and racial research. *Journal of Social Issues, 67*(1), 137–149.

Philanthropy Roundtable. (2005, January/February). Foundations and public policy. *Philanthropy Magazine*. Retrieved from philanthropyroundtable.org/topic/excellence_in_philanthropy/foundations_and_public_policy

Phillips, D. A. (2000). Social policy and community psychology. In J. Rappaport & E. Seidman (Eds.), *Handbook of community psychology* (pp. 397–419). New York: Kluwer.

Phillips, D. A., & McCartney, K. (2005). The disconnect between research and policy on child care. In D. B. Pillemer & S. White (Eds.), *Developmental psychology and social change: Research, history and policy* (pp. 104–139). New York: Cambridge University Press.

Phillips, D. A., & Styfco, S. J. (2007). Child development research and public policy: Triumphs and setbacks on the way to maturity. In J. L. Aber, S. J. Bishop- Josef, S. M. Jones, K. T. McLearn, & D. A. Phillips (Eds.), *Child development and social policy: Knowledge for action* (pp. 11–27).Washington, DC: American Psychological Association.

Pillemer, D. B., & White, S. (Eds.) (2005). *Developmental psychology and social change: Research, history and policy*. New York: Cambridge University Press.

Pope, M. (2012). *Historical timeline for division 44 (1957 to 2012)*. Retrieved from http://www.apadivision44.org/downloads/Div44timeline1957-2012.pdf

Portwood, S. G., & Dodgen, D. W. (2005). Influencing policymaking for maltreated children and their families. *Journal of Clinical Child and Adolescent Psychology, 34*, 628–637.

Price, R. H. (1989). Bearing witness. *American Journal of Community Psychology, 17*, 151–163.

Price, R. H., Cowen, E., Lorion, R., & Ramos-McKay, J. (Eds.). (1988). *Fourteen ounces of prevention*. Washington, DC: American Psychological Association.

Price Waterhouse v. Hopkins (1989). 490 US 228.

Prop 8 Trial Re-enactment, Day 9 Chapter 1 (2010). Retrieved from youtube.com/watch?v=V_Vc2GxwSM0&feature=youtube_gdata

Psychologists for Social Responsibility. (2014). *A brief chronology of PsySR's End Torture Action Committee's initiatives*. Retrieved from psysr.org/about/programs/humanrights/chronology.php

Public Act 07-04, Section 73. (2007). Retrieved from http://www.cga.ct.gov/2007/ACT/PA/2007PA-00004-R00SB-01500SS1-PA.htm

Public Law 104–193. (1996). *Personal Responsibility and Work Opportunity Reconciliation Act of 1996*. Retrieved from http://www.gpo.gov/fdsys/pkg/PLAW-104publ193/pdf/PLAW-104publ193.pdf

Public Law 110-339. (2008). *Healthy Start Reauthorization Act of 2007*. Retrieved from http://www.gpo.gov/fdsys/pkg/STATUTE-122/pdf/STATUTE-122-Pg3733.pdf

Public Law 110-392. (2008). *Comprehensive Tuberculosis Elimination Act of 2008*. http://en.wikisource.org/wiki/Comprehensive_Tuberculosis_Elimination_Act_of_2008

Public Law 111-117. (2010). *Consolidated Appropriations Act of 2010, Department of Health and Human Services* (Division D, Title II), 123 STAT. 3251. Retrieved from http://www.gpo.gov/fdsys/pkg/PLAW-111publ117/pdf/PLAW-111publ117.pdf

Pub Law 111-148, Section 2951. (2010). *Maternal, infant, and early childhood home visiting programs*. Retrieved from http://www.gpo.gov/fdsys/pkg/PLAW-111publ148/pdf/PLAW-111publ148.pdf

Pub Law 111-148, Section 5305. (2010). *Geriatric education and training; career awards; comprehensive geriatric education* (pp. 504–507). Retrieved from http://www.gpo.gov/fdsys/pkg/PLAW-111publ148/pdf/PLAW-111publ148.pdf

Quint, J. C., Balu, R., DeLaurentis, M., Rappaport, S., Smith, T. J., & Zhu, P. (2014). *The success for all model of school reform: Interim findings from the Investing in Innovation (i3) scale-up*. Retrieved from http://www.mdrc.org/sites/default/files/success_for_all_interim_findings.pdf

Raikes, H., St. Clair, S., & Plata-Potter, S. (2013). Early childhood education and care: Legislative and advocacy efforts. In A. M. Culp (Ed.), *Child and family advocacy: Bridging the gap between research, practice and policy* (pp. 107–123). Issues in clinical child psychology. New York: Springer.

Ramey, C. T., & Ramey, S. L. (2010). Head Start: Strategies to improve outcomes for children living in poverty. In R. Haskins & W. S. Barnett (Eds.), *Investing in young children: New directions in federal preschool and early childhood policy.* (pp. 59–68) Washington, DC: Brookings Institution. Retrieved from http://www.brookings.edu/~/media/Files/rc/reports/2010/1013_investing_in_young_children_haskins/1013_investing_in_young_children_haskins_ch5.pdf

Ramey, S. L. (1999). Head Start and preschool education: Toward continued improvement. *American Psychologist, 54,* 344–346.

Ramey, S. L., & Ramey, C. T. (1992). Early educational intervention with disadvantaged children: To what effect? *Applied and Preventive Psychology, 1,* 131–140.

Ramey, S. L., Ramey, C. T., & Lanzi, R. G. (2006). Early intervention: Background, research findings, and future directions. In J. W. Jacobson, J. A. Mulick, & J. Rojahn (Eds.), *Handbook of intellectual and developmental disabilities* (pp. 445–463). New York: Springer.

RAND Corporation. (2015). *News about Getting to Outcomes.* Retrieved from http://www.rand.org/health/projects/getting-to-outcomes/news.html

Rappaport, J. (1977). *Community psychology: Values, research and action.* New York: Holt, Rinehart and Winston.

Rappaport, J. (1981). In praise of paradox: A social policy of empowerment over prevention. *American Journal of Community Psychology, 9,* 1–23.

Reiss, D., & Price, R. H. (1996). National research agenda for prevention research: The NIMH report. *American Psychologist, 51*(11), 1109–1115.

Reppucci, N. D. (1999). Adolescent development and juvenile Justice (Distinguished Contributions Address, 1998). *American Journal of Community Psychology, 27,* 307–326.

Reppucci, N. D. (2011). A tribute to Seymour B. Sarason: Social action and public policy. *Journal of Community Psychology, 40,* 219–222.

Reppucci, N. D., Woolard, J. L., & Fried, C. S. (1999). Social, community and preventive interventions. *Annual Review of Psychology, 50,* 387–418.

Research Caucus (n.d.). *How to organize a congressional briefing.* Retrieved from researchcaucus.org/docs/Organizing%20Congressional%20Briefings.pdf

Reyes, M., Gary, H. E., Jr., Dobbins, J. G., Randall, B., Steele, L., Fukuda, K., . . . Reeves, W. C. (1997, February 21). Descriptive epidemiology of chronic fatigue syndrome: CDC surveillance in four cities. *Morbidity and Mortality Weekly Report Surveillance Summaries, 46*(SS2), 113.

Reyes, M., Nisenbaum, R., Jr., Hoaglin, D. C., Unger, E. R., Emmons, C., Randall, B., Reeves, W. C. (2003). Prevalence and incidence of chronic fatigue syndrome in Wichita, Kansas. *Archives of Internal Medicine, 163,* 1530–1536.

Riccio, J. A., Dechausay, N., Miller, C., Nuñez, S., Verma, N., & Yang, E. (2013). *Conditional cash transfers in New York City: The continuing story of the opportunity NYC–Family Rewards Demonstration.* Manpower Research Demonstration Corporation. Retrieved from http://www.mdrc.org/publication/conditional-cash-transfers-new-york-city interventions

Rich, A. (2004). *Think tanks, public policy, and the politics of expertise.* Cambridge: Cambridge University Press.

Rodríguez, A. (2009). Social policies in Uruguay: A view from the political dimension of community psychology. *American Journal of Community Psychology, 43,* 122–133.

Roper v. Simmons, 543 US 551 (2005).

Rothbaum, F., Martland, N. F., & Bishop-Josef, S. J. (2007). Using the web to disseminate research and affect public policy. In J. L. Aber, S. J. Bishop-Josef, S. M. Jones, K. T. McLearn, & D. A. Phillips (Eds.), *Child development and social policy: Knowledge for action* (pp. 265–280).Washington, DC: American Psychological Association.

Rozell, M. D., & Mayer, J. D. (Eds.). (2008). *Media power, media politics.* Lanham, MD: Rowman & Littlefield.

Rudman, L. A., Glick, P., & Phelan, J. E. (2008). From the laboratory to the bench: Gender stereotyping research in the courtroom. In E. Borgida & S. T. Fiske (Eds.), *Beyond common sense: Psychological science in the courtroom* (pp. 83–102). Malden, MA: Wiley-Blackwell.

Rutherford, A., Cherry, F. C., & Unger, R. K. (2011). 75 years of social science for social action: Historical and contemporary perspectives on SPSSI's scholar-activist legacy [Special issue]. *Journal of Social Issues, 67*(1).

Rutherford, A., & Livert, D. (n.d.). *SPSSI was there.* Retrieved from http://www.spssitimeline.org/

Ryon, S. B., Winokur, K. P., & Devers, L. (2010). *FWSN process and outcome evaluation of the 2007–2009 Connecticut Families with Service Needs Initiative. Final report.* Justice Research Center. Retrieved from http://www.cga.ct.gov/KID/FWSN/Docs/2010/JRC%20Final%20 FWSN%20Process%20and%20Outcome%20Evaluation%20Report.pdf

S. 678 (2009). *Juvenile Justice Reauthorization Act of 2009.* Retrieved from https://www.govtrack.us/congress/bills/111/s678/text

Saïas, T., & Delawarde, C. (2013). The geometrical headache of French policies: Can vertical cultures be tilted horizontally? *Global Journal of Community Psychology Practice, 4*(2). Retrieved from http://www.gjcpp.org/

Sambrano, S., Springer, J. F., & Herman, J. (1997). Informing the next generation of prevention programs: CSAP's cross-site evaluation of the 1994–1995 high-risk youth grantees. *Journal of Community Psychology, 25,* 375–395.

SAMHSA. (2010). Health reform: Overview of the Affordable Care Act. *SAMHSA News, 18*(3). Retrieved from sam hsa.gov/sam hsaNewsletter/Volume_18_Number_3/Affordable HealthCareAct.aspx

SAMHSA. (2013). *Parity: The Mental Health Parity and Addiction Equity Act.* Retrieved from http://beta.sam hsa.gov/health-reform/parity

SAMSHA (2014). *Center for Substance Abuse Prevention.* Retrieved from http://www.samhsa.gov/about-us/who-we-are/offices-centers/csap

Sarason, S. B. (1967). Toward a psychology of change and innovation. *American Psychologist, 22,* 227–233.

Sarason, S. B. (1971). *The culture of school and the problem of change.* Boston: Allyn & Bacon.

Sarason, S. B. (1972). *The creation of settings and the future societies.* San Francisco: Jossey-Bass.

Sarason, S. B. (1974). *The psychological sense of community: Prospects for a community psychology.* San Francisco: Jossey-Bass.

Sarason, S. B. (1986). And what is the public interest? *American Psychologist, 41,* 899–905.

Sarason, S. B. (1990). *The predictable failure of educational reform: Can we change course before it's too late?* San Francisco: Jossey-Bass.

Sarason, S. B. (1995). If I was doing it over again. *Community Psychologist, 28*(3), 13.

Sarason, S. B. (2006). *Letters to a serious education president.* Thousand Oaks, CA: Corwin.

Scott, E. S., Reppucci, N. D., & Woolard, J. L. (1995). Evaluating adolescent decision making in legal contexts. *Law & Human Behavior, 19,* 221–244.

Scott, J., Lubienski, C., Scott, J., DeBray, & Jabbar, H. (2014). The intermediary function in evidence production, promotion and utilization: The case of educational incentives. In K. E. Finnigan & A. J. Daly (Eds.), *Using research evidence in education: From the schoolhouse door to Capitol Hill* (pp. 69–89). Cham, Switzerland: Springer International.

Scott, K. G., Mason, C. A., & Chapman, D. A. (1999). The use of epidemiological methodology as a means of influencing public policy. *Child Development, 70,* 1263–1272.

Serrano-García, I. (1983). La politica publica y los/as psicologos en Puerto Rico. *Boletin de la APPR. VII*(1), 4–6.

Serrano-García, I. (2005). Psicología y política pública: Compromiso y responsabilidad social. *Revista Puertorriqueña de Psicología, 16,* 151–157.

Serrano-García, I., Rodríguez, Y. R., & Pérez, G. G. (2005). Psicologia y politica pulica: 20 anos despues. *Revista Puertorriquena de Psicologia, 16,* 159–190.

Shadish, W. (1984). Policy research: Lessons learned from the implementation of deinstitutionalization. *American Psychologist, 39*, 725–738.

Shank, N., & Tomkins A. J. (1999). *Nebraska child support collection and disbursement system implementation project: Final report.* Retrieved from http://ppc.unl.edu/wp-content/uploads/1999/10/child_support_report.pdf

Shinn, M. (2007). Waltzing with a monster: Bringing research to bear on public policy. *Journal of Social Issues, 63*, 215–231.

Shinn, M., Greer, A. L., Bainbridge, J., Kwon, J., & Zuiderveen, S. (2013). Efficient targeting of homelessness prevention services for families. *American Journal of Public Health, 103*(S3), S324–S330.

Shonkoff, J., & Phillips, D. (Eds.). (2000). *Neurons to neighborhoods: The science of early childhood development.* Committee on Integrating the Science of Early Childhood Development; National Research Council and Institute of Medicine. Washington, DC: National Academy Press. Retrieved from http://www.nap.edu/catalog.php?record_id=9824

Shonkoff, J. P. (2000). Science, policy, and practice: Three cultures in search of a shared mission. *Child Development, 71*, 181–187.

Shonkoff, J. P., & Bales, S. N. (2011). Science does not speak for itself: Translating child development research for the public and its policymakers. *Child Development, 82*, 17–32.

Shragge, E. (2012). *Activism and social change: Lessons for community organizing* (2nd ed.). North York, Ontario, CAN: University of Toronto Press.

Shullman, S. L., Celeste, B. L., & Strickland, T. (2005). Extending the Parsons legacy: Applications of counseling psychology in pursuit of social justice through the development of public policy. In R. Toporek, L. H. Gersein, N. A. Fouad, D. G. Roysircar-Sodowsky, & T. Israel (Eds.), *Handbook for social justice in counseling psychology: Leadership, vision and action* (pp. 499–513). Thousand Oaks, CA: Sage.

Smedley, B. D., & Hectors, H. F. (2014). Conceptual and methodological limitations for health disparities research and their policy implications. *Journal of Social Issues, 70*, 382–391.

Smedley, B. D., Stith, A. Y., & Nelson, A. R. (Eds.). (2003). *Unequal treatment: Confronting racial and ethnic disparities in health care.* Committee on Understanding and Eliminating Racial and Ethnic Disparities in Health Care. Washington, DC: National Academy Press. Retrieved from http://www.nap.edu/catalog.php?record_id=12875

Snowden, L. R. (2012). Health and mental health policies' role in better understanding and closing African American–White American disparities in treatment access and quality of care. *American Psychologist, 67*, 524–531.

Society for the Psychological Study of Social Issues (SPSSI). (2013). *Summer policy workshop.* Retrieved from https://www.spssi.org/_data/n_0001/resources/live/Workshop%20announcement%20.pdf

Society for Research in Child Development (SRCD). (2012). *About the fellowships.* Retrieved from http://srcd.org/policy-media/policy-fellowships/about-fellowships

Society for Research in Child Development (SRCD). (2014). *Strengthening connections among child and family research, policy and practice.* Retrieved from http://www.srcd.org/meetings/special-topic-meetings/1-strengthening-connections

Sommer, T. E., Chase-Lansdale, P. L, Brooks-Gunn, J., Gardner, M., Rauner, D. M., & Freel, K. (2012). Early childhood education centers and mothers' postsecondary attainment: A new conceptual framework for a dual-generation education intervention. *Teachers College Record, 114*, 1–40.

Speer, P. W., Ontkush, M., Schmitt, B., Raman, P., Jackson, C., Rengert, K., & Peterson, N. A. (2003). The intentional exercise of power: Community organizing in Camden, NJ. *Journal of Community and Applied Social Psychology, 13*, 399–408.

Starnes, D. M. (2004). Community psychologists—Get in the arena!! *American Journal of Community Psychology, 33*(1/2), 3–6.

Steinberg, L., & Scott, E. (2003). Less guilty by reason of adolescence: Developmental imma-
turity, diminished responsibility, and the juvenile death penalty. *American Psychologist, 58*,
1009–1018.

Stipek, D. (2013, March 26). Personal interview.

Stolberg, V. B. (2009). Center for Substance Abuse Prevention. In G. L. Fisher & N. A. Roget
(Eds.). *Encyclopedia of substance abuse prevention, treatment, and recovery* (pp. 157–159).
Thousand Oaks, CA: Sage.

Strickland, T. (1996). Moving psychology toward (self) recognition as a public resource: The
views of a congressman psychologist. In R. P. Lorion, I. Iscoe, P. H. DeLeon, & G. R.
VandenBos (Eds.), *Psychology and public policy: Balancing public service and professional need*
(pp. 369–389). Washington, DC: American Psychological Association.

Super, C. M. (2005). The globalization of developmental psychology. In D. B. Pillemer &
S. White (Eds.), *Developmental psychology and social change: Research, history and policy*
(pp. 11–33). New York: Cambridge University Press.

Task Force on Women, Poverty, and Public Assistance. (1998). *Making 'Welfare to Work' really
work*. Washington, DC: American Psychological Association. Retrieved from apa.org/pi/
women/programs/poverty/welfare-to-work.aspx

Tebes, J. K., Amble, P. T., & Baranoski, M. V. (2008). *Evaluation of the residents of Illinois Institutions
for Mental Disease (IMDs)*. Report prepared for Plaintiff class *Williams v. Blagojevich et al. Illinois*.
Retrieved from http://www.clearinghouse.net/chDocs/public/PB-IL-0005-0024.pdf

The National Academies. (n.d.). *Who we are*. Retrieved from http://www.nationalacademies.
org/about/whoweare/index.html

Thomas, J. (2004). 5 psychologists returned to Congress. *National Psychologist*. Retrieved from
http://nationalpsychologist.com/2004/11/5-psychologists-returned-to-congress/10756.
html

Thompson, R. A., & Nelson, C. A. (2001). Developmental science and the media. Early brain
development. *American Psychologist, 56*, 5–15.

Toch, H. (2014). *Organizational change through individual empowerment: Applying social psychology
in prisons and policing*. Washington, DC: American Psychological Association.

Tolan, P.H. (2014). Making and using lists of empirically tested programs: Value for violence
interventions for progress and impact. In L. Carroll, M. M. Perez, & R. M. Taylor (Eds.),
The evidence for violence prevention across the lifespan and around the world: Workshop Summary
(pp. 94–106). Washington, DC: National Academies Press.

Tolan, P. H., Sherrod, L. R., Gorman-Smith, D., & Henry, D. B. (2004). Building protection,
support, and opportunity for inner-city children and youth and their families. In K. I.
Maton, C. J. Schellenbach, B. J. Leadbeater, & A. L. Solarz (Eds.), *Investing in children, youth,
families, and communities: Strengths-based research and policy* (pp. 193–211). Washington,
DC: American Psychological Association.

Tomes, H., & Rickel, A. U. (1996). Psychologists' contributions to the policy process. In
R. P. Lorion, I. Iscoe, P. H. DeLeon, & G. R. VandenBos (Eds.), *Psychology and public
policy: Balancing public service and professional need* (pp. 325–329). Washington, DC:
American Psychological Association.

Tomkins, A. J., Hoppe, R. D., Herian, M. N., PytlikZillig, L. M., Abdel-Monem, T., & Shank,
N. C. (2012). Public input for city budgeting using e-input, face-to-face discussions,
and random sample surveys: The willingness of an American community to increase
taxes. *Proceedings of the European Conference on e-Government, 2*(12), 698–707. Retrieved
from http://ppc.unl.edu/wp-content/uploads/2011/07/PublicInputForCityBudgeting-
Tomkins-et-al1.pdf

Torre, M. E., Fine, M., Alexander, N., Biliups, A. B., Blanding, Y., Genao, E., . . . Urdang, K.
(2008). Participatory action research in the contact zone. In J. Cammarota, & M. Fine
(Eds.), *Revolutionizing education: Youth participatory action research in motion* (pp. 23–44).
New York: Routledge.

Trickett, E., & Beehler, S. (in press), Community psychology misdirected? The case of evidence-based practice. In M. Bond, I. Serrano-Garcia, & C. Keys (Editors-in-Chief), *Handbook of community psychology*. Washington, DC: American Psychological Association.

Trudeau, J., Saunders, L., Andrews, C., Hersch, R., & Oros, C. (1993). *The national evaluation survey of the Community Partner Demonstration Program*. Retrieved from http://www.amstat. org/meetings/ices/1993/invited/VII_JusticeandSubstance AbuseSurveys.pdf

Tsemberis, S. (2010). *Housing first: The Pathways Model to end homelessness for people with mental illness and addiction*. Minneapolis, MN: Hazelden.

Tsemberis, S., Moran, L. L., Shinn, M., Asmussen, S. M., & Shern, D. L. (2003). Consumer preference programs for homeless individuals with psychiatric disabilities: A drop-in center and a supported housing program. *American Journal of Community Psychology, 32,* 305–317.

Tseng, V. (2012). The uses of research in policy and practice. *Social Policy Report, 26*(2), 1–24.

Tseng, V., & Nutley, S. (2014). Building the infrastructure to improve the use and usefulness of research in education. In K. E. Finnigan & A. J. Daly (Eds.), *Using research evidence in education: From the schoolhouse door to Capitol Hill* (pp. 163–175). Cham, Switzerland: Springer International.

Tufte, E. R (2001). *The visual display of quantitative information* (2nd ed.). Cheshire, CT: Graphics Press.

UNL Public Policy Center. (2009). *Taking charge: 2013 final report*. Retrieved from http://ppc. unl.edu/wp-content/uploads/2014/03/TakingCharge2013FinalReport.pdf

US Department of Education. (2013a). *Public Law Print of P.L. 107–110, the No Child Left Behind Act of 2001. Part H- School Dropout Prevention, Sections 1801–1830*. Retrieved from http:// www2.ed.gov/policy/elsec/leg/esea02/pg15.html

US Department of Education. (2013b). *Public Law Print of P.L. 107–110, the No Child Left Behind Act of 2001. SEC. 1825. Strategies and capacity building*. Retrieved from http://www2. ed.gov/policy/elsec/leg/esea02/pg15.html

US Department of Education. (2013c). *Elementary and secondary education: Smaller Learning Communities Program*. Retrieved from http://www2.ed.gov/programs/slcp/index.html

US Department of Education. (2013d). *Public Law Print of P.L. 107–110, the No Child Left Behind Act of 2001*. Retrieved from http://www2.ed.gov/policy/elsec/leg/esea02/index.html

US Department of Health and Human Services. (1993). *Creating a 21st century Head Start Program: The final report of the Secretary's Advisory Committee on Head Start Quality and Expansion*. Retrieved from http://www.bmcc.edu/headstart/21century/index.html

US Department of Health and Human Services. (2001). *Mental health: Culture, race, and ethnicity* (a supplement to mental health: A report of the surgeon general). Rockville, MD: Author. Retrieved from http://www.surgeongeneral.gov/library/reports

US Department of Health and Human Services (2012). Evaluation: Performance improvement 2011–2012. Retrieved from aspe.hhs.gov/evaluation/perfimp/2013/Performace2012.cfm.

US Department of Health and Human Services. (2013a). *Maternal, infant and early childhood home visiting program*. Retrieved from http://mchb.hrsa.gov/programs/homevisiting/

US Department of Health and Human Services (HHS). (2013b). *HHS federal program inventory*. Retrieved from http://www.hhs.gov/budget/2013-program-inventory/federal-program-inventory.html

US Department of Housing and Urban Development. (2012). *The 2011 annual homeless assessment report to Congress*. Retrieved from https://www.onecpd.info/resources/documents/ 2011AHAR_FinalReport.pdf

US Department of Labor. (2013). *Fact sheet: The Mental Health Parity and Addiction Equity Act of 2009*. Retrieved from http://www.dol.gov/ebsa/newsroom/fsm hpaea.html

US District Court. (2000). *Jennifer Gratz and Case No.: 97-CV-75231-DT*. Eastern District of Michigan. Southern Division. Retrieved from https://www.mied.uscourts.gov/PDFFIles/ PJD97cv75231.pdf

US Interagency Council on Homelessness. (2010). *Opening doors: Federal strategic plan to prevent and end homelessness.* Retrieved from usich.gov/resources/uploads/asset_library/ Opening%20Doors%202010%20FINAL%20F SP%20Prevent%20End%20Homeless.pdf

Vincent, T. A. (1990). A view from the hill: The human element in policy making on Capitol Hill. *American Psychologist, 34,* 61–64.

Vincent, T. (2012, June 7). Personal interview.

Vinokur, A. D., Price, R. H., & Schul, Y. (1995). Impact of the JOBS intervention on unemployed workers varying in risk for depression. *American Journal of Community Psychology, 23*(1), 39–74.

Walker, J. (2011). If I'm "the party" where's the cake? The need for comprehensive child—witness court preparation programs. *Center Piece,* 1–6. [The official newsletter of the National Child Protection Training Centers]. Retrieved from http://www.gundersenhealth.org/upload/ docs/NCPTC/CenterPiece/CenterPiece.NL.Vol3.Iss1.pdf

Walker, L., & Monahan, J. (1987). Social frameworks: A new use of social science in law. *Virginia Law Review,* 73(559), 563–567.

Wandersman, A. (2014). Getting to Outcomes: An evaluation capacity building example of rationale, science, and practice. *American Journal of Evaluation, 35,* 87–89.

Wandersman, A., Chien, V., & Katz, J. (2012). Toward an evidence-based system for innovation support for implementing innovations with quality: Tools, training, technical assistance, and quality assurance/quality improvement. *American Journal of Community Psychology, 50,* 445–460.

Wandersman, A., Imm, P., Chinman, M., & Kaftarian, S. (2000). Getting to outcomes: A results-based approach to accountability. *Evaluation and Program Planning, 23,* 389–395.

Weinstein, R. (2013, September 18). Personal communication.

Weinstein, R. S. (2002). *Reaching higher: The power of expectations in schooling.* Cambridge, MA: Harvard University Press.

Weinstein, R. S., and Worrell, F. C. (Eds.) (2016). *Achieving college* dreams: *How a university-charter district partnership created an early college high school.* New York, NY: Oxford University Press.

Weiss, C. H., & Bucuvalas, M. J. (1980). Truth tests and utility tests: Decision-makers' frames of reference for social science research. *American Sociological Review, 45,* 302–313.

Weiss, C. H., Murphy-Graham, E., & Birkeland, S. (2005). An alternate route to policy influence: How evaluations affect D.A.R.E. *American Journal of Evaluation, 26,* 12–30.

Wells, G. L., Malpass, R. S., Lindsay, R. C. L., Fisher, R. P., Turtle, J. W., & Fulero, S. (2000). From the lab to the police station: A successful application of eyewitness research. American Psychologist, 55, 581–598.

What Works Clearinghouse (2014). *Success for all.* http://ies.ed.gov/ncee/wwc/pdf/intervention_reports/wwc_sfa_081109.pdf

Whitebook, M., Howes, C., & Phillips, D. (1989). *The National Child Care Staffing Study: Who cares? Child care teachers and the quality of care in America.* Oakland, CA: Child Care Employee Project.

Whitebook, M., Phillips, D., & Howes, C. (2014). *Worth work, STILL unlivable wages: The early childhood workforce 25 years after the National Child Care Staffing Study.* Berkeley, CA: Center for the Study of Child Care Employment.

Wickizer, T. M., Krupski, A., Stark, K. D., Mancuso, D., & Campbell, K. (2006). The effect of substance abuse treatment on Medicaid expenditures among GA clients in WA State. *Milbank Quarterly,* 84(3): 555–576.

Wilcox, B. L., & Deutsch, A. R. (2013). When evidence and values collide: Preventing sexually transmitted infections. In A. M. Culp (Ed.), *Child and family advocacy: Bridging the gaps between research, practice and policy* (pp. 217–232). Issues in clinical child psychology. New York: Springer.

Wilcox, B. L., Weisz, P. V., & Miller, M. (2005). Practical guidelines for educating policy makers: The Family Impact Seminar as an approach to advancing the interests of children and families in the policy arena. *Journal of Clinical Child and Adolescent Psychology, 34,* 638–645.

Wilson, W. J. (1987). *The truly disadvantaged: The inner city, the underclass, and public policy.* Chicago: University of Chicago Press.

W. K. Kellogg Foundation. (2001). *2001 Annual Report: Growing up.* Retrieved from wkkf.org/~/media/pdfs/annual%20reports/2001%20annualreportpdf.pdf

W. K. Kellogg Foundation. (2002). *Guidelines for influencing public policy.* Retrieved from wkkf.org/~/media/pdfs/migrated/2002/12/2803800.pdf

Wolf, S., Aber, J. L., & Morris, P. A. (2013). Drawing on psychological theory to understand and improve antipoverty policies: The case of conditional cash transfers. *Psychology, Public Policy, and Law, 19,* 3–14.

Wolff, T. (2010). *The power of collaborative solutions: Six principles and effective tools for building healthy communities.* San Francisco CA: Jossey Bass.

Wolff, T. (2013). A community psychologist's involvement in policy change at the community level: Three stories from a practitioner. *Global Journal of Community Psychology Practice, 4*(2). Retrieved from www.gjcpp.org/

Woodhead, M. (1988). When psychology informs policy: The case of early childhood intervention. *American Psychologist, 43,* 443–454.

Woolard, J. L. (1998). *Developmental aspects of judgment and competence in legally relevantcontexts* (Unpublished doctoral dissertation). Department of Psychology, University of Virginia.

Woolard, J. L., Reppucci, N. D., & Scott, E. (1996). *Judgment assessment tool-adolescents* (Unpublished manual). Department of Psychology, University of Virginia.

Yoshikawa, J. (2011). *Immigrants raising citizens: Undocumented parents and their young children.* New York: Russell Sage Foundation.

Yoshikawa, H., & Kholoptseva, J. (2013). *Unauthorized immigrant parents and their children's development.* Migration Policy Institute report. Retrieved from http://www.migrationpolicy.org/research/unauthorized-immigrant-parents-and-their -childrens-development

Zigler, E. F. (2007). Epilogue: Combining basic and applied science in constructing sound social policy. In J. L. Aber, S. J. Bishop-Josef, S. M. Jones, K. T. McLearn, & D. A. Phillips (Eds.), *Child development and social policy: Knowledge for action* (pp. 281–284). Washington, DC: American Psychological Association.

Zigler, E. F., & Hall, N. W. (2000). *Child development and social policy.* Boston: McGraw-Hill.

Zigler, E. F., & Styfco, S. J. (2010). *The hidden history of Head Start.* New York: Oxford University Press.

Zuckerman, D. M., Brown, P., & Nissen, S. E. (2011). Medical device recalls and the FDA approval process. *Archives of Internal Medicine, 171,* 1006–1011.

ABOUT THE AUTHOR

Kenneth I. Maton is a Professor of Psychology and Affiliate Professor of Public Policy at the University of Maryland, Baltimore County (UMBC). His primary areas of research are minority student achievement and empowering community settings. He has taught a graduate-level course on social policy for the past 30 years, received the Special Contributions to Public Policy Award from the Society for Community Research and Action in 2013, and served as lead co-editor of the volume, *Investing in Children, Youth, Families, and Communities: Strengths-Based Research and Policy* (American Psychological Association, 2004).

INDEX